Colored Cosmopolitanism

COLORED COSMOPOLITANISM

The Shared Struggle for Freedom
in the United States and India

NICO SLATE

Harvard University Press
Cambridge, Massachusetts, and London, England   *2012*

Library of Congress Cataloging-in-Publication Data

Slate, Nico.
  Colored cosmopolitanism : the shared struggle for freedom in the United States and India / Nico Slate.
    p.   cm.
  Includes bibliographical references and index.
  ISBN 978-0-674-05967-2 (alk. paper)
  1. African Americans—Relations with East Indians.   2. Racism—United States—History.   3. Racism—India—History.   4. African Americans—Civil rights—History.   5. Minorities—Civil rights—India—History.   6. United States—Race relations—History.   7. India—Race relations—History.   8. United States—Relations—India.   9. India—Relations—United States.   I. Title.
  E185.61.S6185 2011
  305.800973—dc22   2011013395

For Peter Slate

His life was gentle, and the elements
So mixed in him that Nature might stand up
And say to all the world, "This was a man!"
—*Julius Caesar*, Act V, Scene V

Contents

Colored Cosmopolitanism

Introduction

Words like Freedom

Most men today cannot conceive of a freedom that does not involve somebody's slavery.

—W. E. B. Du Bois, *Darkwater*

I N THE SPRING OF 1941, in the midst of the Second World War, Kamaladevi Chattopadhyaya sat down in the "whites only" section of a segregated train traveling through the American South. Just across the Louisiana border, the ticket collector ordered her to move. She asked him why. "That is the rule," he replied, "and you better obey it or you will regret it." She did not move. He walked away angrily but soon returned—subdued, it seemed, by something he had learned. He asked her where she was from, making clear he realized she was not African American. "New York," she said, evasively. "I mean which land do you hail from," he clarified. At this point, she could have proudly explained that she was a distinguished visitor from India, a colleague of Mahatma Gandhi, and a champion of Indian independence and the rights of Indian women, and that she had only a few months before had tea with Franklin and Eleanor Roosevelt. Instead, when prompted to tell the man "from which land she came," Kamaladevi Chattopadhyaya replied, "It makes no difference. I am a coloured woman obviously and it is unnecessary for you to disturb me for I have no intention of moving from here." The ticket collector muttered, "You are an Asian," but he did not bother her again.[1]

By refusing to move, Kamaladevi defied the legalized bigotry of the American South. By proclaiming herself "coloured," she expressed solidarity with the millions of African Americans for whom the brutalities of

---

W. E. B. Du Bois, *Darkwater: Voices from Within the Veil* (New York: Harcourt, Brace, and Howe, 1920): 207.

segregation were a part of daily life. This was more than a fleeting gesture. Kamaladevi understood the efforts of African Americans as crucial to a global struggle against racism and imperialism, a struggle she framed in terms of color. Her self-definition as "a coloured woman" epitomized a colored cosmopolitanism that transcended traditional racial distinctions, positioning Indians and African Americans together at the vanguard of the "darker races." Articulated most eloquently by W. E. B. Du Bois, colored cosmopolitanism appealed to those working to forge a united front against racism, imperialism, and other forms of oppression. Advocates of colored cosmopolitanism fought for the freedom of the "colored world," even while calling into question the meanings of both color and freedom.

In the late nineteenth century, a variety of social reformers began to articulate analogies between the injustices of colonial India and the United States. Inspired by the juxtaposition of emancipation and empire that characterized much of the nineteenth-century world, the discourses that linked Indians and African Americans revolved around the tension between two at times contradictory pairs of analogies. On the one hand, many historical actors compared struggles against racial oppression in the United States with movements against caste oppression in India. In contrast with this race/caste analogy, comparisons between American racism and British imperialism paired African Americans with all Indians. From their inception, connections between Indian and African American freedom struggles were as varied as the struggles themselves.

What does it mean to say that social movements on opposite ends of the world were connected? Ranging from statements of sympathy to coordinated acts of solidarity, the connections analyzed in the following pages often involved selective appropriation and, at times, outright misunderstanding. Many historical actors oversimplified or entirely overlooked the many differences between the social, political, and economic challenges facing African Americans and South Asians. Words like "freedom" or "colored" contain not only distinct histories and competing dreams but also the ability to hide these differences. It is not enough, however, to note that "freedom" meant different things to different people at different times. Rather, the challenge is to understand how historical agents employed such key words to bridge differences and to achieve transnational solidarities.[2]

We must not lose sight of the differences in context and meaning between English words and their closest equivalents in Indian languages: *swaraj* and independence, *azadi* and freedom, *qaum* and community or nation, and so on. To take the most egregious example, the word "caste," from the Portuguese *"casta,"* conflates two distinct social categories: *"varna"* and *"jati."* *Varna* refers to the division of Hindu society into Brahmans, Kshatriyas, Vaishyas, and Sudras, a roughly hierarchical order that excludes Dalits (so-called "untouchables") and the diverse group of peoples known in India as "Tribals." *Varna* literally means "color," a fact that has played a consistent role in racialized conceptions of caste. *Jati,* which comes from the Sanskrit for "birth," refers to the hundreds of endogamous groups, often associated with a particular occupation, that have come to be the preeminent social identifier for many Indians. As the long history of race/caste comparison makes evident, historical actors have creatively and selectively translated between English terms and their counterparts in Indian languages in order to bolster particular arguments.[3]

Recent scholarship has tracked the many linkages South Asians have forged with other regions of the world, particularly within the broader Indian Ocean arena.[4] Historians have also expanded the borders of the American civil rights movement both temporally and geographically, often noting connections between the efforts of African Americans and South Asians.[5] Understanding these connections and their impact on the histories of the United States, South Asia, and the world requires an "interactional history" in which people, ideas, and political pressure flow between regions of the world.[6] The interconnectedness of African American and South Asian freedom struggles must be understood within the larger history of racism and antiracism, of empire and anti-imperialism, of civil rights and human rights, and in connection with key global events, such as the First and Second World Wars and the Cold War. Such a transnational history must not leave behind the nation. The ability of African Americans and South Asians to create links with each other depended on the way they understood their nations and on the diplomatic histories of the United States, the United Kingdom, India, and Pakistan.[7]

The chronology of colored cosmopolitanism demonstrates the interconnectedness of transnational social movements with national histories. Notions of colored solidarity gained popularity within the United States precisely because African Americans, as a minority in a highly racialized society, found hope and inspiration in global solidarities of color.[8] Notions of a "dark" or "colored" world had less immediate purchase in a country such as India where divisions of caste and religion often obscured the workings of the color line. It was, however, independence struggles in India and other parts of Asia and Africa that endowed colored solidarity with political significance. African Americans made colored cosmopolitanism matter at home by inspiring commitment to colored solidarity in countries such as India, whose nonalignment in the Cold War demanded attention in Washington. American politicians cared about colored solidarity only when it threatened to complicate American foreign policy. Ironically, the process of decolonization that rendered colored cosmopolitanism politically powerful also attenuated the bonds of color, as the leaders of newly independent nations came to focus more on maintaining the integrity of the nation-state—an integrity both strengthened and challenged by transnational linkages between freedom struggles.[9]

The diversity of Indian and African American freedom struggles meant that multiple analogies, often contradictory, vied to juxtapose not only "the Indian" and "the Negro" but also "the untouchable," "the Negro worker," or "the Indian woman." At times transnational connections acted as a prism, refracting a narrow focus on a particular injustice into a broader concern for the diverse struggles of a variety of oppressed groups, both at home and halfway around the world. The intersection of multiple oppressions inspired alliances across not only national borders but also social movements.[10] At other times, connections between India and the United States operated as a funnel, narrowing notions of belonging by excluding Dalits, women, or the poor. By forging solidarity across racial and national borders, African Americans and South Asians sometimes challenged and sometimes reinforced prevailing conceptions of race and nation as well as of class, caste, and gender.

Acknowledging the ambiguities of transnational analogies should not obscure the fact that a range of historical actors who struggled against injustice found insight and inspiration in connecting struggles across national borders. When Kamaladevi refused to move on that train, violently enforced hierarchies of power and privilege kept millions of Indians and African Americans in poverty, discriminated against and disfranchised. Jim Crow segregation held sway throughout the Southern United States, locking many Black Americans in a system of peonage all too similar to slavery. Blacks in the North and West faced equally insidious forms of racial segregation and inequality, enforced, as in the South, by the threat of violence. In India, British rule had left the vast majority of Indians impoverished while creating and reinforcing divisions based on religion, caste, and region. While the nature of freedom was debated, most Indians and African Americans knew—this was not it.

The links that African Americans and South Asians forged with each other contributed to the dismantling of the British Raj and of Jim Crow segregation as well as the decline of a racialized global order. Not all South Asians and African Americans benefited equally from these achievements, as the ongoing struggles of Dalits and impoverished African Americans make evident. Many of the characters in this book were themselves relatively elite—their education and status marking the many hierarchies within the Indian and African American communities. But they fought for an expansive emancipation. They fought to redeem words like democracy, *swaraj,* and freedom from a hypocrisy still unvanquished. They rejected not only narrow notions of territorial independence but any conception of freedom that involved somebody else's slavery.

CHAPTER ONE

Race, Caste, and Nation

He was dark, about the colour of a light quadroon, and his full lips, which in a man of Caucasian race would have been brilliant scarlet, had a tint of bluish purple.

—An American woman describing the Indian scholar and social reformer Swami Vivekananda

OVER THE COURSE of the nineteenth century, the decline of slavery coincided with the expansion of empire. Emancipation came to the British Empire in 1833, to Russia's serfs in 1861, to African Americans in 1865, and to Brazil in 1888. As systems of bondage differed widely, so did the degree of freedom granted former slaves. In the United States, after the brief period of hope that came with Reconstruction, former slaves faced a period of economic oppression, legal segregation, and terrorist violence that has been called the "nadir" of the African American experience. The demise of Reconstruction and the rise of new forms of American racial hierarchy coincided with the extension of imperial rule in Asia and Africa. In 1857 Britain's success in brutally repressing a rebellion in India allowed for the consolidation of one hundred years of bloody territorial accumulation. In the winter of 1884–1885 the Berlin Conference divided Africa amongst the European powers. In 1898, after decades of violent continental expansion, war with Spain gave the United States an overseas empire. Old systems of chattel slavery yielded to new forms of imperial bondage.[1]

Theories of racial supremacy that had developed in the context of slavery continued to flourish in an age of color-coded empires. Supporters of the new imperial order celebrated the ascendance of light-skinned Europeans and their descendants throughout much of the world. While disagreeing on which "race" or "people" deserved preeminence, the majority of

---

The Life of Swami Vivekananda by His Eastern and Western Disciples, 6th ed. (Calcutta: Advaita Ashrama, 1989), 406–407, 467.

contemporary ethnologists agreed that Africa belonged under imperial rule. India, on the other hand, posed unique challenges to theorists of racial hierarchy. Some lumped Indians with Africans and other "dark races" at the bottom of the global racial hierarchy. Many scholars chose instead to overlay European racial theories on the complexities of caste, labeling high-caste Indians "Aryan" or "Caucasian" and attributing "Negroid" characteristics to low-caste Indians.

The prominence of caste was only one of many differences between the racialized regimes of British India and the United States. While Indians vastly outnumbered their British rulers, African Americans were a distinct minority. Although the fortunes of African Americans varied considerably within and between different regions of the United States, the diversity of Indians operated at a much greater scale. This crucial difference resulted not only from India's larger population but also from the distinct histories of the United States and India. Slavery did not create a homogenous African American community, but the middle passage and generations of captivity did yield many more commonalities than existed in India during British rule.

Despite these differences, social reformers began to articulate analogies between the injustices of the United States and of colonial India. Some compared American racial oppression with caste in India, pairing African Americans with low-caste Indians. Others compared American racism and British imperialism, juxtaposing African Americans and all Indians, irrespective of caste. The intersection of race, caste, and nation divided opponents of the new imperial order, even while fostering new unities in the pursuit of an increasingly expansive freedom.

In the late nineteenth and early twentieth centuries, Indians, Africans, and their descendants came to share strongly racialized national spaces in South and East Africa, the Caribbean, Europe, and the United States. The intersection of the Indian and African diasporas created opportunities for new antiracist and anticolonial alliances that called into question racial distinctions, national borders, and the nature of diaspora itself.[2] Physical proximity created as much conflict as collaboration. Solidarities between Blacks and Indians faced three distinct obstacles: the differences between racial hierarchies throughout the world (and especially between the United States and India), the fact that many racial systems differentiated between Blacks and Indians, and the abundance of divisions within both the Black and Indian communities. These challenges often overlapped. Some Indians in the United States used racial theories to self-identify as "Aryan" and "Caucasian" and thus to claim legal whiteness, distancing themselves not only from African Americans but from poor and low-caste

Indians as well. Some middle-class African Americans employed a rhetoric of Christian civilization that distinguished themselves from the "backward" millions of Asia and Africa as well as poor and working-class Blacks closer to home. Examining these obstacles to unity reveals the many challenges African Americans and Indians had to overcome to achieve a unified struggle against imperialism, white supremacy, and caste oppression. It was at the height of empire and white supremacy, at a time when many African Americans and Indians found little in common, that forward-thinking individuals laid the groundwork for more inclusive conceptions of belonging and resistance.

The Darker Races

In the second half of the nineteenth century, imperial expansion combined with industrialization to rapidly accelerate a process of global consolidation. Armies, scientists, and missionaries crisscrossed the planet. Interlocking networks of trade, capital, technology, and information bound together distant regions of the earth. Nineteenth-century globalization did not create a world without borders. Rather, as historian C. A. Bayly has argued, "The hardening of the boundaries between nation-states and empires after 1860 led people to find ways of linking, communicating with, and influencing each other across those boundaries."[3] Among the most important boundary-crossing efforts of the late nineteenth century was the rise of a transnational network of white supremacists, whose theories increasingly relied upon the idea of inherent biological differences between endogamous groups of human beings.

In both the United States and colonial India, racial bigotry hardened over the course of the nineteenth century. Many causes can be identified for what was an uneven and heterogeneous but nonetheless persistent growth in American and British racial prejudice. In the United States a backlash against the efforts of abolitionists and the struggles of African Americans, wars with Mexico and with American Indians, and nativist opposition to the inflow of "less suitable" immigrants all worked to sharpen, for many Americans, the importance of a distinctly "Anglo-Saxon" whiteness. The British had not originally understood their empire in strongly racial terms. By the late eighteenth century, however, racial segregation had become a key component of the Raj. In the first half of the nineteenth century a string of successful military campaigns and the rise of a self-assured Christian evangelical movement enhanced the racial chauvinism of the British in India. The aftermath of the rebellion of 1857 demonstrated and further consolidated imperial racism. The color-coding of the British Raj reached its zenith in the decades after 1857. In 1883 the viceroy of India, Lord Ripon, proposed a bill that allowed Indian judges to preside over cases involving "Europeans" in the smaller towns known as *mofussil*. Protest exploded throughout the British community in India, offering a stark demonstration of the prevalence of racism in the Raj.[4]

The histories of white supremacy in the United States and colonial India followed similar trajectories in part because these histories were interconnected. The emergence of the United States as an imperial power strengthened the relationship between British and American racial discourse. In the wake of American victory in the War of 1898, the unity of "Anglo-Saxons" or of "English-speaking peoples" became a favorite topic of imperial propagandists on both sides of the Atlantic. In 1899 Rudyard Kipling encouraged the United States to expand its empire by taking up "the White Man's burden." One enthusiastic advocate of "the White Man's burden," Theodore Roosevelt, told an American audience, "The successful administration of the Indian Empire by the English has been one of the most notable and most admirable achievements of the white race during the past two centuries." By framing his admiration for the British Empire in racial terms, Roosevelt revealed the links between British and American imperialism and the transatlantic discourse on the supremacy of "the white race."[5]

The rhetoric of the "White Man's burden" developed in conjunction with a widespread belief in the general inferiority of the "darker races," a category in which many contemporary theorists situated both Indians and African Americans. The transnational prominence of the word "nigger" epitomized the conflation of dark-skinned people. British residents of the Raj, inspired by white Americans, increasingly denigrated Indians as "niggers." In 1859 a white New Yorker published a book in which he described his arrival in India in racial terms familiar to his audience at home: "On landing in Calcutta I was at once surrounded by a crowd of nearly naked 'niggers.' . . . These gentleman crowded me so much with their black, oily bodies, that I found a vigorous beating with my umbrella necessary to keep them at a respectful distance." Like the word "nigger," notions of blackness linked Indians and African Americans, while disparaging both as filthy, evil, or primitive. In 1899 a British author named Helen Bannerman published a short children's book entitled *The Story of Little Black Sambo*. Bannerman's story, which would eventually be reprinted in more than thirty editions, revolves around a little Indian boy named Sambo who is set upon by four hungry tigers. Later American editions transposed the story to Africa, conveniently ignoring the fact that there are no tigers in Africa. This transformation both revealed and perpetuated the categorization of Indians within a larger assemblage of anonymous dark-skinned savages.[6]

In addition to the widespread use of "nigger" and popular accounts of dark-skinned Sambos, scientific theories of racial hierarchy bound together the trajectories of white supremacy in colonial India and the United States, linking Indians and African Americans within the "darker races." In 1850 the American ethnologist Robert Knox boldly categorized what he called "the races of men." While Knox carefully distinguished between "the Saxon or Scandinavian Race," the "Gipsey, Coptic, and Jew," the "Celtic Race," and "the Slavonian Race," he lumped South Asians and African Americans within "The Dark Races of Men." In his chapter on the "Dark Races," Knox compared India and Africa as benighted regions worthy of colonization. He used the British Raj to argue for the colonization of Africa and exhorted his readers, "See how a company of London merchants lord it over a hundred millions of coloured men in Hindostan." "Since the earliest times," Knox concluded, "the dark races have been the slaves of their fairer brethren."[7] The homogenization of the "darker races" would have lasting consequences, inspiring future advocates of white supremacy and those who opposed them.

While notions of the "Darker Races" linked all Indians with "Negroes," an equally influential effort to categorize human diversity divided certain Indians from others along regional, economic, and caste-based lines. In 1775 Johann Friedrich Blumenbach popularized the idea of a "Caucasian race." He took the name "Caucasian" from the Caucasus Mountains, which he believed had produced "the most beautiful race of men." Despite such arbitrary foundations, the idea of a "Caucasian race" gained currency over time.[8] Many theorists of race classified high-caste Indians as Caucasian, distancing them from low-caste Indians, who were in turn associated with "Negroes." By the mid-nineteenth century scholars had distinguished two large and distinct language families in the Indian subcontinent. This discovery helped inspire "the two-race theory of Indian civilization," in which certain Indians were associated with Europeans, while others were linked with "Negroes."[9]

The popularity of the two-race theory owed much to the renowned Sanskrit scholar Friedrich Max Müller. In a paper given in 1847 at a meeting of the British Association for the Advancement of Science, Müller used linguistics and his analysis of the Vedas, a collection of ancient Indian religious texts, to argue that some Indians were united with Europeans as members of "the Caucasian race." He began his presentation by arguing that a "Caucasian" or "Japhetic" people had invaded India, conquering the original inhabitants. He classified the indigenous population as belonging to "the negro race," and declared, "We generally find that it is the fate of the negro race, when brought into hostile contact with the Japhetic race, to be either destroyed and annihilated, or to fall into a state of slavery and degradation." Connecting race and caste, Müller argued that in the north of India those of "the negro race" were treated as "outcastes." In the most important sentence of his speech he encouraged his British audience to frame their colonizing mission as an extension of the caste system and of "the glorious work of civilization, which had been left unfinished by their Arian [*sic*] brethren." Often associated with the Nazis and other advocates of white supremacy, the word "Aryan" originated in the Vedas. Müller used a rather peculiar reading of the Vedas to associate the word "Aryan" with the "Caucasian" race that he believed included not only his European audience but also many northern and high-caste Indians. The history of Afro-Indian relations reveals the many consequences of a racial science that marked high-caste Indians as "Aryans" and low-caste Indians as "Negroes."[10]

Müller was not the first to argue that certain Indians were related to Negroes. As early as 1792 an officer in the army of the East India Company had written that "a race of Negroes formerly had pre-eminence in India." To support his claim, Francis Wilford wrote, "In several parts of India the mountaineers resemble Negroes in their countenance, and in some degree in their hair, which is curled and has a tendency to wool."[11] In 1882 William Wilson Hunter's *Indian Empire* recited the argument that racial distinctions and especially differences in color had inspired Aryan contempt for the original inhabitants of India. Hunter declared, "India thus forms a great museum of races, in which we can study man from his lowest to his highest stages of culture."[12] Herbert Hope Risley, an ethnographer and colonial official, argued that caste structure was related to "the antipathy of the higher race for the lower, of the fair-skinned Aryan for the black Dravidian."[13] In *The People of India*, published in London and Calcutta in 1908, Risley divided Indians into seven racial types, with fair "Indo-Aryans" the most "advanced" and dark-skinned Dravidians the most "primitive." The Dravidian, Risley claimed, was "recognizable at a glance by his black skin, his squat figure and the negro-like proportions of his nose."[14]

In 1912 an encyclopedic condensation of several generations of scholarship on the Vedas demonstrated how far the Aryan idea had drifted from Müller's original intentions. An article on the word "Varna," which literally means "color," explained the "extreme rigidity of the caste system" as a result of "the difference of colour between the upper and lower classes." The article linked marriage restrictions between "the Sudra" and "the Arya" with "the peculiar state of feeling as to mixed marriages, for example, in the Southern States of America and in South Africa, or even in India itself, between the new invaders from Europe and the mingled population which now peoples the country."[15] By referencing opposition to "mixed marriages" in the United States, South Africa, and contemporary India, the article linked caste distinctions to the supposed antipathy between people of different races. Whereas Müller had used a racial reading of caste to unite Europeans and high-caste Indians as "Aryans," later scholars labeled all Indians a "mingled population," as deserving of racial segregation as Blacks in the American South.

As theorists of the Aryan idea turned to "Negroes" to explain the subjugation of lower-caste Indians, several social reformers compared Indians and "Negroes" while commenting upon caste in India. Unlike Müller, however, many of these reformers advocated solidarity between African Americans and Indians. Building on expansive notions of emancipation, they employed the intersection of race, caste, and nation against imperialism, racism, and caste-based oppression. It would be wrong, however, to argue that whereas ethnologists had compared Indians and "Negroes" in order to justify prevailing hierarchies of power and privilege, reformers strove to unite Blacks and Indians in order to subvert such hierarchies. On the contrary, the rhetoric of slavery and freedom proved elastic. Opportunities for hypocrisy abounded, as some reformers found it easier to denounce the lack of freedom in foreign lands than to confront injustice closer to home.

Emancipations

In 1873 Jotirao Phule drew upon the history of race in the United States to attack caste prejudice in India. An eloquent critic of caste oppression, Phule had authored several books and founded an organization, the Satyashodak Samaj, which aimed to represent the "bahujan" or majority of India that Phule argued had been oppressed by a Brahman elite. Phule titled his attack on Brahmanism *Slavery* and dedicated it

> to the good people of the United States as a token of admiration for their sublime disinterested and self sacrificing devotion in the cause of Negro Slavery; and with an earnest desire, that my country men may take their noble example as their guide in the emancipation of their Shudra Brethren from the trammels of Brahmin thraldom.[16]

In his dedication, as well as in the title of his book, Phule marshaled notions of freedom and slavery to denounce caste hierarchy. His emphasis on the "self sacrificing devotion" of the "good people of the United States" framed emancipation as the end of a noble story. He disregarded the continued plight of African Americans. Phule did not aim to educate his audience about post-emancipation America, however, but to inspire opposition to caste oppression in India.

The significance of a transnational analogy results primarily from its local purpose and impact. In 1849 the influential American business journal *Hunt's Merchant's Magazine,* which often advertised goods produced by American slave labor, declared that the caste system rendered Hindus "the most enslaved portion of the human race."[17] Phule used a similar comparison, but he did so to combat caste oppression rather than, as did *Hunt's Merchant's Magazine,* to dramatize the accomplishments of the British Empire. Phule overestimated the achievement of racial equality in the United States, but he wielded the language of freedom and slavery to oppose the injustices of his own society.

Phule learned of the United States from missionaries, many of whom had been active in the abolition movement and who brought knowledge of American racism to India. In the late 1850s an English missionary known to posterity as "Mrs. Collins" wrote a novel in the South-Indian "princely state" of Travancore. Entitled "The Slayer Slain," the novel was modeled in part on Harriet Beecher Stowe's *Uncle Tom's Cabin.* In Mrs. Collins's version, Uncle Tom became a member of the Pulayan slave caste, and Evangeline St. Claire became a Syrian Christian girl. In 1877 Mr. Collins translated the novel into Malayalam and published it as "Ghatakavadham." Phule himself read *Uncle Tom's Cabin* and wrote, "Anyone who reads this book will have to cry with shame in public like the Marwadi women drawing the pallu of their saree over their heads and will have to sigh and sob."[18]

In November 1879 Mrs. Amanda Smith, a renowned Christian evangelist, born a slave in Long Green, Maryland, arrived in Bombay. In the more than two years she spent on the subcontinent, Smith drew considerable attention from Indians. "During the seventeen years that I have lived in Calcutta," wrote James Mills Thoburn, a bishop in the Methodist Episcopal Church, "I have never known anyone who could draw and hold so large an audience as Mrs. Smith." Smith's journey, like other Christian missionary activity, increased interactions between Indians and African Americans and laid a foundation of mutual awareness. Later generations would construct anti-imperial alliances based on this awareness and on radically different understandings of Christian mission.[19]

As Phule drew on the legacy of abolitionism to support anticaste efforts, so abolitionists used the example of Indians to disprove arguments that legitimated slavery on the basis of race. Speaking before the U.S. Congress, an antislavery activist made reference to Rammohun Roy as "one of the most enlightened and benevolent of the human race now living, though not a white man."[20] By invoking Roy, who had become renowned in the United States as the champion of a reformed monotheistic Hinduism, the speaker aimed to attack a racial hierarchy that denigrated all non-white people. In 1907 a young Mohandas Gandhi drew upon the history of abolitionism in the United States to bolster his early ventures in civil disobedience. A few months after Gandhi initiated passive resistance in South Africa's Transvaal, he published an article praising Henry David Thoreau's use of civil disobedience to protest slavery. In a statement notable for its transnational sympathy if not for its historical accuracy, Gandhi concluded, "Historians say that the chief cause of the abolition of slavery in America was Thoreau's imprisonment and the publication by him of the above mentioned book after his release." A week later Gandhi translated an antislavery passage from Thoreau into Gujarati and published it as an inspiration for his readers.[21]

While Phule contrasted American emancipation with caste oppression, and Gandhi studied Thoreau's opposition to slavery in order to combat racial oppression in South Africa, many African Americans contrasted British freedom with American slavery.[22] Slaves in the British Empire had been freed well before African Americans. In a poem published in 1853 the African American poet Joseph C. Holly deemed the British "Freedom's Champions." In 1901 the African American poet James Madison Bell contrasted American slavery with British emancipation, "when Freedom waved her wand and spoke,/And lo! a million chains were broke."[23]

Not all nineteenth-century African Americans praised the achievements of the British Empire. Well before 1900 Black Americans had begun to forge links with Africa and African peoples around the world, fostering an awareness of the consequences of British imperialism. Some Black Americans began to envision linkages of resistance with Asia. Late in life, William Edward Burghardt Du Bois remembered that it was during his time at Fisk University, from 1885 to 1888, that he "first became aware of a world of colored folk and . . . learned not only of the condition of American Negroes but began to read of China and India." Du Bois recalled that in the fall of 1892, while studying in Berlin, he had begun "to see the race problem in America, the problem of the peoples of Africa and Asia, and the political development of Europe as one."[24] Over his long life, Du Bois would contribute as much as any other individual to forging solidarity between Indians and African Americans.

While Du Bois would never set foot in India, travel to the subcontinent helped inspire other American reformers to link struggles for emancipation in the United States and colonial India. In January 1896, Samuel Longhorne Clemens, better known by the pen name Mark Twain, arrived in Bombay. Clemens would later call India "the only foreign land I ever daydream about or deeply long to see again." His first impressions were not, however, entirely positive. Upon seeing a hotel worker struck by his "European" employer, Clemens wrote in his journal, "I had not seen the like of this for fifty years. It carried me instantly back to my boyhood and flashed upon me the forgotten fact that this was the usual way of explaining one's desires to a slave." Two months later while traveling down the Hoogly River near Calcutta, Clemens once again connected imperialism and slavery. After comparing the mansions of British planters with those of Louisiana plantation owners, Clemens wrote, "The thatched groups of native houses have turned themselves into the negro quarters, familiar to me near forty years ago." Drifting down a branch of the Ganges near the capital of British India, Clemens recognized a familiar pattern of inequalities and concluded, "For six hours this has been the sugar coast of Mississippi."[25]

Samuel Clemens lived through the transition from slavery to empire. His notes on his trip to India reveal his opposition to the most important link between slavery and empire—the idea and practice of racial hierarchy. Clemens was himself not immune to racial essentialism. Of Indians, for example, he wrote, "They seemed a soft and gentle race, and there was something both winning and touching about their demeanor." Clemens's admiration for dark-skinned people starkly differs, however, from the conventional stereotypes of his time. About India, Clemens wrote, "Where dark complexions are massed, they make the whites look bleached out, unwholesome, and sometimes frankly ghastly." "I could notice this as a boy," he remembered, "down South in the slavery days before the war."[26] Thus Clemens again compared the color line in India and the United States, humbling once more the powerful bearers of "bleached out" white skins.

Witnessing the assault upon the hotel worker in Bombay made Clemens recall seeing, at the age of ten, a slave killed "for merely doing something awkwardly—as if that were a crime." Juxtaposing these memories inspired Clemens to write:

It is curious—the space-annihilating power of thought. For just one second, all that goes to make the *me* in me was in a Missourian village, on the other side of the globe, vividly seeing again these forgotten pictures of fifty years ago, and wholly unconscious of all things but just those; and in the next second I was back in Bombay, and that kneeling native's smitten cheek was not done tingling yet![27]

Clemens used the "space-annihilating power of thought" to connect the oppression of African Americans under slavery to that of Indians under empire. Unlike Knox or Risley, Clemens made the Negro/Indian parallel sympathetic to the plight of those whose skins were not as "bleached out" as his own. Like Phule, he argued against injustice to defend a greater freedom. It was travel that allowed Clemens to recognize transnational analogies. The inspirational potential of travel also found embodiment in one of the most renowned Indians to visit the United States in the nineteenth century, the Bengali scholar and social reformer Swami Vivekananda.

Like many Indians in the United States, Swami Vivekananda was repeatedly mistaken for an African American. In 1895 he wrote to a disciple in India, "At Baltimore, the small hotels, being ignorant, would not take in a black man, thinking him a negro. So my host, Dr. Vrooman, had to take me to a larger one, because they knew the difference between a negro and a foreigner." After his first trip to the United States, Vivekananda wrote from London, "That wonderful knowledge of the Americans that identify every black man with the negro is entirely absent here, and nobody even stares at me in the street." Even when his Indian origins were made clear, Vivekananda's color was still an important issue for many Americans. Written reports regularly referred to him as "dark" or "dusky."[28]

A biography prepared by his disciples depicts Vivekananda brushing aside the racial insults he received in the United States "with a grand indifference and what one might call a spiritual hauteur." According to Vivekananda's disciples, Vivekananda embraced African Americans, many of whom saw him as an example of a successful dark-skinned man. They cite the example of "a Negro porter," who asked to shake Vivekananda's hand after explaining that he saw in the Swami "one of his own people [who] had become a great man." We learn that "the Swami warmly clasped his hand and exclaimed, 'Thank you! Thank you, brother!'" The disciples further state that Vivekananda "related many similar confidences made to him by Negroes," and that the Swami refused to explain that he was not Black, preferring instead to be evicted from segregated businesses.[29]

The memories of Swami Vivekananda's disciples may have been shaped by their high esteem for their guru. Nevertheless, newspaper reports as well as Vivekananda's speeches and writings demonstrate a recurring hostility to American racial prejudice, as well as a remarkable pride in his own dark skin. During his more than three years spent in the United States over the course of several visits, Vivekananda repeatedly criticized the treatment of African Americans. These criticisms have been largely forgotten, even as Vivekananda's triumphant visit to the Chicago Parliament of

Religions in 1893 has come to symbolize the antiquity of Indo-American relations. Vivekananda's confrontation with American racism provides a unique perspective on his understanding of the interconnections of race, religion, and caste in India. What emerges is the audacity of a man who embraced the emancipatory potential of transnational, transracial, and transreligious solidarities, even while not completely discarding the racial and caste-based prejudices of his era.[30]

Vivekananda defended India against Western stereotypes of a divided caste-ridden society, even as he used race/caste comparisons to criticize caste divisions. At times Vivekananda repeated elements of the prevailing ethnological wisdom, stressing the purity of races and castes as related phenomena. At other times he expressed skepticism toward these claims or forcefully discarded them. By comparing race and caste, Vivekananda demonstrated the ambiguities in his understandings of both. Although these views might appear self-contradictory, a close reading of his writings, sayings, and speeches reveals a core belief in the necessity of combating inequality and divisiveness. Nevertheless, while Vivekananda's anti-hierarchical vision would prove prophetic, his ambivalences on questions of race, caste, and religion were indicative of the difficulties confronting future reformers.

Vivekananda often aimed his critiques of American racism at Christian hypocrisy, revealing his complicated relationship not only with Christianity but also with Islam. In March 1894 the *Saginaw Courier-Herald* reported that Vivekananda had instructed an audience that Christians did not practice what they preached. He then referenced "the condition of the Negro in the South, who is not allowed in hotels nor to ride in the same cars with white men, and is a being to whom no decent man will speak." Vivekananda's favorite counterexample to the Christian treatment of African Americans involved not Hinduism but Islam. In a speech at the Shakespeare Club in Pasadena, California, on February 3, 1900, Vivekananda told his audience, "The Sultan of Turkey may buy a Negro from the mart of Africa, and bring him in chains to Turkey, but should he become a Mohammedan and have sufficient merit and abilities, he might even marry the daughter of the Sultan." He then made the obvious but nonetheless daring contrast: "Compare this with the way in which the Negroes and the American Indians are treated in this country!" On another occasion Vivekananda told the Universalist Church of Pasadena, "As soon as a man becomes a Mohammedan, the whole of Islam receives him as a brother with open arms." In contrast, he lamented, "In this country, I have never yet seen a church where the white man and the negro can kneel side by side to pray."[31]

Vivekananda used the struggles of African Americans as a touchstone to criticize caste prejudice. In August 1889 he wrote, "It cannot also be doubted that sometimes the Shudras used to be oppressed more than the helots among the Spartans and the negroes among the Americans!" Vivekananda's self-identification as a "Shudra," the lowest rung of the fourfold division of *varnas*, adds poignancy to his comparison between Shudras and "negroes." Vivekananda's many statements on caste vary from praise to trenchant criticism. He once called caste "a natural order" but at another time denounced all forms of caste as "bondage." His views on caste were intimately related to his equally ambivalent understanding of race. In Pasadena, California, in February 1900, Vivekananda compared intercaste and interracial sexual unions, at first seeming to oppose both. Toward the end of his speech, however, he distanced himself from ethnological theories in which caste had preserved the purity of distinct races. Although he believed "racial mixture" proved degrading at first, Vivekananda argued that over time such "intermixture" would prove beneficial. He declared, "The Aryan gives his blood to a race, and then it becomes civilised . . . would you give your blood to the Negro race? Then he would get higher culture." Thus Vivekananda encouraged "mixed-race" sexual unions, a radical suggestion in 1900, even while repeating more conventional beliefs in the relationship between civilization and "blood" and linking "Aryan" Indians to white Americans at the top of a racially demarcated civilization. Vivekananda grappled with racist and casteist hierarchies, unable to completely disown them but equally unwilling to validate them.[32]

Whereas Vivekananda at times asserted that caste distinctions had preserved racial differences in India, at other times he ridiculed the "two-race theory of Indian civilization" and its accompanying association of race and caste. He told one of his disciples, "If I am grateful to my white-skinned Aryan ancestors, I am far more so to my yellow-skinned Mongolian ancestors, and most of all to the black-skinned negroids." Explaining ethnological distinctions between Aryans and Dravidians as the result of a belief in white supremacy generated during the enslavement of Africans, Vivekananda offered a distinctly historical explanation for the interconnectedness of race and caste. He stated, "The Americans, English, Dutch, and the Portuguese got hold of the poor Africans and made them work hard while they lived, and their children of mixed birth were born in slavery and kept in that condition for a long period." Ethnologists, Vivekananda explained, believing that "the same thing happened" in India, imagined the subcontinent "full of dark-eyed aborigines, and the bright Aryan came from—the Lord knows where." Vivekananda mocked Western theorists who believed in a racialized Aryan identity. He proclaimed, "There are patriotic Englishmen who think that the Aryans were all red-haired. . . . If the writer happens to be a black-haired man, the Aryans were all black-haired." For Vivekananda, such theories were "illogical" and "irrational" and deserved ridicule. If the Aryans had invaded a land as large as India, even if it had been full of slaves, "These slaves would have eaten them up, made 'chutney' of them in five minutes."[33]

Vivekananda decried the symbiotic relationship between caste and colonialism. He argued that caste divisions prevented Indians from opposing imperialism, while imperialistic theories of race reinforced caste hierarchy. In a remarkable example of the potential and limitations of transnational analogies, Vivekananda used the life of an African young man to discredit both racial and caste-based hierarchy. He remembered that at the Parliament of Religions "a real African Negro" had given "a beautiful speech." Vivekananda "became interested in the young man" and spoke with him. Later, Vivekananda reported, he learned that the young man was "the son of a Negro chief who lived in the heart of Africa, and that one day another chief became angry with the father of this boy and murdered him and murdered the mother also, and they were cooked and eaten." The boy, Vivekananda explained, fled all the way to the United States. He concluded, "And this boy made that speech! After that, what was I to think of your doctrine of heredity!" Thus Vivekananda reproduced common stereotypes of African cannibals in order to disprove theories of inherent Black inferiority. He used his critique of the "doctrine of heredity" to call for increased education for "Pariahs" in India. Vivekananda's emphasis on education for Dalits was consistent with a long history of claims that the cultural and social shortfalls of low-caste individuals were partly to blame for their oppression. As in his portrayal of African cannibalism, Vivekananda reproduced limiting stereotypes even while marshaling them against prevailing racial and caste-based hierarchies.

Vivekananda's patronizing emphasis on education for Dalits and his recourse to stereotypes of uncivilized Africans help reveal why his most passionate denunciation of American race prejudice came in the form of a plea against radical reform. Vivekananda told an audience at Victoria Hall in Madras, "The history of the world teaches us that wherever there have been fanatical reforms, the only result has been that they have defeated their own ends." In order to illustrate the dangers of radical upheavals, Vivekananda referenced the legacy of the American Civil War. He proclaimed, "No greater upheaval for the establishment of right and liberty can be imagined than the war for the abolition of slavery in America." Vivekananda told his audience that African Americans were "a hundred times worse off today than they were before abolition." He explained, "Before the abolition, these poor Negroes were the property of somebody, and, as property, they had to be looked after, so that they might not deteriorate. Today they are the property of nobody." He concluded, "Their lives are of no value; they are burnt alive on mere pretences. They are shot down without any law for their murderers; for they are niggers, they are not human beings, they are not even animals; and that is the effect of such violent taking away of evil by law or by fanaticism."[34]

Vivekananda understated the horrors of slavery even while powerfully portraying the contemporary plight of African Americans. He failed to recognize that it was not the radical nature of emancipation but the persistence of traditional power structures in the American South that led to the continued oppression of freed slaves. Vivekananda's misguided history is not surprising given that similar interpretations of the aftermath of the Civil War were common in the United States in the late nineteenth century. What merits closer attention are the purposes to which Vivekananda applied American history. Rather than compare African Americans with low-caste Indians or Dravidians, he juxtaposed freed slaves with all Indians—in this case, in order to counsel against radical reform. His emphasis on patience revealed a conservatism at odds with the radical potential of his own ideas.

Vivekananda employed transnational analogies between race, caste, and nation toward a variety of ends. He criticized hypocritical Christians while praising racially inclusive Muslims. He restated ethnological theories of race and caste while portraying India as a racially mixed society and critiquing caste itself. He framed his opposition to British colonialism even while counseling gradual reform. Future reformers would wield the Negro/Indian parallel toward a similar range of goals. The majority of transnational comparisons between Indians and African Americans would reveal ambivalences as profound and persistent as those of Vivekananda.

The Borders of Diaspora

Balanced atop a large globe, dressed in the bright colors of royalty, Jahangir, the fourth Mughal emperor, aims an arrow at the severed head of Malik Ambar, a former slave. This painting, dated 1616, depicts not a historical event but the unfulfilled desire of Jahangir, whose name means "Conqueror of the World," though he never managed to conquer one of his most persistent opponents. Malik Ambar was born in sixteenth-century Harar, Ethiopia. Sold into slavery, he was transported via Baghdad to India's Deccan peninsula. There he created a small but powerful army that contained a large contingent of previously enslaved Africans. Until his death in 1626, Malik Ambar consistently evaded powerful Mughal rulers bent on consolidating power in the Deccan. He continues to be revered by many Indians of African descent, known commonly as Siddis or Habshis, who recognize in him a worthy emblem of the antiquity of the African Diaspora in India.[35]

Many generations after the death of Malik Ambar, close to the turn of the twentieth century, another man was enslaved in East Africa and brought to the Indian subcontinent. In 1954 this man's son, Mohammad Siddiq Mussafar, wrote a book narrating his father's enslavement in Zanzibar and his new life in the province of Sindh, now a state in Pakistan. Mussafar's *An Eye-Opening Account of Slavery and Freedom* reveals a diasporic consciousness that connected Siddis and African Americans. Referring to both Frederick Douglass and Booker T. Washington as *"shidis,"* Mussafar linked them with himself, his father, and other African Pakistanis. He took a special interest in Booker T. Washington's Tuskegee Institute, arguing that Washington's emphasis on vocational training could help the descendants of Africans in Pakistan.[36]

Washington's legacy in South Asia was substantial. While Mussafar employed a racialized conception of diaspora to label Washington a Siddi, most South Asians understood Washington as racially distinct but nonetheless worthy of admiration. In 1903 Anagarika Dharmapala, a Ceylonese Buddhist social reformer, made plans to visit several African American colleges, including Fisk University in Nashville and the Tuskegee Institute. He wrote to Washington, "I am going to have my first experience with your people. I hope it will be pleasant." By referencing Washington's "people," Dharmapala framed his journey as a form of racial encounter. He assumed a racial divide between South Asians and African Americans even while recognizing the potential for intergroup cooperation. Dharmapala was aware of the growing criticisms of Tuskegee from within the African American community. Nevertheless, he hoped to transplant the Tuskegee model of education back to India.[37]

In 1903 an Indian barrister living in South Africa published a long article praising Washington and the Tuskegee Institute even while marking "Negroes" as less civilized than Indians. In that article, entitled "From Slave to College President," Mohandas Gandhi called Tuskegee "an ideal college," an opinion he would repeat throughout his life. Much more than Thoreau's civil disobedience, Booker T. Washington shaped Gandhi's views on African Americans as well as Gandhi's own approach to social change. After chronicling the achievements of Washington, Gandhi concluded, "Such is the work done by Mr. Booker T. Washington, singlehanded, in the face of enormous odds, without a glorious past to look back upon as an incentive which more ancient nations can boast of." Gandhi explained this difference more carefully in a concluding note "to our own countrymen." He stated that Washington's life would "rank higher" than any Indian "for the simple reason that we have a very great past and an ancient civilization." Gandhi explained, "What, therefore, may be and is undoubtedly natural in us, is a very great merit in Booker Washington."[38] In the form of praise, Gandhi thus distinguished Indians and the Indian nation from African Americans. Whereas Mohammad Siddiq Mussafar embraced Washington and Frederick Douglass as *shidis,* Gandhi marked Washington and other "Negroes" as civilizationally distinct from Indians.

Gandhi's elevation of Indian civilization would have surprised Washington, for whom Christianity and Western education served as a model for "uncivilized" regions of the world such as India. While several prominent Indians offered American racism as evidence of the hypocrisy of Christian missions to India, Washington praised the British Empire for supporting Christian missionaries. These different notions of Christian civilization are evident in the divergent responses of Washington and Swami Vivekananda to Momolu Massaquoi, the West African prince who Vivekananda heard speak at the World's Parliament of Religions in Chicago in 1893. Vivekananda reproduced notions of the uncivilized African in order to demonstrate the power of civilization to trump racial differences. But he did not associate civilization with the West; rather, he blamed Western thinkers for imposing false racial distinctions on the practice of caste in India. Washington used the example of Massaquoi, as did Vivekananda, to emphasize the potential expansion of civilization. Washington, however, understood civilization as fundamentally Western and Christian. In an article entitled "Industrial Education in Africa," published in March 1906, Washington praised Massaquoi for trying to bring his "small African tribe" within the "influence of Western and Christian civilization." He then lauded the British for supporting missionary activity in South Africa and India.[39]

It is unclear how much Washington knew about the British Raj. At Andrew Carnegie's palatial home in Scotland, Washington met Lord John Morley, the secretary of state for India. The two discussed, in Washington's words, "parallels between racial conditions in the Eastern and Western world, between the Indians in India and the Negroes in the United States." Writing in 1911 in *My Larger Education,* Washington remembered, "I had never been able to get any definite conception, from what I had read in the newspapers, of the actual situation as between the two races in India, the English and the native Indians, and I was very glad to hear Lord Morley comment on that puzzling and perplexing problem." Washington neither specified Lord Morley's parallels nor offered his own. The few transnational comparisons he did offer between India and the United States served to justify Washington's defense of Jim Crow segregation. In *My Larger Education,* Washington observed that just as different customs in "India or China" deserved respect rather than interference, so segregation in the South should be respected.[40]

Although Washington never visited India, many Indians embraced Washingtonian notions of self-help and group uplift. Washington's works were translated into multiple South Asian languages, including Malayalam, Marathi, Telugu, Hindi, Urdu, Gujarati, and Nepali. K. Paramu Pillai, the headmaster of the Maharaja's high school in Travancore, wrote Washington that Pillai's Malayalam translation of Washington's *Up from Slavery* had been adopted as a textbook. "More than 700 boys and girls, between the ages of 12 and 16," Pillai wrote, "are thereby likely to know something of your labours at Tuskegee, for your race, and I hope they will learn some lessons of self-help therefrom, and learn to recognize the dignity of manual labour and training." Pillai later translated another of Washington's books, publishing it serially in a magazine he edited, and wrote Washington that Madras University had begun using *Up from Slavery.* Pillai is remembered, among other things, for coining the name "Nair Service Society" for the caste-based organization he helped serve, an organization that embodied Washington's emphasis on community self-help. Pillai was but one of several South Asians who wrote Washington, expressing the desire to spread Washington's methods, in the words of one admirer, "all throughout [the] length & breadth of India."[41]

Washington's emphasis on self-help helped inspire Gandhi to move beyond hierarchical notions of race, caste, and nation toward a profound antiracism and a radical conception of the dignity of labor. Early in his career, Gandhi was a "racial purist" who elevated certain Indians as "civilized Aryans" above Black South Africans.[42] Speaking in Bombay in September 1896, Gandhi decried European efforts to "degrade" the Indians of South Africa "to the level of the raw Kaffir, whose occupation is hunting and whose sole ambition is to collect a certain number of cattle to buy a wife, and then pass his life in indolence and nakedness."[43] This was not the only time Gandhi used the pejorative "Kaffir" and the stereotype of the uncivilized African to defend the rights of Indians in the face of white racism. In a widely publicized open letter to the Legislative Council and Legislative Assembly of Natal in December 1894, Gandhi employed the Aryan idea to argue, in his words, that "India is not Africa, and that it is a civilized country in the truest sense of the term *civilization.*"

Despite India's Aryan heritage, Gandhi declared, "The Indian is being dragged down to the position of a raw Kaffir."[44] Gandhi's racial beliefs would evolve, however, in part as a result of his interactions with African Americans and Booker T. Washington in particular.

The history of Gandhi's admiration for Washington reveals both the depth and the limitations of Gandhi's relationships with Black South Africans. In 1901 John Langalibalele Dube opened the Zulu Christian Industrial School, not far from his hometown of Durban, Natal. Modeled on Washington's Tuskegee Institute, Dube's school, later renamed the Ohlange Institute, emphasized technical knowledge, self-improvement, and community solidarity.[45] Only a few years after Dube founded his school, and thirteen months after Gandhi had published an article on Booker T. Washington, Gandhi opened his own model community, the Phoenix Settlement, only a few miles from Ohlange. Gandhi's son, Manilal, visited Ohlange and an African American woman, Catherine Blackburn, who served as superintendent of the student hostel at Ohlange, repeatedly visited Phoenix.[46] Gandhi's lifelong emphasis on rural education and the dignity of labor, first evident at the Phoenix Settlement, resulted in part from his admiration for both Washington and Dube. Dube would later become one of the foremost statesmen of his day, becoming in 1912 the first president of the South African Native National Congress, later renamed the African National Congress. As early as 1905, Gandhi heard Dube speak and concluded, "This Mr. Dube is a Negro of whom one should know."[47]

Gandhi's relationship with Dube both inspired and was inspired by Gandhi's admiration for Booker T. Washington. Gandhi's respect for Washington also influenced his view of other Black South Africans. For example, Gandhi praised the efforts of John Tengo Jabavu, an influential newspaper editor, to establish a new college "on the same lines of industrial training" as Tuskegee. In *Indian Opinion,* Gandhi wrote, "We have already in these columns drawn attention to the excellent and instructive programme carried out by Mr. Booker T. Washington at the Tuskegee Institute in America." Gandhi drew a line of inspiration from Washington through John Tengo Jabavu to Gandhi's own efforts to organize the Indian community in South Africa. He concluded, "If the Natives of South Africa, with all their financial disabilities and social disadvantages, are capable of putting forth this local effort, is it not incumbent upon the British Indian to take the lesson to heart?"[48]

Gandhi's respect for Booker T. Washington and the Washingtonian initiatives of John Dube inspired Gandhi to revise his opinion not only of Black Africans but also of low-caste Indians. During his early years in South Africa, Gandhi believed in both racial and caste purity. On September 8, 1906, Gandhi sent a series of cables protesting a law that required all Indians to register with the government. In the process, he offered a remarkable example of the conflation of race and caste. To the secretary of state for the colonies, Gandhi wrote, "Ordinance reduces Indians to status lower than Kaffirs and much lower than that occupied under Dutch regime." To the viceroy of India, however, Gandhi wrote, "Transvaal ordinance degrading, insulting reduces Indians to a worse status than that of Pariahs."[49] By substituting "Pariahs" for "Kaffirs," Gandhi demonstrated his distance from both Dalits and Black Africans. By 1911, however, he had developed a radically different understanding of "civilization," inspired in part by Washington and Dube, in which expertise in "productive industry" marked Blacks and low-caste Indians as especially civilized. In July 1911 Gandhi declared, "We all live upon the great industry of the Natives and Indians engaged in useful occupations in this country. In this sense they are more civilised than any of us, not excluding European non-producers, inhabiting this continent."[50] After he returned to India, Gandhi's interactions with African Americans would help him develop notions of race and class that extended beyond Washington's often patronizing ideas of racial uplift. Gandhi would be less successful, however, at transcending Washington's influence when it came to matters of caste.

Like Swami Vivekananda, Gandhi reached out to Blacks while maintaining a pride in Aryan civilization that was at times exclusive of Blacks as well as low-caste Indians. Unlike Vivekananda, Gandhi never set foot in the United States. The history of Indians in America parallels, with important differences, the history of Indians in South Africa. Like Gandhi, many Indians in the United States at first attempted to distinguish themselves from Blacks in order to gain respect and legal rights from a dominant white society. As in South Africa, distinctions of caste, class, and religion at times divided the Indian community in the United States. Unlike in South Africa, however, many Indians were able to gain citizenship in the United States by legally proving their whiteness. In order to win the privileges of whiteness, they distanced themselves from poor and low-caste Indians as well as other "non-white" Americans, elevating racial identities such as "Aryan" or "Caucasian" above their identity as Indians.

Race against Diaspora

The history of Indians in America began with a mistake. Christopher Columbus believed he had reached India. Thus a variety of diverse peoples spread across two continents at the opposite end of the world from

India came to be known as Indians. Columbus spawned the first of many confusions in terminology that would influence the experiences of generations of Indians in America. To a remarkable degree, complex questions of race, caste, class, and citizenship came to depend on the meaning of a few key words.

In 1854 the California Supreme Court employed Columbus's mistake to declare that the testimony of a Chinese witness could not be used in a criminal trial against a "white" defendant. At issue for the court was whether a law that expressly prohibited "Blacks, Mulattos and Indians" from providing testimony against whites should be understood to also exclude the testimony of someone of Chinese descent. In a feat of geographic bravado, the court declared, "The name of Indian, from the time of Columbus to the present day, has been used to designate, not alone the North American Indian, but the whole of the Mongolian race." Thus the court used the word "Indian" as a pseudo-scientific bridge between the "Mongolian race" and the "Indians" Columbus had encountered in 1492. The court admitted that such reasoning was flimsy at best. Its decision included the remarkable statement, "Even admitting the Indian of this continent is not of the Mongolian type . . . the words 'black person,' in the 14th section, must be taken as contradistinguished from white, and necessarily excludes all races other than the Caucasian." Thus the court moved to designate the Chinese "black" if they could not label them "Indian."[51]

Well before the United States emerged from the imperial backwaters of Great Britain, people from India had arrived in the New World as sailors and indentured servants. The life of James Dunn, indentured in Calcutta and brought to Georgia, illustrates the dangers these migrants faced in the racialized climate of the American colonies. As an indentured servant, Dunn was legally bound to his master for a set period of years, after which he would be legally free. To Dunn's great misfortune, however, his master died before the end of his indenture. Dunn sought his freedom in court, but his dark skin spoke louder than the few documents he had to prove his right to freedom, and he was sold into slavery.[52]

In part because of prevailing color prejudices, some Indian migrants came to live among African Americans. Some Indians arrived in the United States after having already lived among "Negroes" in Africa or the Caribbean. One Indian man lived with an uncle in British Guyana before making his way to New York toward the end of the nineteenth century. There he established himself in the African American community and married an African American woman.[53]

Beginning in the late nineteenth century, the numbers of Indians entering the United States began to rise. Students, merchants, and religious figures such as Swami Vivekananda came to all regions of the country. By far the majority of Indian migrants, however, settled on the West Coast of the United States and Canada. Mostly young male Punjabi Sikhs, often already seasoned travelers from years of military service, these migrants were neither desperately poor nor especially wealthy. They were attracted by job opportunities, often in the hope of earning enough money to return to India to buy land, marry, and have children. Many worked as laborers in lumberyards or as farmers in the San Joaquin, Sacramento, and Imperial valleys of California. By 1920 several thousand Indians—students, religious figures, merchants, and especially laborers and farmers—were living in the United States, struggling to succeed in an often hostile new land.[54]

Many whites living on the West Coast came to see Indians as they did Chinese and Japanese migrants—as an economic and cultural threat. In 1907 a mob of some five hundred people violently expelled a local population of Indian mill workers from Bellingham, Washington. In 1908 the *San Francisco Call* warned of a "Hindu invasion." Anti-immigration societies such as the Asiatic Exclusion League and the California Joint Immigration League worked to prevent further immigration from India into the United States and to restrict the rights of those Indians already in the country. Due largely to popular anti-immigrant sentiment, India was added to the "barred zone" act of 1917, which severely curtailed immigration from India. Proponents of anti-immigrant sentiment ignored the fact that much of the West Coast had only a few generations earlier been Mexican territory.[55]

Indians in America faced social and economic segregation not unlike that faced by African Americans. In January 1913, real estate brokers in Port Angeles, Washington, published a petition in a local newspaper pledging to not sell any property to "Hindoos and Negroes." In a report for the Department of Labor published in 1923, Indian American author Rajani Kanta Das noted that Indians were routinely forced to live in ethnically segregated ghettos, restricted to the lowest-paying occupations, and denied access to hotels and movie theaters. Despite facing similar forms of discrimination, Indians and African Americans appear to have forged fewer intimate connections on the West Coast than on the East Coast. Das noted that although many Indian men had difficulty finding wives, the majority chose not to marry African American women. Das explained the distance between the communities as the result of "a strong prejudice" among Indians against "associating with the negroes in America." Das traced the prejudice to a "feeling of race superiority and partly to the fact that the negroes are socially ostracised by the Americans themselves." The Indians did not want, Das explained, "to be a party to the racial problem." Even if they did maintain distance from Blacks, the majority of Indians could not avoid "the racial problem," given the discriminatory conditions facing Indians on the West Coast.[56]

Unlike the majority of Indians in the United States, a growing number of middle-class Indians managed to use the binary nature of American race relations to claim the privileges of whiteness. At least sixty-nine Indians gained U.S. citizenship in the years between 1908 and 1922.[57] Since the 1790 Naturalization Act limited naturalization to "free white persons," Indians had to claim legal whiteness in order to win American citizenship. Toward that end, many Indians employed the two-nation theory of Indian civilization to convince American judges of their whiteness. They contrasted themselves not only with non-white Americans but with low-caste Indians in order to gain "Caucasian" status and thus American citizenship.

It was in the segregationist South that Indians first became naturalized citizens. In 1908 Abdul Hamid and Ballal Hussain both gained citizenship in New Orleans. The following year, Abba Dolla attained citizenship in Savannah, Georgia. Dolla, a native of Calcutta whose parents were from Afghanistan, needed to prove that he was "Caucasian." Dolla's doctor offered to testify that Dolla was of "pure Caucasian blood." The presiding judge decided, however, to conduct his own examination. The judge described Dolla as follows: "The applicant's complexion is dark, eyes dark, features regular and rather delicate, hair very black, wavy and very fine and soft." These characteristics left the judge uncertain about Dolla's racial identity. Therefore, he asked Dolla to pull up his shirt sleeves so that he could examine Dolla's skin. Fortunately for Dolla, the judge concluded, "The skin of his arm where it had been protected from the sun and weather by his clothing was found to be several shades lighter than that of his face and hands, and was sufficiently transparent for the blue color of the veins to show very clearly." This physiological evidence proved important in the judge's decision to grant citizenship. It was also important, however, for Dolla to prove that the Savannah community had certified his whiteness. The court noted that Dolla traded "among whites and blacks indifferently" and had asked two African Americans to serve as witnesses to his application. Fortunately, however, Dolla had thought far enough ahead to have purchased a lot in a "whites-only" cemetery in Savannah. His court record cites Dolla's burial arrangements as evidence of his whiteness.[58]

To achieve legal whiteness, many Indians marshaled contemporary race science. In the same year that the court granted Dolla citizenship, another Indian named Bhicaji Balsara also applied for naturalization.

Balsara's lawyers argued that Indians were "Caucasian." Although the court found "no difficulty in saying that the Chinese, Japanese, and Malays and the American Indians do not belong to the white race," it was more difficult for the court to define exactly what groups did belong to the "white race." Stating that more research should be done on the subject of how inclusive the term "white" should be, the court accepted Balsara's arguments, found that he belonged to the white race, and affirmed his admission to citizenship.[59]

The federal government consistently opposed Indian claims to whiteness. As early as 1907, Attorney General Charles Bonaparte declared, "Under no construction of the law can natives of British India be regarded as white persons."[60] In 1909 a judge in Massachusetts noted that government attorneys claimed that Indians should be denied citizenship "because many Englishmen treat them with contempt and call them 'niggers.'"[61] The relationship between British imperialism and American discrimination against Indians was not limited to the arguments of government prosecutors. One Sikh laborer on the West Coast remembered, "One day a drunk *ghora* came out of a bar and motioned to me saying, 'Come here, slave!' I said I was no slave man. He told me that his race ruled India and America, too. All we were slaves."[62] The aggressive drunk connected the privileges of whiteness in the United States and India by using the rhetoric of slavery to assert the universal dominance of whites. By using the word "gora," a popular term for a white person, the Sikh laborer demonstrated his own connection between white oppressors in the United States and in India. He responded to the drunk by belittling whiteness itself, unlike many of the middle-class, high-caste Indians who strove to use whiteness to gain legal status.

In 1910 the U.S. Census declared, "Pure-blood Hindus belong ethnically to the Caucasian or white race and in several instances have been officially declared to be white by the United States Courts in naturalization proceedings." Nevertheless, the census classified Indians with "nonwhite Asiatics," explaining that "the Hindus, whether pure-blood or not, represent a civilization distinctly different from that of Europe."[63] The phrase "pure-blood Hindus" intimated a racial division of Indians based on the purity of their racial and caste lineages. In 1911 the United States Immigration Commission ratified the racial division of Indians in its *Dictionary of Races or Peoples*. The *Dictionary* classified "dark Hindus and other peoples of India" as "Aryans" because of their "Aryan speech" and their "physical type." The *Dictionary* distinguished, however, between types of Indians. It proclaimed, "Dravidians and Veddahs who occupy all of Southern India . . . are extremely low in civilization and approaching the Negro in physical characteristics." The entry for the "Mongolian" race stated, "The Mongolian and the Caucasian are the two largest 'races' or divisions of mankind, the latter being somewhat larger because it includes the greater part of the population of India." Including "the greater part" of the population of India as Caucasian left other Indians outside this privileged racial classification.[64] These geographic distinctions divided Indians by race, echoing the arguments of nineteenth-century theorists of the two-race theory of Indian civilization. Once again high-caste and Northern-born Indians were granted "Aryan" identity, while low-caste and "Dravidian" Indians were associated with the "Negro race."

High-caste Indians won American citizenship by employing this racial reading of caste to distinguish themselves from less "racially" suitable Indians. The phrase "pure-blood Hindus" was linked to caste by Akhay Kumar Mozumdar, the first Indian to gain naturalization on the West Coast. While obliquely referring to the same racial arguments that had bolstered the claims of Dolla and Balsara, Mozumdar relied more heavily on the racial purity of his ancestral caste-based lineage, implying that such purity made him "more white" than most other Indians in the United States. Mozumdar stated, "I am a high-caste Hindu of pure blood, belonging to what is known as the warrior caste, or ruling caste." He distinguished himself from other Indians in America on the basis of caste, class, and religion. Mozumdar argued, "The great bulk of the Hindus in this country are not high-caste Hindus, but are what are called sihks, [sic] and are of mixed blood." Emphasizing the class and religious differences between him and the "mixed blood" Sikhs, Mozumdar stated, "The laboring class, those who do the rough manual labor, are not high-caste Hindus at all, but are in an entirely separate class, having quite a different religion and a different ancestry." He concluded, "The high-caste Hindus always consider themselves to be members of the Aryan race." Largely accepting his claim to racial purity and thus superiority, the court granted Mozumdar citizenship.[65]

The ability of Indians to gain legal whiteness ended in 1923 when the Supreme Court ruled against granting citizenship to a U.S. Army veteran, Bhagat Singh Thind. Like Mozumdar, Thind employed caste hierarchy to claim a privileged racial lineage. He proudly told the court that "the high class Hindu regards the aboriginal Indian Mongoloid in the same manner as the American regards the Negro speaking from the matrimonial standpoint." Thind marshaled American racial prejudice to distinguish himself from "Indian Mongoloids" and to claim legal whiteness. Only a few months earlier, the Supreme Court had denied citizenship to a Japanese individual because he was not "Caucasian." It appeared that Thind needed merely to prove that Indians were "Caucasian," a position several earlier courts had already held and that contemporary racial science supported. Writing for the majority, however, Chief Justice Sutherland concluded "that the words 'free white persons' are words of common speech, to be interpreted in accordance with the understanding of the common man." Bracketing "scientific" arguments as irrelevant, Justice Sutherland explained, "It is a matter of familiar observation and knowledge that the physical group characteristics of the Hindus render them readily distinguishable from the various groups of persons in this country commonly recognized as white." Justice Sutherland thus replaced the scientist with "the common man" as the ultimate arbiter of whiteness, rejecting Thind's appeal to the purity of his caste-based racial lineage.[66]

The United States v. Bhagat Singh Thind carried severe ramifications for those Indians like Dolla, Balsara, and Mozumdar who had already been granted citizenship. After 1923 the government successfully denaturalized the majority of Indians who had previously managed to gain citizenship. The vast majority of the Indians granted naturalization as U.S. citizens came from the educated, relatively wealthy elite. Most Indians were effectively barred from establishing their citizenship as they lacked the social and economic standing to hire an attorney and bring their claims to citizenship into American courts. Nevertheless, the Thind decision carried significant consequences for the entire Indian community. Because the 1924 Johnson-Reed Act would soon decree that any group ineligible for citizenship was also ineligible for immigration, Indians were denied not only the right to become citizens but also the right to immigrate. In some states, Indians came under the jurisdiction of laws that denied non-citizens the right to own or lease land. One of the fortunate few to gain and maintain his citizenship, a lawyer named Sakharam Ganesh Pandit, offered an interview in 1926 in which he compared the treatment he had received to discrimination against Black Americans. The African American newspaper, The New York Amsterdam News, reprinted excerpts from the interview as an article entitled, "Negro Should Create His Own God: Hindu Lawyer Says He Should Be Himself and Not Imitate the White Man." Declaring that Pandit had given "Nordic pride and prejudice . . . a slap in the face," the Amsterdam News demonstrated the potential for the Thind decision to bring Indian Americans and Black Americans together in a common struggle against racial prejudice.[67]

In October 1937, the University of Maryland football team vanquished the previously undefeated Syracuse Orangemen 13 to 0, while Syracuse's star player, Wilmeth Sidat-Singh, sat on the sidelines. Sidat-Singh had been benched after a newspaper publicized the fact that he was Black and not, as his name suggested, a "Hindu." Born in Washington, D.C., to an African American couple, Sidat-Singh gained his last name only after his parents divorced and his mother remarried Samuel Sidat-Singh, a doctor of Indian origin. Raised in Trinidad, Dr. Sidat-Singh studied medicine at Howard University before opening a renowned medical practice in Harlem. As his life makes evident, some Indian immigrants, denied American citizenship on racial grounds, found homes, spouses, and opportunity in African American communities. When Wilmeth Sidat-Singh died as a Tuskegee airman in May 1943, it was his adopted father, the man who had given him his name, who best captured what Wilmeth could mean in death for a country whose racial boundaries his life had challenged. "It is our hope," the stricken father told reporters after his son was buried in Arlington National Cemetery, "that Wilmeth and thousands of others like him are not dying in vain, but that when this war is over America will be a safe place for all people, black and white alike."[68]

The majority of Indians who came to the United States before 1923 chose not to seek citizenship. Many planned to return to India after earning money or gaining an education. In the first few decades of the twentieth century, American colleges and universities attracted a growing number of Indian students. These students often encountered American racial prejudice and brought knowledge of American racism back to India. Unlike the majority of immigrants living on the West Coast, however, the discrimination Indian students faced often resulted not from their being despised "Asiatics" but because they were mistaken for Blacks.

Some Indian students arrived in the United States expecting a paradise of freedom and liberty. Growing up "very poor" in the Tipperah district of rural Bengal, Rash Behari Day developed "a strong love" for the United States by reading the works of Swami Vivekananda. In his travel memoirs, published in 1919, Day remembered thinking of the United States as "a glorious land—the earthly garden of God." His first night on American soil evoked memories of childhood lessons on the American Revolution and inspired Day to proclaim, "The great rule that all men are *born equal* holds true in the United States of America."[69]

Day's pursuit of higher education allowed him a unique opportunity to correct his misguided admiration for American equality. Soon after arriving, Day wrote several colleges about gaining admittance despite his limited funds. Only Booker T. Washington wrote back, and Day soon departed for Tuskegee. Throughout his time at Tuskegee, Day observed Washington closely, once having the opportunity to share an intimate dinner with him. In his travel memoirs, Day portrayed Washington as an austere, extremely busy, and extraordinarily impressive man. Day praised Tuskegee for imparting to students "an indomitable spirit of self-exertion and self-confidence." Failing to note the struggles of the surrounding African American community, Day conceived of Tuskegee as a symbol of American racial harmony. For him, Tuskegee was "the greatest testimonial" of "the American spirit of friendliness towards other nations and races."[70]

Although he experienced racial segregation, Day neither opposed it in person nor critiqued it in his writing. Day's first impressions of race in the American South reproduced common stereotypes of African Americans. He wrote, "There for the first time I saw crowds of American Negroes, and the first impression they gave me was that they are never unhappy." Upon entering a "whites only" restaurant, Day was politely questioned by an African American waiter, curious about Day's nationality. Revealing his own prejudices, Day wrote, "I took him to be a curious ignorant chap and I told him that he would not understand." Only later did he learn that the waiter had been surprised that a dark-skinned man had entered a "whites only" restaurant. Day was not entirely oblivious to his position as a dark-skinned man in a society segregated by skin color. In a railway station, Day noticed that the other passengers were segregated by race. He remembered, "I felt a little uneasy, because my color was dark and I might be violating some rules of the State." When no one protested his presence, however, Day's uneasiness passed.[71]

Unlike Rash Behari Day, other Indian students in the United States forcefully criticized the racial divisions of their host country. During the same years that Day studied at Tuskegee, Shridhar Venkatesh Ketkar pursued a PhD in sociology at Cornell. In 1909 Ketkar published his research. While the majority of his book explored caste in India, Ketkar's years in the United States had convinced him that the United States itself had a "caste system." He outlined the American "caste system" as follows:

1. The blue bloods; 2. The New Englanders; 3. The born gentile Americans; 4. The English and Scottish immigrants; 5. The Irish; 6. Gentile immigrants from other countries of Western Europe; 7. Dagoes (Italians); 8. The Jews; 9. The Mongolians; 10. Negroes.

Ketkar's belief that "Negroes" were at the bottom of the American racial hierarchy helps explain why many of his references to caste in America focused on African Americans. While discussing Indian resistance to intercaste marriage, Ketkar referenced American laws that prohibited marriages between "whites and other races." He noted that many states defined persons as "non-white" if they had one-eighth or more "colored blood." Ketkar ridiculed the foolishness of such a pseudo-scientific distinction by recalling conversations he had shared with "some negro students in Cornell and Harvard Universities." These students told Ketkar that they knew of "several cases of young beautiful mulatto women marrying white men without revealing to them their real composition." Ketkar concluded that, like caste, racial differences depended upon artificial distinctions that were arbitrarily administered.[72]

Ketkar used what he called "the caste system in the United States" to critique the practice of caste in India. Ketkar lamented the fact that "very many of the low castes believe, or are made to believe, that they justly suffer in this condition as a retribution for the sins which they did in the past life." He sarcastically concluded, "How much better it would have been for the whites in the United States, had they taught the negroes the doctrines of Transmigration of Soul and Karma instead of Christianity!" A Chitpavan Brahman, Ketkar approached caste as did many high-caste reformers, lamenting the divisiveness of caste while arguing that caste was too embedded in Indian culture and religion to allow dramatic reforms. Ketkar similarly stressed the embedded nature of race within economic, social, and religious systems.[73]

Like Swami Vivekananda, Ketkar argued that American racial prejudice had contributed to the misguided application of Western racial theories to the history of India. Ketkar wrote, "White races came in contact with dark races in America as they did four thousand years ago in India, and attempts are made to discover the 'color prejudice' in every document of this ancient land." Ketkar critiqued the racialized notions of caste that Akhay Kumar Mozumdar and other Indians used to seek American citizenship and argued that knowledge of American racism had encouraged Indians to divide themselves from other Indians on racial and caste-based lines. He explained, "Hearing of the conditions in the United States, those Hindus who think themselves to be Aryans, wish to demark themselves sharply from those whom they think to be Dravidians."[74]

Neither Ketkar nor Rash Behari Day discussed personally facing racial discrimination in the United States. Their silence should not be taken as evidence that Indian students did not encounter American racial prejudice. In 1922 the student newspaper at the Massachusetts Institute of Technology reported that a "high caste" student had been unable to find housing in "districts where there exists a prejudice against negroes." In Albany, New York, a female Ceylonese student was denied lodging at the local YWCA after being mistaken for a Black woman. She was refused entry even after she explained that she was from Ceylon and had nowhere else to stay the night. In Hartford, Connecticut, a Chinese restaurant refused to seat Indian customers out of fear that white customers would take the Indians to be "Negroes" and would boycott the restaurant.[75]

To avoid suffering discrimination, some Indians donned turbans in order to distinguish themselves from African Americans. One former Indian student, Bharatan Kumarappa, defended the wearing of turbans as "perhaps natural," given the fact that Indians "did not want to be insulted and treated with disrespect." Unfortunately, the desire to not be taken as African American led many Indians to not want "to associate with Negroes or to be found in Negro company." Kumarappa concluded:

> So Indians also often fell into the vicious habit of boycotting the Negro. The air in America was surcharged with it and it was difficult to escape it. But it must be said to the credit of a few Indians I knew that they went out of their way to befriend Negroes. After all, our sympathy cannot but be with those who suffer at the hands of the whites.

Kumarappa's account of his time in the United States, published in Bombay in 1945, was based on some twenty talks Kumarappa had given to friends between February and July 1943, when they were imprisoned in Nagpur Central Jail for protesting British rule. Kumarappa's solidarity with "those who suffer at the hands of the whites" speaks as much to the context of the 1940s as to the years he spent in the United States.[76]

In the years between the First and Second World Wars, relationships between Indians and African Americans grew in number and depth. While some nineteenth-century racial theories had linked Indians and "Negroes" at the bottom of a global racial hierarchy, others had divided Indians, associating the higher castes with Aryans or Caucasians and the lower castes with Negroes. In the racialized systems of South Africa and the United States, many Indians strove to claim the privileges of whiteness by distancing themselves from both Blacks and the lower castes. Racial theories did not only divide, however. Increasingly, a new generation of activists employed a language of racial pride to unite Indians and African Americans in opposition to white racist imperialism. Often this language reified racial divisions, even while fostering interracial and, at times, transracial alliances and calling into question the idea of race itself.

CHAPTER TWO

Racial Diplomacy

> Africa and India, the Blind Samsons, are now awake. . . . The
> cannons of the allies and the central powers have aroused
> them from their long slumber.
>
> —John Edward Bruce, *The Selected Writings of John Edward Bruce*

THE WAR BETWEEN European empires that erupted in August
1914 signaled to many contemporaries the decline of a global
racially coded imperial order. "Watch and wait!" declared the
African Times and Orient Review. "It may be that the non-European
races will profit by the European disaster." The Great War, African American columnist John Edward Bruce prophesied, would end "white domination" throughout the world.[1] Like Bruce's personification of Africa
and India as once powerful Samsons, appeals for unity between Blacks and
Indians in the wake of the Great War often treated the Indian and African
American communities as homogenous units. Advocates of Afro-Indian
solidarity reached across racial categories not to challenge or complicate
these categories but to pursue particular conceptions of race or nation. As
international relations often reinforce the nation even while transcending
it, so racial diplomats presented contested categories such as "Indian" and
"Negro" as settled facts, imbued with transnational respectability.

While recognizing religious and caste diversity in India, many African
Americans praised Indians and the newly famous Mahatma Gandhi for
achieving what appeared to be a remarkable unity of resistance to white
imperial oppression. Gandhi's noncooperation movement, in which
many Indians boycotted British goods and institutions of the Raj, demonstrated the ability of an oppressed people, if unified and organized on

---

John Edward Bruce, *The Selected Writings of John Edward Bruce: Militant Black
Journalist,* compiled and edited by Peter Gilbert (New York: Arno Press, 1971),
152–153.

racial and national lines, to advance amidst the collapse of the old world order. Many Blacks looked toward Gandhi with their own struggles in mind. Black encounters with India in the 1920s defied the dichotomization of the local and the global. As exemplified by Marcus Garvey and his Universal Negro Improvement Association (UNIA), African American engagement with India demonstrated a profound transnational awareness that was simultaneously tightly linked to local and national initiatives. Garvey epitomized racial diplomacy. His frequent references to Gandhi and India served to legitimize Garvey's own efforts to unite "the Negro race."[2]

Indians often used racial diplomacy to refute the claim that religious and caste stratification rendered India not one but many nations. While Black Americans lauded Gandhi for uniting a diverse nation, Indians often compared race in America to caste in India, acknowledging that Indian unity was an incomplete project. They utilized the race/caste analogy to oppose inequalities in both India and the United States. Comparisons between race and caste did not always produce such a double-edged transnational egalitarianism. At times the race/caste analogy operated as a form of transnational self-justification. The conservative potential of race/caste comparison was made clear in the wake of Katherine Mayo's infamous critique of Indian society, *Mother India*. Responding to Mayo, Indians claimed that the racial wrongs of the United States exceeded the injustices of caste, while Americans argued the opposite. Ranking injustice, claiming that the wrongs of others minimized one's own guilt, both Indians and Americans demonstrated the blindness of a racial diplomacy that utilized transnational comparison to defend the nation.

The Great War

The geography of empire meant that the Great War had, from its inception, global implications. Some of the earliest fighting took place in Togoland and German South-West Africa between German, French, and British colonial troops, many of whom were African themselves. In addition to the location of battles, the war gained global significance by mobilizing soldiers from the farthest reaches of the imperial systems and bringing them into contact with each other and with foreign civilians. Indian soldiers fought from German East Africa to Mesopotamia to the forests of northern France. Some 200,000 African American soldiers were sent to the Western Front, although the vast majority were denied the right to fight, restricted instead to equally dangerous but less prestigious noncombat duties. Like Indian and other colonial troops, African American soldiers gave their lives in distant lands for a freedom they were denied at home.[3]

More than the geography of battles and the diversity of soldiers, it was the gap between the rhetoric of the Great War and the reality of racism and imperialism it left unresolved that gave the war global significance. While Woodrow Wilson's defense of "democracy" and "self-determination" inspired hope throughout the world, anticolonial activists struggled against imperial oppression. The conflict between the rhetoric of the war and the experiences of many of the non-white combatants provided new opportunities to anticolonial, antiracist activists who had for many years attempted to forge links between diverse oppressions throughout the world.[4]

On September 25, 1917, an officer in the United States War Department wrote W. E. B. Du Bois to request information on the Indian anticolonial activist Lala Lajpat Rai. Known affectionately as the Lion of the Punjab, Lajpat Rai was one of India's most renowned critics of British imperialism. Considered a dangerous extremist by British officials, Lajpat Rai had been deported to Burma without trial in 1907. When the Great War began, he was in London, about to embark on a brief journey through Europe before returning to India. Instead, with wartime restrictions severely limiting free speech in India, Lajpat Rai found refuge in the United States. He had been to the United States before, staying for a few weeks in the fall of 1905. Nearly a decade later, facing the possibility of imprisonment in India, Lajpat Rai chose to extend his second stay in America for more than five years. He developed friendships with National Association for the Advancement of Colored People (NAACP) founders Mary White Ovington and Oswald Garrison Villard and made a point of meeting a range of African American leaders, including John Hope, the president of Morehouse College, and George Washington Carver, the renowned scientist. Booker T. Washington accompanied Lajpat Rai on a trip to Black communities in the South. Du Bois and Lajpat Rai corresponded, exchanged books, joined the same civic club, and met at both Du Bois's office and his home.

It was a public appearance the two men made together that prompted the War Department to seek information about Lajpat Rai from Du Bois. "Mr. Lajpat Rai seems anxious for trouble," the officer warned Du Bois, before asking, "Did anything of his address bear upon the negro question in this country?" The officer wondered whether Lajpat Rai "was inclined to make trouble here as well as in the world generally."[5] Standing next to Du Bois at the Intercollegiate Socialist Society, Lajpat Rai had proclaimed, "The problem of the Hindu and of the negro and cognate problems are not local, but world problems."[6] If Du Bois understood such a statement as making "trouble," it was a trouble he would have warmly embraced.

No one did more to transform the Great War into a struggle against racism and imperialism than Du Bois. India played a crucial role in his efforts to encourage transnational solidarities between oppressed peoples. Beginning in the late nineteenth century, Du Bois grew increasingly interested in Indian freedom struggles. His interest reached new heights in the wake of the war as Gandhi's noncooperation movement garnered world attention and as Indian Americans and their American supporters gained increasing prominence. The links between the NAACP and Indian American organizations were manifold. For example, Reverend John Haynes Holmes, a founder and board member of the NAACP and a liberal white proponent of racial equality, was also among the most vocal American supporters of India's independence. In July 1921, *The Crisis* quoted Holmes declaring that Gandhi was the "greatest man alive in the world today." Du Bois himself met with K. D. Shastri, the secretary of the India Home Rule League, in New York in 1914 and corresponded with him toward the end of the war.[7]

Indian and African American activists found common ground in their shared opposition to the hypocrisy of wartime pronouncements concerning freedom and self-determination. In January 1921, *The Crusader*, the journal of the Harlem-based African Blood Brotherhood, noted that British troops were "advancing on the Wana Wazirs, a tribe on the North-west frontier of India." *The Crusader* commented acidly, "More self-determination, we suppose."[8] When, in 1921, the Friends of Freedom for India held a national convention in New York, Du Bois echoed the convention's anti-imperial conclusions in *The Crisis*, describing British rule as "opposed to the welfare of all the Indian people."[9] Du Bois's strongest link to India during this period was the founder of the Friends of Freedom for India, none other than Lala Lajpat Rai.

After his first trip to the United States in 1905, Lajpat Rai noted, "The whites have a great prejudice against what are here known as the coloured people." In 1916 Lajpat Rai published a book on the challenges of the United States "with an eye to their practical usefulness for our own development."[10] *The United States of America: A Hindu's Impressions and a Study* dwells at great length on the struggles of African Americans, revealing that Lajpat Rai saw much in the Black condition comparable to the problems India faced. A leading figure in the Hindu reformist organization, the Arya Samaj, Lajpat Rai championed the Samaj's efforts to oppose the wrongs of colonialism while reforming Indian society from within. The Samaj had long challenged caste-based oppression, and Lajpat Rai himself spoke out against caste as an aberration unbecoming the unity of the original Aryas. He contributed to the Samaj's development of an ethnically and religiously based nationalism that aggressively courted Dalits and other low castes while uniting Hindus in opposition to Muslim and Christian missionaries. His evolving views on caste, religion, and nation influenced his perspectives on the struggles of African Americans and were in turn mirrored in his writings on race in America. Using American racism and Black struggles to defend his conception of the Indian nation, Lajpat Rai employed an ambivalent racial diplomacy that condemned injustice in the United States and India, while at times using the former to excuse the latter.[11]

Like Gandhi, Lajpat Rai gleaned from the educational efforts of African Americans—and in particular Booker T. Washington—lessons for his fellow Indians. Lajpat Rai's praise for Washington was, however, limited by his admiration for Du Bois. Lajpat Rai argued that "higher liberal education" and "vocational or industrial" training were both important and depended upon each other. He ultimately stressed higher education, however, by linking Washington with vocational training, and then concluding, in line with Du Bois's judgment, that "Mr. Washington represents in Negro thought the old attitude of adjustment and submission."[12] Lajpat Rai applied his research on African American education to debates within India. A persistent supporter of women's rights, he noted that facilities "for the higher education of the Negro women, are decidedly larger, better, and more liberal than those that exist in India for the education of Indian women."[13] He used the educational efforts of African Americans to bolster his vision for a literate India that did not discriminate against women.

Unlike many Indian reformers, who tended to utilize either the race/caste or the race/nation parallel, Lajpat Rai compared African Americans with both Dalits and with all Indians. However, while he often employed the race/nation parallel to stress Black and Indian initiatives, his use of the race/caste parallel ignored Dalit agency. Lajpat Rai lamented that both African Americans and Dalits were treated as "pariahs" in their respective societies. The word "pariah" came into English from the Tamil "paraiyar," literally meaning "drummer" but referring to a particular low caste in South India. Thus when Lajpat Rai declared "The Negro is the PARIAH of America," he explicitly juxtaposed caste oppression and American racism. In a chapter entitled "Caste in America," Lajpat Rai called it "remarkable" that "as in India, so in America, the discrimination against people of different color (between the Varnas of the Hindus) should be manifested in almost identical ways." Whereas some scholars of race had juxtaposed Blacks and low-caste Indians in order to declare their equal inferiority, Lajpat Rai focused on the oppression of Blacks and of Dalits as problems that needed to be solved.[14]

Despite his opposition to caste oppression, Lajpat Rai's commitment to Hindu unity led him to portray caste inequality as less rigid than American racism. Lajpat Rai used American racism to discredit Christian missionaries and to disarm their criticisms of caste in India. He described support for *The Birth of a Nation,* the notoriously popular chronicle of the origins of the Ku Klux Klan, as "a better and surer index of Christian feeling in this country than any number of books written by Christian missionaries." His distaste for missionaries led him to assert the dubious claim that caste was not as rigid as race. He stated that although the child of a Black woman and a white man was considered Black, the child of a Brahmin father and a Shudra mother achieved a higher social position than Shudra. "The Hindu Aryans of India," Lajpat Rai concluded, "never applied the color bar so rigidly as the Christian whites of the United States of America."[15]

Although he decried white supremacy, like Bhagat Singh Thind and other Indian Americans, Lajpat Rai used contemporary racial theories to claim the privileges of whiteness. In June 1916 he informed several U.S. senators, "It has been acknowledged by the highest scholastic authority in the world, that the Hindus are from the Aryan Stock." Ignoring American racial inequality, Lajpat Rai stated that the exclusion of Indians was "unworthy of the high mindness [*sic*] of this great nation which stands for equal opportunity."[16] In his zeal to defend the Indian nation, Lajpat Rai risked muting his criticism of American racism. In a pamphlet he produced while in the United States, Lajpat Rai declared, "The war has made the Indian feel that, as a British subject, he is really a despicable creature entitled to no consideration at the hands of the other people of the world. Even the negroes (whether in Africa or America) are much better placed than he is."[17]

In the wake of the First World War, many Indians and Americans recognized parallels between British imperialism and American racial hierarchy; both contradicted the rhetoric of the war and yet remained largely unchanged by the outcome of the conflict. Inspired in part by his relationship with Lajpat Rai, Du Bois repeatedly referenced India as one example of the hollowness of Wilsonian rhetoric. In March 1918, in a letter to the editor of the *Internationalist,* Du Bois lamented the fact that there had been "almost no suggestion that the thousands of millions of India, or Africa, and the islands of the sea have any voice or vote." A year later he told readers of *The Crisis* that "Egypt, India and Ireland are not free."[18] When the United States first entered the war, Du Bois encouraged African Americans to "close ranks" and actively support the war effort, in the hopes that such participation would create opportunities for Black advancement. The sacrifices of Black soldiers did not, however, inspire a reduction in racial hostility from white Americans. On the contrary, the achievement of peace in Europe was followed closely by a wave of racial violence in the United States. American racial hierarchy survived "the war for democracy."

Many Indians, including Mahatma Gandhi, experienced a similar pattern of unfulfilled hopes. Having offered support to the British war effort, they found themselves facing increased repression in the aftermath of the war. Indian soldiers fought in large numbers for the British Empire. Many Indians looked forward to achieving representative government in the wake of the conflict. Instead, moderate constitutional reforms were combined with the notorious Rowlatt Act, extending indefinitely the "emergency" suspension of civil liberties that had been enacted during the war. In April 1919, amidst growing protests against the Rowlatt Act, a British brigadier general ordered his soldiers to fire upon a peaceful assembly in Amritsar's Jallianwalla Bagh, a public square surrounded by high walls affording little means of escape. Ten minutes of continuous firing left an official tally of 379 people dead and many more wounded.[19]

Protests against the Rowlatt Act and the blatant violence of British rule culminated in a nationwide noncooperation movement. Beginning in the fall of 1920, nonviolent protesters walked out of schools and government jobs and boycotted public transportation, English-made clothing, and courts of law. Largely orchestrated by Gandhi, these protests gained the Mahatma a position of national leadership and international renown. The African American press covered the noncooperation movement closely, at times debating the applicability of Gandhian nonviolence to the struggle against American racism. More often, however, Black Americans ignored the practicality of Gandhian techniques in the United States and, in a demonstration of transnational solidarity, focused instead on Gandhi's success in India. The first major wave of African American engagement with Gandhi had begun.

Gandhi in Reflection

In December 1921 the final edition of *The Brownies' Book*, a magazine for African American children edited by Du Bois and Jessie Fauset, carried two dramatically distinct accounts of Gandhi and the Indian struggle. The first, a full-page article entitled "'Saint' Gandhi," compared Gandhi to Christ. Written by Blanche Watson, a white American who would soon author her own book on Gandhi, the article reflected the influence of a recent sermon by Unitarian minister and NAACP board member John Haynes Holmes. Holmes had deemed Gandhi the greatest man in the world, and Watson chose that phrase, "The Greatest Man in the World," as her subtitle. Echoing Holmes, Watson presented Gandhi as a modern-day Messiah. "Now, today, on the other side of the world, in far away India," she wrote, "a man is preaching as did Jesus of Nazareth." On the following page of the magazine, Du Bois offered his young readers a similarly sympathetic reading of Gandhi's noncooperation movement. Du Bois, however, emphasized the mass mobilization and the color dynamics of the Indian struggle more than its leadership. He told his young readers, "In India several hundred millions of brown people are much incensed at the injustice of English rule." Only at the end of a dense paragraph on the struggle of the Indian masses did Du Bois add, "Their leader is named Gandhi."[20]

Neither Du Bois nor Watson suggested adopting Gandhian techniques for the struggle against American racial injustice. When, in August 1921, *The Crisis* reprinted an open letter that Gandhi had written to the British people, it did so without making any reference to African American struggles. In June 1922 *The Crisis* reproduced an article by Syud Hossain that declared "India must be free" but made no comparison with the ongoing African American struggle for freedom. If Blacks saw in Gandhi something to emulate, they also saw something worthy of praise in its own right.[21]

This is not to say that Black Americans did not connect the Indian struggle to their own. The Black press regularly made explicit comparisons between British imperialism in India and oppression in the United States. In April 1922 *The Chicago Defender* reproduced an article by Basanta Koomar Roy, an Indian American writer. The *Defender* entitled Roy's piece "Oppressed India, Great Britain's Dixieland," despite the fact that the article itself never made a comparison between India and the Jim Crow South. On the contrary, Roy concluded his article with a different analogy, stating that the princes of India and the Gandhian "revolutionists" may "drive the British out, even as George Washington and Lafayette did in America."[22] While Roy presented the American Revolution as an example of anticolonial rebellion, the *Defender* found India and the land of George Washington equally in need of liberation.

Like some Indian socialists and many Indian communists, many African Americans on the left of the political spectrum tended to view Gandhi suspiciously or to ignore him entirely. *The Crusader,* the organ of the communist-affiliated African Blood Brotherhood, reported favorably on the Indian struggle while giving more credit to Soviet inspiration than to Gandhi. *The Crusader* made evident its lack of interest in Gandhian nonviolence by printing an appeal requesting funds for an armed rebellion in India.[23] In March 1922 the Black socialist newspaper *The Messenger,* edited by A. Philip Randolph and Chandler Owen, stated its interest in "the eventful course of the Indian Liberation Movement." Its opinion of Gandhi was less positive. An anonymously written article in *The Messenger* declared, "He is not a revolutionist. Gandhi is a pure Nationalist." While noting that "the non-cooperation idea in India is something new in social methodology," *The Messenger* stated that many Indians favored the use of force to gain independence. The response of Left-leaning Blacks to Gandhi was far from uniform. In May 1922 the editors of *The Messenger* published a rejoinder to its earlier criticism of Gandhi as a "pure Nationalist." Written by Blanche Watson, the article declared, "Much has been said and written about the economic bases of revolution, but it has taken a 'Saint,'—one who declares that he is a religious man trying to put religion into politics—to come the closest to proving this premise." Watson emphasized the political and economic practicality of Gandhi's nonviolence. Rather than encouraging Black socialists to engage in Gandhian techniques, however, Watson lauded the Mahatma as "a supreme religious teacher."[24]

Many of the articles that were most enthusiastic about Gandhi focused more on his spiritual excellence than on the applicability of nonviolent tactics. While Blanche Watson's "Saint Gandhi" exemplified this approach, even the skeptical Du Bois occasionally warmed to Gandhi's spiritual prowess. In March 1922 Du Bois published a glowing article in *The Crisis* that discussed Gandhi's initiatives at length. The article focused less on nonviolence as a technique of social change, however, than as a demonstration of spiritual achievement. "India has been called a land of saints, the home of religions," Du Bois began. He called Gandhi "an exceptional soul." Du Bois examined the demands of the Indian National Congress and praised noncooperation and nonviolence as strategies to meet those demands. Nonetheless, the article reads more as a highly laudatory biography of Gandhi than as an assessment of noncooperation or strategies of nonviolence, neither of which Du Bois suggested emulating.[25]

The line between praising Gandhi's nonviolence and encouraging its use should not be drawn too strongly. Indeed, the religious framework in which many Americans came to understand Gandhi greatly facilitated Black efforts to utilize Gandhian nonviolence. Take, for example, an article entitled "Gandhi, Indian Messiah and Saint," published in the African Methodist Episcopal (AME) *Church Review* in October 1921 by Reverdy C. Ransom, editor of the *Church Review* and a veteran Black activist. Ransom discussed the noncooperation movement in detail and proclaimed, "The struggle of those long oppressed deserves the sympathetic understanding of every man who waits for a new birth of freedom in every land." He linked Gandhi to Christ, declared, "The spiritual weapon used by Gandhi is intensely practical," and concluded that "if the triumph of India should mean the triumph of the spirit and method of Gandhi then indeed would a new day dawn for all mankind."[26]

Several Black observers praised Gandhi's religiosity while explicitly encouraging nonviolent protest. In December 1921 a columnist for the *Chicago Defender* declared that Gandhi "believes in the doctrine taught by the Christ and turns the other cheek twice and yet again if necessary." Lest its readers fail to make the link themselves, the *Defender* prophesied, "We believe that some empty Jim Crow cars will some day worry our street car magnates in Southern cities when we get around to walking rather than suffer insult and injury to our wives and children." In 1922 the executive secretary of the NAACP, James Weldon Johnson, lauded Gandhi as "a prophet and a saint" in an editorial in *The New York Age*. Johnson declared, "If non-cooperation brings the British to their knees in India, there is no reason why it should not bring the white man to his knees in the South."[27]

In March 1924 African American sociologist E. Franklin Frazier attacked the equation of nonviolence and spirituality in an editorial in *The Crisis*. Frazier did not aim to criticize nonviolent civil disobedience but to denounce a weak nonviolence that glorified passivity. In response to Frazier's article, *The Crisis* received letters of protest, prompting Du Bois to offer Frazier the opportunity to respond in print. While his original article referenced neither India nor Gandhi, Frazier now chose to explicitly discuss the relevance of Gandhi's example to the Black struggle. He asked his readers to imagine that "there should arise a Gandhi to lead Negroes without hate in their hearts to stop tilling the fields of the South under the peonage system; to cease paying taxes to States that keep their children in ignorance; and to ignore the iniquitous disfranchisement and Jim-Crow laws." Frazier prophesied, "I fear we would witness an unprecedented massacre of defenseless black men and women in the name of Law and Order and there would scarcely be enough Christian sentiment in America to stay the flood of blood."[28] Frazier's criticism focused less on Gandhi's techniques than on the violence and hypocrisy of white America that would render nonviolent protest counterproductive or worse. In the wake of the successful nonviolent protests of the 1940s, 1950s, and 1960s, Frazier's doubts might appear unwarranted. However, even during the Second World War, at a time when large numbers of African Americans had moved to the North and West and a more militant spirit pervaded many Black communities, the majority of African American leaders continued to oppose nonviolent civil disobedience, given the potential for violent white resistance. The eventual successes of nonviolent civil disobedience within the United States, successes that were achieved at the cost of great suffering and bloodshed, depended in part on changes in world politics, including India's independence, which occurred decades after Frazier was writing.

Even those who opposed the application of Gandhian civil disobedience in the United States often praised Gandhi and the Indian struggle. Although he described Frazier's counsel against Gandhian agitation as "eminently clear and sound," Du Bois maintained an interest in Gandhi and the Indian struggle more generally. In the same editorial in which he published Frazier's skepticism regarding an American Gandhi, Du Bois recognized "the apostle of passive resistance" in a short piece on "World Leaders" that "Negroes would be especially interested in."[29] Many African Americans praised the unity of Indians in opposition to British injustice. Hindu-Muslim unity won particular admiration. Gandhi received credit for partnering with Indian Muslims who were concerned over the fate of the caliph—the titular head of Sunni Muslims—after Turkey had been conquered by British forces. Gandhi's embrace of the Khilafat cause demonstrated both his shrewd political calculus and his religious pluralism.[30] African Americans, however, tended to explain Gandhi's success at unifying Indians as a result of his personal spiritual power. In July 1921 *The Crisis* wrote of Gandhi, "It is this blameless life of his which has accomplished the incredible—that of bringing together the numerous sects of India."[31]

Gandhi's success at forging Hindu-Muslim unity was not as seamless as many African American accounts indicated. In August 1921 Muslims in the Malabar district of present-day Kerala rose in revolt against their largely Hindu landowners and the British colonial government. The Moplah rebellion, although brutally crushed, demonstrated the potential for violent revolt, as well as the possibility that such revolt would occur along the lines of class, caste, and religion that continued to divide much of India. In February 1922 Gandhi ended the noncooperation movement after nearly two dozen policemen were killed in a single incident in a small town called Chauri Chaura. Coming after earlier outbreaks of violence, the killings at Chauri Chaura convinced Gandhi that his nonviolent movement was becoming increasingly violent and uncontrollable.[32] Gandhi's decision to end the movement disappointed many and gave the British an opportunity to arrest Gandhi and to suppress any further signs of protest. Black Americans continued to debate the Mahatma and his methods, as well as the larger Indian struggle, throughout the 1920s.[33] Coverage of India would reach new heights during Gandhi's next national nonviolent civil disobedience campaign in 1930.

In the aftermath of the First World War, many Black Americans looked toward Gandhi and India not for models of nonviolent protest but for examples of anticolonial activity, spiritual achievement, unity in the struggle against oppression, and integrity in leadership. At a time when a diversity of distinct African American organizations jockeyed for support, questions of unity and leadership were especially important. The largest and most transnational African American organization of the time, Marcus Garvey's UNIA, confronted many of the challenges that Gandhi and the Indian National Congress faced. Both organizations forged solidarities based on a combination of race and nation while reaching out to other oppressed people worldwide. Both strove to create a unified struggle that was nonetheless open to religious and class diversity. Largely unconcerned with nonviolent protest, Garvey looked to India as an example of the rise of an oppressed people and for evidence of the need for unity and strong leadership. Revealing both the power and the limitations of racial diplomacy, Garvey drew upon Gandhi's example to reinforce his own standing as a leader.

Garvey as Racial Diplomat

In addition to politically charged expatriate Indians like Lala Lajpat Rai, the Great War brought large numbers of Caribbean Blacks to the United States. Caribbean immigrants helped internationalize and radicalize urban Black communities, already swelled by new arrivals from the South. Like Indian immigrants, many Caribbean Blacks brought with them a keen awareness of the wrongs of colonialism and especially of the British Empire.[34] Several of the most prominent Caribbean Blacks championed India's cause, none with more flair or influence than Marcus Garvey.

Born in Saint Ann's Bay, Jamaica, in 1887, Garvey traveled extensively, personally encountering the poverty and discrimination that Blacks faced throughout much of the world. In 1914 he returned to Jamaica and founded what would become the UNIA. Like Gandhi, Garvey was strongly inspired by Booker T. Washington. In 1916 Garvey traveled to the United States to raise funds for an industrial school in Jamaica modeled on the Tuskegee Institute. He settled in New York City, where he slowly expanded the UNIA and began publication of its weekly newspaper, *The Negro World*. Between 1917 and 1925, Garvey oversaw the rise of the largest mass movement among African Americans since emancipation. The Garvey movement was not limited to the United States. Branches of the UNIA operated in Africa, the Caribbean, Europe, and Australia. Garvey himself was resolutely transnational in his outlook. He envisioned no less than the unification and worldwide empowerment of the "Negro race."[35] Transnational but not transracial, Garvey's initiatives reinforced racial boundaries, even while opposing racial and colonial oppression. Garvey utilized transnational comparisons with India to defend his conception of Negro unity and his own claims to leadership. He employed a form of racial diplomacy that maintained divisions between "Indians" and "Negroes" while advocating cooperation between these distinct "peoples."

In the wake of the First World War, Garvey regularly referenced the Indian struggle along with other anticolonial movements to illustrate the racial restructuring of the world. The oppressed races of the world were rising toward freedom, Garvey proclaimed. Blacks the world over needed only to organize and mobilize to take their rightful place in the new world order. At the first international convention of the UNIA in New York on August 1, 1920, Garvey declared, "The world is reorganizing, the world is reconstructing itself, and in this reconstruction Ireland is striking out for freedom; Egypt is striking out for freedom; India is striking out for freedom; and the Negroes of the world shall do no less than strike out also for freedom." In August 1921, speaking at the UNIA's Liberty Hall in New York, Garvey welcomed "the news that there is a serious uprising in India, and the English people are marshaling their troops to subdue the spirit of liberty, of freedom, which is now permeating India." While presenting the Indian cause as a struggle for "liberty" and "freedom," Garvey made clear that it was also a racial struggle that Blacks should emulate by unifying the "Negro race." "The conflict between the races is drawing nearer and nearer," he told his audience, "as expressed in the uprising in India."[36]

Many African Americans contrasted the experience of being a minority in a predominantly white country with the Indian experience of being a majority ruled by a small minority of whites. Garvey's emphasis on the African diaspora avoided this contrast. For Garvey, African Americans were "Negroes" and thus, like Indians, constituted a demographically massive group, oppressed despite their numbers, not because of them. Garvey paired references to the "four hundred million Negroes of the world" with numeric estimates of the Indian people to make a prima facie case for racial unity. He marshaled population statistics to present his listeners with hope in the power of large politically oppressed groups.[37]

Garvey lauded the unity of the Indian struggle, despite evidence of its fractures. The "serious uprising in India" that Garvey praised as resulting from the "spirit of liberty, of freedom" was the Moplah rebellion of August 1921, in which poor Muslims battled wealthy Hindu landowners and their colonial protectors. Not only did Garvey overlook the class and religious divisions at the heart of the revolt, he portrayed the struggle as a triumph of Hindu-Muslim unity. He declared, "If it is possible for Hindus and Mohammedans to come together in India, it is possible for Negroes to come together everywhere." Garvey utilized Indian unity to demonstrate the importance of solidarity within what he called the "Negro race."[38]

The juxtaposition of Indian unity and Negro unity marked much of the extensive coverage of Indian struggles in *The Negro World*. Like Garvey, columnist A. H. Maloney used India to emphasize the necessity and the challenge of racial unity. Maloney employed orientalist stereotypes to portray the challenge to Indian unity. He told the readers of *The Negro World*, "Gandhi has to bridge the 2,000 castes, and a score of . . . religious and social ideals. He has to weld into one the proud Parsee, the passive Budhist [*sic*], the belligerent Moslem, and the cold Confician [*sic*]." Maloney compared Gandhi's Herculean task of unification to the equally daunting challenge Garvey confronted in trying to unite the "Negro race." Such comparisons resonated with at least some members of the UNIA. After Garvey was convicted of mail fraud in 1923, the officers of the St. Louis UNIA division wrote President Calvin Coolidge to ask for a presidential pardon. They noted, "Every race has placed someone at the head to guide them," offering, among other examples, that "India honors Ghandi [*sic*]."[39]

Garvey's racial diplomacy—his vision for a partnership between distinct Indian and Negro "peoples"—appealed not only to Garvey's many supporters but to many Indians as well. Garvey hired as a contributor to *The Negro World* and his *Daily Negro Times* an Indian of Caribbean descent, Hucheshwar G. Mudgal, and met with several prominent Indian Americans, including Lala Lajpat Rai and a young Gandhian graduate student, Haridas T. Muzumdar.[40] A student at Northwestern University in his early twenties, Muzumdar became actively involved in bridging the movements of Gandhi and Garvey. After reading about a lynching in the South, Muzumdar could not eat for two days. He approached Garvey, who invited him to give a series of lectures in Harlem. Muzumdar used the opportunity to discuss the noncooperation movement in India and to praise the achievements of African peoples. In May 1922 he discussed "Gandhi and the Future of India" at the UNIA's Liberty Hall and gave "an illustrated talk on India" the following week. *The Negro World* publicized both speeches as "very classic events . . . well worth going to." On May 6, 1922, *The Negro World* published an article by Muzumdar entitled, "Gandhi the Apostle of Freedom." The article emphasized the Mahatma's encounter with "blind color prejudice" in South Africa. Three months later, Muzumdar participated in the UNIA convention in New

York, where he was introduced to the assembly as a member of Gandhi's noncooperation movement. In his remarks, Muzumdar praised the work of the UNIA and observed that "Indians were suffering in the same way as the Negroes of the West Indies."[41]

In January 1922 Garvey invited a Dr. Singh to speak about the Indian freedom struggle at a UNIA gathering in New York. According to *The Negro World*, Dr. Singh stated that Gandhi's movement was successful because it put "into practical application the meaning of the word unity." He compared Gandhi and Garvey as great unifiers and encouraged a "great alliance" between Blacks and Indians worldwide. Reporting Dr. Singh's speech, *The Negro World* declared that India would not be satisfied with being led by "some British white man."[42] One Indian speaker at a UNIA event in October 1920 echoed the antiwhite sentiments so often associated with Garvey by his critics. According to FBI special agent P-138, Garvey introduced the speaker by saying that Indians "were fighting for the same thing that he was fighting for." The Indian speaker praised Garvey "for his courage and determination" and proclaimed that whites "were the en[em]ies of mankind," and that they "should be fought tooth and nail." Such a blanket condemnation of whites contradicted Garvey's frequent statements of respect for all races and his extraordinary admiration for the Irish struggle. Nevertheless, agent P-138's report indicates Indian sympathy with Garvey's strong racialism and his opposition to white hegemony.[43]

On February 4, 1922, a United States intelligence official sent the director of the Office of Naval Intelligence a secret warning. "The present Hindu revolutionary movement has definite connections with the Negro agitation in America," the letter began ominously. As evidence, the official declared that Gandhi and Garvey "were class mates while they were studying in England and in India" and that "Garvey has remained ever since the closest friend, most ardent admirer and the handiest co-worker of Ganti [*sic*], even though they live thousands of miles apart." Even more troublingly, the letter declared, "Both Garvey and Ganti are strong believers in socialism and the revolutionary methods for realizing it."[44] A jumble of falsities, this letter exemplifies the misinformation that underpinned government fears of radical Indian and African American organizations. Although Garvey and Gandhi did both spend time in England, they were not classmates. The two men could not be called close friends, and while both acknowledged class inequality and championed the poor, neither qualified as a "strong believer in socialism." On the contrary, as dedicated advocates of Washingtonian self-help, Gandhi and Garvey were consistently criticized by socialists and communists for failing to sufficiently recognize class inequality.

Garvey evinced little interest in nonviolent civil disobedience. Nevertheless, he frequently referenced Gandhi in his speeches and writings. These references reveal much about Garvey's internationalism and the broader African American encounter with Gandhi. Garvey's interest in Gandhi was manifold. At times Garvey located the Mahatma within a panoply of great racial leaders, in whose company Garvey also placed himself. Often Garvey utilized Gandhi to instruct his audience in the importance of remaining unified behind a leader. In January 1922 Garvey told an audience that Indians had "spent millions and millions, billions of dollars, in the cause of Indian freedom." He stressed that both the wealthy and the poor contributed to Gandhi's cause, and that the Mahatma himself was "held in the highest respect and regard by the people whom he leads." Garvey's message was clear—if African Americans wanted freedom, they needed to support the UNIA as the Indian people supported Gandhi.[45]

By expressing solidarity with India and Gandhi, Garvey presented himself as the representative of "the Negro people." On March 12, 1922, Garvey responded to Gandhi's arrest by offering a classic example of racial diplomacy. Garvey had been arrested for mail fraud only two months earlier. Implicitly comparing himself and Gandhi, Garvey declared, "Gandhi's arrest is nothing unexpected to those of us who understand what leadership means. Leadership means sacrifice; leadership means martyrdom."[46] In 1921 Garvey telegrammed Gandhi, "Please accept best wishes of 400,000,000 Negroes through us their representatives, for the speedy emancipation of India from the thralldom of foreign oppression." Sending telegrams abroad proved an easy way to gain legitimacy and to assert leadership. To the *Madras Mail*, the British prime minister, and even the king of England, Garvey pledged the support of "400 million Negroes" to Gandhi's cause. He signed each telegram as the "Provisional President of Africa."[47]

In 1924 Garvey again telegrammed Gandhi, conveying his sympathies and those of "the Negroes of the world." In his capacity as the chairman of the Fourth Annual International Convention of Negro Peoples of the World, Garvey told Gandhi, "The Negroes of the world through us send you greetings for [sic] fight for the freedom of your people and country." Gandhi published the telegram in *Young India*, under the title "Negroes' Sympathy." He noted, "Theirs is perhaps a task more difficult than ours." Although he did not specify why, and listed only the virtues of "Negroes," his praise spoke to what he saw lacking. Gandhi noted, "They have fine physique. They have a glorious imagination. They are as simple as they are brave." He argued, "There is in them no inherent inferiority as is commonly supposed to be the case." Gandhi concluded, "I know that if they have caught the spirit of the Indian movement, their progress must be rapid."[48] Gandhi made no mention of African American culture or history. Though he did include "a glorious imagination" in his list of virtues, he nonetheless emphasized Black reliance on "the spirit of the Indian movement." As in his article on Booker T. Washington in 1903, Gandhi differentiated Blacks from Indians, even while acknowledging the potential for collaboration between the two peoples. Garvey and Gandhi both wrote as leaders of distinct "peoples." Their transnational connection, rather than transgressing racial borders, allowed them to assert their leadership by presenting "the Negro" and "the Indian" as firmly established categories.

Garvey's emphasis on racial purity, his focus on the uniforms, parades, and other physical trappings of group solidarity, and his occasional praise for Mussolini have led some to portray Garvey's movement as proto-fascist.[49] However, even Garvey's critics recognized that the strength of the UNIA resulted in part from Garvey's ability to tap into larger changes in the world order, changes that would contribute to the rise of fascism but that had already helped spark less chauvinistic nationalisms in India and other colonies. Garvey's contemporaries recognized that he shared as much with Gandhi as with Mussolini. In 1923, in an editorial in *Opportunity*, the organ of the National Urban League, sociologist Charles Spurgeon Johnson described Garveyism as "a black version of that same one hundred per cent mania that now afflicts white America, that emboldens the prophets of a 'Nordic blood renaissance,' that picked up and carried the cry of 'self-determination for all people,' 'India for the Indians,' 'A Free Ireland.'" Johnson's editorial, while strongly critical of Garvey himself, argued that the Garvey movement drew upon legitimate grievances and demonstrated the mobilizing power of a compelling vision. Du Bois similarly criticized Garvey's "bull-headed worship" of race while locating the UNIA within a global process in which "Negroes, Indians, Chinese and other groups" were "gaining new faith in themselves." This "new self-consciousness," Du Bois argued, was leading "inevitably and directly to distrust and hatred of whites; to demands for self-government, separation, driving out of foreigners—'Asia for the Asiatics,' 'Africa for the Africans,' and 'Negro officers for Negro troops!'"[50]

Just as Garvey regularly disputed the claim that his movement was "anti-white," Gandhi would have strongly disagreed that his efforts led "inevitably and directly to distrust and hatred of whites." Nevertheless, the debate between Garvey and his critics resonated in India among those who, like Rabindranath Tagore, preferred a more flexible cosmopolitanism to what they saw as the excesses of Gandhian anticolonial nationalism. In September 1925 *The Servant of India,* a journal of social

reform published in Poona, compared African American and Indian freedom struggles in order to stress the importance of a universalistic humanism opposed to excessive pride in race or nation. *The Servant of India*
lauded Du Bois as "that great American Negro leader," before discussing
an article that *The Crisis* had published on "Temperament." Its author,
Horace Mann Bond, would later become a renowned scholar of African
American education, a distinguished university president, and the father
of the civil rights activist Julian Bond. *The Servant of India* praised Bond
for demonstrating the benefits of "race-consciousness" while warning
against racial chauvinism:

> The writer admits that, as a defense mechanism, the American Negro is de-
> veloping a race-consciousness (in this country we call it Nationalism!)—
> "which is of utility in destroying the submissive and dependent attitude
> hitherto assumed." But, he continues—and how one wishes his words would
> find an echo in the hearts of our people!—"too strong a race-consciousness
> may be as disastrous as none at all. What we should value as more enduring
> and important than any race-consciousness is a realization of ourselves as
> simply and wholly human."[51]

Comparing "race-consciousness" and "nationalism," *The Servant of India*
argued that both could be liberating, if kept subservient to a universalistic
humanism.

Kelly Miller, a respected scholar at Howard University, compared Gandhi and Garvey as racial prophets while, like *The Servant of India*, envi-
sioning a world beyond race. "The leaven of racial unrest is at work all
over the world," Miller wrote in 1924. While Gandhi, "the meek and lowly
Hindu, spoke to the alien over-lord of his race in the language of Moses to
Pharaoh—'Let my people go,' " Miller declared, "Marcus Garvey, a West
Indian Negro, broke suddenly upon us like a voice crying in the wilderness
for the redemption of Africa." Miller did not directly rebuke either Gandhi
or Garvey but did posit an approach to unity that transcended race. He
concluded, "Self-determination is and will be the goal of racial striving,
unless or until, perchance, there arises a moral and spiritual sanction transcending the bonds of breed and birth, which shall ring out the feud of
strife and blood."[52]

Garvey and Gandhi played leading and remarkably similar roles in a
global debate regarding how to oppose white supremacy and imperialism
without succumbing to an equally extreme racialism or nationalism. Both
at times underplayed the internal variety of the "peoples" they claimed to
lead. The movements that Garvey and Gandhi inspired were themselves,
however, remarkably diverse, demonstrating the cosmopolitan complexities of transnational social movements. These complexities are evident in

the interlocking relationships between the UNIA, Indian nationalism, and an even larger, and equally varied, worldwide community—Islam.

In his effort to establish a "grand racial hierarchy," Garvey demanded uniform obedience to the UNIA and its leader. The movement he inspired was, however, far from uniform. The diversity of Garveyism is especially evident in matters of religion, where Garvey himself strove to create an atmosphere tolerant of the religious diversity of Blacks throughout the world. Beginning in the early 1920s, Garveyites began joining the Ahmadiyya movement, a religious community that had begun amongst Muslims in colonial India in the late nineteenth century. Founded by Mirza Ghulam Ahmad, who declared himself the promised Mujaddid or "reformer of the age," the Ahmadiyya movement came to be considered heretical by many Muslims. Although Ahmad did not claim a status on par with the Prophet Muhammad, what he did claim conflicted, in the eyes of many Muslims, with the finality of Muhammad's prophethood. Despite resistance from other Muslims, the Ahmadiyya movement grew both in India and overseas. In 1920 Dr. Mufti Muhammad Sadiq, an Ahmadi missionary, arrived in Philadelphia to convert Americans to the Ahmadiyya's understanding of Islam. Sadiq was most successful in attracting African American converts, especially working-class Blacks in urban communities such as Detroit, Chicago, and Cleveland. The membership of the growing American Ahmadiyya movement drew heavily on local UNIA branches, in part because of considerable institutional support between Ahmadis and the UNIA. In 1923 Sadiq gave five lectures at UNIA meetings in Detroit. Sadiq's successor as editor of the Ahmadiyya newspaper *Moslem Sunrise* reprinted pro-Muslim excerpts from *The Negro World,* which in turn printed his article, "Has Christianity Failed and Has Islam Succeeded?"[53]

The relationship between Garveyism and the Ahmadiyya movement began when Garvey was still a young firebrand in London. There he encountered Dusé Mohamed Ali, an Egyptian Muslim of partial Sudanese descent who edited the *African Times and Orient Review.* Ali's association with an Ahmadi mosque in London most likely introduced Garvey to the Ahmadiyya movement. What is certain is that Ali inspired in Garvey a respect for the anticolonial, antiracist potential of Islam. When Ali came to the United States in the early 1920s, Garvey hired him to write editorials for *The Negro World.* Ali used the pages of *The Negro World* to herald the unity of India and its lessons for other struggling people. "It has become too late for India to accept anything short of complete independence," Ali wrote, "now that India is showing the solid front, and there is no longer an appreciable enmity between Moslem and Hindu." In May 1922 *The Negro World* published a picture of Ali with a delegation of Indian Muslims at the Near East Conference in London. The caption of the photo explained, "These Indian delegates came to the Conference to put forward the Indian demands on behalf of Turkey."[54] These "Indian demands" concerned the same question that inspired the Khilafat movement—what would become of the caliph now that the British controlled Turkey? It was fitting for *The Negro World* to report on the Khilafat struggle and to praise Hindu-Muslim unity. Just as Gandhi and the Khilafat leaders affirmed that one could be a Muslim and an Indian patriot, so Garvey and the Ahmadis would demonstrate that one could be a Muslim and an advocate of Negro unity.

By challenging American racism while asserting Islam's color-blind inclusivity, Ahmadi teachers constructed religious identities that were simultaneously racial and antiracist. In one of the earliest editions of the *Moslem Sunrise,* Muhammad Sadiq offered "the conflict between the Blacks and the Whites in this country" as an example of Christian hypocrisy. Sadiq stated, "In the East we never hear of such things occurring between the peoples." Sadiq failed to acknowledge the many inequalities of "the East" that mapped onto differences of skin color, most notably caste oppression in India. Even within the Ahmadiyya community, tensions remained between African American converts and Muslims from India or other Muslim countries.[55] Nonetheless, Sadiq's depiction of a harmonious East spoke to his vision of Islam as nonracial and inclusive. In an open letter to "My Dear American Negro," Sadiq declared, "Join Islam, the real faith of Universal Brotherhood." The *Moslem Sunrise* reprinted a letter to the editor of the St. Louis *Star* from a Black convert, Sheik Ahmad Din (formally Mr. Nathaniel Johnson), criticizing the racial segregation of Christian churches. Headlined "Moslem View of Color Line," the letter declared, "The question of color must be erased from the church service, in the factory, in the shop and everywhere." In a separate article on Muslim prayer, readers were instructed, "In the Mosque all the Moslems, rich and poor, white and colored stand side by side to pray to their one common Creator and Provider."[56]

The Ahmadi effort to present Islam as a faith in which African Americans could be proudly Black and yet opposed to racial divisions would be overshadowed by the increasing visibility of another unorthodox variant of Islam—the Nation of Islam. Over the course of the 1930s, the Nation of Islam grew in Detroit, Chicago, and other Northern cities, in part by attracting former Ahmadi converts and still-active Garveyites. The Nation of Islam's long-serving leader, Elijah Muhammad, learned from Ahmadi successes and maintained links with South Asian Muslims while creating a distinctive religious community that achieved remarkable success in helping Black men and women transcend drug addiction and crime, achieve economic self-sufficiency, and cultivate individual dignity and group pride. Like the Ahmadiyya movement, the Nation of Islam emphasized the unity of "Asiatic" and dark-skinned peoples. The racial ideology of the Nation of Islam contradicted, however, the inclusivity of the Ahmadiyya movement. Malcolm X's praise of the multiethnic nature of the global Islamic community following his trip to Mecca can be understood as a return to the multiethnic teachings of the Ahmadiyya movement. These teachings remain, however, largely forgotten by the many Americans who equate being Black and Muslim with being a member of the Nation of Islam.[57]

While African American Muslims grew in number and diversity, the challenges to Hindu-Muslim unity in India became increasingly severe. The African American response to the noncooperation / Khilafat movement and Garvey's references to India and Gandhi both emphasized the unity of Indians, and especially of Hindus and Muslims. Defenders of the British Raj, on the other hand, often cited India's religious diversity as evidence that India lacked a common nationality. African Americans and Indian Muslims increasingly found themselves confronting similar questions of minority identity and autonomy. It should not be surprising, therefore, that in the debate regarding the future of Indian Muslims, several leading Indian figures turned to the African American struggle for evidence regarding the status of minorities.

In his presidential address at the Bombay Hindu Conference in December 1925, Lala Lajpat Rai used African American history in an attempt to prevent religious divisions from weakening the Indian nation. At issue was the question of how India's large Muslim minority should be protected from the dictates of the Hindu majority. In 1909 the Morley-Minto reforms had granted Muslims reserved seats in legislative bodies and had taken the further step of guaranteeing that only Muslims would vote to elect representatives to those seats. In his speech Lajpat Rai suggested safeguards for the religious rights of minority faiths but branded communal representation for Muslims a result of "the desire of the foreign rulers to perpetuate our differences and thus make impossible the evolution of a common nationality." Drawing on his knowledge of the United States, Lajpat Rai asserted that despite their large population in New York, Jewish Americans had not asked for communal representation. "The same may be said," he added, "of the coloured people of the U.S.A. who socially form an entirely separate community with whom the white have hardly any social relations at all."[58] Awkwardly, Lajpat Rai argued that since Blacks were marginalized and yet did not receive special legislative representation, Indian Muslims should similarly not be granted communal representation. His analogy could more easily have been turned around to argue that the oppression of American Blacks resulted from their limited representation at all levels of government.

The use of African American history as a cautionary tale regarding the oppression of minorities found an influential advocate in Muhammad Ali Jinnah, leader of the Muslim League and future founder of Pakistan. In December 1937 at the All-India Muslim Students Federation in Calcutta, Jinnah proclaimed, "We do not want to be reduced to the position of the Negroes of America."[59] Thus Jinnah used the oppression of African Americans to warn against the possibility of being an exploited minority. In the wake of the partition of the subcontinent in 1947, it is tempting to read the different analogies employed by Lajpat Rai and Jinnah as evidence of an unbridgeable chasm. It is important to recognize, however, that the Hindu-Muslim unity so consistently praised by African Americans during and in the aftermath of the Great War was neither doomed to be ephemeral nor lacking in legacy.

In addition to Hindu-Muslim unity, Black Americans also praised the intercaste harmony of the noncooperation/Khilafat movement. The subsequent history of religious conflict in South Asia would demonstrate all too clearly that Hindu-Muslim unity would remain a goal only partially achieved. Similarly, the efforts of Gandhi and other leaders of the Indian National Congress to unite Indians of many castes did not translate into a significant reduction in caste-based oppression. African Americans were not alone in overstating intercaste harmony. Indians themselves often did just that while comparing African Americans and Dalits.

Mother India and the Race/Caste Analogy

In June 1925 Taraknath Das told Reverend J. T. Sunderland, "In the Anglo-Saxon world a new caste-system based upon race-hatred and color prejudice has arisen which is going to poison human relations between the people of Asia—particularly, the people of India, China and Japan on the one hand and the world of Whitemanism on the other!" In July 1924, in the Calcutta-based monthly *Modern Review*, Surendranath Das Gupta noted, "American missionaries often condemn the high-caste Indians that they forbid the untouchables to study in school with their children." Acidly, he wrote, "They should not forget what treatment they show to the Negroes in their own schools."[60] As these examples indicate, race/caste comparisons at times highlighted the injustice of racial oppression. Such comparisons, while potentially helping uncover caste oppression, could also be used to defend the practice of caste in India.

In August 1910 Rabindranath Tagore wrote an American lawyer, "It has never been India's lot to accept alien races as factors in her civilization. You know very well how the caste that proceeds from colour takes elsewhere a most virulent form." Tagore elaborated on the word "elsewhere" by saying, "I need not cite modern instances of the animosity which divides white men from negroes in your country, and excludes Asiatics from European colonies." Tagore contrasted the racism of America and Europe with the inclusiveness of India, an inclusiveness that he linked historically with the advent of caste via the two-race theory of Indian civilization:

> When, however, the white-skinned Aryans on encountering the dark aboriginal races of India found themselves face to face with the same problem, the solution of which was either extermination, as has happened in America and Australia, or a modification without the possibility of either friction or fusion, they chose the latter.

For Tagore, caste was a "frictionless" alternative to racism and genocide. After stating that he "need not dwell at length on the evils of the resulting caste system," Tagore instead defended its necessity by arguing, "It served a very useful purpose in its day and has been even up to a late age of immense protective benefit to India." He explained, "It has largely contributed to the freedom from narrowness and intolerance which distinguishes the Hindu religion and has enabled races with widely different culture and even antagonistic social and religious usages and ideals to settle down peaceably side by side." For Tagore, caste harmonized different "races" and allowed India to avoid the divisiveness of Western racism.[61] Such a defensive racial diplomacy marked the controversy surrounding Katherine Mayo's *Mother India*.

Published in 1927, *Mother India* offered a strident critique of Indian society. As she had in an earlier work on American imperialism in the Philippines, Mayo argued that colonization was a force for moral improvement. The majority of Indian responses to *Mother India* combined refutations of Mayo's claims with counterattacks focused on the faults of the West and especially of the United States. To counter Mayo's emphasis on the brutality of caste, several Indian critics of *Mother India* denounced the racial wrongs of the West. In Bombay, K. A. Natarajan published a "rejoinder" to Mother India that branded Mayo a "fanatic apostle (professed) of White domination." C. S. Ranga Iyer's *Father India: A Reply to Mother India* asserted that the "Aryan" invaders of India were "better than the white Brahmins of the twentieth century" who claimed "divine right at home and abroad." Dhan Gopal Mukerji, in his

A Son of Mother India Answers, declared that Mayo's worst inaccuracies were "as fantastic as saying that Miss Jane Addams believes in Negro lynching." In his revealingly entitled *Uncle Sham: Being the Strange Tale of a Civilisation Run Amok,* Kanhaya Lal Gauba proclaimed that the initials "K.K.K." were "well known throughout the world as symbols of terrorism, barbarity and murder." Lal Gauba included two chapters on racial oppression, which he called "the largest blot on the institutions of the American democracy."[62]

Responses to *Mother India* often compared race in America with caste in India. In 1930 the Pacific Coast Khalsa Diwan Society in Stockton, California, published Dilip Singh Saund's *My Mother India.* Saund would later become the first U.S. congressman of Indian descent. "With typical complacency," he wrote, "the Americans declare that there is no caste in the United States. Yet the American negro, although he has a right to vote and to hold office, has absolutely no opportunity to make use of these privileges." Saund referenced laws that prohibited marriage between "whites and negroes," decried the brutality of lynching, and criticized the segregation of schools, churches, hotels, and public transportation. Importantly, Saund told his readers that American racism did not "justify the injustice of caste in India or anywhere else in the world." Like Tagore, however, Saund presented caste in India as better than the near genocide of American Indians or the enslavement of Africans. He wrote, "The Aryan forefathers of India, by giving to the original population of the country a distinct place in its social life, however low, have preserved them on the one hand from extermination and on the other from slavery of person."[63]

Subhas Chandra Bose similarly criticized caste while defending its merits in contrast to Western racism. Bose, however, framed his critique of caste in much stronger terms. In May 1928 Bose declared, "It is in harmonising different angles of view of synthesising different cultures that the special mission of India lies." He continued, "Europe had tried to solve it, but how? What is the record of England and other countries in Africa and Asia and where are the aborigines who had come under the civilizing influence of Europe? How is America solving her Negro problem?" Bose used American racism as an example of the broader failure of the West to deal with the question of difference. India, on the other hand, "had avoided that path and had attempted to solve it according to her lights." The importance of the word "attempted" became clear when Bose proclaimed, "Harmonising of different ethnic groups was sought to be achieved through Varnashrama Dharma. But conditions have changed today and we need a higher and more scientific synthesis."[64] Like Tagore and

Saund, Bose presented caste as the legacy of an ancient effort to harmo-
nize "different ethnic groups." Bose, however, claimed only that harmony
"was sought to be achieved" through caste, not that it actually was.

Within a year of Bose's speech, an American woman asked Mahatma
Gandhi a pointed question: "Is the plight of the untouchable as hard as
that of the Negro in America?" Gandhi's response echoed the argument
that Tagore, Saund, and Bose had made earlier—that caste, despite its
problems, was still preferable to American racism. Gandhi began, however, by seeming to avoid the question. He stated, "There can be no true
comparison between the two. They are dissimilar." His real answer became
apparent when he offered four reasons why the "plight of the untouchable" was in fact not as severe as the treatment of "the Negro in America."
First, he claimed that, in contrast to Jim Crow segregation, no legal discrimination operated against Dalits. Second, he argued that although African Americans were regularly lynched, the "tradition of non-violence" in
India had made such savage violence against Dalits "impossible." Third,
he noted that individual Dalits had become "saints." He wondered if the
United States had "any Negro saints." Fourth, he stated that while the prejudice against untouchability was "fast wearing out," he could only wish
that "the tide of colour prejudice had spent itself in America."[65]

Gandhi's four comparisons between race and caste grossly understated
the brutality of caste oppression in India. His emphasis on the absence of
laws enforcing untouchability, for example, obscured the fact that caste
often operated with the sanction of government authorities and was enforced as regularly and brutally as Jim Crow. Gandhi's optimism regarding the end of untouchability would prove unwarranted, as would his
belief that "the tradition of nonviolence" had rendered "impossible" the
lynching of Dalits.[66] Like Tagore and Saund, Gandhi minimized the ini-
quity of untouchability in an effort to defend India's reputation abroad.
Neither Subhas Chandra Bose nor Gandhi directly framed their references
to American racism as a response to Mayo's work. Their use of American
racism to defend India and caste, however, coupled with the timing of
their statements, indicates a connection to Mayo's infamous accusations.

A more direct response came from Lala Lajpat Rai. On October 6,
1927, Lajpat Rai wrote Du Bois from Lahore to ask for information
about "the treatment of the negroes in the United States and also about
the activities of the Ku Klux Klan." He explained that he was writing a
response to Mother India and was already planning to use a few old copies of The Crisis. He hoped that Du Bois could send articles and photos
documenting more recent atrocities. Du Bois replied on November 9,
sending the last six numbers of The Crisis, as well as a picture of a lynch-

ing. He explained that he was publishing a novel that "touches India incidentally in the person of an Indian Princess," and he forwarded pages of the book for Lajpat Rai's suggestions.[67] Thus Du Bois and Lajpat Rai exchanged help in completing starkly different but nonetheless complementary reflections on injustice in the United States, India, and worldwide. Both accounts responded in their own way to *Mother India*.

Published in 1928, Lajpat Rai's *Unhappy India* used the argument made by Saund, Tagore, Bose, and Gandhi—that American racism was worse than caste prejudice—to attack Katherine Mayo and her book. In a two-part chapter entitled "Less than the Pariah," Lajpat Rai spent almost fifty pages carefully detailing his central claim: "The Negro in the United States is worse than a pariah." Lajpat Rai used the articles Du Bois had sent to give graphic depictions of recent mob violence that he linked to the violence Mayo's work had done to India. Directly after describing a mass lynching in East St. Louis, he wrote, "The extreme mechanization of life in America creates an abnormal craving for crazes, stunts, sensation-mongering and produces yellow journals, and shilling-shockers like *Mother India*."[68] By connecting *Mother India* and lynch mobs to "extreme mechanization," Lajpat Rai made a virtue of India's lack of industrialization while associating Mayo with the degradation of American society.

Even more strongly than Saund, Tagore, Bose, and Gandhi, Lajpat Rai asserted that he was not defending caste. He wrote, "Personally I do not believe in caste. I am in favour of its complete abolition." He condemned untouchability "in the strongest terms possible as an absolutely indefensible, inhuman and barbarous institution, unworthy of Hinduism and the Hindus." A few of Lajpat Rai's comparisons between racism and caste prejudice could be used to critique both, as when he lamented "the treatment the Negro 'citizens' of the United States get from their white 'Brahmins.'"[69] Comparing *Unhappy India* to Lajpat Rai's earlier work *The United States of America* demonstrates the persistence of Lajpat Rai's opposition to both racial and caste-based oppression. Contrasting the two works reveals, however, a distinct shift in Lajpat Rai's emphasis, a shift directly attributable to his need to criticize *Mother India*. In his earlier work, Lajpat Rai had proclaimed, "The Negro is the PARIAH of America." In *Unhappy India*, however, he argued, "The Negro in the United States is worse than a pariah." Shifting from equating wrongs to ranking them, Lajpat Rai transformed a transnational analogy with which he had attacked injustice in the United States and India into a reactionary shield, defending domestic inequality in the face of foreign criticism. By arguing that racism was worse than untouchability, was Lajpat Rai, if not defending caste, at least hindering attempts to abolish it?

Bhimrao Ramji Ambedkar took exactly that stance in a tightly argued pamphlet entitled "Which Is Worse? Slavery or Untouchability?" Ambedkar lamented the fact that "so great a social reformer and so great a friend of the untouchables as Lala Lajpat Rai in replying to the indictment of the Hindu Society by Miss Mayo insisted that untouchability as an evil was nothing as compared with slavery." With lengthy block quotes from Reginald Haynes Barrow's *Slavery in the Roman Empire* and Charles Johnson's *The Negro in American Civilization,* Ambedkar presented a relatively rosy account of slavery that he contrasted with the treatment of oppressed castes in India. He concluded, "There can therefore be no doubt that untouchables have been worse off than slaves."[70]

Just as Lajpat Rai risked underestimating the evils of untouchability, Ambedkar's argument led him to overlook the brutality of slavery. In his conclusion he defined slavery as "an exchange of semi-barbarism for civilization" and proclaimed, "To enslave a person and to train him is certainly better than a state of barbarity accompanied by freedom." By equating white America with civilization, Ambedkar argued that slavery was ultimately a good thing for African Americans. His pamphlet never mentioned the prejudice Blacks faced in twentieth-century America. Similarly, in a small, unpublished essay entitled "Negroes and Slavery," Ambedkar capped over eight pages chronicling the brutal history of slavery with the conclusion: "What is of importance is that these unfree, unprivileged classes have disappeared as a separate class and have become part and parcel of the great Society."[71] By focusing on the brutality of untouchability, Ambedkar overlooked contemporary American racism.

Despite their contrasting conclusions, Lajpat Rai and Ambedkar both used the Negro/Untouchable parallel to rank injustices rather than to suggest new solidarities. Like Katherine Mayo and many of her critics, they utilized transnational comparisons defensively rather than aiming to inspire meaningful collaboration across borders. Epitomizing the potential blindness of such defensive analogies, Mayo herself later wrote that untouchability was "a type of bondage compared to which our worst Negro slavery was freedom."[72] At its best, such a comparison might motivate protest by dramatizing the brutality of caste oppression. Too often, however, ranking injustice shifted the moral focus toward distant wrongs and away from injustices closer to home. Ambedkar, on the other hand, utilized the Slave/Untouchable parallel to further his lifelong commitment to ending caste oppression. Despite his understatement of the brutality of slavery and of later forms of American racism, Ambedkar used the Negro/Untouchable parallel to imagine an India where differences were respected and not punished, an India worthy of the world's respect and emulation.

The Indian response to *Mother India* demonstrated that racial diplomacy could fall into a blind nationalism that aimed to whitewash the
nation and to protect it from any foreign criticism. Garvey's interactions
with Gandhi, while at times similarly embodying the homogenizing potential of racial diplomacy, also revealed the potential for transnational
exchange to encourage intragroup introspection. In May 1926 Gandhi
wrote Amy Jacques Garvey to thank her for sending him the *Philosophy
and Opinions of Marcus Garvey or Africa for the Africans*. A few months
after receiving Garvey's book, Gandhi published an article on "race arrogance," in which he decried "the injustice that is being daily perpetrated against the Negro in the United States of America in the name of
and for the sake of maintaining white superiority." In a demonstration of
his increasing use of the Negro/Untouchable parallel, Gandhi then proclaimed, "Our treatment of the so-called untouchables is no better than
that of coloured people by the white man."[73] Thus, like Ambedkar, Gandhi used an analogy with American racism to underline the injustices of
caste in India. Gandhi would increasingly embrace a notion of "color"
articulated most creatively and consistently by Black Americans. Unlike
the racial diplomacy of Garvey, these new transnational notions of color
would create opportunities for Black and Indian solidarities that eschewed
uniform notions of race.

Recognizing that even the most globally-minded nationalists often
used knowledge gained abroad to bolster their vision for a particular nation does not mean that their concern for the struggles of distant others
was insincere. Dohra Ahmad has criticized Lala Lajpat Rai for discussing
American racism "only when strategically useful." Ahmad concluded
that Lajpat Rai "was not the internationalist that Du Bois wanted him to
be," a judgment that assumes that Du Bois understood internationalism in opposition to the anticolonial nationalism of Lajpat Rai. Ahmad
wrote, "A solidarity politics based upon analogy runs the risk of any
comparative project: namely, that categories under consideration will not
translate neatly into each other."[74] Transnational analogy does not, however, require neat correspondence of categories in order to be productive.
Rather, like translation itself, drawing parallels between disparate struggles
often involved a creative and productive negotiation of difference. Ahmad
is right to recognize that Lajpat Rai's transnational analogies often served
as tools for his anticolonial nationalism. It matters that Lajpat Rai used
transnational analogies for national goals, but it also matters what those
goals were. Ultimately, the historical significance of transnational analogies resulted from the intent of their authors and their influence upon
histories that were often national or local. Criticism of Lajpat Rai should
focus more on the limitations of his nationalist project than on the fact

that his transnationalism was guided by his nationalism. The problem with racial diplomacy is not that transnational analogies were strategically employed but that they were employed to limiting, chauvinistic, or counterproductive ends.

The limitations of racial diplomacy should not overshadow the power of racial alliances to provide hope and meaning in a world divided by race. Traveling through the United States, selling cosmetics and perfumes, Ganesh Rao came to know many African American supporters of the UNIA. In 1922 he wrote a letter to *The Negro World,* praising Garvey and the UNIA and encouraging collaboration between Indians and "Negroes." Rao considered the "growing Negro problem . . . not as a local, or family, or communal, or even national question, but as a portentous universal problem—the problem of the twentieth century." Rao's understanding of the "Negro problem" as universal grew from his belief in the fundamental similitude of the oppression Blacks and Indians confronted. He wrote, "I am one of those millions that are being oppressed by the imperialistic English government. My interest, my responsibility, my duty, has thus impelled me to study the tragic tales of other oppressed peoples, e.g., the Negro, and his future." In order to get to know the "new Negro," Rao claimed, he decided to adopt the "disguise" of a peddler. Implausible but poignant, Rao's effort to present himself as more than merely a traveling salesman reveals how racial diplomacy could empower the individual by endowing local circumstances—in this case, the selling of perfume—with transnational significance. "Peace shall not dawn on this world until Asia and Africa and their ancient peoples are free and enjoy all human rights," Rao concluded. "Oppressed peoples of the world, unite. Lose no time!"[75]

CHAPTER THREE

Colored Cosmopolitanism

> Most men in the world are coloured. A belief in humanity
> means a belief in colored men.
> —W. E. B. Du Bois, *The Negro*

IKE THE BORDERS between nations, racial boundaries have been sites of contact and crossing. Also like national borders, racial divisions have been changed, invented, and erased. In the years between the First and Second World Wars, African Americans and Indians helped engineer one of the most creative and politically significant redefinitions of racial borders in the twentieth century—the invention of the colored world. When, in 1900, W. E. B. Du Bois prophesied, "The problem of the twentieth century is the problem of the color line," he globalized the color line, referring not only to the "millions of black men in Africa, America and the Islands of the Sea" but also to "the brown and yellow myriads elsewhere." Three years later, in *The Souls of Black Folk,* Du Bois again declared, "The problem of the twentieth century is the problem of the color line." In the oft-neglected second half of that famous sentence, Du Bois again chose to globalize the color line, defining it as "the relation of the darker to the lighter races of men in Asia and Africa, in America and the islands of the sea."[1]

In the wake of the First World War, Du Bois's insight became the basis for a transnational initiative to unite the "darker races" in opposition to imperialism and racism. For Du Bois and other Black advocates of colored unity, India was one of the world's most populous "colored" countries and the geographical and racial bridge between Africa and Asia. On their part, Indians had long seen African Americans as an oppressed, but upwardly mobile people, worthy of sympathy and emulation. The pioneering

---

W. E. B. Du Bois, *The Negro* (New York: Oxford University Press, 2007), 110.

scholarship of Du Bois inspired many Indians to express their interest in African Americans in terms of colored solidarity. While the racial diplomacy epitomized by Marcus Garvey strengthened racial borders, expansive notions of color transcended the boundaries between "the Indian" and "the Negro."

Transracial conceptions of color at times defied the idea of race itself. More often, however, appeals for the solidarity of the "darker races" reinforced the importance of race, even while complicating specific racial boundaries or embracing a universalistic humanism. Thus Du Bois could laud the "brotherhood of Negro blood," even while arguing that "a belief in humanity means a belief in colored men." For Du Bois, being "Negro," being "colored," and being human were overlapping, often complementary, identifications. Neither did the transnational reach of colored solidarity limit Du Bois's efforts to secure for Blacks the full benefits of American citizenship. Constructing the colored world involved employing transnational analogies to make demands of the nation, not to abandon national affiliation.[2]

Several Indian and African American activists championed a colored cosmopolitanism through which they framed commonalities of struggle between "colored" peoples fighting for their rights throughout the world. Pratap Bhanu Mehta has located cosmopolitanism between "the logic of assimilation that eroded difference" and "an enclavism that made dialogue impossible." David Hollinger has similarly positioned cosmopolitanism between a universalism that would eliminate difference in pursuit of commonality and a pluralism that would essentialize difference in defense against commonality. At their best, advocates of colored solidarity embodied the middle ground that Mehta and Hollinger understand as central to cosmopolitanism. Their colored cosmopolitanism allowed them to articulate an inclusive humanism that defied narrow, chauvinist definitions of race, religion, or nation while simultaneously defending the unity of "colored" peoples.[3]

In opposition to monolithic notions of group solidarity that elided the struggles of women, Dalits, and the poor, colored cosmopolitans recognized how multiple oppressions intersected and sought to forge alliances across social movements as well as national borders.[4] At times, transnational connections between India and the United States acted as a prism, refracting a narrow focus on a particular injustice into a broader concern for the diverse struggles of a variety of oppressed groups, both at home and halfway around the world. Transnational thinking was not, however, always transgressive at home. Not every reference to the "colored world" reflected a meaningful cosmopolitanism. Examining the diverse uses of the rhetoric of "darkness" as a bridge between Indians and African Americans reveals the importance of distinguishing between ideas of race that included internal diversities and those that did not, between thinkers for whom darkness was colorful and those for whom darkness was colorless.

The Borders of Color

In 1829 David Walker, a free Black man living in Boston, connected "the blacks of Africa" and "the mulattoes of Asia" by contrasting both with their mutual oppressors—the "avaricious, deceitful and unmerciful" whites of America and Europe. Although Walker encouraged the global solidarity of dark-skinned people, his "Appeal to the Colored Citizens of the World" did not fully embrace "the mulattoes of Asia." Walker's emphasis on the African diaspora is evident in his statement that "all the inhabitants of the earth (except, however, the sons of Africa) are called *men,* and of course are, and ought to be, free." Walker's focus on "the sons of Africa" led him to overlook colonization in India and to declare, "The English are the best friends the coloured people have upon earth."[5]

The assertion of similarities between "colored people" did not always extend beyond the African diaspora, nor did ideas of colored solidarity always operate in opposition to racial and economic inequality. Many defenders of white supremacy linked Blacks and Indians—but at the bottom of a racial hierarchy. Despite opposing white hegemony, Indians and African Americans at times similarly denigrated people of color. The Pan-African intellectual Alexander Crummell endowed Blacks with "that permanent *tropical* element which characterizes all the peoples whose ancestral homes were in the southern latitudes; and who may be called 'children of the sun.'" Crummell believed the "tropical element" failed to provide "vigor, hardihood and robustness to a race." His emphasis on the permanency of the "tropical element" raised doubts as to how far the "children of the sun" could progress toward racial "robustness." Nevertheless, unlike white supremacists who castigated the darker races, Crummell aimed to inspire "the children of the sun" to more forcefully pursue their own betterment.[6]

Du Bois similarly marshaled transnational notions of color to encourage African Americans to defend their rights. In 1907 an anonymous editorial in the first edition of *The Horizon,* a publication that Du Bois coedited, described India as "a land of dark men far across the sea which is of interest to us." The editorial characterized India as "the land, perhaps, from whence our fore-fathers came, or whither certainly in some prehistoric time they wandered." In the years to come Du Bois would often revere India as the birthplace of the "Negro race," offering a forceful example of what Judith Shklar has called "subversive genealogies."[7] Having asserted the common racial roots of Indians and Black Americans, *The Horizon* described India as a land where "a white race has conquered brown men," thus juxtaposing two distinct notions of colored solidarity, one based on racial origins and the other based on common histories of oppression. *The Horizon* explained that among Indians there were "two parties . . . in some ways resembling the parties among us. . . . One party says: wait, look for a chance, take all the English give us, and gradually achieve freedom; the other party says: no, freedom now, we are men." Thus *The Horizon* succinctly, if roughly, defined the differences that led to a temporary split in the Indian National Congress. Choosing not to take sides, *The Horizon* rejoiced that "both parties want freedom" and contrasted such unity of purpose with the tensions between conservative African Americans and their militant critics. "With us," *The Horizon* declared, "it looks as though somebody did not want freedom, as though they were actually afraid of it."[8]

Subtitled *"A Journal of the Color Line," The Horizon* offered its readers a transnational and transracial conception of color that bridged freedom struggles throughout the world. One edition included a long extract from a speech by Dadabhai Naoroji before the Indian National Congress. A founding member of the Congress, and the first Indian to be elected to the British Parliament, Naoroji was also an astute critic of imperialism. The African American readers of *The Horizon* were offered the opportunity to sympathize as Naoroji compared imperialism and bondage:

> While China in the East and Persia in the West of Asia are awakening, and Japan has already awakened, and Russia is struggling for emancipation and all of them despotisms—can the free citizens of the British Indian Empire continue to remain subject to despotism, the people who were among the first civilizers of the world?

Having introduced Naoroji's question as "worthy of men who want to be free," the editors of *The Horizon* employed an inclusive construction of color to cast Naoroji's declaration as more than the rumblings of a distant nationalism. Despite the fact that Naoroji did not reference color and that his list of rising nations included neither Africa nor the descendants of enslaved Africans in the United States, *The Horizon* summarized his speech with a call for "colored" unity that Du Bois would repeat throughout his life: "The dark world awakens to life and articulate speech. Courage, Comrades!"[9]

In May 1908 thirty-eight-year-old Mohandas Gandhi employed color as a bridge between Indians and other oppressed peoples. In a debate in

Johannesburg as to whether "Asiatics and the Coloured Races" were "a menace to the Empire," Gandhi redefined the phrase "Coloured Races" to create a larger community of resistance to white racism. He told the audience that he understood "the Coloured Races" as including, in his words, "the Coloured people proper—the Africans and the Asiatics." This would not be the last time Gandhi defined Indians as one of the "coloured races."[10]

Like Du Bois and Gandhi, Dusé Mohamed Ali developed expansive notions of color. On October 21, 1911, Gandhi's *Indian Opinion* published selections from an article by Ali entitled "The Coloured Man in Art and Letters." While Ali offered an international perspective on the achievements of "coloured" authors and musicians, his list of "coloured" geniuses suggested a definition of "color" roughly consistent with notions of "the Negro race."[11] In the aftermath of the Universal Races Congress, Ali founded *The African Times and Orient Review*. In its first issue, Ali expanded his definition of color. He explained that the journal aimed to articulate "the aims, desires and intensions of the Black, Brown and Yellow races," to give voice to "millions of Britain's enlightened dark races." The masthead of the journal proclaimed its devotion to "the Interests of the Coloured Races of the World."[12] Thus, like Du Bois, Ali came to embrace capacious notions of "darkness" and "color" that encouraged unity between a diversity of oppressed "colored peoples."

The African Times and Orient Review strove to become the voice of colored people in Asia, Africa, and the Americas. In anticipation of the first edition, Ali distributed a questionnaire that asked, "Are you of the opinion that a newspaper operated by coloured people—Orient and African—reflecting their opinions and stating their aims and desires, is likely to be appreciated by the British public?" His question assumed a notion of color that connected Asians and Africans, and the vast majority of respondents, including Du Bois and Krishna Gupta, a high-ranking civil servant, either ignored or validated that assumption. Booker T. Washington "wished every success" to "this new and important enterprise." The only response to take direct issue with Ali's casual reference to "colored people" came from Annie Besant, leading Theosophist and social reformer who would soon become a major political figure in India and the first woman to be elected president of the Indian National Congress. "'Coloured men' is a wide term," Besant argued, "and includes very different types, and no one system can be applied to all. Some coloured races are the equals of white races, while others are far more childish." For India, Besant envisioned rapid progress toward "the inclusion of all her educated classes in the governing class." Besant's hesitation to include Indians with "more childish" peoples indicated a condescension toward Africans that, while at times echoed, would be increasingly opposed by Indians in the years to come.[13]

The outbreak of the First World War inspired many to prophesy the dissolution of white hegemony and the rise of the darker world. In November 1914 Du Bois predicted that "considering the fact that black Africans and brown Indians and yellow Japanese are fighting for France and England it may be that they will come out of this frightful welter of blood with new ideas about the essential equality of all men."[14] The attribution of colors to different "races" had already become a Du Bois hallmark, invoking the unity and diversity of what he increasingly designated the "colored world." Du Bois's conception of colored solidarity relied in part on a racial essentialism, crude in its reliance on genealogies of "blood" but defiantly inclusive of those "races," such as Indians, whose ethnological origins remained contested. "The blood of yellow and white hordes," Du Bois wrote in June 1919, "has diluted the ancient black blood of India, but her eldest Buddha still sits black, with kinky hair." By defending the antiquity of Indian darkness, in contrast to those who claimed that the majority of Indians had inherited "Aryan blood," Du Bois brought India within the borders of the colored world. His defense of colored solidarity extended beyond racial roots to encompass a shared history of oppression. Defending the unity of dark peoples, he declared, "We are all one—we the Despised and Oppressed, the 'niggers' of England and America."[15]

The language of darkness at times appealed even to Marcus Garvey. Garvey opposed referring to African Americans as "colored," a word he associated with racial mixture and his integrationist opponents at the NAACP.[16] Notions of "darkness," on the other hand, allowed Garvey to express racial solidarities without referencing "color." When he telegrammed the British prime minister that "four hundred million Negroes are in sympathy with Mahatma Gandhi," Garvey added, "We wish your nation all that is good, but not at the expense of the liberties of the darker and weaker peoples of the earth."[17]

Garvey's newspaper, *The Negro World*, often lauded the rise of the dark world. In July 1921 *The Negro World* published a letter from a reader in Boston that referenced anticolonial struggles in India and other British colonies before proclaiming, "The Englishman ... pats his colored brother on the back and politely treats the poor blacks worse than the Americans."[18] The introduction to Dusé Mohamed Ali's first editorial in *The Negro World* demonstrated the potential for an Islamic universalism that embraced Indian and African American nationalisms, socialism, and an expansive notion of the unity of "the darker races." Readers learned that "India, Asia, and Africa—the strongholds of the darker races are in the throes of a violent proletarian revolt," and that "Nationalism in India, despite Mr. Gandhi's arrest, is proceeding."[19] *The Negro World* often portrayed Gandhi as a leader of the darker races. In March 1922 a columnist in *The Negro World* declared, "The writer likes Gandhi; his people look like mine."[20] One of Garvey's mentors, and a frequent contributor to *The Negro World,* Hubert Harrison proclaimed that Gandhi "stands out among men of all colors today as the greatest, most unselfish and powerful leader of the modern world." Lest the color dynamics of Gandhi's struggle be forgotten, Harrison entitled his editorial "The Brown Man Leads the Way."[21]

Harrison embodied the tension between racial diplomacy and colored cosmopolitanism. Born in the Virgin Islands in 1883, Harrison moved to Harlem, where he became renowned as a street orator. According to the British intelligence operatives who monitored his curbside lectures, Harrison often reviewed "the history of the exploitation of Africa, India and other countries by the Caucasian races."[22] Like Garvey, Harrison used transracial references to bolster his vision of the unity of "the Negro race." Often, however, Harrison aimed not only to unify "Negroes" but to encourage African Americans to recognize their place in a larger colored world. In a collection of his writings entitled *When Africa Awakes,* Harrison asserted that the Great War had concerned "the lands and destinies of the colored majority in Asia, Africa, and the islands of the sea." He called for "a free India" and encouraged his readers to learn from Indian struggles. His knowledge of India came in part from Lajpat Rai, whose *The Call to Young India* Harrison recommended to readers of the *New Negro.* In September 1919, writing with the pseudonym Sayid Muhammad Berghash, Harrison called Indians "the serfs of the British Empire." In December 1921, writing as Hira Lal Ganesha, he called India "the key-stone of the British imperial system." In December 1920, in Garvey's *The Negro World,* Harrison wrote, "India is a sort of seething, raging, but suppressed volcano, with a cover on which the Englishman sits, believing that if he but sits there the fires will no longer burn. But the Hindus believe that some day the wooden cover will burn through and something will get scorched." He told his readers, "We must link up with the other colored races of the world."[23]

Another longtime Garvey supporter, veteran journalist John Edward Bruce similarly championed the unity of the "dark races." Like Garvey, Bruce attacked the word "colored" but embraced a notion of "darkness" that linked Blacks with Indians. "The Oneness of the Darker Races," a speech Bruce wrote in 1918, declared a common "ethnological identity" for "all the darker peoples, of whom there are in round numbers in the world today 947,000,000." The size of his figure indicated that Bruce's notion of "darkness" well exceeded the African diaspora. He recognized the diversity of the "darker peoples," even while emphasizing their common roots. "There are roses, and tulips, and lilies—and honey-suckles," he wrote, "*all* deriving their existence from a common source." As evidence of this "common source," Bruce quoted *Genesis,* asserting that the sons of Ham had originated "the darker races." India played an important role in Bruce's construction of the "darker races." In a speech in 1918, Bruce declared, "The destiny of all the darker races is identical." He decried the "divide and rule . . . policy of England in India and Africa" and encouraged "the merging of the darker races" in order "to bring about a oneness of ideas of sentiments and of action."[24]

On January 2, 1919, the International League of Darker Peoples convened for the first time at the palatial Hudson River home of the self-made cosmetics mogul Madame C. J. Walker. In addition to Walker, the meeting included Marcus Garvey, Reverend Adam Clayton Powell Sr., and the young editor of the *Messenger,* A. Philip Randolph. The league aimed to represent the "darker peoples" at the upcoming peace conference in Versailles. In the league's first and only newsletter, Randolph wrote, "If peace can be secured through a league of free nations, so can the hydra-headed monster—race prejudice—be destroyed, by the darker peoples of the worlds . . . making cause with each other, in one great world body."[25]

As the noncooperation movement heightened African American interest in India and Gandhi, many Blacks chose to express this interest in terms of color. Cyril Briggs, a black communist and leader of the African Blood Brotherhood, a Left-leaning Pan-African organization, told military intelligence interviewers, "Look what the Hindus, another colored race, are doing in India. All these things are factors that help us here, right here in Harlem." Briggs's journal, *The Crusader,* regularly covered developments in India. After Indian troops refused to fight Persian soldiers, *The Crusader* declared, "When colored races refuse to fight each other in the interest of 'white domination of the world,' that domination is surely doomed, and the day of the colored races assured." In March 1922 a *Chicago Defender* columnist discussed Gandhi's arrest in an article entitled "The Rising Tide of Color." The following month, the *Norfolk Journal and Guide* declared, "The readers of the *Journal and Guide* are interested in the millions of East Indians because they are an off-color people seeking a larger measure of self-determination." In May 1922 Du Bois offered one of his most incisive criticisms of the color-coded imperialism of the British Raj:

White Christianity stood before Gandhi the other day and, let us all confess, it cut a sorry figure. This brown man looked into the eyes of the nervous white judge and said calmly, "It is your business to enforce the law and send me to jail; or if you do not believe that the law is right, it is your business to resign." Can you imagine such a judge resigning? Gandhi is in jail. So is English Christianity.[26]

Even Black critics of Gandhi expressed sympathy with the struggles of the "colored people" of India. While arguing against Gandhian methods in *The Crisis*, E. Franklin Frazier nevertheless offered a statement of colored solidarity. He told his readers, "It appears that a disillusioned, but stupid world must undergo another war before white men will learn to respect the darker races."[27]

The rhetoric of color risked homogenizing the "colored peoples of the world." If blanket terms such as "Negro" or "Asian" elided internal diversities, so notions of "dark" or "colored" people seemed to commit an even more grievous amalgamation. While advocates of colored solidarity scorned biological notions of race, their desire to unify antiracist struggles led many to universalize the experience of being dark-skinned in a world of white domination. Just as Garvey often discussed the "400,000,000 Negroes of the world," Du Bois referenced the population of the colored world as if statistics alone could demonstrate unity. In March 1926 he declared, "The number of colored human beings on the earth is 1,150,000,000 while there are but 550,000,000 white people."[28] Did 1,150,000,000 "colored human beings" experience being colored in the same way?

It is easy to dismiss such grand statistics and to trumpet instead the heterogeneity that marked and distinguished different groups of "colored human beings." However, the case of India, which provided a large share of these more than one billion "colored human beings," provides evidence that these numbers could and in fact did matter. Many Indians understood British imperialism as a form of color prejudice akin to what Blacks faced in the United States and elsewhere. They found ample reason to suggest unities of color and, like Du Bois, strove to do so without giving in to racial chauvinism or sacrificing local and national patriotisms. In June 1925 Du Bois published two letters from India in *The Crisis* that together demonstrate the diversity of Indian solidarity with African Americans and the inclusive nature of colored unity as Du Bois himself understood it. One letter, sent by Abdur Raoof Malik in Gujranwala, Punjab, took a distinctly socialist bent while comparing antiracism and anti-imperialism. Malik praised Du Bois for "liberating the Negroes from the bondage of aristocrats and capitalists" and concluded, "The struggle for honorable existence that the American Negroes are now in is

one of the great democratic movements of the modern world. We ourselves being sufferers from the oppression [of] alien rulers naturally view
the struggle of Negroes with great sympathy."²⁹ The second letter came
from the author and editor Benarsidas Chaturvedi. Du Bois had sent
sample copies of *The Crisis* to Chaturvedi in September 1924. In his reply, Chaturvedi told Du Bois, "I entirely agree with you when you say
that the different colored peoples and more especially the Indians and the
American Negroes must get into touch and co-operation with each
other."³⁰ While Malik mirrored Du Bois's understanding of the relationship between economic justice and democracy, Chaturvedi echoed Du
Bois's call for colored unity. Both Malik and Chaturvedi encouraged Afro-
Indian connections while referencing more traditional racial categories
such as "Negroes" or "Indians." Du Bois's decision to publish both letters
together is not surprising, given the fact that he did not see colored solidarity, socialism, and specific racial affiliations as contradictory.

In a letter to Du Bois in January 1925, Chaturvedi wrote that Du
Bois's message "must reach all coloured peoples." He asked Du Bois to
contribute a short note "on the colour problem" for a special edition of
Chand, a Hindi magazine. Chaturvedi added, "I need not tell you that we
feel as strongly on colour problems as the people of your race." Du Bois
responded on October 15, 1925, enclosing a message addressed "To the
People of India":

> Twelve million Americans of Negro descent, grandchildren and great grand-
> children of Africans, forcibly stolen and brought to America, are fighting
> here in the midst of the United States a spiritual battle for freedom, citizen-
> ship and the right to be themselves both in color of skin and manner of
> thought. This is the same terrible battle of the color bar which our brothers
> in India are fighting. We stretch out, therefore, hands of fellowship and
> understanding across the world and ask for your sympathy in our difficul-
> ties just as you in your strife for a new country and a new freedom have the
> good wishes of every Negro in America.³¹

The claim that Indians and African Americans faced "the same terrible
battle of the color bar" boldly glossed over the diversity within and
between Indian and African American freedom struggles. In claiming to
speak for "every Negro in America," Du Bois risked eliding the differences
among Black Americans. Similarly, his reference to "our brothers in India" offered no indication that he recognized the diversity of Indian
struggles. Did "our brothers in India" include Dalits and Indian women?
Nevertheless, Du Bois strove to spark dialogue, not to enforce homogene-
ity, and he succeeded in encouraging many Indians to embrace colored
solidarity and the struggles of African Americans. His legacy in India testi-
fies to the ample inclusivity of Du Bois's notions of color and freedom.

Reading Du Bois moved Amiya Kanti Das to imagine "unity among what is called the colored races." Das offered to write an article on India for *The Crisis,* thereby serving "the cause for which we are all devoted—the advancement of the colored races."[32] Thus Das echoed the title of the NAACP while pluralizing what the NAACP left potentially singular. Du Bois responded that he would be "glad to consider a short article which would explain the present unrest and striving of the Indians so that American colored people could follow the matter intelligently."[33] On December 23, 1927, Shripad R. Tikekar, a journalist in Poona, wrote Du Bois offering a similar article for *The Crisis.* Tikekar declared, "The race problem, I mean the fight between the black races on the one hand and the white people on the other, is keen in India and as such all Indians have a feeling of sympathy toward the 'dark' Americans in their fight against the dominating white people."[34] Tikekar chose to keep "dark" in quotation marks but referred to "the black races" of India without quotation marks or explanation. He assumed Du Bois would recognize the Indian struggle as a conflict between Blacks and whites.

Tikekar and Das, by asking to write for *The Crisis,* provided evidence of the popularity of that journal in India. Demand for *The Crisis* was sufficiently strong to prompt Nazir Ahmad Khan to write Du Bois in 1927 from the Bureau of Information in Gunjranwala, Punjab, pleading for copies of *The Crisis* to satisfy a persistent demand. Subtitled *A Record of the Darker Races, The Crisis* helped bring Indians and African Americans into greater awareness of each other as fellow colored people.[35] *The Crisis* was, however, only one of several ways that Du Bois maintained a leading role in the construction of colored solidarity.

Dark Princess and Race War

In 1928 Du Bois published the novel concerning an "Indian Princess," portions of which he had shared with Lala Lajpat Rai. *Dark Princess* narrates the relationship between Matthew Towns, an African American medical student who abandons his studies in protest after facing racial discrimination, and Princess Kautilya, an Indian princess and the leader of an international alliance of colored people. Having joined Kautilya in striving to unite and liberate the dark world, Matthew becomes embroiled in an effort to destroy a trainload of Ku Klux Klan leaders. After stints in jail and in Chicago politics, Matthew is reunited with Kautilya. The novel ends with the birth of their son, who is deemed the messiah of the darker world.

By tracing the relationship of Matthew and Kautilya, Du Bois presented colored unity as an exciting, important, but fundamentally challenging project. He recognized that any effort to achieve colored solidarity would have to overcome what he called in the novel "a color line within a color line, a prejudice within prejudice."[36] He made intracolored diversity central to *Dark Princess*, repeatedly providing examples of "colored" people refusing the label "colored," or actively plotting to maintain a limited notion of color. Far from negating the cohesiveness of color, however, *Dark Princess* offers a cosmopolitan vision of colored solidarity—cosmopolitan not only in its transnational scope but in its determination to oppose a multitude of oppressions.

From the beginning of the novel, Du Bois framed the relationship between Matthew and Kautilya in terms of color. From the moment he spies her across a crowded cafe, her color predominates: "First and above all came that sense of color: into this world of pale yellowish and pinkish parchment, that absence or negation of color, came, suddenly, a glow of golden brown skin." She was "a radiantly beautiful woman," Du Bois wrote, "and she was colored." Du Bois made a point of locating Kautilya's ancestors in the "black South" of India. "We came out of the black South in ancient days," Kautilya tells Matthew, "and then, scorning the yoke of the Aryan invaders, moved to Bwodpur, and there we gave birth to Buddha, black Buddha of the curly hair." In the darkness and curly hair of the Buddha, Du Bois found an ancient racial connection between African Americans and non-Aryan Indians. Going even further back in time than the era of the Buddha, Du Bois linked African Americans and India, as he had in other writings, by suggesting that the earliest humans had originated in India. With authority, Kautilya declares, "Out of black India the world was born."[37]

In addition to celebrating the aesthetics of darkness and excavating the antiquity of "Negro blood" in India, *Dark Princess* also portrayed colored unity as a response to the denigration of colored people by white supremacists. By having Kautilya labeled "nigger" and "darky" by a white American, Du Bois mapped the transnational reach of white supremacy.[38] He also underscored the political and economic dominance of "the white world." Kautilya introduces her colored alliance to Matthew by saying, "We represent—indeed I may say frankly, we are—a part of a great committee of the darker peoples; of those who suffer under the arrogance and tyranny of the white world."[39] For Du Bois, color and oppression served as overlapping foundations for solidarities of resistance.

Contrary to the critics who argued that *Dark Princess* provided an unrealistic portrayal of seamless colored solidarity, Du Bois rendered prominent the divisions within the darker world. Indeed, Kautilya's "committee of the darker peoples" at first hesitates to include Blacks.[40]

Du Bois's vision for India is most clearly offered in an exchange in which Matthew and Kautilya acknowledge the different histories and opportunities confronting African American and South Asian freedom struggles. "Here in America," Matthew begins, "black folk must help overthrow the rule of the rich by distributing wealth more evenly first among themselves and then in alliance with white labor, to establish democratic control of industry." "In my India," Kautilya answers, "we must first emancipate ourselves from the subtle and paralyzing misleading of England . . . then we must learn to rule ourselves politically and to organize our old industry on new modern lines."[41] Unity did not presuppose uniformity for Du Bois or for the Dark Princess. Neither did his romance with royalty prevent Du Bois from pushing a modernist agenda more reminiscent of Jawaharlal Nehru or Subhas Chandra Bose than of the maharajahs of India.

More than its recognition of intracolored prejudice, the central role given to female agency transforms *Dark Princess* from a tribute to colored unity into a testament to colored cosmopolitanism. Whatever objectification Du Bois risked by celebrating Kautilya's difference is ultimately avoided by Kautilya herself, who refuses to be the object of the novel, choosing instead to be its hero. She saves Matthew on more than one occasion. When four of Kautilya's minions ambush Matthew, one proclaims that Kautilya "is a mere woman—an inexperienced girl." Interrupting this paternalistic lecture, Kautilya arrives, takes control of the scene, and declares, "The Princess will decide."[42] Kautilya defies the equation of masculinity with mobility and femininity with domesticity. Her character is especially striking when compared with the gender dynamics in contemporary novels that explored Black transnational unity, such as Claude McKay's *Home to Harlem* and *Banjo,* where male heroes defined their freedom as the ability to move beyond the reach of women.[43] Du Bois made Kautilya the most well-traveled character in the novel. While Matthew undergoes a series of trials, it is Kautilya who experiences the most complete transformation. Physical mobility allows Kautilya to cross the borders of nations, classes, and races, becoming in the process the Dark Princess.

Transnational and transracial, *Dark Princess* also transcends dichotomies between the secular and the spiritual and between truth and fiction. In the final scene, a preacher reads from the *Book of Revelation,* Matthew's mother chants to Jesus, and three old men emerge from the forest to herald the arrival of a new messiah. Kautilya raises her baby to the heavens and speaks to Brahma, Vishnu, and Siva. Then, a chorus of cheers and trumpets rings from the forest, welcoming the "Messenger and Messiah to all the Darker Worlds."[44] *Dark Princess* leaves readers with a hope so fantastic as to be independent of the practical challenges suggested in the novel. The conclusion does not even attempt to resolve the challenges facing colored unity raised throughout the book. The potential for a color line within a color line remained to haunt readers, as it would continue to occupy Du Bois in his quest to unite the colored world.

In November 1928, less than a year after Du Bois published *Dark Princess*, Lala Lajpat Rai died from a police beating he received while peacefully protesting an all-white commission sent to India to consider constitutional reforms. In *The Crisis*, Du Bois called Lajpat Rai a "martyr to British intolerance" and stated that "every member of the 800,000,000 darker peoples of the world should stand with bowed heads in memory of Lajpat Rai, the great leader of India, who died of English violence because he dared persist in his fight for freedom."[45] Lajpat Rai's newspaper, *The People*, published a special memorial edition in which Du Bois warmly remembered Lajpat Rai's "restraint and sweet temper" and commented, "When a man of his sort can be called a Revolutionist and beaten to death by a great civilized government, then indeed revolution becomes a duty to all right thinking men." Du Bois told his Indian readers that "the people of India, like the American Negroes, are demanding today things, not in the least revolutionary, but things which every civilized white man has so long taken for granted."

Defending the reasonableness of Lajpat Rai's efforts, Du Bois underestimated the radical vision that he and Lajpat Rai shared. Both aimed to end inequalities of race, nation, class, and gender. Neither was satisfied with the prospect of merely adding a colored elite to the circle of wealthy white men who controlled much of the world. In the 1930s it would be Left-leaning Indians and African Americans who would do the most to build upon the linkages forged by Lajpat Rai to develop a colored cosmopolitanism that was aware of diversities internal to the colored world. At the end of his tribute to Lajpat Rai, Du Bois remarked, "I hope that the memory of Lala Lajpat Rai will be kept green in India, and that out of the blood of his martyrdom very soon a free colored nation will arise."[46] Through his growing links with Indians, Du Bois helped ensure that when India gained its independence, many Indians would understand their country as indeed "a free *colored* nation."

In March 1936 Du Bois published an extensive analysis of the relationship between Indians and African Americans in a Bombay journal called *The Aryan Path*. With fascism menacing Europe, this was a significant time to discuss matters of race in a journal entitled *The Aryan Path*.[47] Notions of colored unity had progressed since the days that European ethnographers linked high-caste Indians with other "Aryans" and low-caste Indians with Negroes. Du Bois realized, however, that solidarity between Indians and African Americans remained problematic. He noted the ability of Indians to distinguish themselves from Blacks by flaunting their foreign origins. "An Indian may be dark in color," he wrote, "but if he dons his turban and travels in the South, he does not have to be subjected to the separate car laws and other discriminations against Negroes." On the other hand, Du Bois recognized that Indian immigrants to the United States faced hardships that Black Americans did not face. Of the Indian immigrant, Du Bois stated, "If he should try for employment or for citizenship, or any economic status, he would find the tables quite turned, and that while an African Negro can become a citizen of the United States, an Indian of the highest caste cannot." Du Bois stressed that many "prominent Indians," including Rabindranath Tagore and Lajpat Rai, had gone out of their way to interact with and learn from African Americans. African Americans, Du Bois argued, could learn from "the great struggle for freedom and self-government which has been going on in India." He noted with approbation the fact that several Indians had already attended Pan-African congresses.[48]

Du Bois linked caste in India to hierarchies of color among African Americans. "If India has her castes," he wrote, "American Negroes have in their own internal color lines, the plain shadow of a caste system." Marcus Garvey had similarly argued, "There is more bitterness among us Negroes because of the caste of color than there is between any other peoples, not excluding the people of India."[49] Du Bois and Garvey both used caste in India to highlight color discrimination among Blacks, failing in the process to recognize the severity of caste oppression in India. Du Bois, like Garvey, largely overlooked potential solidarities between Blacks and Dalits. For Du Bois, India's role in the colored world overshadowed the realities of caste inequality. Du Bois used the singular to declare, "India has also had the temptation to stand apart from the darker peoples and seek her affinities among whites. She has long wished to regard herself as 'Aryan' rather than 'colored' and to think of herself as much nearer physically and spiritually to Germany and England than to Africa, China or the South Seas." Du Bois accurately represented the position of many Indians in the United States and India but failed to recognize that many of the Indians who claimed an Aryan past were high-caste, northern-born Indians for whom their Aryan status distinguished them as much from low-caste Indians as from Blacks.[50]

Although he failed to fully acknowledge the severity of caste oppression, Du Bois recognized the potential for injustice to thrive within the colored world. If the "colored peoples" did not respect and protect "their laboring masses," Du Bois wrote, they would ultimately substitute "for the exploitation of colored by white races, an exploitation of colored races by colored men." He concluded, "If, however, they can follow the newer ideals which look upon human labor as the only real and final repository of political power, then, and only then, can the union of the darker races bring a new and beautiful world, not simply for themselves, but for all men." Du Bois once again opposed both "a color line within the color line" and equally divisive anti-white notions of color.[51]

Noting that "the acute problem of the colour-bar" existed "on every continent," the editors of *The Aryan Path* promised that Du Bois's views would be considered "from the Indian standpoint." In May the editors published a reply to Du Bois by N. S. Subba Rao, director of public instruction in Mysore State. Rao praised Du Bois for offering "a moving appeal for a better understanding, greater sympathy, and co-operation between the Negroes of America and the people of India." Rao told his readers that Indians should contribute to Black newspapers and should encourage Black authors to publish in India. Rao's suggestion that "periodical gatherings should be held of representatives of Negroes and Indians as well as of other coloured peoples of the world" went beyond anything Du Bois had suggested in his article but fit well with his conception of the Pan-African Congresses as gatherings of all colored people.[52]

Rao took issue with the suggestion that notions of Aryan identity or color-based prejudices had complicated the relationship between Indians and Blacks. Ignoring evidence to the contrary, Rao asserted, "The people of India do not associate with the term Aryan anything that savours of race or colour, nor is it true that in India black colour is a thing which is despised." According to Rao, "The strangeness which the people of India feel when they come into contact with the people of Africa arises not from any sense of racial superiority, but from nonparity of culture." Revealing his belief in a hierarchy of culture, Rao wrote, "Not that the numerous strata of Indian society are all entitled to feel a sense of superiority over the Africans, or that some sections of the native people of Africa have not elements of culture that take a high place in the scale of values." In Rao's conception, civilized Indians had good reason to look down on the uncivilized at home and abroad. "Broadly speaking," Rao concluded, "one is entitled to hold that for various reasons the people of Africa have remained culturally backward." He did not justify his sudden transition from discussing African Americans to discussing Africans, nor did he enumerate the "various reasons" that explained the supposed cultural failings of Africans. Despite Du Bois's concluding paean to "a new and beautiful world . . . for all men," Rao found Du Bois's notion of colored unity too divisive. He criticized Du Bois for encouraging "the coloured peoples to league themselves against the white races" and, misrepresenting the goal of Du Bois's article, concluded, "To range the forces of the world into two camps, sullen, suspicious, and menacing, is no answer." Taken as a whole, Rao's article endorsed the importance of building bridges between Blacks and Indians and recognized both groups as "coloured peoples" but argued that solidarities of color could too easily become aggressively anti-white.[53]

In October *The Aryan Path* published a response by Du Bois, criticizing Rao's hesitations regarding "colored unity." Du Bois made clear that his ultimate goal was "a real union of all colors and of races," but he argued that colored unity was a necessary means to that end. He championed "inner cohesion and understanding among the coloured peoples." His conception of "inner cohesion" echoed his recent call for Blacks to embrace a form of economic segregation within the United States. Amongst colored peoples, as within the Black community, Du Bois advocated economic and political collaboration.[54] The same edition of *The Aryan Path* contained a "rejoinder" by Rao. While his earlier critique had focused on the risk of racial conflict between white and colored peoples, Rao now chose to question the practicality of colored unity as well. The "coloured people," Rao counseled, "are so divided among themselves that it is hard to believe they will ever arrive at anything like a common understanding." "Let alone the union of coloured peoples in the whole world," Rao wrote, "but consider the unhappy divisions in a country like India, where the people do not agree about such matters as electorates in the political field or music before mosques in that of religion." Thus Rao invoked divisions of caste and religion in India as evidence of the impossibility of colored unity. He rejected an alliance of colored peoples as both anti-white and impractical.[55] Rao's disbelief in the practicality of colored solidarity would prove prophetic. His anxiety regarding a race war, despite being shared by other critics of colored solidarity, would prove needless.

Like Du Bois, many Indians imagined a colored solidarity that did not involve anti-white racial chauvinism. Reading Du Bois's article inspired S. Natarajan, editor of the *Indian Social Reformer,* to send Du Bois a piece that the *Reformer* had published criticizing Paul Robeson for reproducing notions of racial difference between white and non-white races. Across the masthead of the *Reformer,* a quote from William Lloyd Garrison proclaimed: "I will be as harsh as truth, and as uncompromising as justice." Natarajan told Du Bois that the *Reformer* would like to receive any periodicals dealing with "the modern movements among the Negros." He also asked for information on the "Association for Advancement of Coloured Peoples."[56] Like Amiya Kanti Das, Natarajan pluralized the title the "National Association for the Advancement of Colored People." His addition of a final "s" demonstrated his embrace of a notion of color that included a diversity of "colored peoples."

Du Bois's article also helped open channels with the Indian Left. Rammanohar Lohia, secretary of the All India Congress Committee's Foreign Department, wrote Du Bois, "We on our part are equally anxious to establish the closest relations with our Negro comrades of America." Lohia sent Du Bois several editions of the Congress *Foreign Newsletter,* offering to send it regularly. He added, "I hope the letter is of enough interest to the Negro Press to justify reproductions and extracts being made from it." Lohia told Du Bois:

> I am even more anxious to learn of the experiences of your people in their fight for freedom and a higher standard of living. We here attach the highest significance to the Negro Front of anti-Imperialism and, anxious as we are to secure their active sympathy for our cause, we are even more anxious to know in greater detail of the Negro fight and extend it our fraternal support. I would try to give your cause as much publicity in this country as is possible.[57]

Lohia would become an active member of the Congress Socialist Party and, after independence, a prominent Socialist leader. In the early 1950s he traveled to the United States, where he encouraged African Americans to utilize nonviolent civil disobedience against American racism. In the 1960s Lohia returned to the United States and was arrested in Mississippi while participating in a civil rights protest. Throughout his life, in India and in the United States, Lohia opposed oppressions based on race, caste, and class. His letter to Du Bois in 1936 makes evident not only his early sympathy with African American struggles but also the socialist framework in which he expressed that sympathy.

In the United States many appeals for colored unity had originated on the left. In 1925 a diverse assembly of African American labor leaders, journalists, and activists gathered for the founding meeting of the American Negro Labor Congress. The document they drafted noted "with pride the world-wide stirring of the darker races against European imperialism" and declared, "The workers and peasants of India are determined to drive every vestige of British authority from the soil of India." Like many Left-leaning opponents of racism, the Congress linked racial prejudice to class inequality. "Racial antagonism," the Congress concluded, "springs from the present order of society—a society in which less than ten percent of the people own and control everything." The document's signers included Sahir Karimji, a "Fraternal Delegate from Natal Agricultural Workers, South Africa," most likely of Indian descent.[58]

A self-proclaimed disciple of Du Bois, Cedric Dover, would prove to be among the most important links between Black and Indian socialists and, next to Du Bois himself, the most persistent champion of colored cosmopolitanism. It was Dover who suggested to Lohia that he read Du Bois's article in *The Aryan Path*. Dover called himself a "Eurasian," a term he preferred to "Anglo-Indian" as a label for the progeny of British and Indian intimacies. Born in Calcutta in 1904, Dover spent much of his life in England, where he authored an array of books and articles attacking white supremacy and ridiculing biologically based notions of race while imagining a global community built upon color as a marker of shared oppression. Central to this community were a variety of influential African American activists and intellectuals with whom Dover forged collaborations and friendships. In addition to Du Bois, Dover's network included Paul Robeson, Langston Hughes, and Fisk University president, Charles Johnson. Remarkably, despite the richness of his published works and the multiplicity of his contacts, Dover has largely disappeared from the academic record.[59]

Dover's rejection of racial purity began with his analysis of a particular form of racial hybridity—his own. In his first major book, *Cimmerii: Or Eurasians and Their Future,* published in Calcutta in 1929, Dover referenced African Americans in order to encourage Eurasians to embrace their hybridity. He wrote, "The Negro owes his rapidly advancing position mainly to the efforts of mulattoes, among whom Booker T. Washington and E. W. [sic] du Bois are conspicuous examples." For Dover, the achievements of African Americans augured the eventual hybridization of humankind. He prophesied that "the inter-racial difficulties of the world will be solved by the development of mixed breeds, and that the removal of racial friction by marriage will ultimately lead to the peaceful occupation of the whole world by one composite race."[60] Conspicuous here is Dover's use of the future tense. He had not yet abandoned the notion of race but only predicted its future demise.

Dover's encounters with African Americans helped him move beyond race and toward a cosmopolitan conception of color. During the 1930s his focus expanded from the Eurasian community to encompass people oppressed because of their color throughout the world. Dover demonstrated his global vision in 1937 with *Half-Caste,* a landmark tome that combined anthropological critiques of the idea of "race" with a wide-ranging, transnational analysis of the history and culture of people of mixed "ethnicity," a term Dover used to avoid the word "race."[61] *Half-Caste* was cited in a California Supreme Court decision that declared, for the first time, that a law prohibiting marriage across the color line violated the federal constitution.[62] *The Chicago Defender* offered an interview with Dover from London, probably written by George Padmore, entitled "Race Scientist Debunks White Superiority Thesis." Calling Dover a "brilliant Eurasian sociologist" and *Half-Caste* his "magnum opus," the article declared, "This is a book that every intelligent colored man, woman, and child should read. It will give them the intellectual armament necessary to annihilate any jingoist and white racial chauvinist."[63]

Dover's growing interest in African American culture inspired him to visit the United States. He wrote Du Bois in August 1937, noting his desire to meet "Negro personalities" and to "get the feel of Negro life." He told Du Bois, "I am particularly anxious to extend closer cultural contacts between coloured folk, a subject in which you are also so much interested." Du Bois responded that he knew of Dover "by reputation," had received a copy of *Half-Caste,* and planned to read it. Du Bois offered to host Dover in Atlanta. Thus began one of the most important friendships in the long history of relationships between Indians and African Americans.[64]

Dover's journey took him from New England, through New York, and to the Jim Crow South. He visited Howard and Fisk before arriving at Atlanta University to stay as the guest of Du Bois. Dover cabled Du Bois in February 1938 to express his gratitude for Du Bois's "gracious hospitality," but it was in a letter that Dover sent Jawaharlal Nehru that he expressed most fully what he gained from meeting Du Bois. Dover reported finding among Black Americans "a tremendous interest in India and a very definite sense of kinship" with Indians. He declared, "I have personally experienced in Afro-America a mutual bond of understanding and an inspiring feeling of being at home." "My host here, Dr. W. E. Burghardt Du Bois," Dover wrote, "is one of the great pioneers, as you already know, of the movement for closer contacts between coloured peoples." Dover suggested that Nehru and Gandhi send birthday greetings on the occasion of Du Bois's upcoming seventieth birthday. A draft of Dover's letter originally praised Du Bois as leading "this Negro movement for closer contact with Asiatics." By changing "Asiatics" to "coloured peoples," Dover demonstrated that he was learning to see "Negroes" and "Asiatics" as united by color.[65]

Du Bois, Dover, and other advocates of colored solidarity were not content with merely theorizing the colored world. They wanted to build it. If they were to influence politics, then proponents of colored unity needed to gain influence with political figures. In May 1936 Dover sent Jawaharlal

Nehru a copy of George Padmore's *How Britain Rules the Blacks*. Dover asked Nehru if he might send one of Nehru's works to Padmore, as well as Charles Johnson, former editor of *Opportunity* and a distinguished academic at Fisk University. To Nehru, Dover described Johnson as "one of the outstanding men in the Negro world and much interested in India," and he explained, "I am using him to push our propaganda in Negro America."[66] On July 15 Nehru responded, agreeing to have his books sent to Padmore and Johnson.[67] When Nehru came to London, Dover arranged for a small private meeting between Paul Robeson and Nehru. Dover also corresponded with Nehru regarding an article Dover wanted Nehru to write for the African American press.[68] Nehru would eventually become the most prominent and among the most ardent of Indian supporters of African American struggles. He developed his own understanding of colored unity. Like Du Bois and Dover, Nehru defended colored solidarity in part as a response to a history of common oppression. In 1936 Nehru explained "the British upper-class division of the world" as follows:

(1) Britain—a long gap, and then (2) the British Dominions (white population only) and America (Anglo-Saxons only, and not dagoes, wops, etc.), (3) Western Europe, (4) Rest of Europe, (5) South America (Latin races), a long gap, and then (6) the brown, yellow and black races of Asia and Africa, all bunched up more or less together.[69]

Nehru's view that British imperialists saw "the brown, yellow and black races" as equally contemptible influenced his efforts to build an effective coalition of resistance. As prime minister of independent India, Nehru would have the ability to give such a coalition global significance.

Like Du Bois, Dover wrote at times as if a history of being on the wrong side of the color line naturally created bonds of affection between a majority of the world's people. Dover explained the "feeling of unity" between Blacks and Indians as rooted in "colour as a symbol of difference between oppressors and oppressed." "Its binding quality is oppression," he declared, "its impulse the will somehow or other, some day or other, to lay down the heavy load."[70] Dover's belief in the "binding quality" of oppression did not prevent him from assiduously working to connect intellectuals and artists from throughout the world.[71] Dover's own writings include and often combine anthropology, literary analysis, poetry, history, and politics. Trained as an entomologist and a forester, Dover published in the journal *Science* and in the *Proceedings of the Indian Academy of Science*, wrote articles on the sixth-century Black Arab warrior-poet Antarah Ibn Shaddad el-Absi, and authored a book of poems.[72] Dover's ambitions crossed national borders, racial divisions, and disciplinary boundaries. Writing in

1947 in *The Crisis,* Dover stated with a characteristic combination of humility and self-promotion, "*Half-Caste* is not remarkable for its critical understanding of Negro culture, but it is the first book in which another man of color tried to get his comrades in America into focus."[73] In order to clarify why someone named Cedric Dover was identifying himself as a "man of color," the editor of *The Crisis* added "Dover is Eurasian–Ed." in brackets. Dover's conception of what it meant to be a "half-caste" allowed him to be both a Eurasian and, like the many African American readers of *The Crisis,* a "man of color."

In the same year that he published *Half-Caste,* Dover contributed an article to the *Congress Socialist,* the journal of the Congress Socialist Party, a group whose members included Kamaladevi Chattopadhyaya and Rammanohar Lohia. Written under the aegis of the Foreign Department of the Indian National Congress and entitled "Towards Coloured Unity," the article arose from Dover's participation in the World Peace Congress held in Belgium in September 1936. "Towards Coloured Unity" reveals Dover moving from his early focus on "half-castes" to an emphasis on "coloured unity" that would dominate the second half of his career. In order to support "a wider coloured unity," Dover approached the novelist Mulk Raj Anand, a friend and fellow delegate to the World Peace Congress. Dover suggested that the two organize "a meeting of the coloured delegates to consider our special problems." Anand, Dover learned, was already organizing such a gathering with several other delegates. Soon, a group gathered to draft a joint memorandum, signed by delegates representing "Indians, Chinese, Eurasians, Indonesians, American Negroes, West Indians, Africans, Tunisians, Arabs, Jews and other subject peoples." The memorandum attacked "theories of racial inequality," encouraged the granting of "equal civil and political status" to women, and defended the right "of colonial and coloured peoples to organise" on behalf of world peace. For Dover, the memorandum was "the answer to those who believe that 'local loyalties' will prevent the progress of coloured amalgamation." Dover believed that a collaboration of colored peoples would best work in a federalized system that respected local autonomy and diversity. He imagined such a collaboration taking the form of a "Congress of Coloured and Colonial Peoples." His article was reprinted in the journal *Pan-Africa* in 1947 with a note explaining that the original article had been "widely reprinted in India, America and Africa," and that "the passing of a decade has made it still more urgently contemporary."[74]

While defending a global unity based on color, both "Towards Coloured Unity" and *Half-Caste* soundly rejected the idea of distinct races. In "Towards Coloured Unity," Dover's emphasis on "colour" did not exclude any group that continued to suffer from racial, economic, or colonial oppression. In *Half-Caste* Dover methodically dismantled racialist pseudoscience and declared, "There has not been a pure race of our species for at least ten thousand years."[75] Although colored cosmopolitans would consistently find it necessary to defend themselves against charges of "reverse racism," a more fair critique would focus on the practical limits of a discourse largely invented by elites. Colored cosmopolitanism emerged primarily among artists and intellectuals, many of whom traveled widely. The vast majority of Blacks and Indians were denied the means to experience directly a wider world of color. It would be wrong, however, to assert that solidarities of color mattered only to elites. The Black press did much to keep the Indian struggle present in the minds of many African Americans. Those too poor to visit India or to afford a copy of *Dark Princess* might purchase their local Black newspaper, borrow secondhand copies, or discuss the news with friends. Interest in Black America among poor Indians is harder to assess, especially in the pre-independence period. Indian knowledge of African American struggles was surely hampered by the extreme poverty of large numbers of Indians. Furthermore, while Gandhian nonviolent civil disobedience gained worldwide attention for India, Black American struggles were not yet equally well known. Nevertheless, with Booker T. Washington's autobiography being translated into multiple South Asian languages and used as a textbook in the subcontinent, with American missionaries teaching the history of emancipation, and with significant numbers of Indians traveling to the United States, many opportunities existed for Indians of all classes to learn about African American struggles.

The Limits of Cosmopolitanism

While the ideas of Du Bois, Cedric Dover, and other advocates of colored cosmopolitanism increasingly gained adherents, not all Blacks and Indians who encountered notions of colored unity found them persuasive. American immigration policy continued to encourage some Indians to pursue the privileges of whiteness. In 1928 Representative Emmanuel Celler and Senator Royal Copeland introduced bills that would define "Hindus" as legally white and thus worthy of American citizenship.[76] The story of Indians in America demonstrates both the potential for collaboration between Blacks and Indians and the persistence of distrust between two groups with distinct histories and divergent challenges. Conceptions of racial superiority and disparate responses to white supremacy divided the "colored world."

What Du Bois called in *Dark Princess* the "color line within a color line" was dramatically revealed in a controversial letter to *The Chicago Defender* written by one K. Romola, an Indian American living in Chicago, who styled himself the "director" of an "Aryan propaganda society." Romola had noticed the prevalence of stories on India in *The Chicago Defender*, but rather than embrace colored cosmopolitanism, he angrily denounced solidarity between Blacks and Indians. Romola declared, "Too much has been written by the Negro papers, magazines and fourth rate writers like Du Bois, about the darker races, but who in the hell wants to join the caravan with the black ones." Romola explained his distaste for "the black ones" in terms of caste. "Our caste system in India," he wrote, "excludes those who do not belong to the Aryan (white) race and we even here exclude any Indians who live and socialize with the Negro." Romola's casual equation of "Aryan" and "white" had, of course, been soundly rejected by the Supreme Court only seven years earlier in the case of Bhagat Singh Thind. Like Thind, Romola aimed to distinguish high-caste Indians from both low-caste Indians and Blacks. As if his letter was not sufficiently inflammatory, Romola proclaimed, "If we become free in the course of ten or twenty years we are after a slice of Africa too, for the savages there do not have any use for the wealth there." Discarding colored unity, attacking Blacks as poor and unlettered, and suggesting Indian imperialism in Africa, Romola's letter reads at times like a deliberate effort to estrange Black Americans from all things Indian.[77]

Having been exposed to over a decade of mostly positive, at times glowing, accounts of the Indian struggle, Black Americans might have been prepared to discard Romola's rant as the product of one insignificant, if offensive, man. On the contrary, the letters that "poured into the office" of *The Chicago Defender* tended to take Romola as speaking for all Indians. The editors of the *Defender* lamented this response. Having printed Romola's letter under the title "A Hindu Speaks His Mind About Us," they chose to emphasize his singularity even more by entitling a follow-up editorial, "One Hindu Speaks." The "general opinion" of the many letters they received, the editors explained, "was that India is no good, that its people are worse, and that we would be fools to continue showing our interest in that country's struggles." The editors strove to counter such anti-Indian responses to what they noted were the opinions of "one man, and one man only." Rather than offer evidence of Indian support for African Americans, however, the editors emphasized the inability of Indians to disassociate themselves from the colored world. "If we have any kinship with India at all (and we are not saying we have)," the editors wrote, "it is through the common bond of persecution which has been welded around us by those who now dominate world affairs."[78]

While chastising their readers for equating Romola with all Indians, the editors of *The Chicago Defender* nonetheless published several of the letters that continued arriving. One Frank St. Claire of Chicago wrote that Romola "seems to think that none of us has ever read the history of his country when he attempts to class his countrymen as white." St. Claire cited the harsh anti-Indian immigration laws of the United States and other "white" countries. Rather than using this evidence of shared oppression to encourage colored solidarity, however, St. Claire offered his readers a litany of what he took to be India's barbaric customs. He wrote, "The Negro does not marry his babies off while they are yet in the cradle. Neither does he require his widow to burn herself on a funeral pyre, nor does he compel her to bathe in polluted streams."[79] While St. Claire attacked Indian cultural practices, some Black readers responded to Romola's letter by distinguishing Blacks and Indians on racial grounds. These responses echoed Romola's assertion of racial superiority by inverting it. J. Dalton Gilmore of Chicago called Romola a "fatuous jungle ape from the Himalayas" and "a low species of jungle animal." Gilmore attacked caste as "useless sacerdotal idiocy" and "only one of the artificial divisions into which Hindus are restricted by ancient Brahmin religious law." Rather than champion the emancipation of Dalits, however, Gilmore used his critique of caste merely to defame all things Indian.[80]

Not all Black responses to Romola's letter rejected Afro-Indian solidarity. From Toronto, W. H. Beecher wrote, "It hurts Mr. Romola for the truth to be told about the treatment of the Indian people in his country where 325 white men rule 325,000,000 million Indians of all castes and classes." "What Mr. Romola needs to know," Beecher asserted, is that "the American Negro is not seeking to help him or his people any more than any other black people, and no matter how much it hurts him to know his people are black, they are black, all thoughts to the contrary notwithstanding, and he (if he lives long enough) will one day be proud of it."[81] Only one Black respondent to Romola discussed the Indian cause in detail. Moxley W. Willis wrote from Baltimore to counter Romola's claims. Strangely, Willis seemed unconcerned about Romola's many references to Black Americans. Instead, he refuted Romola's portrayal of a religiously divided India.[82]

Several Indian Americans wrote *The Chicago Defender* to disown Romola's sentiments and to reassert Indian solidarity with Black Americans. H. G. Mudgal stated that Romola was "entirely out of touch with not only the recent events in India, but also with the eternal idealism of his country."

To explain Romola's ignorance, Mudgal suggested that he had "been a victim of the white propagandists" of the United States. As the editor of Marcus Garvey's *The Negro World,* Mudgal was in a unique position to refute Romola. He chose, however, not to discuss his own extensive interactions with Blacks in both Trinidad and the United States. Instead he emphasized his high-caste, Aryan identity. Mudgal wrote, "May I as an Indian, as an Aryan, as a Brahman, whose community has been fighting social oppression in India for over 300 (?) years, protest the snobbish tone and content of Mr. Romola's letter." "It is true that Indians are Aryans," Mudgal explained, "and are the only ones entitled to that term." He clarified, however, that "Young India is in the grip of humanism and they care no more for Mr. Romola's caste ideas than they do for his race snobbishness." Mudgal proclaimed, "Young India will fight for humanism and for the freedom of all oppressed peoples in the world, whether it be white oppression, yellow or green oppression."[83] This was not, however, a defense of colored cosmopolitanism. Only Mudgal's address, "355 Lenox Avenue, New York," by placing him in the heart of Harlem, intimated the depth of Mudgal's connections with Black Americans.

Professor G. Rao of Chicago wrote to criticize Romola and to defend India's unity and its solidarity with other oppressed peoples. "The Hindu community of Chicago feels it a shame for a Hindu to write in these terms," Rao wrote. He stated, "I pity a man that has not mixed freely and seen the good that is in the 'Negro' Colored people." Rao praised the "pure, simple, radiant soul" of Du Bois, Paul Laurence Dunbar, and other Black authors. Like Mudgal, he combined a defense of India's unity with an appeal for solidarities between the oppressed. "India is united solidly and has forgotten all of her caste, religious and race differences," Rao wrote.[84] D. G. Madho Singh also defended the achievement of religious unity in India. "We Hindus," he wrote, "have come to a definite understanding with our Mohammedan brothers and in unity we stand for 'love.'" Singh apologized on behalf of Romola, suggested that Romola apologize himself, and encouraged *The Defender* not to publish such inflammatory letters in the future. He declared, "There isn't a civilized man on earth today who feels that he belongs to a superior race."[85] One Muslim reader, L. Rahman, the president of the East Indian Family Club, used Romola as a foil to present the antiracist potential of Islam. Rahman proclaimed, "During the last 1,300 years Islam has exterminated the race and color problems and absolutely effaced color distinctions in the different parts of the world."[86]

By attacking colored solidarity, Romola's letter made evident the prevalence of colored cosmopolitanism. Black and Indian responses to Romola's letter, however, demonstrated that Afro-Indian solidarity faced considerable obstacles. The readiness of some Black respondents to invert Romola's claims of racial superiority, and the near unanimity with which Black respondents were willing to take Romola as a spokesman for all "Hindus," boded ill for the ability of colored cosmopolitanism to gain a large following among Black Americans. Indian respondents to Romola, while uniformly refuting his racial arrogance and especially his caste and religious bigotry, generally failed to invoke notions of color as a marker of shared solidarity. The Romola controversy, while revealing the limits of colored cosmopolitanism, nonetheless provided several grounds to be optimistic about the future of reflections between Indian and African American freedom struggles. Even if they did not speak in terms of color, Indian Americans, Hindu and Muslim, were unanimous in their criticism of Romola. In the years to follow, Indian opponents of unity with Blacks proved to be exceedingly rare.

The construction of the colored world exemplified the fluidity of anticolonial politics.[87] Advocates of colored solidarity, including Du Bois and Dover, encouraged the unity of colored people while defending an antiracist humanism and recognizing the internal diversity of the colored world. Colored solidarity neither conflicted with larger visions of human equality, nor precluded concern for inequalities internal to the colored world. By seeking common ground, some proponents of unity between Indians and African Americans challenged not only white promoters of racial hierarchy but also those Indians and African Americans who pursued a freedom based on, in the words of Du Bois, the "exploitation of colored races by colored men."

Within the "colored world," women, Dalits, and the poor would have to fight to create visions of transnational resistance that did not relegate their own struggles to the shadows. As early as 1920 a group of internationally minded African American women founded the International Council of Women of the Darker Races. Their first public meeting, four years later, included two students from India, who expressed, in the words of The Chicago Defender, "their approbation of the international council and its difficult program."[88] Several of the leaders of the international council would later establish close relationships to leading female Indian political figures, including Kamaladevi Chattopadhyaya and Vijayalakshmi Pandit. Colored cosmopolitanism was increasingly defined and redefined by colored women.

The intellectual and artistic foundations of colored cosmopolitanism threatened to constrain its impact on the intellectual networks in which it flourished. In an editorial in The Negro World entitled "The Darker

World Stirs," the veteran Black socialist and labor leader Frank R. Crosswaith praised struggles in India, China, and Japan. Despite the depth of Black solidarity with "the darker world," Crosswaith argued, "all that we have equipped ourselves to contribute in their struggle for independence are prayers and spirituals, and these weapons (if you call them such) in a world of struggle make as much impression upon a foe as feathers falling on a snow covered field."[89] Crosswaith's editorial appeared in January 1930, only months before Gandhi's dramatic Salt March would once again make India front-page news. India's seemingly rapid progress toward independence offered the hope that even if Black Americans could provide little more than "prayers and spirituals" to the Indian cause, Indians might use their newfound influence to aid Blacks and other members of the darker world.

It was in the 1930s, as his renown once again peaked worldwide, that Mahatma Gandhi intensified his interactions with African Americans. Gandhi met with several Black Americans in India and corresponded with others. His engagement with African Americans and with American racism helped inspire his evolving views not only of race but also of caste. By the Second World War, Gandhi would emerge as an outspoken opponent of white domination worldwide, as well as an increasingly radical critic of caste in India. If the influence of Black Americans on British imperialism approximated "feathers falling on a snow covered field," the impact of Blacks on the shape of the emerging Indian nation proved far more significant.

CHAPTER FOUR

Soul Force

The African must remember the colored Christ. Preachers did
not understand Christ until taught by my Master, Mahatma
Gandhi. Jesus, remember, was not a white man, but an Asiatic
like me.

—Sarojini Naidu

I N MAY 1924 Marcus Garvey's newspaper, *The Negro World*, re-
ported a speech given by the Indian poet Sarojini Naidu at a meet-
ing of the Universal Negro Improvement Association (UNIA) in
Capetown, South Africa. As the meeting opened, an auditorium full of
Black and Indian South Africans sang Christian hymns, including "The
Lord Is King" and one of Gandhi's personal favorites, "Lead, Kindly
Light." The hymns befitted Naidu's speech. Linking Gandhi, Garvey, and
Christ as prophets of pride in dark skin, Naidu offered her audience a
conception of colored unity grounded in an emancipatory reading of
Christian and Gandhian teachings. "The message I bring to my people is
the same message I give to the Negroes," Naidu proclaimed, "that message that Mahatman Gandhi brought out of Africa; that message that
Marcus Garvey is giving the British Dominions to the Negroes of the
world; the same message that Jesus preached nearly two thousand years
ago. Africans, be not ashamed of your black skin." To her audience and
the many African American readers of *The Negro World*, Naidu presented Gandhi as a Christian apostle of colored pride and solidarity.[1]

On January 26, 1930, the Indian National Congress endorsed the goal
of *purna swaraj*, or complete independence. To Gandhi fell the task of de-
ciding how to use civil disobedience to make that goal a reality. He chose
to challenge the government monopoly on the collection and production

---

"Mrs. Naidu, Noted East Indian Poetess, at Great U.N.I.A. Mass Meeting in Capetown, South Africa, Lauds Principles and Leadership of the Association," *The Negro
World*, May 17, 1924.

of salt, a staple whose price particularly affected the poor. Along with a carefully chosen group of followers, Gandhi walked 240 miles from his ashram near the banks of the Sabarmati River to the coastal town of Dandi. The march captured the attention of the world. On April 6 Gandhi reached the sea and gathered a handful of salty sand from the shore. Throughout India, nonviolent protesters began to produce and distribute salt in open defiance of the law.

In the wake of the Salt March, African American interest in Gandhi boomed, revealing both the depth and diversity of Black engagement with the Mahatma. To properly understand the range of African American responses to Gandhi requires careful attention to shifting constructions of race, nation, empire, and, perhaps most crucially, religion. For many Black Americans, Gandhi was a religious teacher who offered spiritual as well as political instruction.[2] The African American encounter with Gandhi was part of a larger American engagement with Indian religion, ranging from American transcendentalism to theosophy. While they contributed to widespread efforts to reconcile Gandhi and Christianity, many African Americans presented the Mahatma as a colored leader opposed to white oppression.

By focusing primarily on Gandhi's impact on African Americans, existing scholarship has largely neglected the ways in which African Americans influenced Gandhi. As a young man, Gandhi used the Aryan idea to distinguish "civilized" Indians from uncivilized Africans. Over the course of his years in South Africa, Gandhi developed a different understanding of civilization, influenced by Booker T. Washington, in which poor and working-class people of all races became exemplars of the civilizing capacity of labor. In the 1920s and 1930s Gandhi's interaction with a variety of African Americans contributed to his growing colored cosmopolitanism and his increasingly outspoken criticism of American racial inequality. While emancipatory conceptions of Christianity strongly influenced many Black perceptions of Gandhi, Gandhi's own religious pluralism allowed him to embrace African Americans as fellow seekers of God.[3] The majority of African Americans who met or corresponded with Gandhi framed their commitment to social change in a religious framework. Many served as Christian pastors or taught religion in Black colleges. Gandhi's conception of African American struggles was shaped by a conception of Black spirituality that he developed largely from his interactions with African Americans.

Gandhi's interactions with African Americans challenged him to revise his understanding of caste in India. While his earliest initiatives aimed to end untouchability while preserving caste, Gandhi eventually came to reject caste itself as detrimental to Indian society and contrary to the true spirit of Hinduism. Gandhi's evolving views on caste were both encouraged and constrained by his relationships with African Americans. While Booker T. Washington helped inspire Gandhi's recognition of the dignity of labor, Washingtonian notions of self-help and social harmony limited Gandhi's efforts to confront caste oppression. As Washington moderated his criticism of racial oppression in order to maintain the support of influential whites, Gandhi tempered his social reforms so as to preserve the support of upper-caste Indians. A key dimension of the long history of relationships between Gandhi and African Americans, analogies between race and caste both advanced and constrained Gandhi's understanding of *swaraj*.

Evangels of *Self*-Deliverance

In the aftermath of the First World War, Indians in the United States galvanized interest in Gandhi among African Americans. Ten years later, in the late 1920s and early 1930s, a new wave of Indian supporters of Gandhi came to the United States, inspired in part by the desire to refute Katherine Mayo's *Mother India*. In collaboration with liberal white Americans who championed both American racial equality and Indian independence, Indian supporters of Gandhi solidified Gandhi's status among Blacks as a "colored" messiah. While shaping African American conceptions of the Mahatma, these ambassadors were equally influential in shaping Gandhi's views of African Americans. They communicated to Gandhi an image of African Americans that, while at times patronizing, increased Gandhi's sympathy with the struggles of African Americans, helping to endow Gandhi's understanding of the Indian struggle with transnational and transracial dimensions.

In 1928, Sarojini Naidu came to the United States to improve American opinion of Gandhi and the Indian National Congress. A renowned poet and a close confidant of Gandhi, Naidu was also a significant political figure in her own right, having been elected President of the Congress only a few years earlier. Naidu conceived of herself as a disciple of Gandhi, spreading a religiously informed message of emancipation that, like Garvey's UNIA, welcomed followers of many spiritual traditions. In a letter to Gandhi from Cincinnati, Ohio, addressed playfully to "My Mystic Spinner," Naidu presented herself as a missionary for the Mahatma, bringing his good news to African Americans. Referencing Harriet Beecher Stowe, the author of *Uncle Tom's Cabin,* Naidu told Gandhi that in Cincinnati "long ago lived a very noble woman who dedicated her genius to the deliverance of the Negros from their pitiful bondage." Naidu wrote, "Mine was, like Harriet Beecher Stowe's, also a message of deliverance from bondage—another version for another land." Referring to herself as a "Wandering Singer," Naidu told Gandhi, "The gospel of the Mystic Spinner as interpreted by a Wandering Singer was from first to last, from the initial to the ultimate word, the evangel of *self*-deliverance from *every* kind of personal, national, economic, social, intellectual, political, and spiritual bondage."

Naidu understood the emancipatory potential of Gandhi's teaching in expansive and explicitly religious terms. She told Gandhi, "I have reached the houses—and I hope the hearts—of the as yet disinherited Children of America, the Coloured population." Referring to Blacks as "Children of America," Naidu evoked Gandhi's own phrase for Dalits, Harijans, or the children of God. The patronizing undertones in both phrases, "children of America" and "children of God," surfaced when Naidu declared: "It breaks my heart to see the helpless, hopeless, silent and patient bitterness and mental suffering of the educated Negroes." Her adjectives—"helpless, hopeless, silent and patient"—denied Blacks agency in a way that high-caste reformers, including Gandhi, often denied untouchables agency. Naidu made the comparison explicit by calling Blacks "the socially and spiritually outcast children of America." Once again she referred to African Americans as children while framing race in America as Gandhi did caste in India—as a spiritual matter.

Naidu's description of African Americans—empathetic, if patronizing—was not without praise for Black initiatives. "They are so cultured, so gifted, some of them so beautiful," Naidu wrote, "all of them so informed with earnest and sensitive appreciation of all that is authentic in modern ideas of life." Naidu described the play *Porgy*, from which the musical *Porgy and Bess* would be written, as "a transcript from life: written and acted by Negroes." She praised the play as "so simple, so true, so heart breaking," and opined, "There is nothing like it in the whole range of modern literature. It is all the tears and all the child laughter of the race and I think it will educate the American white races to a broader consciousness of equality and humanity more powerfully than even Uncle Tom's Cabin did during the days of slavery." By praising *Porgy* as containing "all the tears and all the child laughter," Naidu returned to the stereotype of Blacks as emotional children, needing care. However, her mistaken belief that *Porgy* had been written by Blacks transformed her praise of the play into a recognition of the achievements of Black writers. Furthermore, by arguing that white Americans needed a "broader consciousness of equality and humanity," Naidu explained American racism as a product of white ignorance and inhumanity.[4]

Late in his life W. E. B. Du Bois would credit Naidu with stoking his interest in Gandhi and India. Naidu was only one of several Gandhians who attempted to influence the eminent editor of *The Crisis*. Their encounters with Du Bois manifested the spiritual approach to social change that Du Bois would immortalize in *Dark Princess*. Two years before Naidu visited the United States and *Dark Princess* was published, in the fall of 1926, Du Bois received a long handwritten letter from Simla Hills, India. Its author, a white lawyer from Boston, Richard B. Gregg, had spent the past few years living in India. After six months at Gandhi's ashram and three months at the school of Rabindranath Tagore, Gregg spent a year teaching science and math in a village in the Himalayas. In the 1950s Gregg would become an important source of Gandhian ideas for American civil rights activists. Writing to Du Bois in 1926, he asserted that British imperialism and American racism stemmed from the same root, "the false pride, blindness, and exploiting selfishness of the white races or nations." "More than ever, Gregg wrote, "I am convinced that in essence it is a spiritual and moral attitude which is at fault, and that the only real solution must be in the realm of the spirit." He told Du Bois that he expected "great improvements" in the world because "the fundamental weaknesses of capitalism are rapidly sapping the strength of white 'civilization,' while at the same time the other races of the world are realizing their unity and steadily achieving better organization." As if he were afraid that his emphasis on the spiritual would be lost in the wake of this political analysis, Gregg added in small writing, scrunched between his lines, "These are manifestations of spiritual, inner changes," and scribbled in parentheses, "(I am not a Socialist)."[5] Gregg need not have worried. Du Bois had developed his own mixture of socialism and spirituality, a synthesis he gave narrative form two years later in *Dark Princess*.

A few months before Gregg mailed his letter from Simla Hills, Du Bois had sent Gregg a sample copy of *The Crisis* and a copy of *Darkwater*. Gregg told Du Bois he was reading *Darkwater* "with very great interest" and would loan the book to Charles Freer Andrews, a white Anglican missionary and confidant of Gandhi. After visiting South Africa in 1914, Andrews developed a close friendship with Gandhi, calling him "Mohan," a shortened version of "Mohandas," and becoming intimately involved in every aspect of Gandhi's life.[6] Andrews, Gregg informed Du Bois, "has had much wide experience with the race problem in S. Africa, Fiji, China and here in India" and would be "greatly interested" in *Darkwater*. This was not Du Bois's first introduction to Andrews. In February 1925 *The Crisis* had quoted an article regarding imperial wrongs in British East Africa that Andrews had written for Gandhi's newspaper *Young India*.[7] It was not until 1929, however, that Andrews met Du Bois during a trip to the United States. Their meeting led Du Bois to write Andrews, enclosing letters to Gandhi and Tagore that requested articles for *The Crisis*. Andrews forwarded both notes and told Du Bois that he himself would be happy to write for *The Crisis*. "There is no magazine," Andrews explained, "that has helped me so much to understand the situation in America."[8] In August 1929 *The Crisis* published a speech in which Andrews discussed Gandhi's experiences with racial segregation in South Africa and defended "the Christian principle of racial equality."[9]

In his letter to Gandhi, Du Bois mentioned the pleasure of meeting Andrews and Sarojini Naidu and asked for "a message from you to these twelve million people who are the grandchildren of slaves." Du Bois added, "I know you are busy with your own problems, but the race and color problems are world-wide, and we need your help here." Gandhi responded from Sabarmati on May 1, 1929, with what he called "a little love message." Du Bois published Gandhi's "little love message" in *The Crisis*:

> Let not the 12 million Negroes be ashamed of the fact that they are the grand children of the slaves. There is no dishonour in being slaves. There is dishonour in being slaveowners. But let us not think of honour or dishonour in connection with the past. Let us realise that the future is with those who would be truthful, pure and loving. For, as the old wise men have said, truth ever is, untruth never was. Love alone binds and truth and love accrue only to the truly humble.

Gandhi echoed the reference to slavery that Du Bois had made in his request while offering a distinctly Gandhian pronouncement on the virtues of truth, love, and humility. For the readers of *The Crisis* Du Bois offered his own summary of the Mahatma and his message: "Agitation, nonviolence, refusal to cooperate with the oppressor, became Gandhi's watchword and with it he is leading all India to freedom. Here and today he stretches out his hand in fellowship to his colored friends of the West."[10] While Gandhi offered a philosophical meditation on truth and love, Du Bois praised the militancy of Gandhi's politics.

Like Gandhi, Rabindranath Tagore provided African Americans with an example of an honorable and internationally renowned colored man. Howard University scholar Kelly Miller praised Tagore and declared, "The situation in India is in every particular on a parallel with that of the Negro in the United States." His analysis of Tagore's work allowed Miller to conclude, "The relations of the whiter races to the darker ones constitute one vast problem with local and national complexities and variations."[11] In October 1929 Du Bois published a note from Tagore in *The Crisis*. The poet wrote, "What is the great fact of this age? It is that the messenger has knocked at our gate and all the bars have given way. Our doors have burst open. The human races have come out of their enclosures." African Americans, still very much enclosed in the rigid boundaries of the Jim Crow South or the ghettoes of the North, might demur at Tagore's statement that "the human races have come out of their enclosures." On the other hand, Tagore's words could be read as a prophecy of future change and a call for the kind of colored cosmopolitanism that Du Bois and *The Crisis* had long championed. Along with Tagore's note, Du Bois produced a picture of the poet, introduced Tagore as "colored," and stated that Tagore had "risen to something quite above the artificial limitations of race, color and nation."[12]

Du Bois met Tagore in New York in 1930. According to Du Bois, they "found much in common to discuss concerning the color line which was growing in world importance." While Indians "naturally recoiled from being mistaken for Negroes and having to share their disabilities," Du Bois wrote, "the Negroes thought of Indians as people ashamed of their race and color." Du Bois credited his meeting with Tagore with helping "Negroes and Indians realize that both are fighting the same great battle against the assumption of superiority made so often by the white race."[13] In September 1931 Du Bois sent a year's supply of *The Crisis* to Tagore's university, Santiniketan, and asked for another letter from Tagore for *The Crisis*.[14] In the fall of 1931 Du Bois contributed a short tribute to Tagore for a book produced to celebrate the poet's seventy-fifth birthday. By building on the "beginnings of democracy" laid by Europe and America, Du Bois wrote, "the dark millions of Africa and India can go forward to set new standards of freedom, equality and brotherhood for a world which is in desperate need of these spiritual things." He concluded, "It seems to me that no one has had a finer vision of such a future than Rabindranath Tagore. I greet him in his quest for common justice for all men." While articulating his colored cosmopolitanism, Du Bois framed "freedom, equality and brotherhood" as "spiritual things."[15]

A close friend of both Gandhi and Tagore, C. F. Andrews did much to unite Indians and African Americans in a religiously inspired struggle for "freedom, equality, and brotherhood." Along with Sarojini Naidu, Richard Gregg, and Tagore himself, Andrews served as a conduit between South Asian and African American freedom struggles. In 1929 Andrews visited the Tuskegee Institute. Gandhi's esteem for Tuskegee began as early as 1903. In 1922 Dr. N. S. Hardikar, a medical doctor trained in the United States, who would soon found the influential service organization the *Hindustan Seva Dal* (Indian Service League), wrote Tuskegee asking for information about the school. Robert Russa Moton, principal of Tuskegee, sent Hardikar Tuskegee's annual catalog and other promotional materials.[16] After meeting Andrews in 1929, Moton wrote Gandhi that "India, Africa and America joined hands last night."[17] Andrews also connected Moton with Tagore, arranging a meeting in Philadelphia at which Moton and Tagore discussed exchanging students and professors between Tuskegee and Santiniketan.[18] The *Tuskegee Messenger* summarized the message that Andrews brought as the "plain unadorned story of the two greatest spirits in the world today, Tagore and Gandhi."[19] J. T. Sunderland wrote an article on "Rev. C. F. Andrews in America," which was published in English in the Calcutta journal *The Modern Review,* and in Hindi in the *Hindi Pravas Bharatiya*.[20] Another Hindi journal, the *Vishaal Bhaarat,* published an article on "Andrews in Tuskegee" that offered a history of Booker T. Washington and the founding of Tuskegee and discussed Andrews's vision for cooperation between African Americans and Indians.[21]

During his journeys abroad, Andrews corresponded with the editor of the *Vishaal Bhaarat,* Benarsidas Chaturvedi, a journalist with a strong interest in the Indian diaspora. His letters to Chaturvedi demonstrate that, like Sarojini Naidu, Andrews understood his travels in the United States as an opportunity to connect Blacks and Indians. Also like Naidu, Andrews at times employed racial stereotypes of "the Indian" and "the Negro." On March 9, 1929, Andrews told Chaturvedi, "I am doing my utmost to create a real friendship between the American Negroes who are wonderfully progressive and the Indians, through linking up Tuskegee with Santiniketan."[22] In June Andrews wrote Chaturvedi from British Guiana. "The nature and temperament of the African," he declared, "though differing from the Indian, yet in many ways is akin to it: and it has been one of the greatest wishes of my life to point out that kinship, and to bring about that friendly intercourse between India and Africa in different parts of the world." In explaining the potential for unity between Africans and Indians, Andrews homogenized both groups with racial references to "nature and temperament" and went so far as to suggest a "tropical" disposition that Africans and Indians supposedly shared with other colored people.[23]

While his efforts to connect the Indian and African diasporas were couched in the limiting language of racial diplomacy, Andrews nevertheless fostered solidarities in opposition to the prevailing racial hierarchies of his day. In British Guiana Andrews brought cheers from the crowd when he proclaimed of his time in South Africa with Gandhi, "Believe me, believe me, with my own eyes I saw it—the cause of the African equally with the cause of the Indian." Andrews told his audience that he had related to

Tagore "what he had seen of the great African race in America—about Hampton, Tuskegee, Atlanta, and about his visit in New York where he had met Dr. Dubois and many other great Negro intellectuals as well as great African poets, painters, writers, and novelists who were producing some of the great literature today in America." Andrews told Tagore that he "brought him the good wishes of those great African people, and that everywhere he had gone the names of Tagore and Gandhi were known and loved in every African household throughout the United States."[24] After returning from Guiana, Andrews spent a week at the Hampton Institute, Booker T. Washington's alma mater. The Hampton student newspaper reported that Andrews had "dwelt among the great souls of India, interpreting and thinking, until he too has become, with Gandhi, a symbol of nonresistance and overpowering faith—a believer in Swadeshi, a sympathizer with the oppressed—one with India's mind.[25] Linking "nonresistance and overpowering faith" while praising "the great souls of India," the Hampton student newspaper expressed the blend of religion and politics that C. F. Andrews embodied and that would prove a fertile ground for meaningful interactions between Gandhi and African Americans.

Peanut Milk Politics

On February 24, 1929, African American scientist George Washington Carver wrote Andrews, who was about to end his ten-day visit to the Tuskegee Institute. "Our various, previous conversations, marvelous lectures, followed by our conversation this morning," Carver declared, "all convince me that a new day is dawning for India." To contribute to India's renaissance, Carver outlined a diet involving whole-wheat flour, grits, hominy, and local Indian fruits and nuts. Carver hoped his diet would improve Gandhi's strength. His vision of the diet extended, however, well beyond Gandhi. Referring to the diet, Carver wrote, "You can use it in your school, they will carry it into the various communities from whence they came, bringing to my mind greater health, strength and economic independence to India." He ended by mentioning a kind of milk that could be made from soybeans or peanuts.[26]

Born into slavery, George Washington Carver became one of the most internationally renowned African Americans of his generation, known throughout the world for his innovations in agricultural science, most notably his promotion of dozens of uses for the peanut. Carver had been referred to in Gandhi's newspaper, *Indian Opinion,* as early as 1909.[27] It was the visit of C. F. Andrews, however, that began more than a decade of interactions between Gandhi and Carver, two men treated as saints in their day. Their relationship demonstrates that the African American encounter with Gandhi was multidirectional. Indeed, Gandhi came to see Carver as many Blacks saw Gandhi—as a man of profound personal and spiritual virtue.

It is not surprising that matters of diet provided the foundation for the transnational encounter between Gandhi and Carver. Food played a central role in both men's lives, careers, and faiths. Carver's association of the diet he offered Gandhi with the "health, strength and economic independence" of India reveals a concern for international politics that previous scholarship has failed to note.[28] Carver's grand vision for his diet becomes even more significant in light of the fact that Gandhi himself was uniquely prepared to see the diet in such sweeping terms. Diet played a foundational role—simultaneously religious and political—in Gandhi's vision of his life and work. Gandhi's use of the Sanskrit word "*brahmacharya*" reveals the religious significance of diet for him. Brahmacharya is often translated simply as "celibacy." For Gandhi, however, brahmacharya was best understood in its literal sense—the pursuit of Brahma, the pursuit of God.[29] Sexual abstinence was necessary but not sufficient to the attainment of brahmacharya. Rather, Gandhi encouraged fellow *brahmacharis* to strive for "control in thought, word and action, of all the senses at all times and in all places."[30] Achieving such a demanding goal depended, in Gandhi's mind, upon adherence to a strict diet.

Gandhi connected diet and sexual chastity and linked both to the achievement of brahmacharya. Milk took center stage in these connections. As a vegetarian, Gandhi believed that only milk could provide the strength he needed to be active politically. However, he also felt that milk weakened his ability to be chaste. In his autobiography, written in installments from 1925 to 1929, and in numerous personal letters, Gandhi repeatedly returned to the unfortunate necessity of milk.[31] In the process, he revealed a remarkable compatibility between what he felt he needed and what Carver's diet provided. For Gandhi, milk impeded spiritual independence from the sensual world but aided political independence from Britain. Carver's diet offered the ability to avoid such a conflict, harmonizing religious and political pursuits that both Gandhi and Carver understood to be fundamentally interconnected. For both men a diet could bring "greater health, strength and economic independence."

Carver's discussion of the diet he sent to Andrews provides insight into his own politics and his understanding of Gandhi. Carver mentioned the diet in several speeches in 1930 and at various times afterward. Several newspapers picked up the story, most focusing on Carver's contribution to Gandhi's political efforts. One article proclaimed, "The discoveries of

Dr. George W. Carver, well known creative scientist of Tuskegee, may become a factor in the great fight India is making to free herself."[32] Another declared, "It is, of course, hoped that this menu would add strength and perhaps years of life in which Gandhi could engage in the cause of his country's freedom."[33] The fact that most newspapers connected Carver's diet to Gandhi's politics provides evidence that Carver himself continued to discuss the diet in the political framework that he originally described to Andrews. In 1937, speaking before a scientific conference attended by the governor of Mississippi, Carver again mentioned his diet for Gandhi. Several newspapers reported the event, all using the same revealing language:

> The eminent chemist, born of slave parents in Missouri, and who as a child was stolen and traded for a race horse, also revealed that the lowly Alabama peanut, not the Indian goat, furnishes Mahatma Gandhi with the remarkable strength he possesses. This diet was prepared for him out of peanut milk by Dr. Carver several years ago when Gandhi broke his fast and has since been constantly included. The two correspond regularly.[34]

The words "constantly" and "regularly" make the aforementioned article sound exaggerated. If Gandhi did use the diet, it did not permanently eliminate his need for milk. His correspondence demonstrates that he continued to drink milk throughout his life. However, a detail in Carver's speech provides evidence that in fact Gandhi did make use of Carver's diet, if only temporarily, and that Carver himself understood why Gandhi did so. Gandhi had vowed never to drink milk but reluctantly decided that his vow did not include goat's milk.[35] Carver's reference to "the Indian goat" thus provides evidence that Carver understood Gandhi's dietary needs and was reporting fact when he said that Gandhi had used his peanut milk.

The pursuit of God linked peanut milk to politics and Carver to Gandhi. C. F. Andrews served as a bridge between Gandhi and Carver, helping both men understand the similarities between their views on religion. On February 28, 1929, Andrews wrote Carver to thank him for his letter and for their time together. Andrews concluded his note with a revealing sentence: "I am certain that the soul force which you rightly call Divine Love must some day rule the world for Christ is King and Lord of all."[36] Gandhi often used the phrase "soul force" to translate "satyagraha," a word coined by Gandhi's nephew in response to a contest Gandhi organized through his journal Indian Opinion. Gandhi had been unhappy with the English phrase "passive resistance" as a description of his efforts. He felt "passive resistance" was too reactionary and allowed for the possibility of eventual violence on the part of his followers. Satyagraha, combining the

Sanskrit for "truth" and "holding firm," communicated the more proactive and spiritual meaning that Gandhi attached to his tactics.[37] By stating that Carver translated "soul force" as "divine love," Andrews indicated that the two had discussed Gandhi's understanding of satyagraha and that Carver himself had connected Gandhi's religiosity to his own. Without specific knowledge of each man's religious ideas, we might see a profound disconnect between satyagraha and divine love, the first seeming to involve active will on the part of people, not God, and the latter emphasizing not truth but love. Carver's connection of divine love to satyagraha accurately reflected, however, the blend of religion and social activism that he and Gandhi shared. For both men religion defined the purpose of social reform.[38]

Just as Andrews exposed Carver to satyagraha, so he introduced Gandhi to Carver's faith in God. Soon after leaving Alabama, Andrews wrote Gandhi that Tuskegee was "a real asram, both of prayer and work."[39] His use of the word *ashram* and his emphasis on prayer reveal the religious lens with which Andrews viewed both Tuskegee and Carver. A few years later Gandhi asked Andrews to write an article about Tuskegee for Gandhi's journal *Harijan*. Gandhi called Tuskegee "that wonderful institute" and asked Andrews whether his firsthand experience confirmed the accounts Gandhi had read in books.[40] Andrews responded with two separate articles on Tuskegee. The first lavishly praised the religiosity of Tuskegee and African Americans in general. In the second, entitled "George Carver of Tuskegee," Andrews managed to repeat almost every myth about Carver, while simultaneously touching on many of Carver's most important beliefs. He praised Carver's scientific achievements and emphasized that Carver chose to remain teaching at Tuskegee rather than earn a much higher salary elsewhere.[41] Andrews stressed Carver's humility. He wrote, "Never in my life have I seen one so great in character and achievement and at the same time so modest and retiring in temperament." Such praise seems even more striking coming from such a close friend of Gandhi's. In strong and moving prose Andrews praised Carver's active faith and concluded, "He is one of those about whom it is said: 'Blessed are the pure in heart, for they shall see God.' "[42]

To the end of Andrews's article on Carver, Gandhi appended a revealing note: "The story of Dr. Carver's life has a lesson for us all . . . especially for schoolmasters."[43] The phrase "especially for schoolmasters" highlights a specific lesson Gandhi hoped his readers would take from Carver's life. In 1934, when Andrews's article was published, Gandhi was struggling to recruit teachers to work in poor, rural communities. He was thus well prepared to appreciate Carver's willingness to teach the rural poor for little pay. Carver's self-sacrificing nature does not, however, completely explain Gandhi's praise of Carver. The primary concerns of both men coalesced in the 1930s under the aegis of rural development, giving them many reasons to praise each other's work. Their shared commitment to rural society led to their first direct correspondence. That interaction resulted from and revealed the remarkably similar program of vocational training with which both men addressed the needs of rural people—a program grounded in a theological conception of agrarian sustainability that recognized the need for interdisciplinary approaches to rural poverty but failed to adequately confront the entrenched nature of economic inequality.

Soon after publishing Andrews's article, Gandhi requested more information about Carver and his agricultural work at Tuskegee. He did so via Richard Gregg, the Boston attorney who had written Du Bois from Simla Hills in 1926. Gregg wrote Carver, asking him to send Gandhi several agricultural bulletins. In his letter to Carver, Gregg explained that Gandhi had started a village industries association "to help the Indian peasants to revive some of their indigenous industries and improve their economic position by the use of their own indigenous assets."[44] It was not a coincidence that Gandhi's project so closely resembled Carver's work at the Tuskegee Institute. Gandhi's interest in Tuskegee began during his years in South Africa when he was exposed to the ideas of Booker T. Washington. Writing about Tuskegee, Gandhi often stressed the need for sacrifice and the dignity of labor—both themes that informed his views of Carver.[45] On July 27, 1935, Carver wrote Gandhi, noting with surprise that an earlier letter Carver had sent along with several agricultural bulletins had yet to arrive. He stated he would send more bulletins, and added, "It is indeed a great pleasure and privilege to keep in touch with you. So many people have read your card and have enjoyed it." Carver concluded, "May God ever bless, keep, and direct you in this marvelous work you are doing."[46] Although Carver could have meant "this marvelous work" to refer to all of Gandhi's efforts, the context of the letter indicates that he meant to acknowledge Gandhi's work with the rural poor. On September 2 Gandhi's secretary, Mahadev Desai, wrote Carver to inform him that he had received the first group of bulletins Carver had sent and to apologize for writing to ask for them a second time.[47] Desai's letter demonstrates that Gandhi wanted the bulletins enough to send repeated letters to both Gregg and Carver.

The content of Carver's bulletins helps explain Gandhi's high estimation of him. The bulletins aimed to communicate to rural farmers simple ways they could improve their lives. With that goal in mind, Carver wrote the bulletins with little scientific jargon and published many of them in leaflet form. He used his bulletins to make connections between different fields of knowledge in an effort to confront problems rural people faced. Bulletins addressed how poor farmers could preserve fruit for the winter, produce goods they previously bought, and improve the physical condition of their homes.[48] Gandhi similarly concerned himself with all aspects of rural life. His most renowned experiment in village development, the Sevagram Ashram, aimed to improve every facet of life, from diet and exercise, to the production of food, to the removal of waste. Through the ashram Gandhi fostered a variety of local development projects—what he called "village industries"—such as weaving, pottery, beekeeping, and agricultural experimentation.[49] Like Carver, Gandhi hoped to provide rural people with the means to be economically self-sufficient.

Prayer and other forms of religious practice played a significant role in the communities that both Gandhi and Carver worked to build. It was fitting for C. F. Andrews to call Tuskegee "a real ashram, both of prayer and work." Tuskegee's dedication to regular religious services paralleled the centrality of prayer meetings in Gandhi's ashrams. Carver himself taught a weekly Bible class at Tuskegee for thirty years. Both Gandhi and Carver invested their work on behalf of the rural poor with religious meaning. Carver's bulletins aimed to give poor farmers the means to thrive on their farms, thus protecting a relationship between people and the land that for Carver was both economically and spiritually fulfilling. Similarly, Gandhi introduced the hand-spinning of yarn not only to boycott British goods but also to revitalize a religious connection between people and the production of their basic needs. For that reason Gandhi chose to encourage individual spinning rather than the development of the Indian textile industry. The making of homespun cloth, or *khadi,* was a spiritual practice that Gandhi engaged in daily.[50]

Both Gandhi and Carver saw rural self-sufficiency as a religious end requiring religious means. Both aimed to empower the rural poor without upsetting what they saw as a divinely sanctioned power structure based on harmony between different classes.[51] In hindsight, both Gandhi's and Carver's efforts at rural development seem doomed to failure. Their appeals for charity failed to acknowledge the structural inequalities imposed by the feudal economy of both the American South and rural India. The legacy of slavery and the brutality of Jim Crow vastly compounded the difficulties African Americans faced in achieving economic independence. Discrimination based on caste, widespread inequality, and the brutality of colonialism likewise limited the potential benefits of gradualist reform in India. Their religiously inspired vision of interclass harmony prevented both Gandhi and Carver from effectively confronting rural poverty.

In 1937, only six months after proclaiming his contribution to Indian independence before the governor of Mississippi, Carver demonstrated one vital difference between his approach to injustice and that of Gandhi. Attending a conference as the honored guest of Henry Ford, Carver chose to eat his dinner in the hallway rather than create the uncomfortable spectacle of a "Negro" eating among whites.[52] Although he admired Gandhi's struggles against the British, Carver never attempted to use Gandhian civil disobedience to combat racism at home.

Salt

Between 1930 and 1932, in the wake of Gandhi's dramatic march to the sea, African American interest in India boomed, as the Black press published hundreds of articles on Gandhi and the Indian cause.[53] By confronting the British ban on the production of salt, Gandhi demonstrated the understanding he shared with Carver of the social, religious, and political consequences of diet. It was not the "Alabama peanut," however, but Indian salt, with which Gandhi instructed the world in the power of nonviolent civil disobedience. Gandhi was not the only Indian to inspire admiration in the African American press. In April 1930, as Gandhi reached the sea and nonviolent civil disobedience erupted throughout India, *The Crisis* wrote, "And now let the world sit and watch the most astonishing of the battles of peace which it has ever seen: [t]he civil disobedience campaign in India, led by *Gandhi* and *Nehru*."[54] Sarojini Naidu received considerable press when she assumed leadership of the movement after Gandhi's imprisonment.[55] Gandhi, however, remained the central figure in Black coverage of Indian struggles. Indeed, the Mahatma became a reference point in articles that had nothing to do with India.[56] As during the noncooperation/Khilafat movement, the Black response to Gandhi was neither static nor uniform. Gandhi was seen as a religious figure, a prophet of the dark races, an anti-imperialist, and a bourgeois impediment to mass rebellion. Gandhi's use of nonviolent civil disobedience, while largely responsible for making him a world figure, only partially explains the significance of Gandhi for his African American contemporaries. Calls for a Black Gandhi, increasingly common, often focused not on nonviolence but on the need for strong and determined leadership.[57] Even those who did propose the use of Gandhian satyagraha did little to put their proposals into practice. In the 1930s, at a time of economic depression and violent racial oppression, Gandhi's contribution to African American freedom movements entailed not specific techniques of protest but the hope that comes with a sense of connection to larger struggles.

For some African Americans, Gandhi's spiritual achievements exceeded in importance his methods of protest. In *The New York Amsterdam News,* Kelly Miller declared, "The American Negro can learn valuable lessons from Mahatma Gandhi, who represents the best living embodiment of that mind which was also in Christ." Rather than Gandhian satyagraha, however, Miller endorsed the legal approach to racial inequality pioneered by the NAACP.[58] In *The Chicago Defender,* Drusilla Dunjee Houston similarly praised Gandhi for living Christ's message, while stopping short of suggesting civil disobedience. The Mahatma was "great because he literally follows the teachings of our Master, a thing that our Race might well note, for our leaders do not recognize the power in non-resistance." Houston herself, however, failed to recognize Gandhi's distinction between "non-resistance" and active nonviolent resistance. She argued that "the practice of Christliness will make for us a Race of high place" but emphasized gentleness of spirit rather than civil disobedience.[59]

Langston Hughes also saw Gandhi as Christlike, although that comparison did not inspire his admiration. In 1931 Hughes criticized Gandhi in a poem entitled "Goodbye, Christ."[60] Hughes placed "Saint Gandhi" alongside Aimee McPherson, the infamous Pentecostal leader, and Saint Becton, a Harlem preacher portrayed as a charlatan in Hughes's autobiography *The Big Sea.* All three were "getting in the way of things."[61] His desire to unmask the reactionary potential in organized religion led Hughes to what would prove an unusual criticism of Gandhi for the poet. A year earlier, in December 1930, Hughes had contrasted Gandhi's imprisonment with the spirit of Christmas.[62] In the years to come, Hughes would produce several more poems in praise of Gandhi.

In March 1930 the president of Howard University, Mordecai Johnson, told an audience in Washington, "Gandhi is conducting today the most significant religious movement in the world, in his endeavor to inject religion into questions of economics and politics." To George Schuyler, a columnist for *The Pittsburgh Courier* and the most consistent Black critic of Gandhi, Johnson's analysis of Gandhi was "unadulterated nonsense." Johnson linked Gandhi to what he understood as the best traditions of the Christian faith. In response, Schuyler directly criticized both Gandhi and Christianity. While Gandhian techniques were "mythical and so unsound," Schuyler asserted, Christianity had already done "more to hinder the Negro's advancement than any one single thing." Schuyler suggested that communism was better suited to helping the Black struggle than either Christianity or Gandhi's methods. A reader of the *Courier* challenged Schuyler. "There is nothing mythical," the reader declared, "about an economic boycott that encourages the development of home industries to the detriment of imported goods." The letter, signed only P.T.O., recommended Lala Lajpat Rai's *England's Debt to India* as evidence of the economic injustice of British colonialism in India. In response to Schuyler's criticism of Gandhi's religiosity, P.T.O. gave credit to Gandhi's creative use of the "simple biblical advice" to turn the other cheek, and asked, "Has anyone during the past nineteen hundred years given to the world a more practical and successful interpretation of the Sermon on the Mount?"[63]

While Langston Hughes and George Schuyler both criticized Gandhi's religious politics, other Left-leaning African Americans embraced Gandhi and his religiously inspired approach to social change. Writing in *The Crisis* in 1930, Du Bois proclaimed, "At last India is rising again to that great and fateful moral leadership of the world which she exhibited so often in the past in the lives of Buddha, Mohammed and Jesus Christ, and now again in the life of Gandhi." Gandhi's questionable approach to class inequality did not prevent Du Bois from placing the Gandhian struggle alongside the Russian revolution as one of the two "great events of the modern world." Du Bois concluded, "The black folk of America should look upon the present birth-pains of the Indian nation with reverence, hope and applause."[64] His praise of Gandhi is especially significant given the fact that although *Dark Princess* had established India as a source of great religious and revolutionary meaning, Gandhi played practically no role in the story. What few images of the contemporary Indian freedom movement Du Bois offered in *Dark Princess* were not positive.[65] Gandhi's success at mobilizing large numbers of people, coupled with the American travels of Sarojini Naidu and C. F. Andrews, helped inspire in Du Bois a new admiration for the Mahatma. In October 1931 Du Bois wrote Gandhi, "We are tremendously interested at the effort of the Indian people to achieve independence and self-government."[66]

While Du Bois's interest in Gandhi fluctuated in proportion to Gandhi's success at mobilizing the Indian masses, Du Bois was never inspired to advocate satyagraha. Like Du Bois, the majority of skeptics regarding the transferability of satyagraha nevertheless praised Gandhi's efforts in India. In September 1931, for example, NAACP leader William Pickens called Gandhi "the greatest man of the world and the age" in a highly laudatory article in *The New York Amsterdam News*.[67] Five months later, in February 1932, Pickens published another article on Gandhi in the *Amsterdam News*, this one entitled, "Gandhi-ism and Prayer Will Not

Solve Negro's Problem." Pickens asserted, "Those who see in Gandhi's procedure a model method for the solution of the race problem in the United States are people who reason in shallow analogies." Pickens noted that Indians were in the vast majority in their country, while Blacks constituted a distinct minority in the United States. "If the Negro of Mississippi starts a boycott against working for and trading with white people or against buying or employing any of the facilities owned and controlled by whites," Pickens predicted, "the Negro race would be the very first to freeze and starve." Nevertheless, Pickens concluded, "The American Negro may learn much, in spirit and determination, from the Gandhi movement." Gandhi, Pickens wrote, having "organized and inspired the tremendous movement of 360 million people certainly knows that a leader and his people must not stop with praying in closets and 'sacred places,' but must go forth bravely into the avenues of struggle."[68]

Even those African Americans who endorsed Gandhian nonviolent civil disobedience often focused more on other facets of the Indian struggle. Arthur S. Gray of Los Angeles, for example, wrote *The Chicago Defender*, "We should inaugurate a campaign of nonparticipation in national affairs, civil and political, thereby registering our silent protest." Published with the title "Gandhi-izing America," Gray's letter focused primarily on the need for an independent Black nation.[69] Gray's interest in the Indian struggle inspired him to attend a meeting in Los Angeles with several leading Indian Americans, including Bhagat Singh Thind, Dilip Singh Saund, and the attorney S. G. Pandit. Gray sent a report on the meeting to *The Negro World*, proclaiming "LONG LIVE THE INDIAN REVOLUTION!"[70] The report did not, however, offer suggestions for transplanting Gandhian strategies into the United States.

In *The Negro World*, H. G. Mudgal, the Indian Trinidadian foreign affairs correspondent and subsequent editor, covered Gandhi's struggle closely. Rather than nonviolence, British imperialism in the Caribbean and Africa dominated Mudgal's understanding of the struggle in India. Many of Mudgal's articles praised Gandhi without suggesting adapting his techniques.[71] Mudgal's writing on India was characteristic of *The Negro World* as a whole. When *The Negro World* offered a cover article on Gandhi in June 1930, its title, "Let's Learn Doggedness and Patience from Gandhi," ignored nonviolence.[72] At times *The Negro World* directly argued against Gandhian nonviolence. In an unsigned editorial entitled "The End of British Imperialism," *The Negro World* predicted, "Sooner or later, Mahatma Gandhi and his policy of non-violence will have to give way to the more militant aspirations of the surging masses of India." Readers were instructed that "open revolt in India will mark the beginning of the end of British imperialism, in India, and elsewhere," and that "the age-long domination of the darker peoples of the world will soon receive its death-blow."[73]

Black accounts of Gandhi and the Indian struggle regularly employed notions of colored solidarity. Mary Church Terrell, leader of the International Council of Women of the Darker Races, wrote of Gandhi, "It is gratifying and encouraging to know that the greatest advocate of peace in the world today is a man who belongs to one of the darker races."[74] An article in *The Chicago Defender* reported that several "leading organizations of Harlem" had asked Gandhi to "address them on racial problems." The article declared, "It is the consensus of opinion here that Gandhi will eventually play the part of Moses and lead all of the darker races from the wilderness of bondage into the light of freedom."[75]

Du Bois framed Gandhi and the Indian struggle as central to the aspirations of colored people worldwide. In a two-part article in the fall of 1931, Du Bois outlined India's racial diversity: "Some are Negroes; some are black folk, with straight hair; some are of the Chinese type, and some more nearly the European type." Diversity was not, however, the ultimate reading Du Bois offered of India's racial composition. "The great mass of them are brown people," he stated, "with wavy hair, and allied more nearly to the peoples of Africa and of Asia than to those of Europe." To emphasize the affiliation of Indians with "the peoples of Africa," Du Bois turned to history and the Aryan-invasion theory of Indian civilization. He wrote, "Many black civilizations arose here, like that of the Dravidians and the Sumerians. Invaders came in from the east and west, yellow people and white people." In case his readers did not recall the many odes to the darkness of India and Indians in *Dark Princess,* Du Bois quoted three paragraphs from the novel, beginning, "Out of black India the world was born. Into the black womb of India the world shall creep to die." Having located India within the dark world, Du Bois used his second article to chronicle India's recent history as the story of a dark people rising up against white oppressors. "If we are going to make our way in this modern world," he told his readers, "we must know what the world has been doing to other colored folk and how it has done it, and what they are doing to achieve freedom and manhood."[76]

As Gandhi's reputation grew, so did Black interest in other Indians who visited the United States. In November 1932 Vithalbhai Patel, an important Indian leader and the brother of one of Gandhi's most influential lieutenants, spoke to an African American audience in Memphis, Tennessee.[77] When, in early 1934, Manilal C. Parekh, an author who had written on Gandhi, visited Atlanta to lecture on the Mahatma's message,

The Atlanta Daily World encouraged attendance for all "Atlantans who are interested in what their brown skinned brothers across the waters in India are doing."[78] In addition to the visits of Indians to the United States, Black interest in India received a further boost when several leading African Americans chose to travel to India in the second half of the 1930s. None went with the primary purpose of meeting Gandhi, and yet their encounters with Gandhi became important for them as well as for Gandhi himself. Gandhi had corresponded with a variety of African Americans for years. The opportunity to meet Black leaders in person helped inspire a growing opposition to American racism among influential Indians, including Gandhi himself.

Pilgrims to the Mahatma

A religiously inspired commitment to social change connected several influential Black visitors with Gandhi, creating linkages between Gandhian nonviolence and Black Christianity that Dr. Martin Luther King Jr. would later employ to great effect.[79] It is important, however, to resist reading the travels of African Americans to India in the 1930s solely as groundwork for the 1950s. Recognizing the impact of Black religiosity on Gandhi's evolving views of race and caste returns these journeys to their historical context, opening lines of historical inquiry distinct from, if related to, the transmission of Gandhian nonviolence. Gandhi learned from his visitors as they learned from him.[80]

In 1935 Reverend Howard Thurman and Sue Bailey Thurman and Reverend Edward Carroll and Phenola Carroll traveled to South Asia on a "Pilgrimage of Friendship." Funded by the Student Christian Movements of the United States and India, the pilgrimage gave the Thurmans and the Carrolls the opportunity to serve as ambassadors, not only between India and the United States but also between Indians and African Americans. Reverend Thurman, a leading Black theologian, served as dean of Rankin Chapel at Howard University. Sue Bailey Thurman, a historian and talented singer, had worked for several years on the staff of the Young Women's Christian Association (YWCA). The Carrolls were younger than the Thurmans but no less prepared to make the most of their journey. Reverend Carroll had received his divinity degree from Yale, while Phenola Carroll had received a degree in education and was working as a teacher in Virginia. Even before they sailed for India, their journey became news in the Black press, stoking the already widespread Black interest in India.[81]

The impact of the Pilgrimage of Friendship on Indian perceptions of African Americans also began before the trip had started. A few months before the pilgrimage was scheduled to depart, Madeleine Slade visited the United States. The daughter of a British admiral, Slade had become a devotee of Gandhi, taking the name Mirabehn. Recognizing her closeness to the Mahatma, Howard Thurman arranged for Mirabehn to speak at Howard so that he might learn from her more about Gandhi but also so that she could share her impressions of African Americans with Gandhi. As he had hoped, Mirabehn sent positive impressions of African Americans back to Gandhi, echoing earlier reports the Mahatma had received from Sarojini Naidu and C. F. Andrews.[82]

The Thurmans and the Carrolls departed in September 1935 with Colombo, the capital of present-day Sri Lanka, their first destination in South Asia. Upon arrival Reverend Thurman felt an "inner stirring" that he traced to the fact that "the dominant complexions all around us were shades of brown, from light to very dark." He was in a colored country, where the whites, "despite their authority, were outsiders." At the Law College in Colombo, the chairman of the law club recited the many historical wrongs perpetrated in the name of Christianity, emphasizing slavery and racial oppression, and then challenged Thurman whether if, by acting "on behalf of a Christian enterprise," he had not become "a traitor to all of the darker peoples of the earth." Thurman responded by distinguishing between "the religion of Jesus" and forms of Christianity that had become "imperial." He told his questioner, "My judgment about slavery and racial prejudice relative to Christianity is far more devastating than yours could ever be." Thurman had originally refused to lead the pilgrimage out of concern that he would be expected to portray a rosy portrait of Christianity that ignored racism, imperialism, and other forms of injustice. He agreed to go only after being assured that he could speak his mind freely, which he did throughout the trip, prompting discomfort among some white Americans in India.[83]

Thurman recognized that the "color bar" operated differently in the United States and India. At times, racial hierarchies in India favored the Thurmans and Carrolls as "Europeans" while excluding Indians. At a railway junction en route to Calcutta, for example, the Thurmans discovered that their Indian student companion was not allowed entry in the "European" section of their hotel. In a report he wrote soon after the trip, Thurman compared the color dynamics of British rule in India and the United States, with an eye on where leverage could be applied in pursuit of justice. Thurman wrote, "The Indian is the victim of color prejudice at the hands of a white conqueror who is expressing himself in a land which he has stolen." The "American Negro," in contrast, "along with the American white man, is a foreigner in a land stolen from the American

Indian." When it came to religion, Thurman saw an opportunity for Blacks that Indians did not share. While Indians suffered from "a prejudice which is mixed with fundamental differences in religion and culture," Thurman stated, "both the American Negro and the white man are definitely committed to the same Christian ideal of brotherliness in the light of which unbrotherly practices can be properly classified as sinful and unchristian." Taken as a whole, Thurman's comparisons provided hope that African Americans could succeed in their struggle, despite the fact that they were not a majority in their own land. He concluded, however, on a distinctly pessimistic note, stating that he was filled "with complete despair" by the fact that Americans seemed to be following the British in "becoming mature and reflective" in their "brutality."[84]

The Thurmans and the Carrolls traveled throughout much of India, meeting with eminent public figures, including Tagore and Sarojini Naidu. A few weeks before their departure, in February 1936, they met Gandhi at Bardoli. Gandhi's secretary told Thurman, "This is the first time in all the years that we have been working together that I've ever seen him come out to greet a visitor so warmly." In the conversation that ensued, Gandhi demonstrated a strong interest in African American society and American racial oppression. Thurman remembered, "Never in my life have I been a part of that kind of examination: persistent, pragmatic questions about American Negroes, about the course of slavery, and how we have survived it." Gandhi's secretary recorded a few of Gandhi's questions: "Is the prejudice against colour growing or dying out?" and "Is the union between Negroes and the whites recognized by law?" Thurman remembered Gandhi asking about "voting rights, lynching, discrimination, public school education, the churches and how they functioned." In response, Thurman sketched a portrait of racial prejudice that stressed economic conflict and the spread of racial discrimination beyond the South. An account of Gandhi's interaction with his "Negro guests" was published in *Harijan*, expanding the Indian audience exposed to Gandhi's interest in Black struggles and the responses to his questions offered by Reverend Thurman.[85]

The article in *Harijan*, while demonstrating Gandhi's solidarity with African Americans, also indicated the limits Gandhi had placed on his collaboration with Africans. When asked whether he had included Black South Africans in his satyagraha, Gandhi replied in the negative. He explained, "It would have endangered their cause. They would not have understood the technique of our struggle nor could they have seen the purpose or utility of non-violence." While distinct from the demeaning comments toward Africans that Gandhi had made during his early days in South Africa, this statement nonetheless intimated a cultural condescension dismissive of Africans.

Gandhi's statement that Africans could not have seen "the purpose or utility of non-violence" did not prevent him from proclaiming, after meeting with the Thurmans and the Carrolls, "It may be through the Negroes that the unadulterated message of non-violence will be delivered to the world." The contrast between this prophetic statement and Gandhi's views of Black South Africans indicated a shift in his understanding of "Negroes" that resulted in part from his interactions with African Americans. When Sue Bailey Thurman asked Gandhi how she should react if her brother was lynched, Gandhi suggested nonviolent noncooperation:

> I must not wish ill to these, but neither must I co-operate with them. It may be that ordinarily I depend upon the lynching community for my livelihood. I refuse to co-operate with them, refuse even to touch the food that comes from them, and I refuse to co-operate with my brother Negroes who tolerate the wrong. That is the self-immolation I mean.

By ignoring the consequences of such "self-immolation" for a minority, Gandhi's advice appears grossly impractical. Nevertheless, his advice does demonstrate Gandhi's faith in the ability of African Americans to deliver "the unadulterated message of non-violence" to the world.

Gandhi's respect for Christianity strengthened his belief in the nonviolent potential of Black freedom struggles. He told his guests, "Ahimsa means 'love' in the Pauline sense" and declared, "Seek ye first the kingdom of Heaven and everything else shall be added unto you. The Kingdom of Heaven is ahimsa." At the end of the gathering, Gandhi requested the hymn, "Were You There When They Crucified My Lord?" Sue Bailey Thurman led the singing. The Thurmans returned from India dedicated to spreading knowledge of Gandhi and the Indian struggle. They offered lectures on India throughout the United States and raised funds for a scholarship that brought young African American women to Tagore's school at Santiniketan.[86]

In addition to demonstrating Gandhi's growing interest in Black struggles and the religious foundations of his interactions with many African Americans, the meeting between the Thurmans, the Carrolls, and Gandhi also revealed the continued prominence of comparisons between race and caste. A few weeks before he left for India, Howard Thurman had written to an American supporter of Gandhi that as an African American he could "enter directly into informal understanding of the psychological climate" of Dalits. While recognizing differences between caste in India and race in America, Thurman stated that the experiences of Blacks and Dalits did not "differ in principle and in inner pain."[87] It was not Thurman, however, but Gandhi who raised the issue of caste during their meeting. When asked why his movement had failed to oust the British,

Gandhi stressed the debilitating impact of untouchability. After recording Gandhi's description of the segregation of Dalits, Thurman succinctly noted the overlap between the oppression of Dalits and African Americans: "He was striking close to home with this." Asked how he proposed to counter caste oppression, Gandhi stated that he had adopted a Dalit child and had begun referring to Dalits as Harijans in an effort to reverse the stigma attached to the word "untouchable." Gandhi declared, "I became the spearhead of a movement for the building of a new self-respect, a fresh self-image for the untouchables in Indian society."[88] Gandhi's emphasis on "self-respect," rather than on the legal, economic, and political underpinnings of caste inequality, earned criticism in India and the United States. Like Howard Thurman, however, the majority of African American observers of caste tended to praise Gandhi's initiatives, even as they criticized the continued oppression of Dalits.

In January 1937 Benjamin Mays, dean of the School of Religion at Howard University, and Channing Tobias, a leading Black figure in the Young Men's Christian Association (YMCA), traveled to India to attend the 1937 World's Conference of the YMCA. Like Howard Thurman, Benjamin Mays made of the trip an opportunity to assess racial discrimination in other parts of the world. Onboard the *Queen Mary,* Mays noted the coldness that British passengers showed to Indians and the "lack of prejudice" Indians displayed toward Blacks. He also sensed hostility between Indians and Anglo-Indians, a hostility that he compared to tensions between light- and dark-skinned Blacks. Mays published an account of his journey entitled "The Color Line around the World" in *The Journal of Negro Education.* "It is my firm conviction," Mays wrote, "that the British-Indian situation, though greatly aggravated and complicated on account of caste, is further complicated because the Indians are colored people and do not belong to the so-called 'white race.'" Mays labeled the Raj "imperialism built on racialism."[89]

Like the Thurmans and the Carrolls, Mays met with a variety of leading Indians. He arrived in Bombay in time for the nearby All-India Congress, where he spoke with the Congress president Jawaharlal Nehru and his sister, Vijayalakshmi Pandit, herself a crucial figure in the history of Indo-American relations. With limited time in India, Mays chose to see Gandhi rather than the Taj Mahal. Gandhi later told him, "You chose wisely. When you come to India again, the Taj Mahal will be there. I may not be here."[90] In a ninety-minute meeting with Gandhi, conducted in Wardha on New Year's Eve, Mays asked Gandhi about the practicality of nonviolence on a large scale, as well as about the relevance of nonviolence to a minority confronting an oppressive majority. Gandhi responded by defending the utility of nonviolence on a mass scale. He stated that "a minority can do much more in the way of non-violence than a majority" and, as an example, he offered his own experience in South Africa. Gandhi also noted that Jesus taught nonviolence and declared, "When Daniel defied the laws of the Meads and Persians, his action was non-violent." Clearly impressed by the Mahatma, Mays wrote that Gandhi "did more than any other man to dispel fear from the Indian mind" and concluded, "When an oppressed race ceases to be afraid, it is free."[91]

Although the account of the conversation between Mays and Gandhi published in Gandhi's collected works makes no reference to caste, Mays remembered discussing at length why Gandhi had attacked only untouchability and not caste itself. In his autobiography, Mays wrote, "Gandhi made it clear to me that he was not fundamentally against caste. He believed in caste. He described it as an economic necessity." Gandhi presented caste as a useful "division of labor" while castigating untouchability as a perversion of caste. Mays challenged this assessment, using as evidence his own interactions with Dalits. In Mysore, the headmaster of a school for Dalits asked Mays to visit the school, explaining that he had singled out Mays because he was Black. When Mays suggested that Channing Tobias was also "a Negro," the headmaster replied that Tobias was too light-skinned for the purpose. Mays understood the significance of his dark skin when after eating with the students he was introduced as "an untouchable who had achieved distinction." Mays remembered, "The headmaster told them that I had suffered at the hands of the white men in the United States every indignity that they suffered from the various castes in India and that I was proof that they, too, could be 'somebody worthwhile' despite the stigma of being members of a depressed class." Mays wrote, "At first I was horrified, puzzled, angry to be called an untouchable, but my indignation was short-lived as I realized, as never before, that I was truly an untouchable in my native land, especially in the Southern United States." In his autobiography, Mays offered a scathing assessment of caste, concluding that caste had "done more to retard India" than British imperialism. Mays found caste worse than segregation in the United States where, Mays asserted, there was at least "some social conscience across racial lines." In India, Mays wrote, he could "detect no such social concern across caste lines." "Of course," he added, "Gandhi was an exception."[92]

Channing Tobias also probed Gandhi on questions of caste as well as nonviolence.[93] According to *Harijan,* Tobias told Gandhi, "Negroes in [the] U.S.A.—12 million—are struggling to obtain such fundamental rights as freedom from mob violence, unrestricted use of the ballot, freedom from segregation, etc." When Tobias asked for a message for "my Negro brethren," Gandhi replied, "With right which is on their side and the choice of non-violence as their only weapon, if they will make it such, a bright future is assured." In the midst of his conversation with Gandhi, Tobias raised a question regarding the recent decision of the maharaja of Travancore to open all temples to Dalits. Tobias asked, "Do you think Travancore's example will be followed by other States in the near future?" Gandhi answered, "I shall be surprised if it is not."[94] Tobias did not contest this optimistic assessment of the fight against the exclusion of Dalits from temples. Rather, like Benjamin Mays, Tobias demonstrated concern regarding caste in India, while framing Gandhi as a noble defender of the rights of Dalits. In a letter published in *The Chicago Defender*, Tobias stated that Gandhi was living "in a village of outcasts in order to set the example for high caste Indians to abolish caste."[95] Mays and Tobias, as well as the Thurmans and the Carrolls, offered no indication that they were aware of Indian critiques of Gandhi's approach to caste.

The most renowned critic of Gandhi's approach to caste, Dr. Ambedkar, used the resurgence of American racism in the aftermath of Reconstruction to question whether Indian independence would signal the end of untouchability. In his fierce polemic, *What Congress and Gandhi Have Done to the Untouchables,* published in 1945, Ambedkar offered over three pages on the betrayal of African Americans after the Civil War. After quoting liberally from Herbert Aptheker's *The Negro in the Civil War*, Ambedkar concluded, "The Untouchables cannot forget the fate of the Negroes. It is to prevent such treachery that the Untouchables have taken the attitude they have with regard to this 'Fight for Freedom.' " Ambedkar compared Lincoln and Gandhi, criticizing both. After quoting Lincoln's infamous interchange with Horace Greeley, Ambedkar concluded, "Obviously the author of the famous Gettysburg oration about Government of the people, by the people and for the people would not have minded if his statement had taken the shape of government of the black people by the white people and for the white people provided there was union." While Lincoln was willing to emancipate the slaves to save the Union, however, Ambedkar wrote, "Mr. Gandhi's attitude is let Swaraj perish if the cost of it is the political freedom of the Untouchables."[96] It is fitting that Ambedkar turned to the history of race in America to criticize Gandhi's approach to caste. Understanding Gandhi's evolving views on caste requires probing his use of race/caste analogies often forged through interactions with African American struggles.

The Washingtonian Gandhi

As early as 1910 Gandhi compared racial discrimination in the United States to caste prejudice in India. Lamenting anti-Asian xenophobia, Gandhi attacked such "colour prejudice" as evidence that "the freedom which the Americans boast of is vanishing." Referencing untouchability, he then declared, "The kind of racial discrimination which America practices, we have practiced against our own people in India."[97] In 1928, when questioned by an American woman, Gandhi offered four reasons why the "plight of the untouchable" was not as severe as the treatment of "the Negro in America."[98] Coming in the aftermath of the *Mother India* controversy, when many Indians used American racism to defend caste in India, Gandhi's response to his American interrogator should be read in part as an effort to guard India's reputation. Gandhi's condemnation of American racism should not be ascribed entirely, however, to national pride. His interactions with African Americans inspired in Gandhi a strong and lasting aversion to American racial oppression. His sympathy for the struggles of Black Americans makes it even more significant that, in contrast to his response in 1928, the vast majority of his frequent comparisons between race and caste underscored the severity of caste oppression in India. It was most often to Americans that Gandhi emphasized the injustice of racism. To Indians he stressed the need to confront untouchability. In shifting his use of the race/caste analogy, Gandhi tailored his argument to his audience.

By comparing oppressions of race and caste, Gandhi often aimed to criticize untouchability in India. Writing in *Young India* in 1924, he argued that caste oppression in the South-Indian princely state of Cochin was "much worse" than even the racial policies of the government of South Africa. Lest his criticism of untouchability be interpreted as applying solely to Cochin, Gandhi added, "I have no desire to single out Cochin for its disgraceful treatment of untouchables; for it is still unfortunately common to Hindus all over India, more or less."[99] In 1926 Gandhi published an article on "race arrogance" in which he decried "the injustice that is being daily perpetrated against the *Negro* in the United States of America in the name of and for the sake of maintaining white superiority." In a demonstration of his increasing use of the Negro/Untouchable parallel, Gandhi proclaimed, "Our treatment of the so-called untouchables is no better than that of coloured people by the white man."[100]

Even after *Mother India*, Gandhi continued to use the racial wrongs of the West to criticize, rather than justify, caste oppression in India. In August 1933 the magazine *India and the World* asked Gandhi and Tagore to convey messages on the one hundredth anniversary of the emancipation

of slavery in the British Empire. Both chose to acknowledge the persever-
ance of forms of slavery. While Tagore found slavery "in our plantations,
in factories, in business offices, in the punitive department of government
where the primitive vindictiveness of man claims special privilege to indulge
in fierce barbarism," Gandhi presented untouchability as an especially insidious form of slavery. He wrote, "India has much to learn from the heroes
of the Abolition of Slavery, for we have slavery based upon supposed religious sanction and more poisonous than its Western fellow."[101]

In July 1933 Gandhi published an article in *Harijan* called "An Example to Copy." The example in question was the work of Booker T. Washington's Tuskegee Institute and its predecessor, the Hampton Institute,
founded by Samuel Chapman Armstrong, a former Union general. Gandhi wrote, "There is no doubt that the work of Armstrong at the Hampton Institute and of Booker T. Washington at the Tuskegee is worth
studying by all Harijan workers and Harijans." While he asserted that
"the Tuskegee Institute is a model for Harijans," Gandhi noted that the
analogy did not hold "in all respects." For him, high-caste Indians should
feel an even greater "duty" to help Dalits than "white men" should feel
"towards American Negroes." The key difference for Gandhi was that
caste prejudice in India had been made "a matter of religion" and was
therefore more grievous and intractable. Thus Gandhi again reversed the
argument, which he made four years earlier in 1928, that caste prejudice
was a lesser evil than racism.[102]

Gandhi's understanding of race and caste owed much to his over forty
years of interest in the work of Booker T. Washington. During his years in
South Africa and through his correspondence with George Washington
Carver, Gandhi had learned much about Washington and the work of
Tuskegee. During the 1930s Gandhi continued to educate himself about
Washington and his legacy, often explaining his interest in terms of caste.
In April 1933 Gandhi wished Goparaju Ramachandra Rao, a renowned
atheist and anti-untouchability reformer better known as "Gora", "every success in producing an Indian Tuskegee." He told Rao, "I knew much
about Booker T. Washington even when I was in South Africa and I have
great regard for him." Gandhi cautioned, however, "You have kept before
you a worthy model, but you cannot be an Indian Booker T. Washington.
Only a Harijan can be that." In October 1933 Gandhi wrote C. F. Andrews
asking for articles about Tuskegee. "For the sake of Harijans," he explained, "I have been reading literature about that wonderful institute." In
a conversation with a young Dalit social worker in 1944, Gandhi wrote,
"You have heard of Booker T. Washington. We have to produce better
workers than even him in order to achieve our object."[103]

Washington deserves partial credit for inspiring Gandhi's evolving ideas about caste. While Gandhi continually re-forged his approach to caste in response to a variety of pressures, he repeatedly explained his views on caste by referencing Washington's example. Like Washington, Gandhi taught self-help and vocational education. While Gandhi's strategy for opposing imperialism differed markedly from Washington's accommodationism, Gandhi's attitude to caste oppression, like Washington's cautious approach to racism, emphasized conciliation rather than confrontation. Until late in life Gandhi desired to preserve caste while getting rid of untouchability, a position that paralleled Washington's public endorsement of "separate but equal" racial segregation.

A belief in the dignity of labor, and especially manual labor, was central to Gandhi's praise of Washington and Gandhi's approach to "uplifting" oppressed castes. In 1933, while suggesting that Tuskegee and Hampton were examples "worth studying by all Harijan workers and Harijans," Gandhi proclaimed, "Let it be noted that in both, great stress is laid upon the dignity of manual labour."[104] In 1937 he told a group of Indian educators, "I once more express my satisfaction at your efforts to establish an institute for the *Adi Karnatakas*[105] on the lines of the Tuskegee Institute of Booker T. Washington." He called for "many such institutions all over the country" and encouraged his "educated friends" to recognize "that when they are propagating intellectual culture, they must also inculcate the principle of dignity of labour as is done in those institutions."[106]

Despite his Washingtonian enthusiasm for vocational education, Gandhi recognized the limitations of education via manual labor. In June 1934, at a meeting of Harijan workers in Poona, Gandhi was asked if "it was right to encourage Harijan boys to become B.A.s or M.A.s, when unemployment was rife among graduates, and whether it would not be better if they took to technical education." Gandhi replied that reformers should not expect Harijans to embrace industrial education before other castes. He stressed that academic training "had its own value for Harijans." Nevertheless, Gandhi hoped that "Harijans would study the life and work of Booker T. Washington, whom he looked upon as one of the great men of the world, and draw their inspiration from it." On another occasion Gandhi encouraged industrial education for all children. He stated, "Booker T. Washington tried it with considerable success."[107]

As Washington defended segregation, while aiming to end racial inequality, Gandhi defended *varnadharma*, the division of society into four distinct social and economic groups or *varnas,* even as he attacked untouchability. In the same edition of *Young India,* in which he said that "our treatment of the so-called untouchables is no better than that of coloured people by the white man," Gandhi made clear that his opposition to untouchability did not extend to *varnadharma* as a whole. A correspondent had questioned why Gandhi did not suggest dining across caste boundaries as a practical means of attacking caste. Gandhi responded, "All I have advocated is abolition of the fifth *varna.*" "The untouchables," Gandhi argued, "should, therefore, merge in the fourth division." In the same speech in which he called for many Tuskegees "all over the country," Gandhi encouraged his listeners to provide village children the training necessary to pursue the vocation "to which they were born." That phrase reveals Gandhi's desire to maintain some form of caste, even while ending untouchability.[108]

Gandhi's approach to caste mirrored many of the limitations of Washington's approach to race in the United States. In June 1935 Gandhi told a group of Harijan Sevaks (reformers aiming to end caste oppression) that it would take a long time and much suffering to combat untouchability. He then asked, "And have we tried enough and suffered enough? Look at Booker T. Washington. Have any of us suffered as much as he did?" Thus Gandhi encouraged upper-caste Hindus to change their lives to suffer as Dalits and Blacks had suffered. When asked if Dalits should be encouraged to leave their ghettos and attempt to live among high-caste Hindus, however, Gandhi said, "This is more easily said than done. If all the caste Hindus become reformers your question won't arise. Today the reformers would be powerless to defend Harijans from molestation if they settled in *savarna* quarters." Rather than invite physical confrontation, as he had done repeatedly in struggles against the British Raj, Gandhi preferred less aggressive strategies to touch the hearts of the higher castes. After criticizing the conception that Dalits were inferior, Gandhi offered an analogy that demonstrated his patronizing approach to Dalit advancement. He asked, "Supposing I have a diseased child, what shall I do with it? Shall I discard it, shall I consider it low? No, I shall have to remind myself that it is suffering for my sins, and that therefore it deserves extra care from me." Although he immediately declared that Dalits were "far superior to us," Gandhi's analogy between Dalits and a "diseased child" remained a glaring example of his patronizing attitude toward Dalits.[109]

African American observers of Gandhi often praised his opposition to caste without assessing its strengths and weaknesses. In 1932 Gandhi fasted against a decision by the British government that would have allowed Dalits to elect candidates to the legislatures independently of other voters. Gandhi's fast, while inspiring many caste Hindus to work to end untouchability, forced Ambedkar to abandon separate electorates for

Dalits in exchange for greater numbers of reserved seats. Emphasizing the positive consequences of the fast without discussing the lost opportunities, many supporters of the Mahatma turned the fast into an iconic moment in his struggle against untouchability. C. F. Andrews wrote Benarsidas Chaturvedi that Gandhi's fast had "impelled" him to dedicate his life "to removing 'untouchability' in the West, i.e., the Colour Bar."[110] Du Bois wrote, "There is today in the world but one living maker of miracles and that is Mahatma Gandhi. He stops eating, and three hundred million Indians, together with the British Empire, hold their breath until they can talk sense. All America sees in Gandhi a joke, but the joke is America."[111] Praising Gandhi for his opposition to untouchability allowed African Americans to find inspiration for their own struggles. But in lauding Gandhi uncritically, many Americans, Black and white, forfeited the opportunity to pressure Gandhi to confront the limitations of his approach to caste oppression.

The African American press was not always uncritical of Gandhi's views on caste. During the 1920s Gandhi avoided either advocating or criticizing inter-dining and intermarriage between castes. Instead, he repeatedly stated that neither was a part of his strategy to end untouchability.[112] In contrast, in the book he finished at Tuskegee in 1929, C. F. Andrews presented Gandhi as opposed to inter-dining and intermarriage. Andrews quoted Gandhi as saying, "I would never give my consent to such a marriage, because it would be contrary to my ideas of religion thus to transgress the boundaries wherein we were born."[113] If Gandhi opposed inter-dining and intermarriage between castes in India, then what did Gandhi think of Blacks and whites eating together and marrying each other? Gandhi responded to that question in a statement published in 1934 by the *Baltimore Afro-American* in which he claimed that either Andrews had been misunderstood or had incorrectly communicated his views. Gandhi wrote, "Prohibition against other people eating in public restaurants and hotels and prohibition of marriage between coloured people and white people I hold to be a negation of civilisation."[114] In fact, Andrews's assessment of Gandhi's outlook accurately represented Gandhi's early views on caste. By the 1930s, however, Gandhi had begun to change his opinions and by the 1940s he would openly advocate inter-dining and intermarriage as a means to ending untouchability.[115]

It is difficult to distinguish the influence of Washington or other African Americans from the other factors that shaped Gandhi's evolving perspectives on caste. A stronger case can be made that Gandhi's admiration for Washington, in conjunction with his interactions with other African Americans, played a decisive role in furthering Gandhi's commitment to a transnational conception of colored solidarity. One of Gandhi's most impassioned references to Washington came in a discussion of racial prejudice in Gandhi's *Satyagraha in South Africa,* most of which was written in Yeravda Central Jail from November 1923 until February 1924. Discussing discrimination against Indians in South Africa, Gandhi declared, "The dislike of the brown races has at present become part and parcel of the mentality of Europeans." As an example, Gandhi wrote:

> Even in the United States of America, where the principle of statutory equality has been established, a man like Booker T. Washington who has received the best Western education, is a Christian of high character and has fully assimilated Western civilization, was not considered fit for admission to the court of President Roosevelt and probably would not be so considered even today! The Negroes of the United States have accepted Western civilization. They have embraced Christianity. But the black pigment of their skin constitutes their crime, and if in the Northern States they are socially despised, they are lynched in the Southern States on the slightest suspicion of wrongdoing.[116]

After the outbreak of the Second World War, and especially after American entry in the war, Gandhi's pointed criticism of American racism would take on new significance as American politicians worried about the impact of American racism on foreign opinion of the United States. During and after the war, Gandhi's example would help inspire a wave of nonviolent civil disobedience that brought Jim Crow even further into the glare of world opinion. Through his influence on Gandhi, Booker T. Washington contributed to efforts that far exceeded his own.

Kamaladevi Chattopadhyaya with her son. Courtesy of Nina Menon and Neel Chatto.

Lala Lajpat Rai in 1915. Author's collection.

Cedric Dover, behind the wheel, in front of the Victoria Memorial, Calcutta. Author's collection.

Langston Hughes and Cedric Dover at Fisk University, November 1947. Courtesy of the Manuscript, Archives, and Rare Book Library, Emory University.

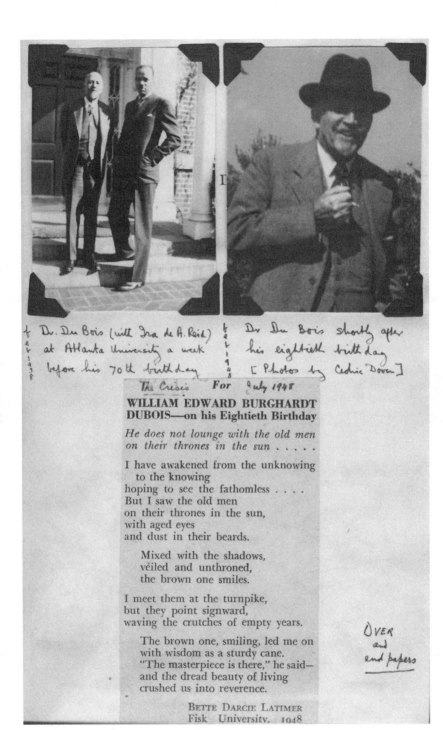

D. Du Bois (with Ira de A. Reid) at Atlanta University a week before his 70th birthday

Dr Du Bois shortly after his eightieth birthday [Photos by Cedric Dover]

The Crisis   For July 1948

WILLIAM EDWARD BURGHARDT DUBOIS—on his Eightieth Birthday

*He does not lounge with the old men
on their thrones in the sun* . . . . .

I have awakened from the unknowing
   to the knowing
hoping to see the fathomless . . . .
But I saw the old men
on their thrones in the sun,
with aged eyes
and dust in their beards.

   Mixed with the shadows,
   veiled and unthroned,
   the brown one smiles.

I meet them at the turnpike,
but they point signward,
waving the crutches of empty years.

   The brown one, smiling, led me on
   with wisdom as a sturdy cane.
   "The masterpiece is there," he said—
   and the dread beauty of living
   crushed us into reverence.

          BETTE DARCIE LATIMER
          Fisk University. 1948

OVER
and
end papers

A page from Cedric Dover's personal copy of W. E. B. Du Bois's *Dusk of Dawn*, illustrated with photos of Du Bois taken by Dover. Courtesy of the Manuscript, Archives, and Rare Book Library, Emory University.

African American soldiers in Calcutta. Note the disparity in wealth between the soldiers and their rickshaw pullers and the advertisement in the background for *Tarzan's New York Adventure*. Courtesy of the U.S. National Archives and Records Administration.

African American soldiers driving a convoy across the Ledo road. Courtesy of the U.S. National Archives and Records Administration.

Note that it is only the "Hindu woman" whose experience with American racism requires explanation. Kenesaw M. Landis, graphics by Tom P. Barrett, *Segregation in Washington* (Chicago: National Committee on Segregation in the Nation's Capital, 1948).

"It's all right to seat them, they're not Americans." A 1961 Herblock Cartoon, copyright by The Herb Block Foundation. Note that the man's turban and the woman's clothing, akin to a sari, distinguish them as most likely South Asian.

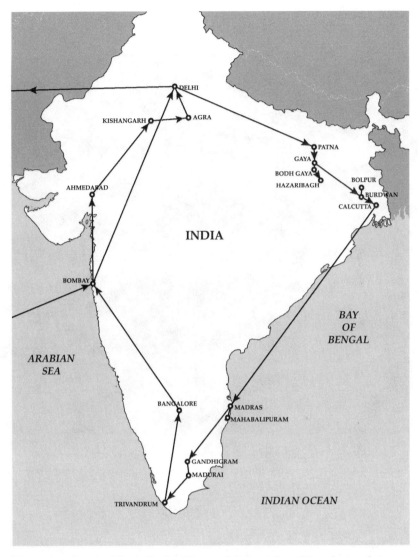

The route taken by Martin Luther King and Coretta Scott King during their trip to India in 1959. Credit: Jesse Wilson.

Reverend Ralph Abernathy with Ahmed Meer, Montgomery, Alabama, 1960. Stoned by angry whites, the church billboard retained a distinctly appropriate message. Courtesy of Ahmed Meer.

Ahmed Meer, Martin Luther King, Coretta Scott King, Suchetana Kripalani,
J. B. Kripalani, and Jaswant Krishnayya at Morehouse College, Atlanta, 1960.
Courtesy of Ahmed Meer and Jaswant Krishnayya.

SNCC sit-in leaders learning from veteran Indian activists. Martin Luther King
and J. B. Kripalani on far right. Courtesy of Ahmed Meer and Jaswant
Krishnayya.

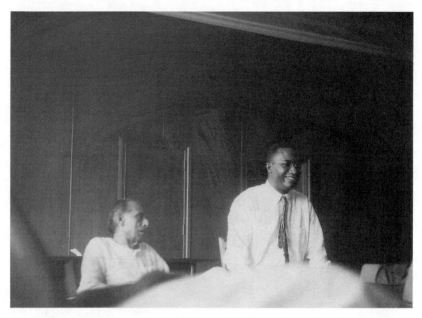

J. B. Kripalani: and Lawrence Reddick at a SNCC training at Morehouse College. Courtesy of Ahmed Meer.

Pauli Murray in 1941, one year after she engaged in her own "satyagraha" on a bus in Virginia. Courtesy of The Schlesinger Library, Radcliffe Institute, Harvard University.

(1) India
    Textile mills
    man - 2¢ a day
    women - 1¢ " "
    child 7¢ - " "

(3) Ghandi
    imprisoned
    7 times since
    the war.

(2) 370,000,000

War Without Violence

India	Am. Negro
majority	minority two races living side peacefully by side
tradition	
non-violence Christian ethics	
civil disobedience	told that we move too fast; upset friendly relations between races
willingness to sacrifice for your ideal — to change heart of enemy	
well disciplined movement	lack of well disciplined movement
non-violent direct action	legalistic movement NAACP - through court tests
unified labor movement	dual Jim-Crow unions

Notes taken by
P.M. on Non-Violence
March 1940

A chart Murray prepared in March 1940, comparing African American and Indian struggles. "Notes taken by P.M. on Non-violence," dated March 1940, "Petersburg Bus Incident," File 86, Box 4, Pauli Murray Papers. Courtesy of The Schlesinger Library, Radcliffe Institute, Harvard University.

In the spring of 1945 Deton Brooks, an African American reporter for *The Chicago Defender*, asked Mahatma Gandhi, "Is there any special message you would care to send to the Negro people of America?" Gandhi replied, "My life is its own message." These words, shortened to "my life is my message," adorn the front of the Mahatma Gandhi Memorial in Washington, D.C. Unlike several other quotations at the Gandhi memorial, the words "my life is my message" are neither explained nor dated—fitting testimony to the fact that Gandhi's relationship with African Americans remains only partially remembered. Photo by author.

CHAPTER FIVE

Global Double Victory

The Allies have no moral cause for which they are fighting, so long as they are carrying this double sin on their shoulders, the sin of India's subjection and the subjection of the Negroes and African races.

—Mahatma Gandhi, 1942

ON JULY 1, 1942, Mahatma Gandhi wrote Franklin Delano Roosevelt. Although beginning "Dear friend," Gandhi came quickly to the point. He told Roosevelt, "I venture to think that the Allied declaration that the Allies are fighting to make the world safe for freedom of the individual and for democracy sounds hollow so long as India and, for that matter, Africa are exploited by Great Britain and America has the Negro problem in her own home."[1] Beginning in 1942 Gandhi repeatedly connected the oppression of African Americans to the subjugation of India in order to expose the hypocrisy of the stated war aims of Great Britain and the United States. As Gandhi's letter to Roosevelt indicates, Indian solidarity with African Americans contributed to Indian estrangement from the Allied cause. The long history of connections between Indian and African American freedom struggles took on new meaning in the context of a war fought in the name of freedom.

Connecting the war abroad against fascism to the war at home against racism, African American leaders strove to leverage Indian opinion in order to pressure American officials, including President Roosevelt, to take concrete steps toward achieving racial equality in the United States. On December 7, 1941, the liberal New York daily, *PM*, declared, "If England is haunted by the problem of India, so are we haunted by the problem of our resident 12,000,000 Negroes."[2] This analogy would not have surprised African American readers accustomed to finding similar compari-

Interview to Preston Grover, June 21, 1942, *Collected Works of Mahatma Gandhi*. The CWMG are available on-line at www.gandhiserve.org/cwmg/cwmg.html.

sons between British imperialism and American racism in Black newspapers. That morning, however, some five thousand miles away, on the shores of Pearl Harbor, the Japanese navy made Britain's imperial dilemmas of vital strategic importance to the United States. Britain's troubles were no longer merely analogous to American problems; they were American problems. In particular, the fate of India came to be seen by many Americans as crucial to the success of the Allied cause, especially after Singapore fell to the Japanese in February 1942. That month the African American newspaper, *The Pittsburgh Courier,* began a "double victory" campaign to achieve racial equality in the United States by linking victory overseas against the Axis with victory at home against racial oppression.[3]

For many Black Americans, "double victory" entailed victory against imperialism throughout the world. Comparisons between the Axis powers and American racists served to dramatize American hypocrisy, establishing a connection between the war abroad and the war at home that was entirely figurative. In contrast, the anti-imperial dimensions of global double victory inspired the more powerful claim that the defeat of America's enemies hinged on the defeat of American racism. India often provided the crucial link in this causal chain. If Americans did not reform their racial policies, advocates of global double victory argued, then Indians would come to see the United States as yet another racist imperial power and would embrace the Japanese claim that its colonization of much of Asia was a liberation struggle against white colonial powers.[4]

The global double victory campaign was predicated on the notion that the plight of African Americans could influence the way Indian leaders viewed the United States. American State Department officials attacked this reasoning on the grounds that caste-based prejudice against dark skin would inspire Indians to distance themselves from Blacks, an argument with considerable historical support. Since the First World War, however, many prominent Indians had come to embrace a colored cosmopolitanism that linked Blacks and Indians in a common struggle against white oppression. During the war, Indian leaders, including Gandhi and Nehru, publicly endorsed solidarity between Indians and African Americans. In August 1942 the dramatic announcement of the Quit India movement, the last nationwide civil disobedience movement before independence, provided an opportunity for both Indians and African Americans to strengthen the bonds of color.

The deployment of American soldiers to India, many of whom were African American, provided unique opportunities to advocates of global double victory while revealing the limitations of colored solidarity. In early 1942 the United States began amassing military personnel in the

Indian subcontinent. Over the next three years more than two hundred thousand American soldiers came to live and work in India.[5] More than twenty-two thousand of these soldiers were African American.[6] The army prevented the majority of African American soldiers from serving in combat. Treated as second-class citizens at home, African American men and women found themselves laboring abroad as second-class soldiers. Indians who had before only read of American racial discrimination, or perhaps knew a friend who had witnessed it, now found Jim Crow segregation in their own cities. Many came to see in American racial oppression a reflection of British imperialism. Meeting in a time of profound social transformation, when famine, poverty, and political rebellion convulsed much of India, African Americans and Indians did not always encounter each other as friends, let alone as partners in a common fight against injustice. Some African American soldiers felt treated as "outcastes" by Indians. Indian civilians often resented the presence of foreign troops—both white and Black. These conflicts only render more significant the ability of many Indians and African Americans to forge relationships based on mutual sympathy, colored cosmopolitanism, and a shared history of oppression.

The Diplomacy of Double Victory

No one did more to make India central to a global double victory campaign than Walter White, the executive director of the NAACP. White used Indian opposition to American racism to pressure American politicians, afraid of losing India to Japan, to grant equal rights to African Americans. The advantages of this strategy, as well as its limitations, are evident in White's response to one of the most important diplomatic failures of the war. In the spring of 1942 American pressure helped convince Winston Churchill to evince a commitment to Indian "constitutional reform" by sending Sir Stafford Cripps to India.[7] A noted liberal and friend of Nehru, Cripps was charged with the difficult task of securing the support of the Indian National Congress for the war effort without being able to offer the Congress any substantive changes in British policy toward the Raj. He arrived in Delhi on March 22, 1942, and left for London from Karachi on April 13, 1942. Before Cripps left India, it was already evident that his mission had failed. Writing about the failure of the Cripps mission, the *Baltimore Afro-American* declared, "If Britain has thus failed to solve her India problem it can be said with equal justice that we in America have failed to solve our Negro problem."[8] Recognizing the power of this analogy now that the United States had entered the war, Walter White used it to pressure the Roosevelt administration to support Indian independence and American racial equality by arguing that both goals were necessary to ensure Allied victory.

On April 28, two weeks after a crestfallen Cripps left Karachi for London, White penned a "very confidential" letter reporting a conversation that he had shared with the British ambassador to the United States, Lord Halifax. The letter went to a roster of eminent and influential African Americans, including W. E. B. Du Bois and A. Philip Randolph. During his conversation with Halifax, White reported, he had suggested an elaborate plan that he believed could help assure "colored peoples throughout the world that in the post war world they would share in the benefits of the struggle now being made." He envisioned an American version of the Cripps mission in which President Roosevelt would send an official commission to India to help resolve the crisis between the British and the Indian National Congress. "As a preliminary to their departure and as proof of the sincerity of the United States on the matter of color," White suggested, "President Roosevelt would take a sweeping and unequivocal stand against discrimination on the basis of color in the United States." Thus White directly connected Indian independence and the achievement of racial justice in the United States. Further demonstrating his belief in the unity of Indians and African Americans, White suggested that the commission include a "distinguished American Negro who is unmistakably Negro." By referencing someone "unmistakably Negro," White effectively eliminated himself as a potential candidate for the job. White's light skin, blond hair, and blue eyes had allowed him to pass as white while reporting on lynching in the South. In his letter White noted that he had already asked for an appointment with President Roosevelt in order to discuss his plan. He asked each recipient of the letter to serve as a potential candidate for the committee that would travel to India.[9]

The responses White received to his letter ranged from enthusiastic to lukewarm, but taken as a whole they demonstrated the broad support for Indian independence that existed among African American public figures. On April 30 John W. Davis, president of West Virginia State College, wrote White that his proposal was "of world-wide significance." Agreeing with White's transnational conceptualization of color, Davis asserted, "The failure to include people of color, whether in America, Australia or India, realistically in the democratic concept of government is partially responsible for the present world turmoil." Having linked the plight of colored peoples to the outbreak of war, Davis concluded that "one of the results of the present war must be the inclusion of people of color (Indians and Negroes everywhere) in the world-wide democratic benefits."[10] A few days later, Carl Murphy, president of the *Baltimore Afro-American*, also approved White's proposal and agreed to be on the list of potential Blacks to be sent to India.[11]

On May 2 Du Bois sent a brief and overtly formal response. "My dear Sir," he told White, "Any duty which the President of the United States may lay upon me, I will be glad to perform to the best of my ability. Very respectfully yours, W. E. B. Du Bois."[12] The brevity of this response speaks more to the strained relationship between Du Bois and White than to Du Bois's views on the importance of Indian independence. On the same day that he wrote White, Du Bois authored an article in *People's Voice* declaring that the "British Empire has caused more human misery than Hitler will cause if he lives a hundred years." Du Bois told his readers, "It is idiotic to talk about a people who brought the slave trade to its greatest development, who are the chief exploiters of Africa and who hold four hundred million Indians in subjection, as the great defenders of democracy."[13] On May 5 R. O'Hara Lanier, dean of instruction at the Hampton Institute, wrote White that he appreciated his proposal, but that "some definite statements from the President" were necessary to make it effective. Only if the journey was based on a real potential for change, he asserted, would it help improve the "morale of the darker races throughout the world."[14] A. Philip Randolph similarly wrote, "I think the Commission idea to India is good providing something fundamental about racial discrimination here in [the] U.S.A. is done by the President." Although Randolph did not want to personally serve on the commission, he told White, "I think your observations on India are sound."[15] Only a few months later, Randolph would initiate the first effort to utilize mass-based Gandhian nonviolence to combat racial injustice in the United States. Although a fundamentally different approach to bridging Indian and African American freedom struggles, Randolph's initiative would employ the same claims of colored unity central to White's diplomatic approach to global double victory.

White organized a collaborative effort to present Indian independence and American racial equality as vital to the war. He discussed his plan for an American Cripps mission with millionaire philanthropist Anson Phelps Stokes, who confirmed that "an American Negro would be considered by Great Britain and by India as an acceptable member of the Commission." He told White, "I happen to know that when an American friend of mine met Gandhi he asked him particularly about how Dr. Du Bois was."[16] White also shared his plan with Wendell Willkie, the Republican presidential nominee in 1940. A month later, at the annual conference of the NAACP in Los Angeles, Willkie declared, "Today it is becoming increasingly apparent to thoughtful Americans that we cannot fight the forces and ideas of imperialism abroad and maintain a form of imperialism at home."[17] In May White attended a conference at Lincoln University, a historically black college in Pennsylvania, along with Pearl S. Buck, eminent author and expert on Asia, William Hastie, the special assistant to the secretary of war on racial affairs, and Krishnalal Shridharani, an Indian American sociologist, whose works on Gandhi would help inspire the use of nonviolent civil disobedience against American racism. The conference emphasized the interconnections between the cause of "colored" peoples at home and abroad and the importance of that cause to the war effort.[18]

The precise causal links between victory abroad against imperialism and the Axis and victory at home against racism proved controversial, even among advocates of global double victory. On May 5 Pearl Buck telegrammed White that he should "make clear" that his "chief concern is in world issue because present emphasis on home situation while very important is perhaps a little too heavy." By questioning White's link between Indian independence and the achievement of American racial equality, Buck struck at the heart of White's conception of global double victory. She offered a more limited framework for linking the war abroad and at home. Buck suggested that White focus on gaining American support for Indian independence. She argued that the collapse of the British Raj and the rise of an independent India would ultimately benefit Black Americans.[19]

In spite of Buck's hesitations, White continued to assert that progress toward racial equality at home was necessary to ensure Indian support in the war. His efforts to enlist the help of Eve Curie, daughter of the famous French scientists, reveal the determination with which White defended his conception of global double victory. Curie, a renowned writer and journalist, had recently traveled to India. White prepared a memo based on his conversations with Curie that he hoped to use to demonstrate to President Roosevelt Indian concern for African Americans. Curie, however, complicated White's plans by editing the memo, eliminating sections comparing Jim Crow segregation in the United States to "a somewhat parallel situation in India" in which the Saturday Club of Calcutta "boasts of the fact that no colored man (which includes Indians) has ever crossed its threshold." White strove to present Curie's findings in the most alarming light, bending her memories when necessary to support his argument that Indian support in the war hinged on the struggle against American racism. Curie commented that "the high-caste Indians believe themselves to be superior to everybody, including all white people. Thus, any untoward acts by prejudiced American whites based on color would be disastrous to American-Indian relations." White employed this statement to argue that American racism was a threat to Indo-American relations. It could, however, just as easily be used to argue that high-caste Indians would feel no sympathy with Black Americans. The strongest statement in White's memo survived Curie's red pen. "Wherever she went in India," White wrote, "Mlle. Curie found that Indians were keenly aware of the treatment of the Negro in the United States and of the inequality between races based on color, which the Indians believed to characterize thought and action in the United States." This statement succinctly encapsulated the basic premise with which White aimed to persuade American politicians that domestic race reforms were in the nation's foreign policy interests. American racism, he and Curie agreed, influenced how Indians perceived the United States.[20]

On May 4, two days after he first spoke with Curie, White wrote directly to President Roosevelt, linking the defense of India with the attainment of racial justice. As he had done in his conversation with Lord Halifax, White suggested sending to India an African American representative "whose complexion unmistakably identifies him as being a colored man." To justify the inclusion of an African American member, White stated, "The treatment of Negroes in the United States is among the most frequently publicized and mentioned topics of discussion in India regarding the United States." "While the people of India do not think of themselves as Negroes," White explained, "they are keenly aware of the inequality of races based on skin color, from which they too have suffered." White stressed that Japanese propaganda routinely used incidents of American racism to court Indian sympathy. He told Roosevelt, "Your sending of the commission to India might conceivably lead to the drafting of a Pacific Charter which will assure to all the peoples of the world that the era of white domination of colored peoples is ended." White's conception of a Pacific Charter extended the principles of the Atlantic Charter, a widely publicized document, signed by Roosevelt and Churchill in August 1941, which defended "the right of all peoples to choose the form of government under which they will live." Although African Americans and Indians had long been denied that very right, Churchill and Roosevelt did not apply the promises of the Atlantic Charter to racial minorities in the United States or to the colonized peoples of the British Empire.[21]

As if a Pacific Charter was merely a minor suggestion, White offered, in his words, "an even bolder proposal." He outlined for Roosevelt a conference in the Pacific between Roosevelt, Nehru, Gandhi, the president of the Indian National Congress, Maulana Abul Kalam Azad, General Chiang Kai-Shek, and, perhaps, White added, Chakravarti Rajagopalachari. The preponderance of Indians in White's proposed Pacific Conference spoke to the centrality of India in his vision of global double victory. His inclusion of Rajagopalachari, a highly respected moderate who had supported the Cripps proposals, demonstrated White's knowledge of Indian politics.[22] Regardless of whether the president chose to hold a conference himself or to send a commission to India, White suggested that he first give "a sweeping declaration, perhaps in the form of a fireside chat, to be translated into specific action against discrimination from which colored peoples now suffer within the United States." White took this suggestion almost verbatim from a letter he had received from Roy Wilkins. Adding his own emphasis on color, White explained the importance of such a statement in terms of its impact "upon the colored peoples of the world, who constitute four-fifths of the world's population."[23]

White's ability to use colored solidarity to generate political change at home and abroad depended on the degree to which Roosevelt and his advisors believed that the fate of India's army and resources hinged on American racism. Would lessoning the plight of African Americans prevent Indians from siding with Japan? In May the undersecretary of state, Sumner Welles, told White that his plan was "of the highest significance" and, in White's words, "as possibly being the step which might be the turning point in the war." On June 2 Welles told White that President Roosevelt was "enthusiastic about the proposal to send a commission to India and believed it would be of very real value." Although Welles reassured White that his plan had been warmly received, Welles wrote the president criticizing White's ideas and noting that State Department staff opposed the plan "on account of well-recognized racial prejudices on the part of Indian leaders themselves." "Indians, despite their dark complexion," Welles told Roosevelt, "do not regard Negroes as their equals."[24]

Having learned of the opposition to his plan, White wrote Pearl Buck for her opinion on Indian racial views. The State Department, White told Buck, had concluded that the "people of India consider American Negroes to be in the same class with India's untouchables, and that they for this reason would resent the presence of an American Negro, however distinguished, on the commission." White asked Buck if this was an accurate assessment of Indian opinion or merely "the typical white bureaucratic interpretation."[25] White also wrote Krishnalal Shridharani for his opinion "as to what would be the reaction in India if a distinguished American Negro were included at any time in the future on a delegation from the United States to India." Two days later, Shridharani telephoned that sending a Black representative to India "would have the best possible effect."[26] Having gathered such evidence, White wrote to Adolf Berle, the assistant secretary of state, questioning the argument that Indian leaders looked down on African Americans.[27]

White's protestations did little to convince the Roosevelt administration of the connection between domestic race relations and Indian support in the war.[28] White's efforts did, however, help encourage opponents of American racism and advocates of Indian independence to see their struggles as related. After his secret meeting with Halifax was leaked to the press, a number of sympathetic articles were published in the United States and London, further spreading the idea that Black and Indian struggles were linked.[29] Reporting on White's initiative, one African American columnist called for "more and more public opinion and pressure to insist on extension of the Atlantic Charter to encompass all peoples, all colonies . . . and all colors." Another took a more cynical view, declaring that the "time for colored people to press for rights is when whites are scared."[30]

In part because of White's initiatives, the global double victory campaign expanded even as plans for an American Cripps mission faltered. White helped inspire broad support for Indian independence among African Americans. It would be wrong, however, to explain African American solidarity with Indians as resulting entirely from the initiative of elite leaders like Walter White. Grassroots support for the anti-imperial dimensions of the double victory campaign was epitomized in July 1942, well before White's efforts were made public, when an African American woman speaking at a community meeting on Long Island declared, "We can tell you what Hitlerism is because we know it. We face it every day." Expanding her comparison between fascism and American racism to include imperialism, she added, "The cancer is here in Great Neck, in Nassau, and it's in India and in China, too."[31] None of the reports on White's meeting nor White himself ever explained that the idea to contact Halifax may well have originated with the director of a funeral home. On April 7, 1942, two weeks before White met with Halifax, L. G. Robinson, the president of the Angelus Funeral Home, wrote White suggesting that the NAACP contact Halifax to request that the British government grant India its freedom.[32] As Robinson's letter makes evident, Walter White and other Black public figures responded to African American support for India as much as they inspired it.

The Color of *Swaraj*

The State Department's claim that "racial prejudices" would have biased Indians against an African American diplomat contradicted the statements of India's most renowned leader. American entry in the war inspired

Mahatma Gandhi to make clear his opposition to American racism, an opposition grounded in more than forty years of reading about and meeting with Black Americans. In February 1942 Gandhi received a series of agricultural bulletins written by George Washington Carver. Gandhi received Carver's bulletins from a visitor with whom he initiated this pointed conversation:

> *Gandhi:* "But even this genius suffers under the handicap of segregation, does not he?"
> *Visitor:* "Oh yes, as much as any Negro."
> *Gandhi:* "And yet these people talk of democracy and equality! It is an utter lie."
> *Visitor:* "But Dr. Carver is never bitter or resentful."
> *Gandhi:* "I know, that is what we believers in non-violence have to learn from him."[33]

Recorded by Gandhi's secretary, Mahadev Desai, and published in *Harijan* under the title "British and American Nazism," this conversation reveals how the war altered the purpose to which Gandhi put the Negro/Indian parallel. While continuing to encourage Indians to learn from the struggles of African Americans, as he had done throughout the 1930s, Gandhi increasingly used the treatment of "the Negro" to unmask American racism. In June Gandhi told a reporter for the Associated Press of America, "The Allies have no moral cause for which they are fighting, so long as they are carrying this double sin on their shoulders, the sin of India's subjection and the subjection of the Negroes and African races." He proclaimed, "You have yet to abolish slavery!" The reporter asked, "In the United States, you mean?" Gandhi answered, "Yes, your racial discrimination, your lynch law and so on."[34] It was less than two weeks later that Gandhi told President Roosevelt that Allied declarations sounded "hollow so long as India and, for that matter, Africa are exploited by Great Britain and America has the Negro problem in her own home." Walter White could not have engineered a more perfect demonstration of the need for Roosevelt to pursue a global double victory.

Indian opposition to American racism extended well beyond Gandhi. In January 1943 John Davies, political aide to Joseph Stilwell, commanding general of the China-India-Burma theater of the war, finished an extensive report, detailing his meetings with a variety of Indian public figures. The Davies memo reveals that opposition to American racism cut across divisions of caste, religion, and political orientation. Davies informed General Stilwell that Dr. Ambedkar, the renowned Dalit leader, was "fully conscious of the color issue and resentful on that score." Although Ambedkar and the Congress took starkly different approaches to caste oppression, Davies portrayed both as concerned about American racism. Davies quoted C. Rajagopalachari "that the white races could not afford to continue antagonizing the colored races." Davies concluded, "The Congress conservatives—as well as other Indians—are beginning to wonder if they may not have to face a racial fight for liberation from white domination." According to Davies, Indian color-consciousness transcended religious divisions. Pothan Joseph, the Christian editor of the Muslim League's weekly publication, *Dawn,* "mentioned with fierce resentment white domination of the colored peoples of the world." Davies warned General Stilwell that "insofar as color is identified with a condition of economic and political servitude, it can be a powerful emotional factor contributing to a future war."[35]

While detailing widespread Indian opposition to racial oppression, the Davies memo did not directly counter the State Department's claim that Indians would look down on an African American diplomat. Increasingly, the State Department and other branches of the federal government were provided direct evidence that Indians resented American racism. It is necessary, however, to distinguish between Indian opposition to discrimination against Indians and a broader opposition to racism in general. In the summer of 1943, an Indian visitor named Mr. Pereira was denied service in a restaurant in Virginia. He complained directly to the State Department. On July 19, 1943, the American Consulate in Bombay wrote to the secretary of state describing the impact of prejudice on Indian businessmen as "disastrous." The report explained that many Indians "were treated as Negroes in the United States and often returned with deeply entrenched anti-American feelings." The report mentioned that American companies had advised Indian employees to always wear turbans in order to distinguish themselves from African Americans, not a procedure likely to improve Indian respect for the United States.[36] Nevertheless, the consulate's letter, like the protests of Mr. Pereira, did not directly demonstrate Indian concern for the plight of African Americans. In the first decades of the twentieth century, many Indians had criticized American racism while striving to distinguish themselves from Blacks in order to avoid discrimination. They had, in other words, cautiously donned their turbans. Since the First World War, however, increasing numbers of Indians, many prominent public figures, chose to speak out against all forms of American racism while expressing solidarity with African Americans.

The Second World War inspired many Indians within the United States to publicly express sympathy with the struggles of African Americans. In the spring of 1943 Taraknath Das, a veteran of the Ghadar movement who taught history at the College of the City of New York, spoke to a congressional panel about America's "double standards of international morality." Speaking against the Chinese Exclusion Act, Das took the opportunity to pursue larger claims about racial injustice in the United States. In an effort to discredit Das, Congressman A. Leonard Allen of Louisiana asked, "Would you go as far as to say that we should dine with those of Ethiopian race and accord to those people every social privilege?" Unlike earlier Indians who had distinguished themselves from African Americans, Das answered, "Yes. It will do a man honor to dine with a man like Booker T. Washington or Dr. Carver, as President Theodore Roosevelt did, and made the greatest example of what America stood for." In the spirit of double victory, Das used the context of the war to underline the injustice of American racial discrimination. He argued, "Since the American people declared that they did not believe the superior race theory of the Nazis, there should be no discrimination against any individual because of race, creed or country of origin."[37]

In addition to the hypocrisy of the allies, ideas of color as a marker of shared oppression inspired solidarity between Indians and African Americans. The Davies memo quoted several Indians critiquing the oppression of "colored" people throughout the world. For Kamaladevi Chattopadhyaya, one of the most articulate champions of colored cosmopolitanism, being a woman, being a socialist, and being "colored" were all vital to her identity and her sense of purpose. Her nearly two years in the United States allowed her to reach out to African Americans as a "coloured woman" who had dedicated her life to opposing not only imperialism and racism but gender-based oppression as well. When the war began, Kamaladevi had just returned to London after walking out of the International Women's Conference in Copenhagen in frustration over its silence on the issue of imperialism. A friend and fellow champion of Indian independence suggested that she raise American awareness of British imperialism and thus "strike a few blows for India."[38]

Kamaladevi's plans did not escape the attention of British officials. A letter from the Royal Empire Society to Lord Zetland, the secretary of state for India, complained that Kamaladevi's politics were "distinctly anti-British." The letter, now in the British Library, contains a revealing note scribbled across its top: "Can we take any action to prevent this woman going to the U.S.A.?"[39] The answer came in a letter from one intelligence operative to another, explaining that although Kamaladevi was a "keen Socialist and an ardent champion of the Women's Movement," she was not "sufficiently fanatical to be classed as 'Left-Wing.'" Furthermore, the letter continued, "She has powerful friends in the

United Kingdom who would, no doubt, object if she were refused permission to go to the United States."[40] Thus, after careful review, Kamaladevi Chattopadhyaya was granted the right to visit the United States. Secretly, British authorities kept track of her visit, producing in the process valuable records for the historian.

Kamaladevi's British spies must not have been happy with the warm welcome she received from influential Americans. Kamaladevi met with Supreme Court justices Hugo Black and Felix Frankfurter, as well as with several members of Congress. She spoke on the radio in New York City and delivered the convocation address at Kansas University. She attended the presidential inauguration of Franklin Roosevelt in Washington as well as a convention of Roosevelt's rivals, the Republican Party, in San Francisco. Kamaladevi went out of her way to meet a range of American women, touring the women's section of Sing Sing Prison and traveling to Arizona to talk with the famed birth control advocate Margaret Sanger.[41]

Among Kamaladevi's strongest supporters were Christian Americans for whom opposing war, imperialism, and racism were religious commitments. On December 17, 1939, Kamaladevi spoke to the Community Church in New York City. She was introduced by John Haynes Holmes, who almost twenty years earlier had famously called a relatively unknown Mohandas Gandhi the "greatest man alive in the world today." Holmes, who had helped found the NAACP, exemplified the vitality of an older liberal Christian commitment to combating racial prejudice in the United States and abroad.[42] On January 3 Kamaladevi had dinner with the War Resister's League, whose president, A. J. Muste, was in attendance. Like John Haynes Holmes, Muste used a Christian vocabulary to fight racism at home and overseas. In the next two decades he would play a central role in bringing Gandhian nonviolence to the African American struggle.[43]

In her private meetings and her public speeches, Kamaladevi repeatedly urged Americans to support Indian independence. Her message found receptive audiences throughout the United States. A professor of sociology at Hobart College in Geneva, New York, wrote Jawaharlal Nehru after hearing Kamaladevi speak. "She lectured in the Coxe Hall auditorium to a capacity house," the professor reported, "and when she finished there was the most prolonged cheering I ever heard there." He concluded, "This wonderful woman inspired us with the spirit of the Indian movement for independence and we shall do our best to carry its meaning to others." Nehru himself wrote Kamaladevi in September 1940 that he had been "following with great interest" her "extraordinarily interesting time in America."[44]

Kamaladevi's efforts to influence American opinion of India did not deter her from publicly demonstrating sympathy with the struggles of African Americans. In December 1939 she denounced British imperialism at a special gathering of the Harlem branch of the NAACP. Beneath a photo of Kamaladevi and Walter White, a newspaper covering the event quoted Kamaladevi offering a classic statement of colored solidarity: "We condemn imperialism and oppression in South Africa and in any other part of the world; because of our color we feel a racial kinship with the other colored peoples." Kamaladevi chose to travel through the American South and made a point of staying only with African American families. Her sympathetic interest in the struggles of "colored" Americans drew attention from both African American and Indian newspapers. *The Chicago Defender* kept its readers apprised of Kamaladevi's efforts, calling her "Gandhi's Aide" and "India's foremost woman leader." *The Bombay Chronicle* called Kamaladevi's decision to stay with African Americans in the South "a daring and unusual procedure because of the strong prejudices against Negroes in that part of the country." The paper concluded, "Coming close to the Negro groups, she has considerably endeared India to these struggling people."[45]

Kamaladevi's public solidarity with African Americans was indeed "daring." When she refused to give up her seat on a Jim Crow train in Louisiana, Kamaladevi risked more than her own safety. Her actions could have alienated Americans receptive to the idea of an independent India but defensive when pressed about injustices closer to home. There is no evidence that Kamaladevi criticized American racism in speeches before white audiences or in her meetings with American politicians. Nevertheless, Kamaladevi's courage in meeting with Black leaders and staying with Blacks in the American South contrasts sharply with the caution of Madame Chiang Kai-shek, who came to the United States at the end of 1942. Like Kamaladevi, Madame Chiang aimed to garner American support for her country by establishing cordial relationships with a range of distinguished Americans. Unlike Kamaladevi, Madame Chiang chose to distance herself from African American activists, lest she alienate Southern politicians.[46]

In a series of books and articles published after she returned to India, Kamaladevi encouraged Indians to support African Americans and other oppressed colored peoples.[47] Partially inspired by the arrival of American troops in India, several Indians published accounts of their negotiations of the American racial landscape, educating the Indian public about American racism and the struggles of Black Americans. In 1943 Left-leaning author K. A. Abbas published in Bombay a book about his American experiences based on articles he had originally published in 1939. Abbas used a Langston Hughes poem, "The Darker Brother," to title a chapter on African American struggles. Abbas told his readers that he found "White superiority lurking even in the most educated and advanced section of the American people." As an example, Abbas narrated his own experiences with racial prejudice. On a train from Los Angeles to New York, a young boy beckoned Abbas to an open seat in the dining car. The boy's mother, however, proclaimed loudly, "No, not him. He is a nigger." Looking around the dining car, Abbas noticed "a suppressed bitterness" on the face of the African American waiters. After a manager informed the woman that Abbas was a "Hindu," she responded, "Oh, that is different. You can sit here, young man." Abbas was, in fact, not a Hindu but a Muslim. For many Americans "Hindu" was a racial term, one that in this case offered escape from the indignities forced upon African Americans. Abbas, however, like Kamaladevi Chattopadhyaya, refused to use his foreignness to distinguish himself from African Americans. He told the woman, "But it is not different. Now I refuse to sit on the same table as you."[48]

Abbas combined his critique of American racism with an awareness of class inequalities. He argued that communists were relatively free of racial discrimination, criticized Northern capitalists for exploiting poor African Americans, and compared the "colored bourgeois" to "the Indian capitalists who saw in nationalism a means of their economic gains." Abbas criticized the rhetoric of colored solidarity for obscuring the rightful preeminence of class. In 1938 he served as an Indian delegate to the World Youth Congress, a gathering in New York of some five hundred young people committed to international cooperation and opposed to war. Abbas found the Black delegates at the youth congress "friendly, reasonable and enthusiastic for the cause of India's freedom." With other Indian and African delegates to the congress, Abbas attended a reception given in Harlem by the Ethiopian World Federation, an organization founded in 1937 to coordinate the African American response to the Italian invasion of Ethiopia. In front of "a huge gathering," Abbas remembered, a fiery speaker "invited us to join a coloured world front against all White people and said in so many words that when we gained ascendancy we should do [sic] the white races exactly what they had done to us." This suggestion was met with great applause, much to the discomfort of Abbas. When his turn to speak arrived, Abbas began by expressing "the sympathy of India for Ethiopia and assuring the American Negroes that we were with them in their struggle for the attainment of complete political, social and economic equality in their country." He told the audience, however, that global oppression was "not a question of colour at all" but of the "historical inter-relation between imperialism, militarism, capitalism, and fascism." Abbas directed the audience to examine the root causes of racism rather than the divisions between white and "coloured" peoples.[49]

Many colored cosmopolitans opposed overt anti-white sentiment while, unlike Abbas, defending colored unity. In 1939 Cedric Dover published *Know This of Race,* a careful refutation of the idea of "race" and an exploration of racial prejudice, based on lectures he had given at Cambridge University. Dover began *Know This of Race* with an analogy between racism in Nazi Germany and the United States: "The European Jews are being driven back to the ghetto in the name of race. The American Negroes are still confined to ghettoes in the name of race. Everywhere men are scorned, segregated and persecuted in the name of race."[50] Dover dedicated *Know This of Race* to Paul and Eslanda Goode Robeson— both of whom Dover had come to consider close friends. In 1943 Dover dedicated an entire broadcast on All-India Radio to praising Paul Robeson. Dover described for his Indian audience when, in 1928 on a rubber plantation in British Malaya, he first heard Robeson performing his landmark tune "Ol' Man River." "As the rich notes floated out above the rubber trees, silencing the crickets," Dover remembered, "I sensed behind them the pressure of a people whose tragedy became mine."[51]

Like the Robesons, Dover embraced a leftist politics that recognized inequalities of race and class as interconnected. In *Know This of Race,* Dover connected racism to class inequality by arguing that "racial theories seek to justify the inequalities of capitalist society: to rationalise privilege and oppression on the one hand, and to compensate the masses for their sufferings and feelings of inferiority on the other."[52] On All-India Radio, Dover praised Robeson for remaining "a man of the people among the people" and concluded, "More than an artist, he is a worker, struggling with other workers."[53]

A transnational conception of color underpinned Dover's antiracist socialism. In 1943 Dover published *Hell in the Sunshine,* a wide-ranging assessment of the war in the Pacific that linked the "shooting of Negroes and Indian nationalists" as examples of the hypocrisy of British and American war aims. In a chapter entitled "Eastern Unity to Coloured Unity," Dover wrote, "I have tried to bring the lives and problems and aspirations of the coloured peoples under imperialism into one perspective." Like Walter White, Dover argued that the Allies faced losing the propaganda war with Japan if they continued to praise democracy while oppressing "coloured peoples."[54] It was not Walter White, however, but

W. E. B. Du Bois that Dover credited with inspiring his understanding of colored unity and the intersection of race and class.

Du Bois was a colored cosmopolitan before he was a socialist. By 1928, when Du Bois published *Dark Princess,* his socialism and his colored cosmopolitanism had come to reinforce each other. In *Black Reconstruction in America,* published in 1935, Du Bois argued that African Americans shared a "common destiny" with "that dark and vast sea of human labor in China and India, the South Seas and all of Africa; in the West Indies and Central America and in the United States—that great majority of mankind, on whose bent and broken backs rest today the founding stones of modern history." Du Bois framed "darkness" as the result of oppression and marginalization. His reference to "that dark and vast sea of human labor" included all those who had been forced into the shadows of the global economy.[55] In *Dusk of Dawn,* published in 1940, Du Bois told his readers that the history "of our day" can be "epitomized in one word—Empire; the domination of white Europe built on the economic control of labor, income and ideas." In opposition to "white Europe," Du Bois arrayed the "kinship" of the colonized. He wrote, "The real essence of this kinship is its social heritage of slavery; the discrimination and insult; and this heritage binds together not simply the children of Africa, but extends through yellow Asia and into the South Seas." By expanding his understanding of empire and slavery so that the two categories overlapped, Du Bois used history to unite the struggles of African Americans and other non-white peoples. He drafted a list of "widely wished-for" events among imperialists: "the probable extermination of Negroes, the failure of Japanese Imperialism, the incapacity of India for self-rule, collapse of the Russian Revolution."[56] By portraying what imperialists wanted, Du Bois instructed his readers what they should work against. Significantly, the "collapse of the Russian revolution" concluded the list. For Du Bois, as for Dover, colored solidarity did not preclude but encouraged class solidarity.

Since the Depression, links between the African American Left and the Indian Left had increased in number and significance. Some Black and Indian leftists, like Du Bois and Dover, reached out to each other within the framework of colored cosmopolitanism. Others, most notably Jawaharlal Nehru and Paul Robeson, chose to frame their solidarity in terms of a common struggle against fascism in all of its forms. In 1940 Nehru wrote Du Bois that he was "greatly interested in the future of the American Negroes." As a student in England, Nehru had "come across" a book written by Du Bois. Nehru remembered "the powerful impression" it had on him and sent his good wishes "for the advancement of the Negroes of

America."[57] In April 1942 Nehru cabled the Council on African Affairs (CAA), the Left-leaning, anti-imperial organization led by Paul Robeson and Max Yergan. A year earlier, in March 1941, Kamaladevi Chattopadhyaya, herself a member of the Congress Socialist Party, had spoken at a meeting of the CAA alongside Robeson and Yergan.[58] Without referencing the conception of color that Kamaladevi often employed, Nehru's telegram championed an expansive conception of "true freedom" implicitly opposed to the "freedom" that the Allied powers so often lauded but only partially honored. Nehru wrote, "All good wishes for success against fascism, imperialism and establishment of true freedom everywhere. Recognition equal rights, opportunities all races and peoples."[59]

His relationship with Black leftists, and especially with Paul and Eslanda Robeson, deepened Nehru's solidarity with Black struggles. Nehru met the Robesons for the first time in London in 1938. His admiration for Paul Robeson grew extensively over the next decade, deepened through Nehru's friendship with Eslanda Robeson, with whom he exchanged a series of letters that grew increasingly intimate over time. After having lunch with Nehru in London, Eslanda wrote him, "To be able to talk, freely, with some one who has the same interests we have, and who understands our peculiar problems and background, is more than a treat."[60] Nehru also received a steady stream of news about Paul Robeson from Rajni Patel, who met Robeson while studying law and working for the India League in London in the late 1930s. In a letter to Nehru on May 6, 1939, Patel lauded Robeson as a singer and as a human being, before adding that Robeson himself had praised Nehru as "one of the few greatest men in the world." A few months later, Patel wrote Nehru that he and Robeson had shared tea and had again discussed Nehru in "a fond and affectionate manner."[61]

In the winter of 1939, Patel traveled to the United States with Kamaladevi Chattopadhyaya. Like Kamaladevi, he raised awareness of India's cause while reaching out to African Americans. Patel received assistance from Eslanda Robeson, who helped him find speaking engagements at African American universities. From London, Patel had written Nehru praising Eslanda as "a wonderfully vital person." From New York, Eslanda wrote Nehru describing Patel as "very popular and very well thought of here." She told Nehru, "I have had reports on him from all over the country."[62] Throughout his time in the United States, Patel sent his own reports to Nehru, writing from New York, Minnesota, and Honolulu, inevitably mentioning Paul Robeson.[63]

After returning to India, Patel was immediately arrested, in the words of his jailers, for "anti-British and anti-war propaganda activities." From the Yeravda Central Prison in Poona, he continued corresponding with Nehru, who sent him fatherly advice on how to cope with imprisonment. Even behind bars, Patel managed to share news of Robeson with Nehru. After learning from American friends that Robeson had been denied entry into a cafe, Patel wrote Nehru a passionate denunciation of American racism. He proclaimed, "I know the terrible plight of the Negroes (eleven million of them) and I could give you some unbelievable bloodcurdling incidents from my own experience." Patel concluded, "Whenever I think of the terrible cruelties and injustices they—[Robeson] and his people— have to suffer my whole being revolts and I burn with anger and have no pity left in my heart for the system that breeds such diseases."[64]

Many of the African Americans Patel interacted with had already developed a strong interest in India. In November 1939 Patel wrote Nehru that Robeson's understanding of contemporary Indian politics had impressed him "immensely." Patel mentioned meeting Max Yergan, whom he described as "a very fine Negro scholar." Yergan, Patel added, still remembered meeting Nehru in India in 1928. Yergan told Patel, "Nehru is one of the few men in the world who has left a profound impression upon me."[65] The Quit India movement triggered an outpouring of support from African Americans for Indian independence, an outpouring that was communicated to Indians, further strengthening Indian sympathy with Black struggles. Expressions of solidarity reflected back and forth, solidifying transnational conceptions of color and reinspiring advocates of global double victory.

Gandhi in Harlem

On August 8, 1942, the All-India Congress Committee called for widespread civil disobedience. Throughout the country, Indians began to purposefully disobey laws and were imprisoned in large numbers. The last major civil disobedience movement in the colonial era, the Quit India movement, had begun. In his speech the previous day, Gandhi provocatively proclaimed, "I do not regard England, or for that matter America, as free countries." He explained, "They are free after their own fashion, free to hold in bondage the coloured races of the earth."[66] Jawaharlal Nehru also emphasized the racial dimensions of the Indian struggle. After noting Churchill's penchant for praising the "Anglo-Saxon race," Nehru declared, "There is too much talk of majesty and dignity of the Anglo-Saxon race or the German race or the Italian race. There are other races also in the world and we have had enough of such talks. This racial superiority can no more be tolerated."[67]

While most American newspapers closely covered the outbreak of civil disobedience in India, it was the African American press that recognized the racial framework in which Gandhi, Nehru, and other leading Indian figures positioned their struggle. Black interest in India had risen dramatically during the noncooperation and civil disobedience movements, and it peaked again in the wake of the Quit India declaration. On September 26 over eighty Black intellectuals sent President Roosevelt a joint letter encouraging him to take decisive action to resolve the crisis in India.[68] That same day, sociologist and *Pittsburgh Courier* columnist Horace Cayton told readers of *The Nation,* "It may seem odd to hear India discussed in poolrooms in South State Street in Chicago, but India and the possibility of the Indians obtaining their freedom from England by any means have captured the imagination of the American Negro." In October the *Courier* published the results of a poll in which 87.8 percent of ten thousand black respondents answered yes to the question, "Do you believe that India should contend for her rights and her liberty now?"[69]

Committed to both American democracy and Black racial identity, African American defenders of Indian independence employed expansive definitions of both color and freedom. The Quit India movement reinvigorated Black efforts to link Indian independence and racial equality as necessary components of a global double victory. After his proposal for an American Cripps mission faltered, Walter White continued to warn American politicians that American racism threatened the "loss" of India. On August 8, the day of the Quit India resolution, White told a subcommittee of the Senate Judiciary Committee that banning the poll tax would show "the people of India and South America whose support we need, that democracy here is living and expanding."[70] After the British imprisoned Gandhi and Nehru, White refused to deliver a speech solicited by the Office of War Information as a way of countering Japan's use of American racism as propaganda. To the Office of War Information, White explained, "Arrests leave me with nothing convincing to say."[71] On August 10 White telegrammed President Roosevelt, "It is apparent that Japan won a great victory in the Pacific Saturday when Gandhi, Nehru and Azad were thrown into prison because they too wanted and demanded for people of India the same freedom the British Government is fighting to preserve for white Englishmen." *The Chicago Defender* carried the full text of White's telegram and noted that Dr. Vishnu V. Oak, an Indian professor of economics and sociology at Wilberforce University, a historically black college, had sent Roosevelt his own message supporting White's telegram. *The Chicago Defender* warned its readers, "If

India's cry for freedom is smothered, the position of the Negro people the world over will become increasingly precarious; more than that, the cause of democracy for which our own beloved America and her allies are bleeding, will be irreparably jeopardized." On August 31 White again admonished Roosevelt that the Indian situation was "one of the most important problems confronting the United Nations and one which has considerable bearing upon the race question in the United States."[72]

White's advocacy dovetailed with the grassroots colored cosmopolitanism of many NAACP members. On August 21, 1942, H. W. Sewing, a member of the NAACP in Kansas City, Missouri, wrote White to suggest a week of "sympathy for India" in which African Americans would wear armbands or badges that declared their support for India and would barrage both Roosevelt and Churchill with letters demanding "immediate Indian freedom." Sewing stated that "the cause of Indian freedom is identified with the cause of our freedom" and repeatedly expressed what he called the "identity of interest between the Indian people and the Negroes of the United States."[73] On September 10 an NAACP member told Roy Wilkins, *The Crisis* editor, "Your column on the Indian question was a good piece of work. Our leaders are on trial not to fail the colored peoples of the world."[74]

Conceptions of colored unity proved central to how many Blacks connected Indian freedom to their own. Linking colored solidarity to the achievement of democracy, *The New York Amsterdam News* declared, "To the coloured races throughout the world, Gandhi is the living and dynamic symbol of the struggle for freedom, justice and democracy."[75] In 1943 journalist Roi Ottley proclaimed, "The condition of the black man in the United States has become the barometer of 'democracy' to the colored leaders of the world, and even suggests to them—should certain Fascist-minded elements here have their way—the sort of 'democracy' which may dominate the new world a-coming." As an example, Ottley stated, "Did Gandhi not say, 'The [white] Allies have no moral cause for which they are fighting, so long as they are carrying this double sin—the sin of India's subjection and the subjection of Negroes'?"[76] By inserting the word "white" into Gandhi's quote, Ottley underlined the opposition to racial hierarchies that he and Gandhi both shared.

The increasing stridency with which Indian leaders criticized American racism, coupled with the concerted efforts of Walter White and other Black leaders, convinced many Americans of the interconnected nature of the "colored world." Mainstream publications began to frame India's bondage as, in the words of *Time* magazine, "a symbol of despair for millions of the colored peoples of the earth." Oswald Garrison Villard wrote in *The Christian Century* that India's independence would produce "a wonderfully stimulating and inspiring effect, not only in India but among all colored peoples." The reverse argument—that domestic racism threatened the war effort by alienating "colored" nations—also took hold. In a special issue entitled "Color: Unfinished Business of Democracy," the progressive magazine *Survey Graphic* juxtaposed the struggles of African Americans and other colored peoples. Even *Fortune* magazine, not known as a champion of colored solidarity, declared, "The Negro's fate in the U.S. affects the fate of white American soldiers in the Philippines, in the Caribbean, in Africa; bears on the solidity of our alliance with 800 million colored peoples in China and India; influences the feelings of countless neighbors in South America."[77]

The demographics of colored solidarity could produce tangible political gains by pressuring reluctant American politicians into action and by providing Black Americans, long aware of the perils of being a minority, the confidence of a majority. In a speech entitled "White Supremacy and World War II," given on the last day of the NAACP's annual meeting in Detroit in 1943, Walter White stated that a "high official" of Britain's India Office had told him that "Nehru and Gandhi and the other leaders of the fight for freedom of India's three hundred and fifty million people would never be freed from prison until they confessed guilt of treason and insurrection for daring to demand that India's millions receive as well as fight for freedom." Such mass incarceration provided "the Japanese propagandists with superb material to convince the one thousand million colored peoples of the Pacific that the white nations of the world are liars and hypocrites when they say that this is a war for the freedom of all men everywhere."[78] White's references to "India's three hundred and fifty million people" and "the one thousand million colored peoples of the Pacific," like many other numeric estimates of "colored" nations, ignored the internal diversities of "coloured" peoples, although not without purpose. White's ability to mobilize African Americans and the Roosevelt administration depended on his presentation of India as a unified colored country within a larger unity of colored peoples.

A few months into the Quit India movement, Walter White received a letter questioning the NAACP's seeming unconcern with caste. The letter deemed caste "the great curse of India" and challenged White, "As representing the colored people, I am wondering whether you have considered these oppressed millions in India and what their plight might be."[79] Whether White replied is not known. One answer to White's correspondent was supplied in an editorial by Deton Brooks, a reporter for *The Chicago Defender.* Brooks acknowledged caste oppression as well as

India's religious divisions while defending both Indian unity and the solidarity of non-white peoples. How could a global solidarity of color succeed if India, the largest "colored" country in the world, was divided along lines of caste and religion? Brooks parried the challenge of India's internal diversity by subsuming it within a larger narrative of colored resistance to the "deep rooted prejudices" that biased both British and American leaders against "any non-white group." Brooks acknowledged India's internal diversity while asserting an Afro-Indian solidarity based on a common struggle against white supremacy.[80]

Black expressions of colored solidarity both revealed and obscured the internal diversity of India. A. M. Wendell Malliet, a native of Jamaica and a leader in the Council on West Indian Affairs, told readers of *The New York Amsterdam News,* "The bonds of unity, brotherhood and common fellowship between the brown and black millions of India and Africa are being drawn closer together." As evidence of this coming together, Malliet quoted from an interview he conducted with Abdul Aziz, a Muslim missionary from Bengal. While Aziz defended the solidarity of Indians and Africans in terms of global Islam, Malliet stressed secular notions of color. Although neither Malliet nor Aziz discussed the future of the Muslim minority in India, their divergent views made clear the uneasiness of the relationship between Pan-African and Pan-Islamic visions of transnational unity.[81]

The rhetoric of colored solidarity homogenized not only Indians but also African Americans. Note the singular tense in the following evocative plea, published in *The Chicago Defender* two weeks after the Quit India resolution:

> The sympathy of Negro America pours all-out for India. The demands of India are just. There are no "buts," nor can there be any. Negro America supports India's demands. Negro America knows that the independence of India will aid the cause of the United Nations in the fight against Hitler and Hitlerism. It will aid the cause of colonial freedom; the cause of Africa and of black men in these United States. The cause of freedom and democracy is indivisible. We stand with India in order to do honor to our own demands for full and complete equality.

While referring to Negro America as undifferentiated, this editorial itself demonstrates the diversity of African American responses to Indian struggles. The editorial defended Indian independence in the context of global double victory, powerfully asserting the transnational indivisibility of freedom. Unlike many declarations of global double victory, however, the editorial concluded by encouraging its readers to join a "people's war" against the "powerful monopolists" who oppressed Indians and African Americans.[82]

Many Left-leaning African Americans saw India's cause as a "people's war." In May 1941 Richard Wright, Paul Robeson, Countee Cullen, Max Yergan, and some 160 other African American public figures on the left issued a statement castigating "the British war makers" for enslaving "Africa, India, the West Indies, and other colonial areas in a cruel bondage often infinitely worse than the oppression known by Negroes in America."[83] In 1943 Paul Robeson wrote, "After the defeat of the fascists and their allies, the United States will have to cope with the fact that the harassed people of India and the British West Indies will be free, and that Africa will occupy a different position in the post-war world."[84] Like Nehru, Robeson rarely framed solidarity between Blacks and Indians in terms of color, instead emphasizing class solidarity and anti-imperialism. Two weeks after the beginning of the Quit India movement, Albert Parker told readers of the *Militant,* "The cause of the Indian masses in this struggle is the cause of the oppressed toilers everywhere." "Negro workers," Parker declared, "the Indian struggle is yours too."[85] In the *Daily Worker,* Paul Robeson defended the importance of India to the struggle against colonialism. Max Yergan, as the president of the National Negro Congress, wrote directly to President Roosevelt that "we see etched in blood in India the stake which oppressed people all over the world have in this war of liberation."[86] At the end of August, *The Negro Quarterly* organized a joint discussion of "India and the People's War" and "Africa and the Atlantic Charter." The discussions were led by Angelo Herndon and Kumar Goshal, both Left-leaning activists.[87] Goshal also participated in an "Aid-India Rally," organized by the Council on African Affairs and headlined by Paul Robeson. Four thousand people attended the rally, including Channing Tobias, Max Yergan, and Councilman Adam Clayton Powell.[88]

The fiercest criticism of Gandhi among African Americans came from the Left. Yet even Black critics who attacked Gandhi as being too conservative expressed strong support for the Indian cause.[89] While some Black socialists accused Gandhi of neglecting the people, Gandhi accused Indian communists of forgetting about the colored peoples. Although originally opposed to the war, Indian communists became enthusiastic hawks after Hitler's surprise invasion of the Soviet Union. In June 1944 Gandhi asked Puran Chandra Joshi, the general secretary of the Communist Party of India, whether "the meaning of 'people' in 'people's war'" included "India's millions, or the Negroes in East, South or West Africa, or the Negroes of America?" Joshi responded, "People in people's war means all peoples the world over without exception. It, of course, includes India's millions and also the Negroes wherever they be." Gandhi was not so easily convinced. He replied, "The chief actors among the Allied powers are by no means inclined towards real democracy."[90]

The increasingly widespread Indian solidarity with other colored peoples resulted in part from the publicity in India of widespread African American support for Indian independence. On April 16, 1942, Walter White telegrammed the All-India National Congress: "PROBLEMS ARISING FROM PREJUDICE BASED ON SKIN COLOR FACE PEOPLES THROUGHOUT WORLD AND MUST BE SOLVED TO END PERMANENTLY GREED OF ALL EXPLOITERS." In September 1942 R. Lal Singh, editor of the Los Angeles newspaper *India News,* wrote White for a statement on India. White offered a powerful question: "Why is it heroic and noble for the British to fight for their freedom; and criminal for the Indian to fight for theirs?" Singh gathered similar statements of support from other Black figures, compiling a press release that documented sympathy for Indian independence among Black leaders.[91]

Singh's press release began with a resolution from the 33rd annual conference of the NAACP calling for the application of the Atlantic Charter and Roosevelt's four freedoms to India and other colonized peoples "so that the dark-skinned and colonial peoples may be given greater hope of real political democracy and freedom from economic exploitation." Quotations from a variety of Black figures demonstrated the prevalence of the idea of global double victory. Paul Robeson wrote, "American Negroes must have all their rights, for this is the way to lick Hitler. India must be freed, for this is the way to lick Hitler." Channing Tobias, the YMCA leader who had traveled to India to meet Gandhi, asserted "the importance to the cause of the United Nations of immediate action on the freedom of India." Du Bois proclaimed, "There is no justification for this horrible war, if it does not mean autonomy for India now." According to the renowned Black poet Countee Cullen, "England's refusal to give India her freedom now is a mockery of the freedoms which the Allied Nations claim they are fighting to make assured for all peoples." As he had previously in poetic form, Cullen juxtaposed Gandhi's famous declaration, *Karenge ya Marenge* (We will do or die) with Patrick Henry's cry, "Give me liberty or give me death!" Langston Hughes responded with a classic statement of global double victory: "It just does not make sense for the Allied leaders of the Western World to make beautiful speeches about freedom and liberty and democracy with India still enchained and Negroes still jim-crowed and neither group permitted to participate with fullness and enthusiasm in the war effort of the United Nations." He declared, "Freedom for India is not only a military need, but a moral need to lift the fighting spirits of all who want to believe in freedom *for all.*"[92]

More eloquently than most, Langston Hughes located Black and Indian struggles within a worldwide movement for freedom. Writing in *The Chicago Defender* in January 1943, he stated, "Now is when all the conquered nations of Europe are asking for freedom. Now is when the Jews are asking for it. Now is when America is fighting to keep it. Now is when Nehru and Gandhi are sitting in jail silently demanding it for India." Hughes concluded, "How can anyone expect American Negroes not to catch the freedom fever too, is beyond me." On February 10, 1943, Gandhi began a three-week fast while imprisoned. Hughes responded with a poem that compared oppression in India with American racism.[93] Hughes's concern for India arose not from narrow hopes of future reward but from an expansive vision of united struggle against oppression worldwide.

Like their counterparts in the Black press, Indian journalists did much to facilitate mutual solidarity between Blacks and Indians. On July 18, 1944, Pasupuleti Gopala Krishnaya, editor of *The Orient & the USA*, a publication based in New York, wrote Walter White that he was sending a dispatch to Indian newspapers on "the American Negro, the war and the future." He asked White for information and explained, "In India there is [an] extraordinary and genuine interest regarding the Negro people at large and especially in this country."[94] Indian journalists helped inspire Black support for India. Beginning in 1942, Kumar Goshal published a regular column in *The Pittsburgh Courier* entitled "As an Indian Sees It." Goshal attacked American racism and British imperialism as harmful to the war effort. In an article entitled, "To the Allied Leaders: 'You Can't Beat Hitler By Protecting Jim Crow,'" Goshal compared riots in Harlem to the struggle in India as protests against the "anomaly of bondage in the midst of freedom."[95] Other column titles included, "Lynchings and Beatings Mar War Effort on Home Front," and "Oppression of India Will Weaken United Nations against Japanese."[96] Goshal defended Indian independence against charges that India was hopelessly divided. In one article, he wrote, "Surely the people of the United States should be the last ones to point the finger of scorn at the Indians for discrimination against minorities!"[97]

In 1944, near the end of his landmark book *An American Dilemma,* the Swedish social scientist Gunnar Myrdal declared, "This War is crucial for the future of the Negro, and the Negro problem is crucial in the War." Myrdal noted, "The smoldering revolt in India against British rule had significance for the American Negroes, and so had other 'color' incidents in the world conflict." By framing Indian struggles as a "color incident," Myrdal nodded toward the similarities between American racism and

British imperialism. By placing the word "color" in quotations, he maintained a skeptical distance from those who, like Du Bois or Cedric Dover, championed the solidarity of colored peoples. Myrdal believed that African American connections with other "colored" peoples were vague, emotional, and without a "definite pattern." Myrdal argued that the sentiments of African Americans were only "a minor part of the international implications" of race in America. "The main international implication," for Myrdal, was "that America, for its international prestige, power, and future security, needs to demonstrate to the world that American Negroes can be satisfactorily integrated into its democracy."[98] Thus, like Walter White, Myrdal argued that American racial prejudice hurt American foreign policy. Unlike White, however, Myrdal failed to recognize the many ways in which African Americans themselves influenced the way the world understood their struggles. He neglected the relationship between the sympathy African Americans expressed toward other colored peoples and the reverse solidarity in which others expressed support for African Americans. Myrdal thus overlooked the key dynamic that linked the war and African American struggles.

During the Second World War, African Americans helped strengthen Indian opposition to American racism, laying the foundation for independent India's support for Black freedom struggles. While the efforts of Indian and African American activists converged upon a global double victory campaign, large numbers of African American soldiers traveled to India. The American military ensured that Jim Crow traveled with them. While exporting segregation throughout the world, the army struggled to minimize the consequences of that segregation on America's reputation in "colored" countries such as India. Army propaganda failed to convince many Indians, who developed friendships with African American soldiers while seeing American racism with their own eyes.

A Jim Crow Army in India

"The easy-going social democracy of the Americans, their generosity with their resources, personal and official, may have had a greater impact on India than could be imagined at the time." So declared the third and final volume of the United States Army's official history of the China-Burma-India theater of World War II. Americans, it was argued in the volume, were walking "suggestions that not every society insisted on rigid caste distinction."[99] According to President Roosevelt's personal advisor to India, Indians were learning a different lesson from their encounters with Americans. In 1943 William Phillips wrote Roosevelt that "as time goes on, Indians are coming more and more to disbelieve in the American gospel of freedom of oppressed peoples." "Color consciousness," Phillips warned, "is also appearing more and more and under present conditions is bound to develop."[100] Such contrasting views on the impact in India of American soldiers evidence a complicated reality that resulted from the fact that there was not one but two American armies in India—one white and one Black.

From the day they registered for duty, African American soldiers faced racial discrimination, both official and unofficial. Jim Crow followed African American soldiers abroad, where they often traveled on segregated ships, ate in segregated mess halls, slept in segregated tents, and labored and fought in segregated platoons.[101] In India, Black troops built the Ledo road, transported arms and equipment from the ports of Calcutta, Bombay, and Karachi, and worked to prevent a Japanese advance—all in segregated units. One Black sergeant, Jeffries Basset Jones, worked as a truck driver, ferrying supplies and weapons over the perilous Ledo road. "During the monsoon," Jones remembered, "the mud on the Ledo was worse than driving on ice." While narrating his own wartime service, Jones recalled the equally dangerous work of the African American engineers and laborers who used bulldozers and shovels to construct and maintain the narrow mountainous roads. Despite the fact that the vast majority of drivers were African American, Jones remembered, the first honorary convoy to travel the completed road had only one African American driver. Segregation was maintained even in remote areas of Assam, close to Japanese-controlled Burma, where the segregated Ninth Cavalry, long known as "buffalo soldiers," patrolled the jungle on horseback.[102]

Army segregation in India was not absolute. Life for Black soldiers could be "friendly and hospitable," especially in Calcutta, where the largely female Black Red Cross staff managed the Cosmos Club and where Black piano player Teddy Wetherford regularly performed with an Indian band at the Grand Hotel.[103] Nevertheless, American racism fundamentally structured the experiences of Black soldiers in India. Joseph E. Davies was stationed on the opposite side of the Hoogly River from Calcutta. His work consisted of traveling to the King George docks by truck, loading equipment, weapons, and supplies, and driving from the docks to warehouses or to an air base. White troops, Davies remembered, were billeted in hotels or had camps with easy access to the city. The 4052nd, on the other hand, was kept far from Calcutta and thus had a more difficult time getting into the city for recreation. Once they were in the city, African American soldiers were limited to a segregated Red Cross club.[104] Louis Douglas, private first class in the Army Air Force from Marion, Indiana, also found racial prejudice in India. Soon after arriving in India, he and a group of Black soldiers traveled to a theater outside of Bombay where they encountered a group of white Americans who taunted them, calling them "nigger."[105] Evelio Grillo, a Black soldier of Cuban descent, served thirty-two months in Assam. Although he faced fourteen bouts of malaria and was twice bombed by the Japanese, Grillo found most difficult the racial discrimination practiced within the army. Throughout his life, he maintained "a certain bitterness, because it was unbelievable the way we were treated."[106] Herman Perry, another Black soldier who resisted Jim Crow, met a more tragic end. After killing a white officer, twice escaping custody, and living in the jungle, married to a Naga girl, Perry was hung by the army in India in the spring of 1945.[107]

African American soldiers resisted the racial inequality and discrimination they faced in India. At the end of August 1945 the headquarters of the India-Burma theater forwarded to Washington a secret report discussing the "participation of Negro Troops in the Post-War Military Establishment." The report concluded, "Racial sensitivity is noticeable among almost all Negro officers, and easily leads to agitation, non-cooperation, and charges of racial discrimination."[108] African American soldiers refused to quietly accept unequal treatment. Black soldiers in the Army Air Force actively complained when their rest camp facilities were inadequate, and even after their facilities were improved, they continued to complain about segregation.[109] Another secret army document revealed the ability of African American newspapers, in conjunction with supportive Black officers, to inspire Black troops to protest. Dated November 21, 1944, the report warned that "inadequate recreational facilities" were causing "dissension among negro troops." After quoting a white officer that "white troops were treated better than Negro troops, both in the way of recreational facilities and the amount of rest allowed," the report stated, "The negro chaplain of SOURCE's group, Captain A. C. Jones, did much to stir up racial hatred by asking and urging Negro troops to request unreasonable things. Another source of agitation was a Negro newspaper, published in Pittsburgh, which was allowed to be delivered and which caused much discontentment on the racial question and gave very little actual news." Thus the army's report indicated the important roles that officers (Chaplain Jones) and the African American press (*The Pittsburgh Courier*) played in encouraging protest.[110] Consistent protests regarding discriminatory treatment by military police led to positions for Black MPs being created near the end of the war. Protests also led the military to find a new rest camp site near Calcutta for Black troops.[111]

Protests did not, however, succeed in combating the importation of Jim Crow practices into India.

In the spring of 1945 a new Red Cross swimming pool in Calcutta was opened on a segregated basis. One Black soldier wrote home that the "Master Race" had built a swimming pool while racially segregating its use, and that 95 percent of the officers were of the "Master Race" and thus received better benefits.[112] A group of African American soldiers organized a boycott, convincing the majority of Black soldiers to avoid the pool even on those days when it was reserved for "colored" troops. The commanding officer of the Base Section blamed Deton Brooks, a reporter for *The Chicago Defender*.[113] Brooks, while taking no credit for the boycott, did his best to publicize it, sending two articles to *The Defender*, one of which declared, "Dixie tradition won a smashing victory last week when it was announced that the palatial swimming pool, newly-built in Calcutta, would be run on Jim-Crow basis." When Black soldiers were excluded from a Fourth of July celebration at the pool sponsored by the Red Cross, nearly the entire staff of the Cosmos Club, the Black Red Cross club, signed a letter of protest sent to Red Cross headquarters. Several of the volunteers, including Geraldine Smith, a teacher from Chicago and the assistant director of the Cosmos Club, resigned in protest.[114] On its part, the army's report presented the segregation of the pool as equitable, adding, "Complaining of segregation, however, Negroes have completely boycotted the pool." The word "however" implied that the demands of African American soldiers were unreasonable. In addition, a reader twice crossed out the word "completely," as if such an excision could limit the forcefulness of the boycott. Further minimizing the importance of the protest, the report referred to the boycott as a "token Negro protest." Finally, the word "Negro" was crossed off. Thus an effort by African American soldiers and Red Cross volunteers to protest the inequality of Jim Crow segregation in Calcutta was rendered as a colorless "token protest."[115]

The army tried to present the experiences of African American soldiers in the best possible light, in part out of concern for Indian opinion. In 1942 the War Information Bureau produced a "propaganda film of coloured troops, their activities, recreational facilities and mode of living in India." Shot in Karachi and finished in Bombay, the film aimed to improve Indian views of the American army. Army strategists recognized that many Indians viewed American soldiers as perpetuating British imperialism, if not presaging some form of American rule. The Davies memo, prepared in anticipation of large American troop deployments in the subcontinent, demonstrated the breadth of Indian opposition to

American racism. Another army document drew on the Davies memo to declare that Indians were beginning "to project the role of mastery from the British to all white men and to identify the colored skin as a symbol of servitude."[116]

Even before large numbers of American troops arrived in India, Walter White shared his concerns regarding the foreign consequences of American racism with General Frederick D. Osborn, chief of the Special Services branch of the War Department. White wrote, "We have had disturbing rumors of occurrences in India and China caused by the racial attitude towards colored peoples of some of the American white troops from Texas, Mississippi, Louisiana, and Arkansas which have been sent to the Far East." On June 16, 1942, White publicly declared that he had heard "disturbing rumors . . . of Southern soldiers treating Indians and Chinese as they are accustomed to treat with impunity Negroes in darkest Mississippi." White's concerns about American segregation abroad led him to plan to visit Black soldiers in the United Kingdom and various British colonies, including India. His desire to meet with Gandhi and Nehru and his vocal support for Indian independence inspired considerable anxiety within the British government.[117]

For over fifty years scholars, social reformers, and political figures had rhetorically juxtaposed the freedom struggles of African Americans and Indians. The war thrust British imperialism and American racism into direct contact and, for the first time, brought large numbers of African Americans to India. Not all Indians welcomed the arrival of Black troops. A reporter for the *New York Times* found a disjunction between the colored cosmopolitanism of African American soldiers and the feelings of Indians toward African Americans. "The Negroes have their troubles," the reporter explained, "for the Indian people do not know how to treat them. Negroes think of East Indians as colored, like themselves, but the Indians have other ideas."[118]

Dan Burley, an African American pianist and journalist, visited Calcutta during the war and was disturbed by the "marked attitude of aloofness the average Indian showed towards black-American soldiers." He found a "superiority complex" directed against Blacks "in every caste of Indian life with the emphasis on the upper class Indian." Burley placed partial blame on the "many fantastic stories" concerning Blacks that were "circulated by the American white man among Indians of all classes." Still, Burley argued, "Indians should be the last people on earth to discriminate or to be influenced by those who want such an attitude to exist among coloured peoples, all of whom were oppressed and exploited." Burley asked one Indian acquaintance, "Can't there be a unity of ideals between the African-

American, the Indian, Burmese, Chinese, Malayan and others of the coloured races of the world?" "After all," he pleaded, "I belong to a dark group, you belong to one, and as the average Black-American feels, there should be a sense of kinship among us all that would bring us closer together on grounds of mutual interest." Burley's Indian interlocutor responded curtly, "You are powerless and we know it over here."[119]

The army's report on segregation in India noted two sources of conflict between African American soldiers and Indian civilians: labor disputes and sexual relations with Indian women. Several officers mentioned assaults by African American soldiers upon Indian laborers. There is no evidence that such tensions were more common in "Negro" units than in white units. In regard to questions of sex, however, white officers tended to stress differences between African American and white soldiers, echoing the common stereotype of the lascivious Black male. Others traced tensions between Blacks and Indians "to the fact that native persons here are of a dark race, and the negro fails to respect their rights and privacy, and seeks more openly to obtain satisfaction for his sexual desires than he would with a populace of Europeans." In opposition to these claims, some officers denied that Black soldiers were especially aggressive in their pursuit of Indian women. "While Negro troops have a tendency to pursue Indian women," the commanding officer of the Army Air Forces wrote, "as a whole they have caused no more trouble to Military Police than White soldiers."[120]

In Calcutta a handful of incidents occurred in which Black soldiers seriously wounded Indian taxi drivers, although there is no evidence that race played a factor in these assaults. Bengali anti-black prejudice was revealed in rumors that black soldiers kidnapped children and, according to at least one confiscated letter, ate them.[121] Although more likely a result of unequal pay, one African American soldier remembered caste as a component of tensions with Indian soldiers. Corporal Charles Pitman remembered, "The East Indian troops we encountered under British command would have nothing to do with Negro soldiers. They looked upon us as outcasts." He added, however, "The Indian people were cool to us at first but once they found we were not like the lies told about us they became friendly."[122]

A variety of sources support Pitman's more optimistic conclusions, revealing that despite the prevalence of tensions between Indians and African American soldiers, the presence of Black troops in India reinforced Indian solidarity with African American struggles. Soon after African American soldiers began arriving in India, *The Chicago Defender* noted, "Native Indians are reported charmed and pleased with their influx, because not only do they realize that these uniformed men are there to defend their country, but the Indians realize also that these dark men are their brother from across the sea."[123] Deton Brooks offered a largely positive assessment of relations between Black soldiers and Indians. At a social club for Black soldiers in Karachi, for example, he noted that Indians regularly attended dinners and dances with Black troops.[124] In Bombay the communist paper *People's War* reported on a meeting between a racially diverse group of American sailors and local Indian activists. After discussing the "Negro problem" with the American guests, one Indian reporter realized that "Freedom for All" was "becoming the watchword of this war all over the globe." The following year, the *People's War* reported on the Detroit race riot. "With the Japanese attack on the United States," the paper concluded, "the Negroes almost unanimously took up the position that their contribution to the defeat of fascism would advance their cause, as it was the cause of all coloured and subject peoples."[125] In its enthusiasm to promote the anti-fascist struggle, *People's War* overlooked the fact that many African Americans—like their Indian counterparts—remained deeply skeptical about fighting for freedom in Europe when so much remained to be done at home. Nevertheless, by linking the war to the struggle for racial equality, *People's War* advocated a global double victory, grounded in connections between "colored and subject peoples" worldwide.

The army's report on segregation in India concluded, "All except one of the major area commanders of this Theater agree that Negroes get along with civilians (predominantly dark-skinned) in India-Burma Theater as well or better than do White troops." As an example of amicable relations between Indians and Black soldiers, one officer stated, "Negroes frequently are invited to attend native civilian parties to which White troops are not invited." Others reported that Black troops were "invited to the best Indian homes." Another officer declared, "Negro troops of this command gave no trouble in relation to Indian civilians; both being of dark color the clashes usually prevalent between Whites and Blacks were not present."[126] Such repeated emphasis on the importance of darkness as a bridge between Indians and African American soldiers could be explained as another indication of racial prejudices on the part of white officers. However, the specificity of examples of positive interaction these officers offered suggests that African American soldiers and Indians were able to forge solidarities, based in part on colored cosmopolitanism and a shared opposition to racial oppression.

In 1944 a confidential army intelligence report warned its readers, "Natives of India closely watch any indication of American discrimination against the Negro soldiers." Based on the testimony of an American businessman who had lived in Calcutta from 1937 until 1944, the report explained that African American soldiers "in the natural course of conversation" often discussed with Indian civilians the injustices that they faced at home. In addition to sharing conversations with African American soldiers, Indian civilians directly witnessed official army segregation and the racism of individual white American soldiers. By 1943, the anonymous informant claimed, Indians in Calcutta "were constantly bringing up the subject of racial prejudice in the United States when talking to American citizens." Speaking of American racial discrimination, he warned, "Natives who have had any formal education have evidenced a great interest in the problem since it has a corollary with the problem between British and natives in India." The informant had worked for the Indian Red Cross for six months in 1944. He used his experience to reveal a dimension of the African American boycott of the Calcutta Red Cross club that other army documents had failed to recognize. He explained that denying Blacks entry to the club touched an especially raw nerve with Indians who themselves had recently been denied use of British recreational clubs.[127]

Calcutta newspapers reveal widespread Bengali interest in American race relations. Several papers offered regular coverage of race in the United States, in addition to reporting on the activities of black soldiers in Calcutta.[128] The racial segregation of American troops found Indian critics outside of Calcutta as well. Frene Talyarkham, a columnist for the *Sind Observer,* an English language paper published in Karachi, used her column "Strictly Feminine" to publish an "open letter to the Unknown American soldier." Talyarkham spoke directly to the "pale face" American GI suffering from "that dread fever—anti-Negro—a fever which is a hundred times more dangerous than any jungle malady." After criticizing white troops not only for their prejudices but for refusing to discuss them openly, Talyarkham proclaimed, "To us it is indeed shocking and disappointing to find that you Americans are still suffering from Negro hatred—you, who have always stood for democracy, freedom and liberty." Talyarkham ended her column with advice and a warning:

> Remember that the colored soldier is fighting for you, not against you. Remember, he is your countryman. He has a right to breathe the same air as you. He, too, has a birthright. Remember all these things, soldier, because you are fighting and dying for the ideals of democracy, at least so it is said. When peace comes, we shall be waiting and watching.[129]

In 1954 African American author Jay Saunders Redding quoted Talyarkham's column in his book *An American in India.* After Talyarkham's warning, "we shall be waiting and watching," Redding added, "And when the peace did come and America's relations with Russia deteriorated, the Communists were quick to promote the conviction that the Indian people waited and watched in vain." Thus Redding argued that American racial discrimination contributed to the spread of communism in independent India. Like Talyarkham, Redding pointed to the role that World War II played in shaping Indian opinions of American racism. He stated that Indians "knew the catalogue of race hatred compiled by American officers commanding Negro troops in India during the war."[130] Redding linked the knowledge of American racial discrimination that Indians gained during the war to the widespread opposition to American racism that Redding himself encountered throughout India in 1954. He argued that Indian opposition to American racial oppression was too embedded to be easily undone and too important to be overlooked. If Americans wanted to check Soviet advances, they would have to combat racial injustice at home.

The strategy of utilizing the Cold War to achieve racial equality originated during the Second World War when advocates of global double victory creatively employed the threat of losing India to Japan as a tool to pressure recalcitrant American officials. During the Cold War, civil rights activists employed the same tactic, arguing that Indian support in the Cold War hinged on the achievement of American racial equality. Ultimately the global double victory campaign had little impact on the timing of Indian independence, but it did influence independent India's foreign policy by strengthening Indian concern for American racism and the plight of the "colored world" more generally. Indian opposition to American racism helped compel American politicians and government officials, afraid of "losing" India to communism, to dismantle the most blatant forms of racial discrimination. By strengthening Indian opposition to American racism, the global double victory campaign contributed to the successes of the American civil rights movement.[131]

Looking ahead to the postwar period should not obscure the hopes and failures of global double victory activists during the war. An observer in 1945 would have rightly concluded that the global double victory campaign had largely failed to influence decision making in the White House or at Whitehall. To assess fully the significance of global double victory during the war requires, however, looking beyond power politics and high diplomacy. On July 4, 1944, Gandhi told an American reporter, "Freedom for India will bring hope to Asiatics and other exploited nations. Today there is no hope for the Negroes, but Indian freedom will fill them with hope."[132] An overemphasis on the strategic dimensions of global double victory fails to acknowledge the importance of the hope that came with belonging to a worldwide movement. In 1942 Horace Cayton stated, "Whereas for years Negroes have felt that their position was isolated and unalterable, some of them are now beginning to feel that dark people throughout the world will soon be on the march."[133] Indians, including Gandhi himself, played a crucial role in inspiring that feeling of global colored unity.

In the spring of 1945 Deton Brooks, *The Chicago Defender* reporter the army blamed for instigating the boycott of the Calcutta swimming pool, arranged a brief interview with Gandhi. Using the respectful "Gandhiji," Brooks asked, "Is there any special message you would care to send to the Negro people of America?" Gandhi replied, "My life is its own message." Taken alone, these words speak eloquently to Gandhi's optimism about the unity of his life and the transnational applicability of his ideas. In his interview with Brooks, however, Gandhi immediately added a more somber note. He said, "My life is its own message. If it is not, then nothing I can now write will fulfill the purpose." Gandhi's words were printed in *The Chicago Defender,* along with his assertion that "We are fast approaching a solution to the troublesome race problem." "Indicating that his own life stands as a beacon of hope to all underprivileged peoples who are fighting injustice throughout the world," Brooks told his readers, "Gandhi, by his remarks, sent a message of cheer to the Negroes of the United States."[134] After India gained independence, African Americans would help revitalize the race/caste analogy, reminding Indians, as Gandhi himself did, that *swaraj* was not merely the absence of foreign rule but the presence of justice and democracy for all of India's citizens.

CHAPTER SIX

Building a Third World

Gandhi and Nehru have been heroes in Mississippi no less
than in Bombay.
—St. Clair Drake, "Brother India"

N AUGUST 1946 African American sociologist St. Clair Drake reminded readers of *The Pittsburgh Courier* that African Americans
had long understood "India's fight as an integral part of the struggle everywhere against white imperialism and political domination."
Drake was disturbed, however, by "some mounting evidence that a Free
India might conceivably act somewhat different from an India in the
throes of a struggle for independence." Indian students in the United
States had "a tendency to shun Negroes as though they were lepers."
Shifting his focus to South and East Africa, Drake castigated Indian merchants and money lenders who had developed "a very bad record of exploitation." "When Gandhi and Nehru support the fight against jim-
crow of Indians in Africa, but fail to speak out against the terrible
exploitation of Negro natives there (some of it by Indians)," Drake told
his Black readers, "we have reason to fear for the future."[1]

Drake's article carried the subtitle, "Undoubtedly Brother Goshal Will
Answer the Question Raised Here by Bro. Drake." Since 1942 Kumar Goshal had published a weekly editorial in *The Courier* entitled "As an Indian
Sees It." Goshal responded to Drake's concerns in two separate editorials.
He stated that when he spoke at an African American church in Detroit, he
found that a "large Indian population" regularly attended events at the
church. Far from allaying Drake's concerns, however, Goshal agreed that
Blacks should worry about the future of independent India. He portrayed
the Indian struggle as a temporary alliance of "conservatives, liberals, and

St. Clair Drake, "Brother India," *The Pittsburgh Courier,* August 3, 1946, 7.

radicals," an alliance that had already begun to dissolve as freedom approached. Relating Indian support for Black struggles to India's domestic politics, Goshal asserted that it was the Indian Left who would best serve the cause of freedom worldwide. He did not attempt to comfort Drake or the Black readers of *The Courier* but, rather, challenged them to prevent the U.S. government from bolstering Indian "reactionaries."[2]

In the wake of Indian independence, advocates of colored cosmopolitanism strove to make India a bulwark for the rising colored world. Aware that Afro-Indian solidarity was the fragile product of many years of concerted effort, internationally minded activists such as Cedric Dover and Kamaladevi Chattopadhyaya appealed to the Indian public and to Indian power brokers, especially Jawaharlal Nehru. They strove to make August 15, 1947, a turning point not only for India but also for Indian unity with the colored world. Colored cosmopolitans opposed racism without fully abandoning the claims of race. In part because colored cosmopolitanism appealed most strongly to those on the left, socialists and communists continued to play a central role in bridging African American and Indian freedom struggles, even as the onset of the Cold War made their position increasingly tenuous.

In combination with Indian independence, the Cold War endowed Indian colored cosmopolitanism with the potential to advance racial equality in the United States. With India under British rule, advocates of global double victory had little leverage to force changes in American government policy toward racial discrimination and inequality. After 1947, however, Indian opinion helped pressure American presidents, Supreme Court justices, and diplomatic officials, afraid of losing the propaganda battle of the Cold War, to resolve civil rights crises and to instigate significant domestic reforms.[3] The link between the Cold War and American civil rights depended on the degree to which Afro-Indian solidarity worried powerful figures in the United States. Would American racism complicate relations with independent India? A bloody partition had rendered colonial India not one but two independent nations—both confronting not only endemic poverty and political instability but also millions of dispossessed refugees. The need for American aid provided a powerful incentive for Indian officials to temper their critiques of American racism. Nevertheless, old relationships between Black and Indian leaders and the prevalence of an expansive conception of Indian freedom inspired a significant, if muted, opposition to American racism on the part of Nehru and other Indian government figures. This muted opposition was amplified in importance by India's strategic significance and by Nehru's effort to chart a middle course between American and Soviet influence. At the same time, Indian public opinion pressured Indian leaders to express solidarity with African Americans while itself worrying American politicians concerned with India's position in the Cold War.

By inspiring Indian opposition to American racial oppression and communicating that opposition to American politicians, African American activists linked the Cold War and the civil rights movement. Even Blacks who traveled to India to "represent" the United States attempted to serve as advocates of global double victory by alerting the American public to Indian opposition to American racism. They faced the challenge of defending the United States in the propaganda battle of the Cold War while facing tough questions from Indians regarding American racial oppression. For them, as for Indian government officials, the demands of the nation strained and at times eclipsed the bonds of color.

When challenged with questions regarding race in the United States, Americans in India, white and Black, often responded by criticizing caste inequality. The opportunity for meaningful reflections between Black and Dalit struggles was largely lost, however, as race/caste comparisons became little more than defensive maneuvers in the Cold War. Cold War civil rights advocates, while successfully applying pressure on American diplomats to confront American racism, did little to assist the struggles of low-caste Indians. National political figures in India had already denounced untouchability, outlawing it along with any discrimination based on caste. Thus international pressure at the top levels of government had less potential benefit in India than in the United States.

The failure of the Cold War civil rights framework to address caste oppression productively was part of a larger failure that resulted from the nature of the Cold War itself. In the United States, anticommunist witch hunts narrowed the vocabulary with which Blacks and Indians expressed solidarity. Although Left-leaning colored cosmopolitans did the most to inspire the Indian concern that undergirded Cold War civil rights, the two Black figures most admired in India, Paul Robeson and W. E. B. Du Bois, were both harassed by the American government and largely abandoned by mainstream civil rights organizations such as the NAACP. In India and other "non-aligned" former colonies, notions of a "Third World" promised to avoid the dichotomies of the Cold War but, like the renowned Asian African Conference, held at Bandung in April 1955, nevertheless fell victim to the same hegemonic notions of the imperial nation-state that motivated both Cold War superpowers. The achievements of Cold War civil rights and of the Third World, while significant, failed to realize the full potential of the long history of connections between Indian and African American freedom struggles.[4]

Indian Independence and Colored Cosmopolitanism

On February 23, 1948, a diverse assembly of distinguished scholars, activists, and community leaders gathered at New York's Roosevelt Hotel to celebrate the eightieth birthday of W. E. B. Du Bois. A small group of notables, including Fisk University president Charles Johnson, NAACP president Arthur Spingarn, and a young historian named John Hope Franklin sat at the front of the room, alongside Du Bois, looking out on the crowd from an elevated platform. A "Eurasian" writer born in Calcutta in 1904 and originally trained as an entomologist might seem to be out of place on the dais. Cedric Dover, however, had earned his place on that platform. Since his first visit to the United States in 1937, Dover had deepened his friendships with many African Americans while writing and speaking against prevailing hierarchies of race and nation. In 1947 Dover moved to Nashville, Tennessee, to teach at Fisk University, a prestigious African American college, where Du Bois himself had studied. In addition to teaching at Fisk and the New School for Social Research in New York, Dover spoke to a variety of nonacademic audiences, consistently promoting a global alliance of "colored" peoples.[5]

Dover organized the Du Bois birthday gala with the express purpose of celebrating the leadership Du Bois had long offered the colored world. In a letter to Du Bois written in 1946, Dover called Du Bois "the most internationally minded man the coloured world has ever known." He suggested a selected edition of Du Bois's writings, to be called *Eighty Years a Black Man,* that would become "a one-volume classic which coloured men everywhere, and those whites who sense what is happening, will treasure as *their* book."[6] In November 1947, six months before the birthday gala, Dover wrote Du Bois that "it would be a cultural and political tragedy for the colored peoples of the world if we allowed your eightieth birthday to pass without some major acknowledgment to your inspiration and labour, which would be at once an expression of our own solidarity and a token of our regard for the elder brother of the whole coloured family."[7] As Dover had hoped, the birthday party became a celebration not only of Du Bois but of the colored world he had for so long championed. The highlight of the evening for Dover came when he conveyed birthday greetings from Jawaharlal Nehru, prime minister of a newly independent India. "India will always remember," Nehru wrote of Du Bois, "his sympathy during her struggle for freedom." Of Nehru's birthday salutation for Du Bois, Dover would later write, "It was a greeting for a people, as well as its greatest representative. It also seemed to me a promise for the future."[8]

Dover strove to redeem Nehru's "promise" by making independent India a bulwark for the rising colored world. When Yusuf Meherally, former mayor of Bombay and a leading Congress Socialist, visited New York for medical treatment, Dover wrote Du Bois suggesting that an official NAACP committee visit Meherally and issue a press statement that might "find its way into several papers here and in India and would greatly help our 'feeling' of solidarity."[9] Dover also attempted to enlist the help of Nehru himself. On June 7, 1948, he wrote Nehru, thanking him for the birthday telegram Nehru had sent Du Bois and proclaiming that "a cumulative effect has resulted from the realisation that such a message from the highest level in India was a token of a larger interest and sympathy." Dover suggested that Nehru invite distinguished African Americans to India. At the top of Dover's list, not surprisingly, was Du Bois. Dover also suggested the philosopher and cultural critic Alain Locke, the sociologist E. Franklin Frazier, the painter Aaron Douglas, and the poet Arna Bontemps, whose "family background," Dover noted, "includes some East Indian mixture." Dover emphasized the ability of these Black cultural diplomats to improve American opinion of India. He assured Nehru that they would "influence public opinion when they return." Dover forwarded Du Bois his letter to Nehru, to which Du Bois responded, "It would certainly be a realization of my life's ambition to be able to see and know India."[10] Du Bois would, however, never visit the subcontinent. Nehru agreed that inviting "eminent Negroes" to India was "a valuable suggestion" but hesitated to implement the plan, citing "weather and other conditions."[11] As we will see, Nehru's willingness to devote time and resources to Black struggles was limited not only by the demands of a newly independent nation but also by his desire to not upset the American government.

In his efforts to make the Indian nation a champion of Black struggles, Dover aimed well beyond influencing Nehru and other government officials. He strove to generate a cultural bond between Blacks and Indians. In 1947, Dover published a book in Bombay entitled *Feathers in the Arrow: An Approach for Coloured Writers and Readers*. *Feathers in the Arrow* was based upon an article Dover had originally published in *Phylon: The Atlanta Review of Race and Culture*. *Phylon* had been founded by Du Bois in 1940, and it was to Du Bois that Dover dedicated *Feathers in the Arrow*, lauding "the muscular scholarship Dr. Du Bois has devoted for six decades to the causes, potentialities and unity of the coloured world." In November 1947 Dover sent Du Bois a copy of *Feathers in the Arrow*. In the acknowledgments, Dover wrote, "In the dark yesterdays no group in the United States supported the Indian struggle more sympathetically and energetically than the Negroes." Dover promised, "We shall not forget this debt.

And, as our fortunes change, we will not neglect to repay it."[12] Dover's "we" spoke for all those recently free of the British Raj, including citizens of Pakistan. The "fortunes" Dover saw changing were those of an independent South Asia, understood not as a grouping of nation-states but as the beginning of a free and independent colored world.[13]

Dover's *Phylon* article was entitled "Notes on Coloured Writing." By revising it for publication in Bombay, Dover demonstrated one of the key themes of his "Notes"—that writing across racial and national boundaries offered unique opportunities for the "coloured" author. "Notes on Coloured Writing" and *Feathers in the Arrow* contain Dover's most revealing explication of colored cosmopolitanism. In what had become for Dover a standard refrain, he proclaimed, "If we have penetrated the question of 'race,' we must deny the very existence of human races." For Dover, denying "race" did not entail repudiating racialized unities. His was a counterracist racialism. Dover explained:

> We must combat racialism, and its attendant inhumanity and degeneration, wherever we meet it, whether it comes from the Great Race or ourselves. And yet we must in a sense be "racial" in our immediate loyalties and consciousness, and we must first seek our wider alliances amongst peoples bound to us by the symbol of colour and the facts of circumstance. That is to say we must be both "racial" and anti-racial at the same time, which really means that nationalism and internationalism must be combined in the same philosophy.[14]

A partial cosmopolitanism, partial toward "the symbol of colour," guided Dover's search for unity in difference. By striving to be "racial" and "anti-racial," "national" and "international," Dover called into question rigid boundaries of "race" and "nation." Having complicated these categories, Dover put them to work in the global struggle against inequality and injustice. His colored cosmopolitanism left room for "racialism" and "nationalism" as long as races and nations continued to struggle against various forms of racism and imperialistic nationalism.

Although he aimed to articulate a colored solidarity that avoided "racialism, and its attendant inhumanity and degeneration," Dover's writings at times employed dubious notions of culture that approximated the racialism he denounced. Charles Glicksberg, associate professor at Brooklyn College, attacked Dover's equation of race and culture in a detailed response to *Feathers in the Arrow,* published in *Phylon* in 1951. In his "Notes on Coloured Writing," Dover framed colored solidarity as a response to what he saw as the impossibility of full engagement with white "American" or "British" cultures. Glicksberg rightly criticized Dover's definition of culture, defending the ability of Black Americans to produce

American literature of the highest quality. Glicksberg chose to aim his strongest ire, however, at a less worthy target—Dover's notion of colored unity. Glicksberg labeled as "exasperating moonshine" what he took to be Dover's belief in "a mysterious correspondence of cultures, a profound calling of color to color, blood to blood." Glicksberg criticized Dover for propagating a "mystical, blood-and-soil theory of language" that, Glicksberg argued, logically "culminates in the racist doctrines of the Nazis." He acknowledged that Dover "would certainly repudiate such an interpretation," but he failed to properly credit Dover for his denunciation of racial chauvinism.[15]

The crude, chauvinistic notion of colored solidarity that Glicksberg critiqued bore little resemblance to Dover's antiracialist project. In a response to Glicksberg, published in *Phylon,* Dover attempted to defend the possibility of being "'racial' and anti-racial at the same time." Dover argued that colored solidarity would serve as a bridge between local solidarities and a global universalism. "This is the paradox that naïve internationalists do not understand: that the 'narrow' but richly conceived things," he wrote, "are those that gradually move toward universality." Dover embraced universality as a goal to be achieved through, and not at the expense of, more limited affiliations. He and Glicksberg were not as opposed to each other's ideas as they believed. Both strove to envision unities that allowed for internal diversity and sought a world free of rigid hierarchies and open to multiple loyalties.[16]

As an author and contributing editor for the journal *United Asia,* which began publication in Bombay in 1948, Dover strove to encourage Indians to understand themselves as part of a large and vibrant colored world. In June 1953 Dover organized a "Special Symposium on the American Negro." With essays by an impressive range of scholars, including Du Bois, John Hope Franklin, Charles Johnson, and Alain Locke, the symposium treated its readers to a diverse examination of African American history, society, and culture. In keeping with Dover's emphasis on the arts, the symposium abounded with poetry, including pieces by Sterling Brown, Countee Cullen, and Claude McKay. Langston Hughes contributed a short anthology of his twelve favorite poems, as well as a selection of his own work. Photographs of African American sculpture and painting were reproduced from Alain Locke's *The Negro in Art.* The symposium embodied Dover's belief in the power of art and literature to inspire Indian solidarity with African Americans.[17]

Contributions to the "Symposium on the American Negro" ranged from ringing endorsements of colored solidarity to skeptical assessments of the claims of color. In a revealing note, the editors of *United Asia* wrote that "the presence of pigment on human skins marks out Asia (and Africa) from the rest of the world as markedly as the oceans separate them on the map." They asked, "Is there any significance in this?" and answered, "We do not know."[18] The editors referred to the United States as a country where racial prejudice was "rapidly passing," a claim both supported and contested by the symposium itself. Charles Johnson's foreword credited international opinion with narrowing racial inequalities in the United States. Beneath a photo of himself with Jawaharlal Nehru, he explained that "the political codes are naturally responsive to international opinion, which grows more and more interested in the status and achievements of American Negroes."[19] Johnson did not explain how American "political codes" responded to international opinion, but the fact that the symposium concluded with an essay by the American ambassador to India revealed one important link between foreign opinion and domestic politics. Ambassador George Allen's essay demonstrated a sensitivity to Indian criticism that had been heightened by the Cold War.[20]

In an ambitious introduction to the symposium, Dover defended colored unity while offering a less optimistic portrayal of domestic American politics than the editors, Charles Johnson, or Allen. Since the days of slavery, Dover declared, African Americans had "survived every violation that human viciousness could invent." He praised African Americans for noticing "every injustice, every achievement, in the farthest corners of the 'coloured world.'" In particular, Dover noted the decades of sympathy and support African Americans had shared with the Indian struggle for independence. It was a shame, Dover wrote, that "no Indian group, political or otherwise, has seriously tried to repay the debt we owe to so many Negro friends."[21] In his writings and his editing and through his personal contacts, Dover strove to encourage Indians to repay the "debt" he felt they owed African Americans. In the context of the Cold War, even a vocal minority of Indians had the potential to influence American domestic policy. Still, Dover's efforts alone would have been too insignificant to inspire a robust opposition to American racism among the Indian public or within the smaller circles in which Indian foreign policy was determined. Dover was, however, far from alone in encouraging Indians to support African American struggles.

Kamaladevi Chattopadhyaya forged connections between independent India and the larger colored world. After her visit to the United States, Kamaladevi repeatedly criticized American racism and praised the initiative of African Americans. In 1946 she published *America: The Land of Superlatives*. At the beginning of a chapter dedicated to African American struggles, Kamaladevi wrote, "The biggest blot on the fair name of America is the problem of the Negro." She located the "negro problem" not only within the context of American democracy but within the global "struggle between the dispossessed coloured world and the ruling white." Importantly, it was not the injustice of American racism but the democratic initiative of African Americans that Kamaladevi declared most worthy of global attention. "Rarely in history did an enslaved people get so quickly democratic-minded," she proclaimed, "and that is why this emancipation-revolution has a world importance far beyond its local and national character."[22]

Kamaladevi praised African Americans for the colored cosmopolitanism she herself demonstrated. She linked the transnational initiative of African American artists with their ability to assert cultural pride "in a broad national and international setting, not a crude racialism." Kamaladevi explained the transnational significance of contemporary African American initiatives in terms of the intersection of racism with other forms of oppression. She linked American racial discrimination to economic inequality and offered her readers an extended analysis of the economic bases of racial prejudice. Of African American art, she wrote, "When it speaks for economic equality and social justice, it speaks for the peoples of the world." For an example she turned to Paul Robeson:

> For when Paul Robeson sings he becomes something more than a singer. He transcends all human limitations and becomes the disembodied melody, which knows neither colour nor race. He interprets the ageless, deathless spirit of his lost land of Africa, his priceless heritage, before which even the hooded order of bigotry and hate spontaneously retreat.

In her praise of Robeson, Kamaladevi revealed the dual nature of her colored cosmopolitanism. She commended Robeson for transcending "colour" and "race," before lauding him for interpreting "the deathless spirit of his lost land of Africa, his priceless heritage." Kamaladevi articulated a colored cosmopolitanism that accommodated both a universalistic humanism and a more particular pride in the social, cultural, and historical roots embodied in racial identification.

After encouraging her Indian readers to learn from African Americans, Kamaladevi suggested that African Americans would benefit from the liberation struggles of Asians and Africans. She wrote:

> Soon Africa too, will come back, and come into her own, and the dark ones will cease to be the "untouchables" of the world. The international colour line has been challenged and stormed by Asia. No more the colonials will allow themselves to be jim-crowed the world over and their country looted under pseudo-slogans. The Negro problem will only cease when the colour-line of imperialism vanishes.[23]

Thus Kamaladevi placed the struggles of African Americans in a global framework in which "colonization" was akin to "Jim Crow." Kamaladevi's reference to "untouchables" reminded her readers of India's own legacy of "Jim Crow." By comparing African American struggles simultaneously to the efforts of Dalits and of all Indians, Kamaladevi demonstrated the potential of colored cosmopolitanism to combat multiple injustices. She used analogies of struggle between Indians and African Americans to situate Indian nationalism within a broader opposition to the intersection of imperialism, racism, and oppressions based on gender, class, and caste. It remained to be seen how much Kamaladevi's endeavors, or those of other colored cosmopolitans such as Cedric Dover, could influence politics in the United States or India. Kamaladevi and Dover, like many advocates of Afro-Indian solidarity, were socialists. Ironically, it would be American fears of international socialism, and especially of the Soviet Union, that would endow colored cosmopolitanism with political power.

The Cold War and Color

In April 1953 Walter White received a letter that suggested that since India was "so vitally important to world stability and future security," the NAACP should "appeal to India as they are a dark race, to help our people in America." The letter came from one L. T. Lucas, of Buffalo, New York. "This is just a little thought from a small person," Lucas wrote earnestly. "I hope this little note will mean something."[24] The strategy that Lucas described, leveraging India's strategic importance to the United States to achieve domestic racial equality, had already become central to White's efforts as the executive director of the NAACP. During the Second World War, White had used the possibility of losing India to the Japanese to pressure reluctant American politicians into taking action to combat American racism. India's independence, coupled with the onset of the Cold War, invested Indian criticism of American racial oppression with new power. To have an impact on American politics, however, the opinions of Indians, especially powerful Indians, had to be communicated to Americans in positions of influence. As the Cold War came to increasingly dominate American politics at home and abroad, White emerged as one of the leading voices arguing that Indian support for the "free world" depended on the extension of full citizenship rights to African Americans.[25]

White's knowledge of India and his connections with powerful Indians grew rapidly during the 1940s, in part as a result of White's friendship with an influential Indian American businessman named Jagjit (J. J.) Singh. During the war, Singh emerged as one of the most prominent and politically savvy Indian American leaders. Singh's India League of America lobbied for Indian independence and the civil rights of Indian Americans, especially the rights to citizenship and immigration that Indians had lost in 1923 when Bhagat Singh Thind's claims to whiteness were rejected by the Supreme Court. Singh and White shared a passion for connecting the struggle for democracy abroad and at home. They also shared a roster of powerful white supporters and a talent for politics. The two quickly became friends. In June 1944 White accepted a position on the National Advisory Board of the India League.[26] Two months later Singh held a party for White and his family and afterward lauded White as "one of the outstanding negro leaders in this country" and "a perfectly delightful man."[27] In February 1945 White praised Singh and the India League in *The Chicago Defender*. White admitted that "most Indians still believe themselves more Aryan than the whitest-skinned, bluest-eyed Nordic," but he concluded that "the more intelligent ones like Singh begin to realize that 'white superiority' applies not only to black men in the United States and Africa but to brown and yellow men all over the world as well."[28] A few months later, when the India League received a request from Yusuf Meherally for information on "friends of India" in the United States, the India League responded by introducing Walter White.[29] In June 1947 White invited Singh to sit on the platform at the Thirty-Eighth Annual Conference of the NAACP.[30]

Masters of publicity, both White and Singh strove to influence public opinion and worked together to generate links between Black and Indian newspapers. When Devadas Gandhi, son of the Mahatma and the editor of the influential *Hindustan Times,* visited the United States, Singh telegrammed White inviting him to attend a luncheon in Chicago with Gandhi and Ramnath Goenka, an Indian newspaper publisher. After the luncheon, White telegrammed the publishers of *The Chicago Defender, The Pittsburgh Courier,* and the *Baltimore Afro-American,* alerting them that Gandhi was going to call each of them, and asking them to offer their support for India. White's efforts to connect Gandhi with these influential Black editors proved successful. On June 6, 1946, Carl Murphy of the *Afro-American* sent his contact information to Gandhi in care of the NAACP. On May 18 *The Chicago Defender* printed an interview with Gandhi, headlined "Gandhi's Son Asks Negro Aid for People of India." The *Defender* quoted Gandhi that there was "sympathy in India for all the colored peoples of the world." "The Negro people of America especially have our most whole-hearted support and sympathy for their progress," Gandhi declared. This expression of solidarity found tangible manifestation in the consistent coverage the Indian press gave to incidents of racial discrimination in the United States.[31] The following week *The Defender* carried a large photo of Devadas Gandhi, explaining that he sought "the continued aid of the American Negro people in the struggle for freedom of India's millions." In response, an African American pastor, the Reverend J. H. Edmondson, wrote *The Defender,* asking for J. J. Singh's address so that he could discuss Gandhi's appeal. The paper forwarded the request to the NAACP, which provided Singh's address to Reverend Edmondson.[32]

After Indian independence, White and Singh continued to work together, although their joint initiatives increasingly focused on securing American aid to India rather than on connecting Black and Indian struggles.[33] It would be inaccurate to draw a sharp line between White's general concern for India and his efforts to use Indian opinion to advance Black struggles. His frequent efforts to demonstrate India's importance in world affairs were related to the link he asserted between India and American racial equality. In February 1951 White telegrammed Senators Tom Connally and Guy Gillette that aiding India would demonstrate "to colored peoples of Asia, Africa, and South America as well that we favor freedom, food, and security for all men everywhere."[34] That same month, Clarence Mitchell, director of the Washington Bureau of the NAACP, encouraged the House Foreign Affairs Committee to provide aid to India. Taking his words directly from a letter from White, Mitchell declared, "We have a magnificent opportunity to show that neither race or place of birth is a determinant of American democracy and generosity."[35] White attempted to enlist J. J. Singh in advancing the connection between Indian opinion, the Cold War, and American civil rights. In May 1949 he complimented Singh on a speech he had given but added, "I kept waiting for you to point out that one of the reasons for the spread of communism in China and other parts of Asia is due in part to the lowered prestige of the United States and faith in democracy because of discrimination in America."[36] Singh may have taken White's advice, although there is evidence that Singh was all too aware of the dangers of linking Indian and African American struggles. As early as 1942, Singh had written Nehru, "In sending the representatives of India to the United States, it may be borne in mind that they should not be of too dark a complexion, because we have the Negro problem in this country."[37] The need to temper solidarities of color in order to gain American support only became stronger after India gained independence.

In the context of the Cold War, conflicts between colored solidarity and the demands of the nation-state challenged Indians and African Americans, particularly liberal anti-communists like Walter White. In 1949 White was presented with an ideal opportunity to use the Cold War to advance racial equality. Along with twenty-eight prominent Americans, White toured the world as part of "America's Town Meeting of the Air," a popular radio show. The strong interest in American race relations that the tour encountered provided White with an opportunity and a challenge. He strove to respond to questions regarding race in America in such a way as to emphasize the need for change, but without providing fuel for Soviet propaganda. In Karachi, White stated, "As an American Negro, I am deeply aware of the grave shortcomings of my own country so far as democracy for minorities is concerned." Making clear that his criticism was of American racism and not the United States itself, White put his comments to work in the Cold War. He asserted that "under democracy, minorities can fight against injustice. We are doing that in America and we are making progress." White's assurance of "progress" did not mollify a young Pakistani man, who told the panel, "You talk a great deal about your American type of democracy. But we all know what it means. We know that if a colored man even looks at a white woman in the United States, he is lynched." When a panelist responded by referencing White's relationship with Poppy Cannon, a white South African, a Pakistani woman sitting next to Cannon told her that her relationship with White was "the best argument for your American democracy."[38] It was, therefore, not surprising that White announced his marriage to Cannon on their first morning together in New Delhi. Thus a marriage that was deeply controversial in the United States among both whites and Blacks came to be employed in South Asia as a demonstration of American racial progress.

White's success at defending America's image abroad prompted the State Department to invite him to travel to India again to respond to ongoing critiques of American racism. The State Department regularly received reports that, in the words of the American consul general in Bombay, "The color question is of intense interest in India."[39] In October 1952 a State Department official sent White an article by Norman Cousins, the editor of *The Saturday Review of Literature*. Cousins had recently returned from a trip to India and Pakistan, where he found that the practice of "race prejudice and discrimination" was the "number one" topic of discussion about America. The State Department hoped that White could counter what Cousins called the "general impression that the American people have a superiority race complex."[40] White's efforts to define American racism as an impediment to American foreign policy did not, however, always receive praise from the Foreign Service. At an education conference of the UAW-CIO in 1952, White discussed the case of a man from Ceylon who "because his skin was dark" had been "humiliated in Nashville, Tennessee, and other parts of the South." The Ceylonese man became "so embittered . . . against the United States and against the democratic process itself," White reported, "that he became active in the Communist Party in Ceylon and is one of the leaders of Communism there." White's comments were published in the UAW-CIO's magazine *Ammunition*, prompting the public affairs officer of the American Embassy in Ceylon to protest that although a Colonel C. P. Jayawardana, chief of the Ceylon Boy Scouts, had been "embarrassed on a number of occasions during his visit to the United States, and in a report to the State Department gave a full account of the incidents in which he was humiliated because of the color of his skin," he was, however, still very friendly toward the United States. White refused to back down. He explained that he had never referred specifically to Jayawardana, and that his information came from an unimpeachable source.[41]

As during the Second World War, White allied with other Americans eager to connect American foreign policy to the achievement of domestic racial equality. He found a uniquely influential ally in Chester Bowles, the American ambassador to India from 1951 to 1953 and from 1963 to 1969. As the governor of Connecticut, Bowles had made clear his commitment to racial equality by desegregating the National Guard.[42] As ambassador to India, Bowles repeatedly argued that American racism undercut American initiatives abroad. In November 1951 Bowles told White, "I have met up with many questions on racial intolerance in the United States. In fact, it is a sure-fire question every time I speak."[43] From India, Bowles twice sent White copies of his progress reports.[44] In his *Ambassador's Report*, a book published in 1954, Bowles wrote, "Almost invariably the number one question was, 'what about America's treatment of the Negro?'" Although he himself was sufficiently liberal to worry about being tarred as a "communist-sympathizer," Bowles often referenced the communist menace in order to highlight the importance of protecting Indo-American relations.[45]

The link between the Cold War and civil rights received publicity from the liberal white editor of *The Atlanta Constitution*, Ralph McGill, who traveled to India in the winter of 1951–1952. McGill penned a series of articles that were later published as a book. Like Walter White and Chester Bowles, McGill found many Indians concerned about American racial discrimination. Although he presented these concerns as uneducated and driven largely by Soviet propaganda, McGill used them to highlight foreign awareness of American racism. McGill recalled for his readers the response Chester Bowles had given a group of "Communist students" who had asked why "all the congressmen in the United States belonged to the Ku

Klux Klan." Bowles answered that not more than half a dozen belonged, in McGill's words, "to that notorious and un-American organization which has been branded by the United States itself as a subversive group." Narrating this incident, McGill attacked the Klan, even while underestimating the prevalence of American racism in the U.S. government.[46]

Even as they encouraged Americans to combat racism lest they lose India to the Soviets, Walter White, Chester Bowles, Ralph McGill, and other liberal anti-communists strove to persuade Indians that America was progressing toward racial equality. Their optimism regarding race in America often evoked skepticism from Indians. A conversation McGill reported with a railway guard deserves quoting at length:

"American?" he asked.

"Yes," I said, "the Southern part."

"That's where the colored people live?" he asked, in pretty fair, but somewhat difficult-to-follow English.

"That's right," I said.

"They can't walk on the sidewalks, can they?" he queried, "or go in the shops?"

"Oh yes," I said, "things are not perfect, but much of what you read here is exaggerated."

"I read about a lot of them getting shot by men in masks."

"Not a lot of them," I said, "and the men in masks are gangsters like your own dacoits."

Placing this conversation in a Cold War context, McGill noted that the railroad guard gained his information from *Blitz*, a Left-leaning newspaper, based in Bombay, which regularly criticized the United States. McGill's version of their conversation, while presenting the guard as duped by communist exaggerations, nevertheless indicated the persistence with which many Indians denounced American racism.[47]

In an article published in *United Asia* in February 1953, Chester Bowles presented the United States as a diverse country that had gradually overcome many forms of discrimination and would soon defeat prejudice against Blacks. The text boxes chosen by the editors of *United Asia* to accompany the essay contradicted such a rosy account of American progress. Bowles described the American North as a place where "slavery had never had a firm hold and where rapidly expanding industries and agriculture offered jobs for all." In contrast, readers were offered a text box entitled "The Negro in the North," in which Otto Klineberg's *Characteristics of the American Negro* was quoted: "In the North the Negro is granted theoretical equality, but there is little personal contact between the races and little interest in the Negro on the part of the whites." African Americans, Bowles concluded, "are Americans, and determined to work out their problems as Americans." In contrast, a text box on "The Negro Newspaper" quoted P. L. Prattis, editor of *The Pittsburgh Courier:* "The nation is divided into two groups, a majority group and a minority group." What Bowles presented as a gradual process of national unification, Prattis described as a "battle for survival" within a deeply divided nation.[48]

In 1949, Prattis traveled to India for seventeen days, writing a daily account of his experiences, and publishing these accounts in consecutive issues of the *Courier.* Prattis revealed for his readers the depth and extent of Indian opposition to American racism while using Cold War tensions to underline the importance of Indian opinion. In one article, for example, Prattis discussed an edition of the *Hindustan Times,* the newspaper edited by Devadas Gandhi, in which three separate articles discussed American racial discrimination. Prattis contrasted these articles with the extensive coverage the *Hindustan Times* offered Russia's Pushkin Day, a celebration of the renowned Russian poet. Prattis reminded his audience that Pushkin was "a Negro," thus underscoring the fact that while Indians learned about American racism, they were also learning to view the Soviet Union as racially inclusive.

Prattis placed Indian opposition to racial discrimination in the context of the Cold War without himself participating in the anti-communist witch hunts increasingly common in American discourse. By drawing on the concern that Jawaharlal Nehru expressed for Paul Robeson, Prattis courageously offered his readers muted sympathy for leftists such as Robeson. Over lunch one day, Nehru expressed his desire that Robeson would visit India and asked Prattis how Robeson was viewed by Black Americans. Prattis told Nehru that "Negroes were proud of Robeson, regardless of his extreme political position, but they could not afford to follow him." Prattis added that "in the light of the present attitude in the United States toward communism" it was dangerous for Blacks to cooperate with communists, "even though it might be right in principle." Thus Prattis avoided the risks of directly embracing embattled leftists, but without offering support to their anti-communist opponents.[49]

Even more than Jawaharlal Nehru, it was Kamaladevi Chattopadhyaya that emerged in Prattis's articles as an icon of Indian support for Black struggles. On his third day in India, Prattis met Kamaladevi at her home. In his article that day, he mentioned Kamaladevi's travels to the United States, noted her book, *America: The Land of Superlatives,* and described her as a "woman of immense power."[50] In his portrayal of Kamaladevi, Prattis offered his readers an overwhelmingly positive image of an Indian socialist. One summer night, after sharing dinner, Prattis and

Kamaladevi shared a long conversation in her garden. "We had mused over the color problem all over the world," Prattis wrote, "and I had sought to obtain from her something of her feeling." He explained his curiosity by telling his readers, "You can never be sure that these other coloured people will feel like we do in the United States." Prattis assumed that his readers would accept his nonchalant reference to Indians as "coloured." Throughout his time in India, he made reference repeatedly to the darkness of Indian skin tones, often contrasting that darkness with the cultural preference for lightness expressed in matrimonial ads or portrayed in films with "milk-white" actors.[51]

Kamaladevi's view on "the color problem" demonstrated the ability of her colored cosmopolitanism to bridge an expansive humanism with a belief in solidarities of color. She began by stating, "Not as an Indian, but as a human being, my innate self-respect would suffer if I were not moved by the sufferings of others who are persecuted because of their color." Thus Kamaladevi utilized a universalistic notion of humanity to explain her sympathy with the victims of racism worldwide. Her universalism did not prevent her from offering a more focused understanding of colored solidarity. *Courier* readers followed along as Kamaladevi held out her "pretty, plump, brown arm," pointed to her skin, and proclaimed, "Every time prejudice is shown against any colored people, I look at myself and I know that I am a victim, too."[52]

Readers moved by Prattis's extensive portrait of Kamaladevi's colored cosmopolitanism needed only to glance at the next page of *The Courier* to learn more. There, Kamaladevi again blended a universalistic humanism with a ringing endorsement of colored solidarity in a special message to the African American readers of *The Courier*. She explained her desire to publish in the paper as a way to reach out to African Americans, who "like ourselves in this vast continent of Asia are waging the great battle of humanism." She concluded, "The Indian people have pledged to work and strive for a world order from which the vestiges of tyranny and exploitation be it racial or territorial are banished. For our own freedom assumes a reality only when the rest of mankind becomes genuinely free."[53] Kamaladevi offered her African American readers a vision of freedom unbound by national borders and rooted in the transnational history of Indian nationalism.

Kamaladevi's colored cosmopolitanism should be distinguished from Indian concerns regarding the discrimination that Indians faced in the United States. A report on segregation in Washington, produced by the National Committee on Segregation in the Nation's Capital, gave many examples of foreign visitors harassed on account of race. One concerned an Indian woman who was refused service at a soda fountain after being mistaken as Black. When she explained that she was from India, however, she and her husband were offered apologies and tea. An accompanying graphic stressed the ambivalent nature of Indian racial identity in the United States. In the graphic, which portrayed several foreigners being refused service on account of color, only the Indian woman was given an asterisk explaining her inclusion with the phrase, "Dark-skinned foreigners are often embarrassed."[54] When the Indian ambassador G. L. Mehta was harassed at the Houston Airport in August 1955, the story made headlines in the United States as well as India. When an Indian businessman was denied service at the cafeteria at Washington National Airport, he complained to the Indian Embassy. An American friend of his, also a prominent businessman, wrote undersecretary of state, Dean Acheson, and two U.S. senators to complain. The State Department in turn wrote airport authorities that racial discrimination could "seriously affect our relations with friendly and important countries."[55] To inspire more far-reaching changes would require demonstrating that the Indian public or, more importantly, Indian power brokers cared about Black Americans and not just the discrimination that Indians themselves faced in the United States.

The Constraints of Power

In January 1947 Jawaharlal Nehru dispatched a secret note to the first Indian ambassadors to the United States and China. "In the U.S.A. there is the Negro problem," he wrote. "Our sympathies are entirely with the Negroes." Nevertheless, Nehru explained, representatives of India "must avoid any public expression of opinion which might prove embarrassing or distasteful to the Government or people of the country where they serve."[56] Expressing "sympathies" for African Americans without embarrassing the American government would prove to be a difficult task, not only for Indian ambassadors but also for Nehru himself.

During the war and in its immediate aftermath, Nehru repeatedly expressed solidarity with African Americans. In August 1945 he asked a Black journalist to "remember" him "to all of the Negroes of America." Nehru praised the "valiant struggle" of African Americans to obtain their "cherished birthright" and concluded, "In many ways our problems are kindred."[57] In August 1946, soon after he was named to head the interim government of India, Nehru met with a journalist from *The Chicago Defender* at Gandhi's ashram in Wardha. Nehru, the journalist wrote, "often wondered if the people of America realized how much they suffered in the world's estimation because of their ill-treatment of the Negro." Toward the end of the interview, Nehru declared, "To the Negro people of America I send the greetings of my own people, and my assurance of our sympathy in their cause."[58]

Indian independence transformed Nehru from an anticolonial freedom fighter to the leader of a nation-state. The need to maintain cordial relations with the United States strained his solidarity with Black struggles. In the fall of 1949 Nehru undertook his first visit to the United States. His itinerary included neither meetings with Black leaders nor visits to Black communities, a fact not lost on the African American press. *The Chicago Defender* noted that the Indian press had "taken Pandit Nehru and his sister, Madame Vijaya Pandit, the Indian Ambassador to the United States, to task sharply already because he is not meeting any Negroes during his visit to America."[59] Most commentators blamed not Nehru, however, but the American State Department, which had planned Nehru's visit. In an editorial entitled "To Understand America, Nehru Should Visit Negro Ghettos Too," Langston Hughes remembered meeting Nehru in Paris years earlier. "Being no stranger to slurs, insults, and even violence, having lived through the colonial days of British India," Hughes declared, "Nehru might well feel quite at home in Nashville; Jackson, Mississippi, or Dallas, Texas."[60]

Some two months earlier, well before Nehru arrived in the United States, Roy Wilkins, editor of *The Crisis* and a powerful figure in the NAACP, wrote a letter to Nehru's sister, the Indian ambassador to the United States, Vijayalakshmi Pandit. Wilkins sought to arrange a "private, off-the-record dinner" in New York with Nehru and a select group of guests. "Pandit Nehru may wish on this occasion," Wilkins wrote, "to express his concern over the impairment of American prestige throughout Asia, Africa, and the Pacific because of American racial policies." Two days later Walter White held a dinner for Pandit at his house to talk about the Nehru/NAACP meeting. By October 7 a secret meeting with Nehru had been set for November 5, 1949. Ralph Bunche signed the invitations, which explained that in Paris the previous spring Nehru had expressed to Bunche his desire to meet with Americans to discuss "the repercussions in Asia of America's racial practices." Bunche wrote potential guests that Nehru was "concerned that the greatest propaganda weapon of the Communists in their struggle for power throughout Asia has been the news of racial strife in the United States." Nehru's official tour would end on November 3. He was staying until November 5 in order to attend the NAACP meeting.[61]

As planned, two days after Nehru's visit officially ended, White and Bunche co-chaired a private meeting between Nehru and a roster of eminent

Americans, the vast majority Black, at the Park Avenue home of Mrs. Robert Lehman, a wealthy philanthropist. In addition to Vijayalakshmi Pandit, participants included Arthur Spingarn, Roy Wilkins, and Louis Wright, all of the NAACP; Robert C. Weaver, a professor at New York University; Mrs. Robert Vann, the publisher of *The Pittsburgh Courier;* and Claude Barnett, director of the Associated Negro Press. Nehru received a brief overview of African American history from such eminent figures as Ralph Bunche, Mary McLeod Bethune, the founder of the National Council of Negro Women, and Mordecai Johnson, the president of Howard University. William Hastie, the governor of the Virgin Islands, detailed the legal aspects of the Black struggle. Lester Granger, the director of the National Urban League, described the rapid urbanization of Black communities. George Weaver of the Congress of Industrial Organizations (CIO) discussed the integration of labor unions. Nehru listened attentively and asked questions. While clearly demonstrating his commitment to Black struggles, however, he also admitted the limits on that commitment imposed by his official position. Nehru explained that while his speeches in the United States had broached questions of race and color in general terms, he had purposely avoided discussing African American struggles. According to the Associated Negro Press, Nehru "said he felt it would have been highly improper for him to come into another country, especially on an official visit and venture to criticize the internal policies of that country." The demands of Nehru's position did not prevent him from attending the meeting, however, or from concluding it with an automobile tour of "the good and the bad" in Harlem. The following day Nehru was presented with a life membership in the NAACP. Speaking at the gala event, Walter White said that the celebration had been achieved "without help from the State Department and, in fact, in spite of the State Department."[62]

Nehru's interactions with African American leaders strengthened his solidarity with Black struggles but did not significantly increase his willingness to risk India's relationship with the United States by forcefully denouncing American racism. Perhaps the most significant consequence of Nehru's trip was the recognition it gained in the Black press, and the symbolism Nehru provided to many African Americans. Robert Shelby shook Nehru's hand for a brief moment outside of Chicago's City Hall. Shelby wrote *The Chicago Defender* that Nehru's "warm handshake" was "a confession of his sincere regard and a feeling of interest of the Negro in the United States." "In spite of his nobility," Shelby wrote of Nehru, "he did not fail to recognize a member of the minority group of the African descent."[63]

As the leader of the Indian delegation to the United Nations and the ambassador to the United States and Mexico, Vijayalakshmi Pandit also found it necessary to mute her previously outspoken support for Black struggles. Pandit won wide admiration among African Americans during and in the aftermath of the war. In early 1945, on her way to attend the Pacific Relations Conference in Hot Springs, Virginia, Pandit saw signs indicating "For Whites" and "For Colored" that reminded her of when benches labeled "For Europeans Only" had been common in India. She later remembered, "I insisted on using the 'Colored' toilet because I was so angry, though I was assured that there was no need for me to do so." Scheduled to speak at Baltimore's Lyric Theater, Pandit refused until the normally segregated space was opened to Blacks, who then turned out in large numbers to hear her speak.[64]

African American newspapers covered Pandit's travels extensively, reporting her frequent statements of Afro-Indian solidarity. *The Pittsburgh Courier* quoted her declaring, "The happiest moments I have spent in America were those when I was at dinner in Harlem. I felt that I was at last with my own."[65] In *The Chicago Defender*, Walter White reported that Pandit had been warned that "she would injure India's cause if she identified it with the Negro's struggle for freedom." She replied, "I am colored myself and so are my people." In the spring of 1945 White and Du Bois shared lunch with Pandit and J. J. Singh in San Francisco, where Pandit unofficially represented India at the founding convention of the United Nations. White and Du Bois expressed their support for Pandit by refusing to be photographed with the "official" Indian delegates, "the stooges of the British Empire," in Du Bois's words. Even St. Clair Drake, while questioning India's commitment to Blacks, noted Pandit's "warmth" toward African Americans.[66]

Pandit's relationship with Paul and Eslanda Goode Robeson, which had begun in London in 1938, continued during and after the war. In 1943, when Pandit's daughters came to study at Wellesley, they stayed in the Robeson home in Enfield, Connecticut. Two years later the girls attended a party held by the Council on African Affairs to celebrate Eslanda Robeson's book *Journey to Africa*. At a United Nations meeting at Lake Success in New York, Paul Robeson greeted Pandit with a big hug, lifting her off her feet. She recalled that "the sight of this black man, famous though he was, embracing me so affectionately, shocked" her UN companions. "As far as I was concerned," she explained, "I was too pleased at seeing Paul to notice other people's looks!"[67]

In 1946 India led an effort in the General Assembly of the United Nations to censure South Africa. As the leader of the Indian delegation, Pandit received warm praise in the Black press, which often compared apartheid and Jim Crow. After discussing Pandit's critique of apartheid at the

UN, Harry Greene, a columnist for the *Washington Star,* told his readers, "A description of the Indian's situation in South Africa might lead one to think that Madame Pandit was speaking of Negroes in Washington." As St. Clair Drake perceived, however, Indian foreign policy focused primarily on the treatment of Indians in South Africa and largely avoided direct comparisons with racism in the United States. "For our part," Nehru wrote, "we did not intend raising the Negro issue, but it was not possible to tone down our opposition on the South African question because the Americans might feel uncomfortable."[68] It was the restraint expressed in the first half of this sentence that St. Clair Drake found worrying.

The need to secure American support did not prevent Pandit from offering to help the NAACP place a petition protesting American segregation before the United Nations. In September 1947 Du Bois sent Pandit a copy of the petition via Walter White.[69] Pandit replied, "I shall certainly do what I can to help you place this before the Assembly of the United Nations or the Economic and Social Council." The Indian press helped publicize the petition. Hugh Smythe at the NAACP reported to Cedric Dover that "a representative for a chain of sixteen Indian newspapers has obtained the petition with the promise of reporting it and the event in the local papers of his chain in India." Nevertheless, there is evidence that Du Bois was skeptical of India's support. His papers include a note that may have accompanied his letter to Vijayalakshmi Pandit. "India knows well," Du Bois wrote, "that the ambition of the real leaders of the United States is to succeed Great Britain as ruler of the Colored World in Asia and Africa." He added, "But perhaps India is not so clearly informed as to the deeper causes of this ambition in the long conditioning of America to color prejudice because of Negro slavery and the caste system which still persists here." Du Bois concluded, "India is not apt to be aware of our existence."[70]

When Pandit returned to the United States as the Indian ambassador in 1949, she received an abundance of awards and distinctions from African American admirers. In accepting these awards, she chose her words carefully so as to not overtly critique the United States. Nevertheless, by repeatedly attacking racial discrimination, even if only in general, Pandit made clear her ongoing support for Black struggles. On June 3, 1949, Pandit received an honorary degree from Howard University before an audience of approximately ten thousand. The degree's citation, written by Howard's president, Mordecai Johnson, praised Pandit for her outspoken opposition to racial oppression in South Africa.[71] Accepting her degree, Pandit told the audience, "Because freedom is indivisible, there can be no lasting freedom for any nation until liberty is assured to all races, peoples and communities." Ralph Bunche was also honored during the ceremony.[72] In July 1949 Bunche won the prestigious Spingarn Medal from the NAACP. Pandit was chosen to give him the award in front of twelve thousand spectators at the Fortieth Annual Conference of the NAACP at the Hollywood Bowl. Pandit stated that Indians had "made common cause with all oppressed peoples during the days of our national struggles." She proclaimed, "We feel today that our newly acquired independence is limited by the lack of freedom that still exists in many parts of the world."[73]

Like Nehru, Pandit at times muted her critique of American racism in order to avoid controversy. In November 1950 Pandit participated in a panel in New York sponsored by the United Negro College Fund. She remarked that "many people in India think of America as a land where the coloured people are not given any opportunities and they are exceedingly discriminated against." Rather than suggesting ways to eliminate American racism, Pandit encouraged the audience to "try and sell your democracy to us—to us of the East." She blamed Hollywood, not American racists, for harming the image of the United States abroad.[74] Earlier that year, W. E. B. Du Bois accused Pandit of compromising her commitments to Black Americans. When she spoke in the United Nations on behalf of Indians and Blacks in South Africa, "We Negroes of America rose to applaud her." Over time, however, according to Du Bois, "Mrs. Pandit realized that while it was popular here to defend Indians in South Africa, it was never popular to defend Negroes anywhere." As an example, he offered a speech Pandit had given to "one of our colored sororities," in which she, according to Du Bois, said that "she did not go along wholly with what Negroes in America were saying and trying to do; that she advocated patience and waiting." The audience, Du Bois wrote, "felt insulted and cruelly disillusioned."[75]

Even as she muted her criticism of American racism, Pandit offered her African American audiences the hope that resulted from feeling part of a large and resurgent colored world. As a powerful woman of color, Pandit's example carried special meaning for African American women. Descriptions of Pandit's beauty, often emphasizing her "darkness," combined with tributes to her leadership, worked to subvert the equation of beauty with whiteness and power with masculinity. On May 19, 1951, a large photo of Pandit covered the front page of *The Pittsburgh Courier Magazine*. The accompanying article, written by Gertrude "Toki" Schalk, carried the byline, "She Brings Real Ability to Her Exacting Job . . . and Once Again Proves That Women Can Hold Their Own in Any Profession." In a series of articles, Schalk portrayed Pandit as a beautiful and powerful colored woman. She called the "sun-beige Ambassador" with "liquid darkness" in her eyes "one of the most beautiful women in the world" and declared, "Madame Pandit, gorgeous one from India, takes American Negroes to her heart and is 'one of them.'" The majority of African American commentators on Pandit presented a woman whose beauty and grace were matched with a sharp intelligence and a talent for leadership. The emphasis of the Black press on Pandit's gender was not surprising, given the fact that Pandit often presented herself as a powerful woman and regularly discussed, at times too optimistically, the ability of Indian women to attain positions of power.[76]

Pandit developed strong ties with Mary Mcleod Bethune, the founder of the National Council of Negro Women. In November 1945 Pandit spoke at the Tenth Annual Meeting of the Council, telling a large audience that when she arrived in the United States she discovered that "the Four Freedoms meant one thing for the white people and another for Negroes." Pandit was made a life member of the council and told the delegates that she wanted Indian women to attend the annual workshops and women of the council to go to India.[77] In April 1951 Pandit received an award from Bethune-Cookman College, given by Mary Mcleod Bethune herself. The citation praised Pandit as "the foremost feminine figure in the complex structure of international affairs of this age." At the Fourteenth Annual Convention of the National Council of Negro Women, Bethune again gave Pandit an award. The citation praised Pandit for her "courageous and unyielding stand" in support of the Indian people as well as "the universal representation" that Pandit had "given to womanhood and the oppressed peoples of the world."[78]

The "universal representation" that Pandit offered was limited, as it was for Nehru, by the demands of official office. It would be wrong, however, to discount the significance of the sympathy expressed by Pandit and Nehru, limited though it was. Indian solidarity with African Americans gained significance in the context of the Cold War, in large part because of the efforts of African Americans who inspired and publicized Indian criticisms of American racial oppression. Several influential African Americans traveled to India, where they strove to present Indian support for the United States as dependent on the achievement of racial equality. African Americans in India during the Cold War, especially those representing in some capacity the United States, faced a difficult task not unlike that of Nehru and Pandit. They strove to represent the "interests" of their country, interests often framed in the terms of global power politics. Such representation involved understating the extent and viciousness of racism in the United States. Like Indian public officials, Black diplomats struggled to balance their national loyalties with a transnational conception of freedom.

(Black) Americans in India

In March 1950 an article on the front page of *The Pittsburgh Courier* declared, "India Would Welcome Negro Ambassador." "The Indian people are very proud of their color and feel closer to the darker people," the article explained. The story focused on an interview with Nehru, who stated that he would "welcome" an African American ambassador from the United States. Nehru made clear, however, that he could not formally request a Black ambassador, as such a request would broach the legitimate bounds of diplomacy. Asked about India's "attitude toward racial discrimination," Nehru "pointed to the firm and unequivocal stand his country had taken for racial equality as shown in her constitution, her laws and actions." He said nothing about racial discrimination in the United States. Nehru mentioned that he was a lifetime member of the NAACP but again stopped short of directly commenting on racial inequality in the United States. Despite Nehru's careful comments, his words were sufficient for *The Courier* to present India's leader as a champion of Black Americans. The article suggested sending a Black ambassador to India as a way to "bolster sagging American prestige" in India and "knock the props from beneath most Communist argument."[79]

Concerned that many Indians sympathized with Black struggles, the State Department sent several African Americans to India to generate pro-American sentiment. In 1949 Edith Sampson, an African American attorney, later to become the first Black American UN delegate, traveled to India as part of the same "Town Hall" radio program tour in which Walter White participated. Because of her eloquence and because White's light skin weakened his ability to speak "as a Negro," Sampson became the central figure in the tour's response to questions regarding race in America. In Delhi she responded to questions regarding American racism by agreeing that the United States needed to change and noting that foreign pressure could help. "I think one of the great instruments in quickening the pace of the American white man is the report that we at the Town Hall are going to take back to white America," she said. Sampson declared that the United States could not win "the confidence of Asia's dark-skinned millions, if they continue to read about discriminatory practices in America."[80]

After her trip, Sampson continued to use her experiences abroad to present the Black freedom struggle as a crucial front in the Cold War. It was, however, her defense of the United States that garnered wide publicity. In 1951 a *Reader's Digest* article offered a glowing portrait of Sampson, entitled "Thorn in Russia's Side." Supreme Court Justice William O. Douglas remembered that a speech that Sampson gave in New Delhi on August 16,

1949, created "a profound impression." "She made it clear," Douglas remembered, "that while she would fight for the rights of her people at home, she would stand for no criticism of America abroad by reason of the color issue."[81] Not all accounts of Sampson's time in India were positive, however. In *The Pittsburgh Courier* P. L. Prattis criticized Sampson for presenting race relations in too positive a light. Friends who heard her speak in Delhi, Prattis wrote, were "utterly disgusted" that she "had apologized for the acts of White Americans against Negro Americans."[82]

Like Sampson and Walter White, several African American visitors to India leveraged Indian opinion to present American racism as a Cold War liability, even while at times whitewashing American racial oppression. In 1955 the U.S. government arranged for the African American journalist Carl Rowan to travel to South Asia to respond to criticisms of American racism. In a letter to his wife, Rowan described Indians as "the most argumentative, abrasive, know-it-all fucking people that I have ever met in my life." What inspired Rowan's antipathy toward Indians, strangely enough, was their persistent criticism of American racism. Later in life, Rowan explained that during his trip to India he was "still naively optimistic about the willingness of the South to accept the end of Jim Crow."[83] His optimism, coupled with his desire to defend the United States, inspired Rowan to denounce Indian critiques of American racism as the result of communist propaganda and a misguided faith in colored solidarity.

Rowan's account of his journey, *The Pitiful and the Proud*, published in 1956, presented the majority of Indian views of the United States as uneducated and exaggerated, even while offering several sympathetic examples of the depth of Indian knowledge about race in America. Rowan recited the stories of several Indians who had themselves suffered racial discrimination in the United States. In Madhya Pradesh, for example, a former justice of the State High Court explained that he was denied access to a dining car in Louisiana in 1937. Rowan also offered his own critiques of American white supremacists. After a group of students in Calcutta asked about the persistence of segregation in Louisiana, Rowan declared that "the politicians of Louisiana were a lot more narrow-minded, a lot more bigoted and a lot more stupid than the general population."[84]

Rowan criticized the notion that "India today is leading a world campaign for people of color everywhere," but he did not fully reject colored solidarity. In Assam, Rowan encountered a "thick-lipped, dark-skinned newsman named P. E. Shanker," who explained that after seeing Rowan's picture in the paper, he had looked at his "dark hand" and said, "Here comes one of us." Rowan dismissed such "'bond of color' nonsense." He asked Shanker, "If I accept your theory that we colored people are all alike in a good way, is it not logical for someone else to accept the bigot's theory that we are all alike in a bad way?" Despite his criticism of colored solidarity, Rowan appreciated that "thousands of Indians bore a deep, honest feeling of kinship" for African Americans. Rowan remembered a meeting with the Trivandrum District Journalists Association, before which President A. Govinda Pillai read a letter which, in Rowan's words, "was calm and seemed to have arisen from no propaganda motives." The letter read:

> Above all, we are happy to have in our midst the representative of a race, which against tremendous odds of prejudice, persecution and malice, is making very rapid headway and reaching fullest human development. It is no idle racial pride that prompts me to claim that the future of the world rests on the Asiatic and African races in a degree larger than that of the past. In a war-worn, war-weary world all efforts of peace get the largest number of votaries from the coloured races whose bitter experience of human misery and bondage have rendered them more susceptible to the nobler side of human character.

Rowan was "strangely touched by the display of emotion with which this letter was presented." Although he "saw in the letter many elements of danger," he knew that "deep down inside" he "shared the hopes of these young men that the day had come when the world's colored races would make a great contribution toward their own freedom and to the welfare of mankind."[85]

It is easy to criticize African Americans like Carl Rowan or Edith Sampson who chose to defend the United States against the charges of Indian critics. Rather than fostering Indian concern about American racism, such apologists chose to understate racial inequality in the United States or to exaggerate America's progress toward racial equality. Of course if Rowan or Sampson had publicized the scale and intransigence of racism in the United States, their funding would promptly have been cancelled. While helping to explain their public stance, such a contingency should not be used to defend it. A stronger defense, paradoxically, begins with the fact that Black visitors proved rather ineffective in changing Indian opinions. Indian audiences remained too adamant in their opposition to American racial prejudice to be swayed by fleeting examples of progress. Rather, it was American audiences who were most influenced by the accounts of Black travelers in India. By publicizing Indian concern regarding American racism and arguing that American racial discrimination contributed to the spread of communism in independent India, Sampson, Rowan, Walter White, and others encouraged Americans to reject racial oppression as harmful to American foreign policy.

In 1952 the American State Department arranged for African American author Jay Saunders Redding to tour India. As with Carl Rowan, Redding's trip was funded in the hope that he would improve Indian opinion of the United States. Upon arrival in India, Larry Wilson, an African American foreign service officer, warned Redding that race was "a bigger issue in the thinking of the rest of the world than Americans have let themselves believe." Wilson noted, with a hint of anger, that many Americans who visited India seemed unaware that they were "dealing with *colored* people in a *colored* country." Redding himself was asked "more than once whether the Negro community of America would join with the colored peoples of the world in a war against the white man." "The Indian people believe," Redding wrote, "that American policy is opposed to the 'liberation and rise' of the colored peoples of the world." Before his trip, Redding felt that he had, as he put it, "escaped" the bonds of race. Redding had published an earlier book entitled *On Being Negro in America,* but he called his account of his travels *An American in India.* Traveling to India forced him to realize that his escape from race was only partial. He could not cease being a "Negro," even if he tried to be merely an "American in India."[86]

Indians refused to let Redding forget American racism or his own racial identity. On his first night in India, while exploring Bombay in a horse-drawn carriage with a white American woman named Rena Mark, Redding was approached by an Indian man, who asked, "By you 'frika?" Redding responded, "Not Africa. America." Rejecting this national identification, the man reached into the carriage, took Redding's hand, and pulled back Redding's sleeve to expose his forearm. "A slow smile of recognition and wonder trembled like a light on his dark face," Redding wrote. "Same like me," the man said, "Like by you." "All at once," Redding remembered, "I knew I was closer to this nameless man than I could ever be to Rena Mark." In contrast to Carl Rowan's criticism of colored unity, Redding concluded, "The barriers of language, culture and national birth dissolved before it, and I stood face to face with an indestructible truth: the color of my skin was still the touchstone. I did not like it." During a meeting with a dozen Indian lawyers and academics, a professor told Redding that he had decided to refuse a position at a university in Texas after some Americans had encouraged him not to speak English very well and to wear a turban so as not to be mistaken for a Negro. Redding asked his American readers, "What was there to say? This was no lie to answer with a ringing, contradicting truth. My heart raged with hatred of this thing I knew, and ached with the necessity to admit it."[87]

Edith Sampson, Walter White, Carl Rowan, and J. Saunders Redding were only a few of the many Black Americans who visited India during the Cold War. Even African Americans who did not travel to India as "official" representatives experienced the transnational double consciousness of being a Black American overseas. In 1952 Dorothy Irene Height, a leading figure in the National Council of Negro Women, traveled to Delhi to serve as a visiting professor at the Delhi School of Social Work. "I went as a colored person," she later remembered, "but I was an American. And so I had it both ways." On her first day on the job, a student asked her why the university had sent "an inferior person." The student added, "I thought they were sending an American." When Height responded, "Well, I am an American," the girl replied adamantly, "But you're not an American, you're a Negro." This interchange gave Height "the opportunity to open up the whole discussion of what it means to be an American, what it means to be a black American, and the like."[88]

Before her trip to India, Height recalled, she had "never seen that many colored people." In India she could "look at the equivalent of two or three city blocks and see only colored people." Height found such a proliferation of color "just unbelievable" and "very exciting." She explained, "I always had felt that I was part of a large group, but I had never had that experience of being part of this large a group."[89] Height's perception of Indian women as beautiful allowed her to embrace her own beauty as a colored woman. "The women looked like empresses in their saris," Height remembered, "the rich darkness of their skin setting off magnificent jewel tones in their silks." She wrote, "All through my childhood the 'beauty' of whiteness had been drummed into me. Yet at this moment in Alipur, how peculiarly wan and lifeless a white person would have looked."[90] The aesthetics of dark-skinned Indian women also attracted the attention of Carl Rowan, who recalled "shy, well-hipped maidens with smooth dark skin and dazzling black hair tied by tradition in one long braid."[91] J. Saunders Redding similarly made much of the beauty and darkness of Indian women. At a women's college in modern-day Kerala, Redding remembered a dance: "Two of the dancers seemed to me especially beautiful—both dark and statuesque, one with a chiseled Nubian cast of features, and the other with a startling dark translucence, like black light."[92]

Despite praising the darkness of Indian women, Redding recognized that being a dark woman in India entailed a considerable burden. At a party, Redding met a wealthy and accomplished woman whose name he remembered as Mada Dyal. Redding described her as "a dark saturnine beauty." "The light winked in her black hair," he wrote, "And her skin glowed like light chocolate-colored marble. She was exquisite. Many years of careful breeding had gone into her making." Redding's reference to "breeding" animalized Dyal's beauty. Unlike Dorothy Height, Redding sexualized the darkness he found in Indian women. Nevertheless, his description of Dyal, taken as a whole, focused as much on Dyal's intelligence as on her beauty while stressing the challenge of being a woman, and especially a dark woman, in India. As the party ended he asked her why she had not married. Speaking "almost with rebuke," she stated, "I am thought too dark for the men of my caste, and I will not marry outside it."[93] Thus Redding revealed that the challenge of being a dark woman existed in India as well as in the United States. In her memoirs Dorothy Height would write of women of color: "No matter what our circumstances or where in the world we live, we must daily fight against forces that wish to keep us down because of our skin color, our gender— or both." In India Height confronted the multiplicity of oppressions based on more than race and gender. She remembered helping privileged Indian students "learn something about how to work with people of lower class and caste."[94] In addition to the intersection of race and gender, old analogies between race and caste gained new significance in the aftermath of Indian independence and the onset of the Cold War.

Race, Caste, and the Cold War Nation

In 1928 Indian authors had responded to the criticisms of caste in Katherine Mayo's *Mother India* by attacking American racism. Their purpose was not to achieve racial equality in the United States but to defend India against the assessment of outsiders like Mayo. During the Cold War Americans similarly employed critiques of caste for defensive nationalist purposes. In 1948 the American Consul in Madras wrote the secretary of state that "an oft-repeated answer by the recent Consul General at this post to questions about the 'color problem' in the United States was 'Yes, it's almost as bad as it is in India.' This often caused such embarrassed confusion that the subject was immediately dropped."[95] The race/caste analogy once again came to serve nationalist ends. Americans responded to Indian opposition to American racism by referencing caste oppression in India. They presented American racism as a purely national problem in a world where each nation should confront its own shortcomings rather than pressure others to confront theirs.

Blacks who strove to defend the United States without defending American racism found caste especially useful, as it offered a means to respond to Indian challenges without directly defending American racism. Black visitors in India often asserted that American racial oppression was less severe, or at least no more severe, than caste oppression in India. Consider, for example, what inspired Edith Sampson to declare in Delhi, "I would rather be the lowliest, most downtrodden Negro in the United States than one of your Untouchables."[96] The context of Sampson's statement, as a response to questions about racism in the United States, makes evident that her reference to caste was employed in defense of the nation. On his part, Carl Rowan denied using caste "as an excuse for, or mitigating factor in regard to, American racial discrimination." As an example, he wrote, "I admitted to Indians that, as reported in my book, I *had* grown up in a town where, as a Negro, I couldn't get a drink of water in a drug store unless the fountain clerk could find a paper cup. I also told them how I had visited Manimangalam, an Indian village, where untouchables could not draw water from the well." Although Rowan claimed that he did not use caste as a "mitigating factor," his many references to caste in *The Pitiful and the Proud* operated primarily to parry Indian questions regarding race in America.[97]

Like Carl Rowan, *Pittsburgh Courier* columnist George Schuyler used caste to shield American racism from foreign criticism. In an article in which he argued that "each nation has its own prejudices and discriminations," and thus that American racism did not deserve the world's condemnation, Schuyler offered as evidence that "India's castes are notorious."[98] A month later Schuyler defended Edith Sampson against the criticism of P. L. Prattis. Schuyler asserted that when African Americans were chosen to go abroad, they should "speak as an American," not as a Black American. He equated being American with defending America against charges of racism. As an example of a minority leader who pursued justice within the nation rather than appeal to international opinion, Schuyler offered Dr. Ambedkar, whom Schuyler called "the brilliant leader of India's outcasts and untouchables." Schuyler asserted that if Ambedkar was chosen as an ambassador from India to the United Nations, "it is highly unlikely that he will so far forget his position as to wash his country's dirty linen (the treatment of his people) before the world audience."[99]

Ambedkar had long used African American history to better understand and dramatize the struggles of Dalits in India. Since 1928, when Ambedkar inverted Lala Lajpat Rai's suggestion that American racism was worse than caste oppression, Ambedkar had moved from ranking wrongs to recognizing historical lessons in the Black struggle. In 1943 he denounced the denial of equal rights "to Negroes in America, to the Jews in Germany, and to the Untouchables in India."[100] In 1945, in his fierce polemic *What Congress and Gandhi Have Done to the Untouchables,* Ambedkar compared Lincoln and Gandhi as leaders more focused on national unity than the freedom of oppressed minorities. In 1946 he wrote W. E. B. Du Bois, "There is so much similarity between the position of the Untouchables and the position of the Negroes of America that the study of the latter is not only natural but necessary."[101] With Ambedkar as the chair of its drafting committee, the Indian constitution would outlaw untouchability as well as any discrimination based on caste. Ambedkar and other Indian legal authorities studied American attempts to use the law to achieve racial equality.[102] The Indian constitution went further than American law by reserving seats in the legislatures for the lowest castes and declaring that the state "shall promote with special care the education and economic interests" of those "castes and tribes" officially deemed to occupy the lowest position in Indian society.

Although infusing their pronouncements with an optimism that would prove largely unjustified, several leading Indians were nonetheless willing to admit that the inequalities of caste in India and race in the United States were comparable. In a book entitled *Ambedkar Refuted,* C. Rajagopalachari wrote that improvements in the treatment of Dalits did not "compare ill with what has been done in America for Negroes."[103] Rajagopalachari chose his words carefully in order to avoid apologizing for caste injustice. In 1945, when it was suggested to her in an interview that the closest thing to Dalits in America "might be the Negroes," Vijayalakshmi Pandit responded that in India the state was fighting untouchability.[104] Before independence, many Indians suggested that the end of British rule would facilitate the fight against caste oppression. In August 1945 Nehru was asked by an African American war correspondent, "Will the caste system continue to retard India's progress?" Nehru responded, "Not under a modified Socialist system."[105] In August 1946, in the midst of a discussion of American racism, Nehru told a *Chicago Defender* columnist, "We in India, in our own long past, have been guilty of suppressing large numbers of our own people. That is the problem of the Harijans."[106]

Some commentators used the concept of caste to attack racism in the United States. In 1942 Lin Yutang, a Chinese scholar, wrote that "Americans laugh at the hopeless ignorance of Hindus in their attitude toward untouchables. But if the white treatment of Negroes in America is not caste, I do not know what caste is."[107] In 1948 the report of the National Committee on Segregation in the Nation's Capital quoted an unnamed Indian visitor, "I would rather be an Untouchable in the Hindu caste system than a Negro in Washington."[108]

Like a double-edged sword, comparisons between racism and caste oppression could be employed to criticize both. In November 1951 Ambassador Chester Bowles told Walter White that he often answered Indian questions "on racial intolerance in the United States" by saying, "You have your own deep prejudices here in India for which you have suffered profoundly. We have an equally serious problem in America, and we have suffered also."[109] Unlike the American consul general in Madras, who used the race/caste analogy to produce "such embarrassed confusion that the subject was immediately dropped," Bowles neither claimed that caste was worse than racism nor attempted to silence discussion of both "deep prejudices." Similarly, a review of Robert Penn Warren's *Segregation* published in *United Asia* compared the violent response to the attempted integration of Little Rock High School to the burning of several Dalit villages in Ramanthpuram, Tamil Nadu. The review made clear that both atrocities deserved condemnation.[110]

Between February and July 1943 Bharatan Kumarappa was imprisoned in the Nagpur Central Jail for his opposition to British rule. There he gave some twenty talks to his fellow political prisoners about his time as a student in the United States. In 1945 Kumarappa published these talks as a book in which he labeled "the negro problem . . . one of the most serious problems in the national life of the United States." Kumarappa connected American racism to injustices of class and caste in India. He concluded, "America has a long way to go before it can come anywhere near the tyranny we have practised in regard to the Harijans." He asked his readers, "Shall we now complain if other nations treat us as untouchables, brahmins of the purest blood though we may be?" Kumarappa's concern for the inequalities of caste did not prevent him from criticizing British imperialism. On the contrary, he again used an analogy with African Americans to defend the right of all Indians to govern themselves. Kumarappa declared, "Britain treats us in much the same way as America treats its Negroes."[111] By using the race/caste and race/colony parallels to encourage his readers to combat caste oppression, imperialism, and racism, Kumarappa demonstrated that transnational solidarities could oppose multiple injustices.

Often, critics of American racism used "caste" as an analytical category without exploring caste in India. A poor understanding of caste limited even the most extended comparison between race and caste. In his monumental study, *Caste, Class, and Race,* the African American sociologist Oliver Cox presented caste as a rigid social system that had changed little since ancient times. "No one ever discusses, far less questions, the caste system," Cox wrote, overlooking the concerted efforts of

Ambedkar and others to challenge caste in India. By presenting Indian society as static, Cox aimed to highlight the dynamism of race in America and thus to refute the caste school of American sociology on race, and especially its most renowned figure, Robert Park. Cox criticized the "definite ring of fatality and mysticism in Park's discussion of the stability of race relations in the South," linking that fatality to "the false outlook derived from the caste belief." Rather than reveal that Park was as wrong about caste as he was about race, however, Cox largely accepted a reading of caste in India as unchanging and eternal, using it as a foil to present race as dynamic and contested.[112]

Unlike caste, Cox argued, race was modern and linked to capitalist exploitation. Race was "not an abstract, natural, immemorial feeling of mutual antipathy between groups, but rather a practical exploitative relationship."[113] The greatest insight of *Caste, Class, and Race,* its emphasis on the embeddedness of racial oppression within American political economy, became overshadowed as advocates of Cold War civil rights increasingly embraced narrow notions of "civil" as opposed to human rights. Mainstream civil rights organizations and activists acquiesced in and at times contributed to the red-baiting of prominent Black activists, including Paul Robeson and W. E. B. Du Bois, the two African Americans most revered in India.[114] Edith Sampson, for example, was asked in India why she omitted Du Bois and Robeson when discussing famous African Americans. She told an audience in Delhi that Robeson had joined "a lunatic fringe in America" and had "forgotten that he owes a great deal to our democracy." Sampson was far from alone in championing Cold War civil rights while alienating the African American leftists who inspired the Indian concern that helped make the achievement of civil rights a Cold War necessity.[115]

The Limits of the Third World

On June 12, 1956, testifying before the House Committee on Un-American Activities, Paul Robeson transformed an investigation into his loyalty to the United States into an opportunity to proclaim the rise of the colored world. His congressional inquisitors cited a speech Robeson gave in Paris in 1949 in which he reportedly said that African Americans would never fight against the Soviet Union. Robeson responded by noting that he had spoken alongside Dr. Yusuf Mohamed Dadoo, an Indian South African leader, and that their audience included "students from various parts of the colonial world, students who since then have become very important in their governments, in places like Indonesia and India, and in many parts of Africa." When pressed on his statement concerning

Black Americans, Robeson instead offered a global declaration of colored autonomy: "Four hundred million in India, and millions everywhere, have told you, precisely, that the colored people are not going to die for anybody: they are going to die for their independence."[116]

In India admiration for Robeson remained strong despite the efforts of the U.S. government. In the spring of 1958 Indira Gandhi began organizing a "Paul Robeson Day." While Nehru supported the effort, Ellsworth Bunker, the American ambassador to India, promptly wrote Secretary of State John Foster Dulles that he would work to have the celebration cancelled. The American consul general in Bombay pressured M. C. Chagla, chief justice of the Bombay High Court and the president of the Robeson celebration committee, to cancel the event. Chagla refused. Similar pressure applied to India's ambassador to the United States in Washington also failed, although Ellsworth Bunker did tell Dulles that "All-India Radio and the Indian press had been instructed to play the celebration down." Robeson's passport had been confiscated by the American government. After it was returned, Vijayalakshmi Pandit gave him a reception at the Indian embassy in London.[117] The continued admiration in India for Robeson indicates the power of colored solidarity to survive the pressures of the Cold War.

Although he never visited the subcontinent, Du Bois similarly remained respected in India throughout the years in which he was persecuted in the United States. In 1953 one Indian visitor wrote Du Bois that meeting him was "so inspiring that I, a Hindu, felt as if I were leaving one of our sacred temples when I took leave of you." Recognizing the prevalence of Indian admiration for Du Bois, Cedric Dover mobilized Indians as part of a larger effort to gather international support for Du Bois. In March 1951 Dover wrote Du Bois that he was *"extremely worried"* after learning that Du Bois had been charged with illegally representing the interests of international communism and indicted under the Foreign Agents Registration Act. Du Bois responded, "It is a great opportunity for a courageous stand." Dover then sent a letter of support to forty newspapers throughout the world, as well as to several Indian friends, including the novelist Mulk Raj Anand and the journalist Iqbal Singh.[118] At a conference in England, Dover contributed to a resolution that condemned as "flagrant violations of human rights"

> (a) the secret trial of prominent Service officers, intellectuals, and other workers for peace and democracy in Pakistan; (b) the trials of the Telengana peasants; (c) the indictment and humiliation of the pre-eminent Negro American scholar, leader and champion of all the Asian and colonial peoples, Dr. W. E. B. Du Bois.

By juxtaposing the persecution of Du Bois with violations of human rights in Pakistan and India, this resolution marked a major shift in analogies between Indian and African American freedom struggles. American racial inequality had long been compared to British colonialism. After 1947, in contrast, activists like Cedric Dover compared the oppression of African Americans to the wrongs of the governments of India and Pakistan. This new emphasis on human rights as opposed to the rights of the nation was evident in a separate resolution that praised Du Bois for fighting for "justice and human well-being" as well as "the full emancipation of his own people and complete democracy for all men." Dover sent both resolutions to Du Bois, who replied that he was "thrilled."[119]

As Du Bois's day in court approached, Dover wrote that he wished he "were an American who could stand at your side on that day." He prepared a message from Indian writers:

> We *Indian* writers, gratefully speaking for ourselves but echoing the feelings of that vast company which owes so much to your long struggle for human rights, humbly yet proudly send you our heartfelt good wishes on this day. Your deep scholarship and uncompromising heroism have brought the whole struggle for peace, justice and decency nearer to victory—and your wise and courageous role in this struggle will never be forgotten.

The letter was signed by eminent authors, including Mulk Raj Anand, Mahomed Ashraf, Munib Rahman, Iqbal Singh, and Dover himself. Although Du Bois was acquitted, the State Department denied him a passport, effectively barring his ability to leave the country until 1958. When Du Bois was returned his right to travel and visited England, Dover corresponded with Shirley Graham Du Bois, calling their visit "a great event in my life." On July 12 Dover wrote to Du Bois, noting that Paul Robeson, whose passport had recently been returned, had already arrived in London. Dover told Du Bois that the Robesons were "bubbling over" with joy. "As we ride through the streets," he wrote, "Paul every now and again bursts into a chuckle of deep-throated but incredulous delight."[120]

The commitment of Du Bois and Robeson to leftist politics influenced their understanding of Jawaharlal Nehru and his government. In 1946 Nehru sent Du Bois a book about Gandhi. Du Bois responded warmly, "I shall treasure it among my most valued possessions." He told Nehru, "You have the sympathy of myself and my people in the great work that you are attempting to do for India."[121] Three years later, however, in anticipation of Nehru's visit to the United States, Du Bois and W. Alphaeus Hunton, a leading figure in the Council of African Affairs, joined Kumar Goshal, Howard Fast, and other Left-leaning intellectuals in sending Nehru an open letter protesting "wide-spread violations of civil liberties" in India. The letter noted "the appeals of progressive trade unions, peasant and political leaders now incarcerated in the jails of India," and expressed concern regarding "the mounting evidence of wholesale denial of civil liberties and basic democratic rights under your administration."[122] When Nehru visited the United States, Du Bois did not try to contact him. "I was grievously disappointed," he explained, "at the number of persons in jail in India, because of their political and economic beliefs." "Nehru is a socialist," Du Bois asserted, "but he cannot carry out socialism here against capitalists like Patel."[123]

The shifting politics of the Cold War and the persistent evidence of Nehru's socialism inspired a change, however, in Du Bois's view of the Indian leader. In 1953 Du Bois told L. N. Rao, a member of the Servants of India Society, that he respected Nehru and Vijayalakshmi Pandit despite the detention of labor activists in India after independence. He also mentioned warmly India's efforts to secure peace in Korea.[124] In December 1956 Du Bois sent Nehru a note of gratitude. "I write to thank you deeply for your visit to the United States," Du Bois began. "Your restraint and your insistence on peace and equality among men was needed in this land where the voice of Asia as well as that of Africa has long been ignored." Du Bois praised V. K. Krishna Menon as "a tower of strength for the Darker Nations" who had "for this reason met much of the force of American color prejudice." Menon, India's ambassador to the United Nations and future defense minister, was criticized in the United States for his pro-Soviet leanings. Du Bois made clear his own views of Soviet benevolence. "We are not yet equal citizens, but conditions are improving and real emancipation is in sight," he wrote Nehru. "For this we have to thank the rise of the Soviet Republics and the rise and growth of free India." Du Bois explained that he had been "deeply disturbed" at Nehru's "jailing of Communists." "But as progress toward Socialism developed," Du Bois wrote, "I understood better the vast task which confronted you and the courage and persistence with which you were accomplishing the great end of making India a great and leading nation." Du Bois explained that his "long desire" to visit India had been "frustrated by the fear of my government lest if I were allowed to travel abroad, I would tell the truth about the still existent Color Bar in this Nation."[125]

Paul Robeson's relationship with Nehru was also strained by the Cold War. Beginning in the late 1930s Nehru and Robeson had forged a friendship based in part on a shared enthusiasm for socialism. After Indian independence, however, Robeson increasingly contrasted Chinese "freedom" with Indian vacillation. "The Chinese people have their freedom and they are going to keep it," Robeson wrote in October 1951. "The Indian people, the Indian masses," on the other hand, "watch and weigh their chances."[126] Speaking before the National Negro Labor Council in Cincinnati, Robeson defended China's "freedom," before declaring that "hundreds of millions" of Indians were telling Nehru, "Stand your ground for the Indian people, don't sell yourself to the imperialists wherever they may be, for you may not be there if you do."[127] Robeson's ambivalent opinions of India and Nehru, like those of Du Bois, indicate that Left-leaning advocates of colored solidarity were liable to subordinate notions of color to the imperatives of the Cold War. As Nehru's relationship to the Soviet Union improved, so did Robeson's opinion of Nehru. In 1955 Robeson praised Nehru for his warm comments on the Soviet Union.[128]

The Cold War dynamics that influenced Du Bois and Robeson as well as their critics permeated the Asian-African Conference, held in Bandung, Indonesia, in April 1955. A month earlier *United Asia* had published an article by Du Bois entitled "Pan-Africanism: A Mission in My Life." Could Bandung, a meeting of representatives of twenty-nine Asian and African countries, culminate Du Bois's long efforts to forge a colored world? In his opening address, the leader of independent Indonesia, President Sukarno, welcomed the delegates by saying, "This is the first intercontinental conference of coloured peoples in the history of mankind!" In a gathering fractured by Cold War tensions, opposition to racism proved a powerful common bond. It was, however, neither its emphasis on color nor its "intercontinental" nature that made the Bandung conference unique. Rather, what distinguished Bandung from earlier gatherings such as the Pan-African congresses or the meetings of the League against Imperialism was that the majority of delegations in Bandung represented independent nations. The focus of the meeting on national representation effectively sidelined much of Africa, then still under colonial rule.[129] Independence endowed former colonies with significance on the world stage while transforming anticolonial "freedom fighters" into nationally minded statesmen. The Bandung conference, while "a conference of coloured peoples," was also a meeting of nations, in which a unified opposition to imperialism and racism was complicated by international politics and Cold War diplomacy.

The focus of Bandung on national representation made ambiguous the role African Americans might take in the gathering. In January 1955 Walter White asked Nehru and Vijayalakshmi Pandit if "outsiders" would be permitted to attend the conference.[130] Pandit replied from London that White and his wife, Poppy, were the only two Americans officially invited.[131] White's fragile health prevented him from accepting the invitation. Claude Barnett, owner of the Associated Negro Press, told his Washington correspondent that he did not want her to attend the conference, as it would have a "pink tinge."[132] Nevertheless, several prominent African Americans did attend the conference, and the Black press covered it closely. Their reports demonstrate the tension between colored solidarity and Cold War loyalties that marked the gathering at Bandung.

Several Black observers chose to prioritize the Cold War above solidarities of color. In a lengthy report Carl Rowan noted Sukarno's reference to color but chose instead to emphasize Cold War tensions. He dismissed as communist propaganda the comments of a Ceylonese woman who had asked, in Rowan's words, "Now how does anyone here expect the United States to strike boldly against racial discrimination in Africa? The Americans are too busy practicing it at home."[133] Adam Clayton Powell, the outspoken Black congressman from Harlem, similarly prioritized America's standing in the Cold War. Although the State Department attempted to prevent Powell from traveling to Bandung, once there he defended American race relations. Powell went so far as to declare, "Why, it's a distinction to be a Negro in America nowadays."[134] In *The Pittsburgh Courier*, Max Yergan, who had repudiated his socialist past while working to gain anti-communist credentials, reported from Bandung that "any persons who entertained ideas of Bandung as representing color or territorial solidarity were most certainly on the losing side." Yergan portrayed Nehru as an apologist for the communist powers.[135] An anonymous editorial on Bandung in *The Courier* decried "sentimentalism about color and race as a cement presumably binding the non-white world together." The editorial dismissed references to "color and race" as nothing more than "convenient propaganda footballs."[136]

Were the many critiques of racism and imperialism that studded the conference merely "propaganda footballs"? The final communiqué of the conference castigated "racial segregation and discrimination" and recognized "the equality of all races."[137] Many observers left with the hope that decolonization would undermine oppressions based on race throughout the world. The African American press consistently described the conference as the first gathering of the "World's Darker Peoples."[138] The NAACP sent a greeting to Bandung that declared, "We salute this effort of the darker people to emerge as an independent world force in the struggle for order, dignity and peace among nations."[139] Even anti-communists, such as Max Yergan and Adam Clayton Powell, while defending the United States at Bandung, strove to present racial equality as a Cold War necessity.[140]

Recognizing the centrality of race and color at Bandung, the African American author Richard Wright chose to entitle his account of the conference *The Color Curtain*. Wright presented the conference as responding to legitimate historical grievances. Nevertheless, he distanced himself from the emphasis on race and religion, "vague but potent forces," that he felt characterized the conference. At Bandung, Wright saw "a racial and religious system of identification manifesting itself in an emotional nationalism which was now leaping state boundaries and melting and merging, one into the other."[141] Wright's belief that an "emotional nationalism" was "leaping state boundaries" failed to recognize the preeminent place of the nation-state at Bandung. The Asian-African Conference had become a pageant of newly independent states in which non-national movements found inspiration but little official recognition. As the widespread press that the conference received in African American newspapers makes clear, the inspirational significance of the conference should not be understated. Nevertheless, as colonies continued to become independent states, inequalities of power and privilege within the postcolonial nation, inequalities often based on class, gender, religion, or caste, would increasingly challenge the narrative of national achievement so prominently displayed at Bandung.[142]

After Bandung, decades of efforts to construct a colored world survived in a reduced form in new notions of a Third World. Constructed in tension with the American and Soviet blocs, the "First" and "Second" worlds, the Third World epitomized the efforts of newly independent nations to maintain their independence while revealing the primacy of the Cold War and the preeminence of the nation-state. In building a Third World rather than a colored world, former anticolonial activists often marginalized questions of intranational injustice. Transnational connections aimed at an expansive freedom became overshadowed by international efforts to achieve a narrowly national independence. The meaning of the Third World for Dalits, African Americans, and other marginalized "minorities" remained unclear.

"Old, deep, sad eyes, looking out of black faces in America, turn towards India with a look of love and understanding—and hope." So wrote William A. Rutherford, a Black businessman from Chicago, in *United Asia* in 1950. "Spiritually, India is to the American Negro and other suppressed peoples of the world," Rutherford wrote, "what the new state of Israel is physically to world Jewry; a bulwark justifying, encouraging and defending their aspirations and struggles against the variously clothed vehicles of tyranny and oppression." Rutherford concluded that "only once in eternity will black America find the champion and the brother it has found in India."[143] Rutherford's warm praise failed to acknowledge the continuing challenges of caste and poverty within India, as well as the constraints imposed on Indian support for African Americans by the Cold War. Nevertheless, his view of India as the champion of Black freedom was not unfounded. Although Indian support for Black struggles was far from uniform, and Indian public figures often muted their solidarity with African Americans, the Cold War endowed even India's divided and at times muted support with the power to advance African American freedom struggles.

In 1967 Rutherford agreed to a request from the Reverend Martin Luther King Jr. to direct the Southern Christian Leadership Conference, a civil rights organization that King helped found. King's creative adaptation of Gandhi's legacy gained support from white Americans and from throughout the world, nowhere more so than India, while tapping into older channels of inspiration that linked African Americans with the wider colored world. Civil disobedience, often framed in Gandhian terms, would create many of the crises through which the Cold War civil rights framework gained traction. While the attainment of Cold War civil rights focused largely on high policy, the movement that emerged in Montgomery, Alabama, in 1955 was a mass movement. Beginning during the Second World War, dozens of activists and thinkers, including many Indians, contributed to creatively re-adapting Gandhi's legacy for the ongoing African American freedom struggle.

CHAPTER SEVEN

Nonviolence and the Nation

> I don't think the Gandhi influence was direct in Montgomery
> where nobody even knew about Gandhi except Martin Luther
> King. The woman who didn't move on that Montgomery bus.
> She just didn't know why she didn't move.
>
> —"A well-known public figure," quoted in Harold R. Isaacs,
> *The New World of Negro Americans*

FIFTEEN YEARS BEFORE Rosa Parks refused to give up her seat on a bus in Montgomery, Alabama, two young Black women were arrested on a bus near Petersburg, Virginia. Like Parks, both women were already actively engaged in the struggle for racial equality. By the time they boarded an old bus bound for Durham, North Carolina, in late March 1940, Pauli Murray and Adelene McBean had long discussed how they could most effectively challenge racial segregation. The poor condition of their bus gave them the opportunity to translate their thoughts into action. Seated near the back of the bus, directly over a wheel, the two young women suffered with every bump. When McBean began to feel a sharp pain in her side, she and Murray occupied seats in the middle of the bus. The driver told them to move back. They refused and, after a lengthy debate with the driver and local police officers, were arrested. Murray wrote friends, "We did not plan our arrest intentionally. The situation developed and, having developed, we applied what we knew of *Satyagraha* on the spot." In her memoirs, Murray remembered that when she and McBean were arrested their knowledge of *satyagraha* was "sketchy" and they had "no experience in the Gandhian method."[1] Like Murray, many Americans would learn the "Gandhian method" in the process of applying it against racial injustice. Less a rigid system than a series of guiding principles and a source of inspiration,

Harold R. Isaacs, *The New World of Negro Americans* (New York: The John Day Company, 1963), 52.

Gandhian satyagraha would be reinvented in restaurants, department stores, buses, and jails throughout the United States.

Since the early 1920s advocates of racial justice in the United States had debated the possibility of launching satyagraha against American racism. Gandhi's dramatic Salt March reignited these debates in the early 1930s. It was not until the 1940s, however, that Americans first began to significantly experiment with using Gandhian techniques to combat racial discrimination. Several of the tactics associated with Gandhi, notably boycotts and marches, had long been employed by African Americans.[2] What was new in the 1940s was the degree to which Gandhi's example motivated and shaped the ongoing struggle for racial justice.

Many civil rights activists and their liberal supporters opposed the introduction of Gandhian techniques. They noted that while Indians were a majority in India, Blacks constituted a minority in the United States. Some suggested that African Americans lacked the "tradition of nonviolence" that Gandhi had successfully tapped in India. Lastly, many argued that while the British were at times violent in their efforts to maintain imperial rule, British tactics paled in comparison to the brutality that American white supremacists had employed and would employ to defend white hegemony. Aware of the differences between colonial India and the United States, and conscious of the great challenges that faced Gandhian satyagraha in America, many civil rights activists nevertheless strove to learn from Gandhi and the Indian struggle.

Given the widespread doubts of many advocates of racial equality and the fierce opposition of white supremacists, attempts to employ Gandhian satyagraha in the struggle for racial justice proved remarkably successful. Understanding these successes and their limitations requires challenging the equation of Gandhi with nonviolence. Many movement participants were drawn less to Gandhian nonviolence (*ahimsa,* or non-harm) than to Gandhian nonviolent civil disobedience (satyagraha). From the early 1920s until the mid-1960s, for the vast majority of civil rights activists, the question was not whether to employ Gandhian nonviolence or the violent tactics of Mao or Che but whether to adopt Gandhian civil disobedience in addition to the lawsuits and lobbying of the NAACP. More than merely a symbol of nonviolence, the Mahatma was seen by many as a "colored" leader who challenged white racism with radical techniques of mass protest and confrontation.

Tracing the legacy of Gandhi in the long civil rights movement challenges the dichotomy between "integration" and Black nationalism. By claiming their rights as American citizens and creating crises in which foreign opinion came to bear, Black protests rendered politically significant old solidarities with Africa and India. Thus Black "integration" with the United States was facilitated, not challenged, by Black "integration" in the larger colored world. In addition to helping link the Cold War and the civil rights movement, connections with India helped movement leaders, and especially Dr. Martin Luther King Jr., forge a vital middle ground in which Blacks could embrace colored cosmopolitanism while reaching out to white allies. Gandhi was a "safe" figure for many whites and yet a paragon of colored activism for many Blacks. By utilizing the racial bipolarity of Gandhi's image in the United States, King built upon the efforts of colored cosmopolitans such as Du Bois and Cedric Dover who had for generations constructed notions of color that were antiracist and anti-imperial but not anti-white.

In the early 1940s several interconnected organizations introduced Gandhian satyagraha into the struggle for racial justice in the United States. While creatively drawing on a variety of links to India, these organizations lacked equally strong connections to African American communities. Bridging the gap between Gandhian activists and the organizing traditions of Black communities, African American labor leader A. Philip Randolph announced near the end of 1942 that his March on Washington movement (MOWM) was considering launching nationwide nonviolent civil disobedience. Widespread concerns that Gandhi's efforts were too radical and would incite violence prevented Randolph's efforts from materializing. When the Montgomery bus boycott began in 1955, however, many observers recognized in the boycott and its young spokesman, Dr. King, the fruition of Randolph's plans and other earlier attempts to bring Gandhian satyagraha to the United States.

King embraced Gandhi's legacy, making it his own. In addition to nonviolence, he adopted the anticolonialism and colored cosmopolitanism that had long linked Black and South Asian freedom struggles. During his trip to India in 1959, King confronted the brutal realities of caste and poverty in independent India. He increasingly expanded his understanding of nonviolence to include opposition to the violence of poverty and war. The boundaries of nonviolence were further enlarged by the student activists who founded the Student Nonviolent Coordinating Committee (SNCC) in the spring of 1960. Tracing the legacy of Gandhi for King and the members of SNCC demonstrates the multifaceted meanings that nonviolence attained in the movement.[3]

The equation of Gandhi with nonviolence overshadowed the continued relevance to Black struggles of Indian anticolonial nationalism, economic self-sufficiency *(swadeshi),* and colored cosmopolitanism at the very time that these ideas found new relevance with the emergence of

Black Power on the national stage. Despite the expansive and heterogeneous notions of nonviolence popular in SNCC, Gandhi's legacy was increasingly restricted to a narrow conception of nonviolence, often unnecessarily defined in opposition to armed self-defense. This limited notion of nonviolence contributed to the rejection of Gandhi and Indian nationalism by many advocates of Black Power who might otherwise have found much common ground with the ongoing Indian struggle. For some, Gandhi ceased to be the radical antiracist activist and symbol of colored liberation that inspired both A. Philip Randolph and Martin Luther King. He became instead an icon of ineffectual tactics and irrational love for the enemy. For many, Gandhi and the larger Indian struggle became overshadowed by violent rebellions in Cuba, China, Vietnam, Algeria, and elsewhere.

While a younger generation of Black Power activists rejected Gandhian nonviolence, Black Power itself influenced protest movements in independent India. The Dalit Panthers, an organization founded in Bombay in 1972, took more than merely its name from the Black Panthers. Just as many civil rights activists understood their efforts as building upon the battle against colonialism, many South Asians came to see the civil rights movement and Black Power as part of a global struggle to achieve freedom and democracy, a struggle they continued to wage in postcolonial India and Pakistan.

War Without Violence

On a sheet of paper, dense with writing, Pauli Murray grappled with what lessons India might offer the African American struggle. Written in March 1940, the same month that Murray and McBean were arrested, Murray's "notes on nonviolence" demonstrate that even the most ardent champions of Gandhian techniques recognized many obstacles to implementing satyagraha in America. Defining what an American satyagraha could and should entail challenged Gandhian activists to reconcile the many differences between Indian and African American freedom struggles. Murray noted India's population (370,000,000), the number of times Gandhi had been imprisoned since the First World War (7), and the amount earned in Indian textile mills by men, women, and children (26, 18, and 7 cents per day, respectively). Then she produced a grid with columns labeled "India" and "American Negro." Each row of her grid contained a comparison, most of which indicated that nonviolent civil disobedience had a higher likelihood of success in India than in the United States. Murray noted that while Indians were a majority in their country, Blacks were a minority in the United States. She contrasted India's "non-violent direct action" with the "legalistic movement [of the] NAACP," and the relatively "unified labor movement" in India with the "dual Jim-Crow unions" of the United States. Murray's grid mostly contained a list of differences, as if she was considering obstacles to her plans. The closest she came to recognizing a point of commonality involved comparing the "tradition of nonviolence" in India with the single word "peaceful" in the column labeled "American Negro."[4]

Gandhian satyagraha meant much more to Murray than merely "nonviolence." After her arrest, Murray wrote friends in New York that she and McBean were "most anxious to discuss with you the Satyagraha technique as applied to ourselves in this situation." Asked to explain how she had applied satyagraha, Murray replied with an extensive list of ten ways that she and McBean had employed a "strict application of Satyagraha." Murray's list included her and McBean's efforts to win the sympathy of white passengers and the police, their willingness to be arrested, and their "educational work with negro prisoners." While in jail, Murray and McBean had sent a letter to the jailer, politely demanding sheets, towels, soap, and some of their belongings. They also shamed male prisoners, housed in an adjacent cell, into apologizing for harassing female prisoners.[5] Challenging injustice, accepting imprisonment, and seeking to educate as many people as possible—this was the core of Murray's understanding of satyagraha.

Although her "notes on nonviolence" had contrasted nonviolent civil disobedience with the "legalistic movement" of the NAACP, Murray's own actions in the wake of her arrest demonstrated that she understood satyagraha and the law as complementary tools. She actively pursued the possibility that her case would be used by the NAACP to win a court ruling banning segregation on interstate buses. Upon her arrest, Murray wired her aunt and adoptive mother, Mrs. Pauline F. Dame, in Durham: "Easter greetings. Arrested Petersburg warrant Greyhound Bus. Don't worry. Contact Walter White."[6] The national office of the NAACP became interested in using Murray and McBean's case to test the constitutionality of segregation on interstate buses. Top NAACP figures, including Charles Hamilton Houston, Thurgood Marshall, and Walter White, corresponded with each other and local lawyers regarding the case. Murray was well aware that the case might be used to set legal precedent. In a letter to Murray and McBean, their lawyer had suggested that theirs could be a "far reaching case," a phrase Murray underlined.[7] Bold and creative, Murray imagined winning not only their criminal case but also a subsequent civil case against Greyhound, the proceeds from which she planned to donate to further activism. She hoped to use a combination of civil disobedience and legal suits to bankrupt companies that practiced segregation. Hers was no narrow conception of satyagraha.[8]

Ultimately the NAACP chose not to pursue the case to the Supreme Court. When, however, in 1946, the Supreme Court ruled that segregation in interstate travel was unconstitutional, the case, *Morgan v. Virginia,* involved a young Black woman who had refused to give her seat to a white couple on a bus in Virginia. Murray worried that the NAACP had been dissuaded from pursuing her case by a negative first-person account of Murray's behavior during the arrest written by a white student and published in *Opportunity,* the magazine of the National Urban League. The most damaging detail in the account would not have been missed by the NAACP despite the fact that the writer himself was oblivious to its significance. The article described Murray as a young man. At a time when lesbian, gay, bisexual, and transgender (LGBT) individuals faced severe repression *within* social justice movements (an injustice only partially remedied today), Murray had striven to keep her sexual identity private. The fact that she was dressed like a man provides one potential explanation for why the NAACP chose not to pursue the case. The fact that the presiding judge had dropped the most constitutionally relevant charge provides another explanation. If Murray's sexual identity did inhibit the actions of the NAACP, it would not have been the last time that Gandhian advocates contributed to the civil rights movement, despite facing discrimination based on sexual orientation.[9]

While Murray pursued her legal case, she simultaneously considered partnering with the editor of a local Black newspaper to begin a mass-based Gandhian movement. The editor of the *Carolina Times,* Lewis E. Austin, in Murray's words, "a firebrand if there ever was any," had asked Murray and McBean to "fight this race battle by starting a Ghandi-type of movement among Negroes." Ultimately Murray decided against attempting to initiate nonviolent civil disobedience. In a letter to friends that outlined her vision for an "American Satyagraha movement," Murray made clear that while she was excited by the potential of mass-based Gandhian civil disobedience, she believed such an effort required careful planning. The first step in Murray's "American Satyagraha movement" entailed meeting with an Indian American sociologist, Krishnalal Shridharani. Shridharani, a veteran of Gandhi's Salt March, had published his Columbia University dissertation in 1939 as *War Without Violence: A Study of Gandhi's Method and Its Accomplishments.* Murray read *War Without Violence* soon after it was published and credited Shridharani's book with inspiring her to ponder applying Gandhian nonviolence "to the racial struggle in the United States."[10] After consulting with Gandhian advisors, Murray proposed gathering "prospective American Satyagraha-ites for further discussion." This discussion phase would be followed by the creation of a "program for action" and "a statement of principles." Murray then suggested official correspondence with Gandhi, a step she believed would provide prestige to the American movement while gener-ating advice from the Mahatma. Then Murray proposed a "call for mem-bership" and the development of an official movement organ.[11] Member-ship came last in Murray's plan. She focused more on the careful study of Gandhian techniques than on the development of local organizational capacity, neglecting the possibility that the organization for a Gandhian satyagraha could originate within Black communities.

The early 1940s witnessed many efforts to combat American racial oppression with Gandhian nonviolent civil disobedience. The majority of these initiatives failed to engage the organizing traditions, creativity, and courage within Black communities. They were, however, inspired by strong and significant ties to India. In the fall of 1939 the viceroy of British India, Lord Linlithgow, unilaterally committed the Indian army and India's resources to the Second World War. Four Methodist mission-aries in India—Jay Holmes Smith, Paul Keene, Ralph Templin, and Lila Horton Templin—responded by sending Linlithgow a letter of protest. Lest the British government restrict the activities of Methodist mission-aries in India, the Board of Foreign Missions of the Methodist Church promptly recalled Smith and Keene. The Templins left India a few months later.[12]

Undaunted, Jay Holmes Smith decided to found an ashram in Harlem, inspired by Gandhi's blend of religious practice, local community service, and nonviolent protest. In India, Smith and Templin had worked to blend Gandhian satyagraha with Christianity, calling the product "Krista-graha." In Harlem, Smith understood his mission as "the rediscovery of original Christianity and its application to such problems as war and ra-cial justice in our time." His ashram included daily Christian worship and Bible study. The ability of ashram residents to blend Gandhian prac-tice and Christianity resulted in part from Gandhi's own religious plural-ism. Their efforts received support from a network of Gandhian Chris-tians that the Mahatma himself had cultivated for decades. Ashram residents gained advice from Muriel Lester, a British pacifist who had lived in one of Gandhi's ashrams and was then serving as the secretary of the International Fellowship of Reconciliation (FOR), a Christian pacifist organization founded during the First World War. Lester helped the ash-ram residents draft a training course in nonviolence, which also benefited from close readings of A. J. Muste's *Nonviolence in an Aggressive World*. Muste, who became the executive director of FOR in 1940 and who had dined with Kamaladevi Chattopadhyaya as president of the War Resister's League that January, practiced a Christian nonviolent activism. He visited the ashram and helped transmit needed funds from renowned missionary and scholar E. Stanley Jones.[13]

The residents of the Harlem Ashram organized an interracial "pilgrimage" to the Lincoln Memorial, strove to end racial discrimination in housing and at YMCAs in New York, and demonstrated against the poll tax in Washington, D.C.[14] The poll tax protest, which occurred in May 1944, brought ashram residents together with eighteen Black ministers in a march around the Capitol building. An ashram memo defined the protest as "one of our most heartening adventures in the application of the way of Jesus and Gandhi to the struggle for racial justice in America." The ashram held a summer training course, after which one Black pastor wrote, "I don't know any experience in my life that has been so helpful as my two weeks at the Ashram."[15] As the poll tax demonstration and the summer training course make evident, the ashram's efforts to partner with Black pastors met with some success.[16] Connections between the ashram and Black organizations remained, however, too few in number and small in scale to be of great significance.

The limited growth of the ashram and, in particular, its inability to attract larger numbers of Black residents resulted in part from the leadership style of J. Holmes Smith himself. Furthermore, many of the most talented young Black Gandhians believed that the ashram should be under "negro leadership" or should at least have an interracial management.[17] The Gandhian austerity of the ashram may have further contributed to its inability to attract larger numbers of residents. One of the ashram's most influential African American residents, James Farmer, later mocked its self-imposed poverty and remembered that the ashram "was as incongruous in Harlem as the Bucket of Blood Bar, which faced it, would have been on a street in Bombay."[18] Another Black resident of the ashram, none other than Pauli Murray, also bristled at the more austere elements of the ashram. In her diary Murray discussed a troubling episode in January 1941 that began as she was about to smoke a cigarette in the ashram. Haridas Muzumdar, who had through books and lectures for over a generation introduced Americans to Gandhi, touched her on the shoulder and told her, "No smoking." Murray went upstairs to smoke with Adelene McBean, missing in the process a visit from A. J. Muste and his wife. The next morning she wrote in her diary, "I agree with Haridas that we must have discipline, but it must be self-imposed, not dictated from without." Murray concluded, "If the ashram is to become a convent or a monastery, then I have no place here."[19]

If the Harlem Ashram had been the only organization attempting to employ Gandhian techniques against American racism, its impact would have been minimal. The ashram was part of a larger movement, however, that succeeded at challenging Jim Crow practices in many cities of the North and West while developing leaders and models of protest that would prove crucial to later civil rights protests. The challenges of the ashram, in particular, its inability to establish strong roots within Black America, inhibited the larger Gandhian movement of the early 1940s. Nevertheless, analyzing the larger world of Gandhian initiatives demonstrates the significance of what the Harlem Ashram did best—introducing young activists to sources of Gandhian inspiration.

Ahimsa Farm, founded in June 1940 by six students from Antioch College, epitomized the potential of young activists galvanized by the Indian freedom struggle. The students were inspired by an Indian sociology professor at Antioch, Manmatha Chatterjee, who donated five thousand dollars to fund a small ashram outside of Cleveland, which the students named Ahimsa Farm. In addition to learning from Professor Chatterjee, members of Ahimsa Farm met with A. J. Muste, J. Holmes Smith, and Krishnalal Shridharani, who gave them a signed copy of *War Without Violence*.[20] Like the residents of the Harlem Ashram, members of Ahimsa Farm mobilized against racial discrimination, collaborated with African American activists, and achieved limited but meaningful success. In the summer of 1941 Ahimsa Farm residents worked with several Black organizations, including the East Mt. Zion Baptist Church and the local NAACP branch, to desegregate the Garfield Park swimming pool in Cleveland. On a hot Sunday afternoon an interracial group entered the pool. Despite the sweltering heat, once the interracial bathers entered, everyone else exited the pool and stood around the rim. Some of the onlookers began to yell "fight," and the integrated bathers left the pool and were surrounded. One of the young Blacks, Herman Wooley, proceeded to give a speech on "democracy as it applied to minority rights," a tactic that effectively disarmed much of the crowd's animosity. A few weeks later another group of integrated bathers entered the pool. This time the attempt to get everyone out of the pool failed. The effort to desegregate the Garfield Park pool demonstrated the potential of collaboration between Gandhian activists and African American organizations.[21] Could such collaboration be accomplished on a larger scale?

In February 1942 James Farmer sent A. J. Muste a long letter encouraging FOR to launch a large-scale Gandhian campaign against racial segregation. Farmer argued against "an uncritical duplication" of Gandhi's efforts in India. Nevertheless, Farmer emphasized several direct lessons that FOR should learn from Gandhi, including the importance of balancing mass participation with "satisfactory discipline and unity" and of cultivating a "religious base." Farmer's emphasis on Gandhian unity inspired him to begin small. Farmer and half a dozen other young people, Black and white, began meeting in Chicago to discuss how to apply Gandhian nonviolence to the struggle for racial equality. The group, which came to be called the Congress of Racial Equality (CORE), read Shridharani's *War Without Violence,* discussing it chapter by chapter. In his letter to Muste, Farmer had noted Shridharani as an inspiration. He had also acknowledged the efforts of J. Holmes Smith and the Harlem Ashram, where Farmer himself would soon come to live. Ashram residents had themselves collectively read *War Without Violence* and had received a visit by Shridharani himself. The overlapping relationships between individuals such as Shridharani, Farmer, Murray, and Muste, as well as organizations such as FOR, Ahimsa Farm, the Harlem Ashram, and CORE, demonstrate the interconnected nature of efforts to enlist Gandhi's example in the struggle for racial justice in the United States.[22]

Soon after its founding in 1942, CORE emerged as the most dynamic organization engaged in translating Gandhian satyagraha into the American context. In May the group began to implement sit-ins in restaurants in Chicago. In addition to Farmer, key leaders included Bernice Fisher and Homer Jack, both white divinity students at the University of Chicago, and George Houser, a white staff member of FOR. CORE grew quickly, in part by affiliating with local organizations and in part by tapping the resources and personnel of FOR. In addition to Houser and Farmer, CORE's links with FOR included a young Black pacifist named Bayard Rustin, who would become one of the most influential conduits between the Indian freedom struggle and efforts to employ nonviolent civil disobedience within the United States. In 1942 and 1943 Rustin traveled the country spreading the word about FOR and CORE and encouraging local protest movements.[23]

In cities across the North and West, integrated CORE chapters challenged segregation in restaurants, skating rinks, movie theaters, and other public arenas. CORE did not attempt a major Southern campaign, however, until 1947. On April 9 of that year, sixteen men, eight white and eight Black, left Washington, D.C., on a "journey of reconciliation" organized by George Houser and Bayard Rustin. Traveling through Virginia, Kentucky, Tennessee, and North Carolina, the integrated group tested compliance with a recent Supreme Court decision outlawing segregation on interstate travel. Arrested in North Carolina, Rustin and another Black freedom rider were sentenced to thirty days on the chain gang, while two white riders received ninety days. In the time between his sentencing and when he had to report to the chain gang, Rustin traveled to India, where he was warmly received by leading Indian figures, including Jawaharlal Nehru. Although contributing to Indian knowledge of the burgeoning civil rights movement, the "journey of reconciliation" failed to gain significant nationwide attention or to inspire widespread acts of protest throughout the South. The limitations of the journey of reconciliation spoke to the limitations of CORE, which were in turn emblematic of the majority of efforts to employ Gandhian satyagraha in the early 1940s. Gandhian activists had been unable to mobilize Black communities on a large scale, especially in the South. The closest they came to sparking a nationwide grassroots movement involved a brief, but historically significant, partnership between FOR and one of the premier civil rights leaders of the early 1940s, A. Philip Randolph.

Mobilizing the Masses

In June 1941 President Franklin Delano Roosevelt signed Executive Order 8802, prohibiting racial discrimination in the defense industry and establishing a Fair Employment Practices Committee. By threatening a march on Washington, A. Philip Randolph, the founder of the Brotherhood of Sleeping Car Porters, had pressured Roosevelt to guarantee that the economic opportunities of the war would be equitably shared. Randolph understood the power of mass mobilization and used the threat of protest to maintain pressure on the Roosevelt administration. After the beginning of the Quit India movement in August 1942, Randolph increasingly turned to Gandhi as a source of inspiration and tactics for the MOWM. Near the end of that year, Randolph announced that in six months the national conference of the MOWM would consider launching a nationwide civil disobedience campaign modeled along Gandhian lines. Randolph's plans garnered vocal opposition from many Blacks and liberal whites and ultimately failed to develop into action.

While demonstrating the significant obstacles to utilizing Gandhian satyagraha in the United States on a national scale, Randolph's efforts laid a foundation for the successes of similar initiatives in the 1950s and 1960s. Randolph framed the lessons of Gandhi as Christian in spirit and American in practice. At the same time he used the language of colored solidarity to explain his commitment to Indian independence and to encourage Blacks to join a global movement for the freedom of the oppressed darker races. Randolph imagined a mass-based Gandhian satyagraha grounded in colored cosmopolitanism and led by an all-Black organization in partnership with white liberals and Gandhian activists. He demonstrated that transnational linkages could reinforce a Black militancy that exceeded the American nation while making claims upon it.

Randolph aimed to emulate Gandhi's successful mobilization of the Indian masses. In September 1942, one month after the outbreak of the Quit India movement, Randolph outlined his vision of a "Negro Liberation Movement" in a speech to the Policy Conference of the MOWM. He called for picketing, marches, and civil disobedience and proclaimed, "Witness the strategy and maneuver of the people of India with mass civil disobedience and non-cooperation and marches to the sea." While Randolph's references to Indian civil disobedience were most directly inspired by the events of the past month, his reference to "marches to the sea," evoking Gandhi's Salt March of 1930, demonstrated Randolph's awareness of the history of the Indian struggle for independence.

In early January 1943 banner headlines in African American newspapers across the country reported Randolph's plans to launch a civil disobedience campaign inspired by Gandhi. Black readers were encouraged to consider a variety of nonviolent protest tactics, including eating in "whites-only" restaurants and boycotting segregated train and trolley cars. "If they are ejected they should not fight back," several articles declared, "but during that week Negroes should constantly keep up their program of refusing to enter Jim Crow cars and waiting rooms in an orderly, peaceful and quiet manner."[24]

Randolph's emphasis on order and peacefulness did not prevent critics from arguing that Gandhian civil disobedience was too radical and would alienate white liberals and incite violence from white supremacists. An editorial in *The Atlanta Daily World* opposed satyagraha as "revolutionary and radical" and unlikely to work given the manifold differences between the struggles of Indians and African Americans.[25] In April *The Pittsburgh Courier* published a poll in which 70.6 percent of African American respondents opposed a "non-violent civil disobedience campaign" as not likely to help Blacks. According to *The Courier*, many felt that "Gandhi's way," while suited to "the way of the Oriental mind," was "not suited to the temperament of the American Negro."[26]

Several of the key disagreements between supporters and detractors of Randolph's plan were made evident in a pair of editorials in *The New York Amsterdam News*. The first, published on March 13, 1943, and written by W. E. B. Du Bois, opposed Randolph's plan to launch civil disobedience along Gandhian lines. Du Bois noted that while Indians were an overwhelming majority in the subcontinent, African Americans were a distinct minority in the United States. In addition, Du Bois argued, "Fasting, prayer, sacrifice and self-torture, have been bred into the very bone of India for more than three thousand years." He explained, "That is why the fasting to death of a little brown man in India today is world news, and despite every effort to counteract it, is setting four hundred millions . . . a-quiver and may yet rock the world." Differences in "culture patterns," Du Bois believed, meant that a similar effort in the United States "would be regarded as a joke or a bit of insanity." Du Bois's use of the phrase "little brown man" echoed Frederick Fisher's influential biography of Gandhi. Unlike Fisher, however, who had striven to present Gandhi as "Aryan," despite his brown skin, Du Bois used the phrase "little brown man" to communicate the combination of skepticism and respect with which Du Bois looked toward Gandhi as a "colored" leader.[27]

Du Bois's skepticism regarding Gandhi stretched back at least to the publication in 1928 of *Dark Princess*, a book whose many references to India contained only a few passing and largely negative references to the Mahatma. *Dark Princess* had, however, offered a compelling vision of transnational antiracist revolution grounded in cultural, religious, and racial fluidity. In contrast, in his *New York Amsterdam News* editorial, Du Bois framed Gandhian methods as ill suited to the American context by treating Indian culture as seamless, unchanging, and foreign. Du Bois failed not only to recognize Gandhi's cosmopolitanism but also the greatest lesson of *Dark Princess*—that creativity, having long transgressed the fluid boundaries of culture, could yield novel forms of protest. Like the respondents to *The Pittsburgh Courier* who distinguished between "the Oriental mind" and "the temperament of the American Negro," Du Bois overlooked the degree to which Americans, and particularly Black Americans, could make satyagraha their own.

On May 29 Ralph Templin, the Methodist missionary who had contributed to the founding of the Harlem Ashram, responded to Du Bois's reservations regarding Gandhian nonviolence in a letter to *The New York Amsterdam News*. Templin countered Du Bois's claim that civil disobedience was culturally inappropriate for the United States by stating that Gandhi had borrowed many of his ideas from abolitionists, including Henry David Thoreau. Templin argued that civil disobedience was an American original; its use in India demonstrated its universality, not its cultural particularity.[28] Although Templin overstated the American roots of satyagraha, his defense of the universal applicability of Gandhian nonviolent civil disobedience was prophetic. Creative attempts to adapt satyagraha to American conditions had already begun. These attempts would bear fruit in the 1950s and 1960s, in part because of the continuing efforts of Ralph Templin, A. Philip Randolph, and the many other American advocates of satyagraha already active during the war.

Randolph's strongest support came from those pacifists who had already begun experimenting with Gandhian nonviolence in the struggle for racial justice. A. J. Muste congratulated Randolph for his "vision, intelligence and courage" and compared Randolph's plans to the "epoch-making" movement Gandhi initiated in South Africa.[29] J. Holmes Smith called Randolph a "distinctly American Gandhi" and published an article in the *Christian Century* magazine defending the MOWM. Randolph, in turn, asked for Smith's guidance in the use of nonviolence, and the two met in person to discuss the implementation of nonviolent civil disobedience.[30] In April 1943 Randolph sent Charles Wesley Burton, the chairman of the Chicago division of the MOWM, to a conference in Detroit on the use of nonviolent civil disobedience against American racism. Speakers at the conference included Haridas Muzumdar, A. J. Muste, and E. Stanley Jones.[31] A few months later, Jones advocated nonviolent protests in one of the closing speeches of the widely publicized "We Are Americans Too" nationwide conference of the MOWM, held at Chicago.[32] At the same conference, William Stuart Nelson, James Farmer, J. Holmes Smith, Bayard Rustin, and the national executive secretary of the MOWM, E. Pauline Myers, all discussed "Non-violent goodwill direct action—what it is and how it can be applied to abolishing Jim Crow."[33]

Many opponents of racial oppression, both white and Black, chose not to support Randolph's proposed civil disobedience. This opposition demonstrates the radical nature of Randolph's plans. In response to Randolph's announcement that the MOWM would consider a civil disobedience campaign, FOR solicited the opinions of a variety of leading American liberals as to whether Blacks should practice "organized, non-violent civil disobedience to Jim Crow." Edited by James Farmer and published with an essay by A. J. Muste as a double issue of the *Non-Violent Action News Bulletin,* the responses to FOR's questionnaire were decidedly mixed. In his influential *Moral Man and Immoral Society,* published in 1932, theologian Reinhold Niebuhr had suggested Gandhian techniques for the struggle against racial injustice.[34] In response to FOR's query, however, Niebuhr discouraged civil disobedience and instead suggested a campaign "which has the support of the law." Haridas Muzumdar defended the right of African Americans to use civil disobedience but asked if "goodwill and reconciliation" had already been sufficiently exhausted. Oswald Garrison Villard stated that he was "opposed to Negroes practicing non-violent civil disobedience at this stage of their development." Blacks were not "emotionally ready."

While only a few respondents strongly rejected the idea of utilizing non-violent civil disobedience, many suggested that civil disobedience would prove effective only after concerted efforts to train protesters in nonviolence. Many respondents cited Gandhi in order to clarify what they saw as the weaknesses of an American satyagraha. For Buell S. Gallagher, the president of Talladega College, the difference was simple: "India has a Gandhi and we have none." Several stated, as had Du Bois, that Indian culture better suited nonviolence. Others stressed the extreme violence of American white supremacists. An unnamed professor in a southern Black college explained, "In India, Gandhi is jailed; in Georgia, he'd be lynched."[35]

In the early 1940s, in the midst of the Quit India movement, Gandhi was perceived by many as a radical revolutionary. Only later did he become associated primarily with nonviolence. While emulating Gandhian tactics, Randolph was forced to defend his goals and techniques as more moderate than Gandhi's. In a series of newspaper editorials, Randolph stressed that the "non-violent, good-will direct action" under consideration by the MOWM was a "modified expression" of what Gandhi had taught.[36] He explained that while Indian leaders sought a transfer of power, the MOWM aimed merely to achieve equality within the United States. Randolph emphasized that he wanted to uphold, not undo, the American constitution. He advocated the most moderate version of what many had come to see, largely as a result of the writings of Krishnalal Shridharani, as Gandhi's method. Protesters would be trained before entering a segregated restaurant. If refused service, they would calmly seek an explanation. If verbal persuasion failed, they would file a lawsuit. Only then would the group return to engage in what Randolph, echoing the famous CIO protests of the 1930s, called a "sit-down strike."[37]

Confronted by charges that Gandhian techniques were foreign and, in the midst of war, unpatriotic, Randolph presented his tactics as distinctly American. He entitled his proposed week of nonviolent protests "I am an American, too," and he stressed, perhaps too optimistically, the unifying potential of civil disobedience. "Instead of hindering the war," Randolph argued, "it will help the war by developing a deep sense of national unity because it seeks to achieve what the war seeks to achieve, namely, democracy."[38] In an article that contained a large photo of Gandhi, Randolph dubbed his version of Gandhian tactics "constitutional obedience" and strove to present them as Christian. He acknowledged that Gandhian satyagraha had been criticized as "a strategy which was born in a foreign and oriental situation." Randolph parried, "By the same token of reasoning one could condemn Christianity and reject it as a product of an oriental clime. Jesus Christ, like Gandhi, was born in the eastern world."[39]

Randolph's plans to employ Gandhian nonviolence failed to materialize. Widespread resistance to the idea of civil disobedience, grounded in the justifiable fear of white supremacist retaliation, convinced Randolph and his advisors to table their civil disobedience campaign. By announcing a bold, nationwide initiative, rather than beginning small and working with a few select Black communities, Randolph forfeited the opportunity to demonstrate the feasibility of a satyagraha based in the Black community.[40] Nevertheless, the MOWM raised the visibility of Gandhian nonviolent civil disobedience, preparing the ground for later initiatives, including Randolph's own successful efforts to desegregate the military in 1948. In June of that year, only months after Gandhi was killed, Randolph joined with FOR to create a League for Non-Violent Civil Disobedience against Military Segregation.[41] Randolph became the chairman of the league, with Bayard Rustin and George Houser of FOR serving as executive co-secretaries. As in 1943, Randolph issued bold statements threatening massive civil disobedience. He told a congressional committee, "In resorting to the principle of direct-action techniques of Gandhi, whose death was publicly mourned by many members of Congress and President Truman, Negroes will be serving a higher law than any passed by a national legislature in an era when racism spells our doom."[42] After Truman issued an executive order ending segregation in the military, Randolph canceled his plans for civil disobedience.[43] As in 1941, Randolph demonstrated that threats of mass protest could produce tangible results.

Even as he strove to present Gandhian satyagraha as distinctly American, Randolph championed Indian independence as a vital component of the global struggle for democracy. His efforts to implement Gandhian satyagraha must be understood as one facet of a multidirectional transnational relationship. Like Randolph, the majority of individuals and organizations that strove to learn from Gandhi simultaneously worked to end British colonialism in India. Wielding colored cosmopolitanism and an expansive notion of freedom, American Gandhians positioned the burgeoning civil rights movement and the Indian independence movement within the larger struggle to end racial and imperial hierarchies throughout the world.

In the spirit of global double victory, Randolph argued that victory against racism and imperialism was a vital component of victory against fascism. At the Policy Conference of the MOWM in September 1942,

Randolph proclaimed, "Unless this war sounds the death knell to the old Anglo-American empire systems, it will have been fought in vain." The conference passed a resolution supporting Indian independence, calling for the release of arrested Indian leaders, and demanding an immediate end to the "the wanton murder of the Indian masses."[44] The following month, Randolph told a meeting of the American Federation of Labor that it was "pure hypocrisy to talk of this war as being fought for democracy while India is continually oppressed by British autocracy."[45]

Like Randolph, the majority of activists committed to utilizing Gandhian nonviolence in the United States understood their efforts as part of a global struggle against injustice in which attaining India's independence was central. Ahimsa Farm members followed the Quit India movement closely and discussed ways of traveling to India to participate in Indian civil disobedience protests.[46] Members of the Free India Committee, headquartered at the Harlem Ashram and including residents of Ahimsa Farm, considered using fishing boats to launch a "non-violent expeditionary force" to India and promoted wearing Gandhi caps emblazoned "Free India Now."[47] A Harlem Ashram document praised Indians, Puerto Ricans, and Blacks for fighting "imperialistic exploitation" and "that white domination which is akin to it." Ashram residents worked with the Free India Committee to organize pickets of the British consulate and embassy.[48]

Pauli Murray also spoke out in support of Indian independence. After her arrest, Murray wrote a friend, explaining that she wanted to contact an Indian student who was scheduled to speak at the Southern Negro Youth Conference in New Orleans. "We want to get in touch with him," Murray explained, "and let him know that already the technique of the Indian movement is being put into action as a test for its adaptability to the American minority struggle." The student was Rajnikant Patel, Kamaladevi Chattopadhyaya's travel partner, who did much to solidify the relationship between Paul Robeson and Jawaharlal Nehru. In August 1942 Murray wrote Krishnalal Shridharani, "I want you to know how deeply sympathetic I am, and many other Negroes are, to the point of view you expressed in the India crisis." As a delegate to the International Student Assembly in Washington, Murray helped pass a resolution calling on Great Britain to grant India "political freedom," despite the fact that Eleanor Roosevelt asked Murray to oppose the resolution. Soon after the beginning of the Quit India movement, Pauli Murray sent a letter to the editor of the *New York Herald Tribune,* supporting Indian independence and proudly noting that "13,000,000 of our own Negro citizens" and every "outstanding Negro leader" were "intensely interested in how the United Nations handle the Indian question."[49]

Even critics of Randolph's plan supported Gandhi and the Indian cause. While opposing the application of Gandhian civil disobedience in the United States, Du Bois expressed sympathy with Indian anticolonialism. He exhorted his readers, "Remember that we American Negroes are the bound colony of the United States just as India is of England."[50] Many of Randolph's critics, while questioning the applicability of Gandhian satyagraha, nevertheless recognized the Indian struggle as an antiracist movement of colored people. In 1944 Du Bois declared, "The greatest color problem in the world is that of India, with its 389 millions of colored folk, under the domination of Great Britain."[51] *The Pittsburgh Courier* wrote, "In India there are 390 million colored folk and about 250,000 white people; while in the U.S.A., there are 120 million white folk and 13 million colored folk." Thus while arguing against the relevance of Gandhian tactics to a minority, *The Courier* paralleled Blacks and Indians as colored people.[52]

While many Black commentators portrayed the Indian cause as vital to the worldwide struggle of the darker races, some recognized Randolph's proposed civil disobedience as part of that global initiative. Lucius C. Harper, writing in *The Chicago Defender* in July 1943, offered Randolph, Gandhi, and Nehru as leaders of a "ferment of discontent" on the part of "members of the colored races throughout the world."[53] On September 4, 1942, a few weeks after the beginning of the Quit India movement, Pauli Murray told readers of *The Call*, the organ of the Socialist Party, "The eyes of the colored peoples of the world, including our own national minority of Negroes, are fixed upon India today."[54] A few days after the Quit India movement was launched, Murray wrote Randolph, "Even on vacation, the Indian situation haunts me." Murray suggested that the MOWM initiate a rally to protest India's plight and encouraged Randolph to publicize his support of the Indian cause.[55]

Randolph often positioned his efforts within what he called "the world-wide problem of color and exploitation." A few weeks after Gandhi initiated the Quit India movement, Randolph told an audience at the Mid-West Headquarters of the YWCA in Chicago, "Colored people of America, the West Indies, and Africa should support this grim, determined and courageous battle for freedom of the Indian people under the gallant, wise and dauntless leadership of Mohandas K. Ghandi." Indians, he asserted, "constitute one of the great oppressed and exploited sections of the darker races of the world."[56]

Randolph's colored cosmopolitanism provides a transnational context in which the contested racial dynamics of his movement appear in a new light. Limiting the MOWM to Blacks helped protect the organization from the control of white communists but drew the ire of many of Randolph's opponents. One critic, *Chicago Defender* editorialist John Robert Badger, linked Randolph to Krishnalal Shridharani's *Warning to the West,* a book about the potential for a future world war between whites and non-whites. Calling Randolph a "Negro isolationist" and a "racist," Badger criticized Randolph for perpetuating the "race war bug-bear." As evidence, Badger quoted from a speech Randolph had given at an NAACP convention in Louisiana: "Now the darker races are not only fighting for the right to live and the right to be free, they are entering the struggle for power, world power."[57] Randolph's call for power to the darker races prefigured later invocations of "Black Power," a phrase that would, like Randolph, be criticized as "racist." For Randolph, colored cosmopolitanism was neither anti-white nor anti-American. While encouraging "the darker races" to struggle for their freedom, neither Shridharani nor Randolph sought a global race war. On the contrary, Randolph's relationship to Indian struggles, while strengthening his sense of colored solidarity, simultaneously facilitated Randolph's efforts to partner with white Gandhians. More than a decade would pass before the African American residents of Montgomery, Alabama, would demonstrate that large numbers of Blacks could withstand violent retaliation without resorting to self-defeating violence. The Montgomery movement would produce a leader who, like Randolph, embodied Gandhi's multifaceted legacy. Even more successfully than Randolph, Dr. Martin Luther King Jr. used Gandhi's legacy to balance his roles as a Black leader, an American leader, and a world leader.

Montgomery's Mahatma

On December 1, 1955, an African American seamstress and local NAACP leader named Rosa Parks was arrested for refusing to give up her seat on a bus in Montgomery, Alabama. Black leaders, having long awaited an opportunity to protest the daily indignities Blacks faced on Montgomery's buses, quickly organized a city-wide bus boycott. For 381 days, some 50,000 Montgomery Blacks stayed off the buses, many walking miles every day. The boycott brought national and international attention to a twenty-six-year-old pastor named Martin Luther King Jr., whom many came to see as a Black Gandhi.

It is difficult to distinguish what Gandhi meant to King from the history of how King made use of Gandhi to craft a particular public image. King had encountered Gandhian ideas as a student at Morehouse College and at Crozer Theological Seminary, where his advisor was a pacifist. In early November 1949 King heard A. J. Muste speak at Crozer. Afterward the two had "a pretty heated argument," according to one of King's classmates, who later remembered, "King sure as hell wasn't any pacifist then." The following year King heard Mordecai Johnson, the president of Howard, speak in Philadelphia. King found Johnson's account of Gandhi "so profound and electrifying" that he immediately "bought a half dozen books on Gandhi's life and works." Or so King remembered it in 1958, in *Stride toward Freedom,* a work that explained King's relationship to Gandhi largely as a result of King's personal intellectual journey. Ironically, while the text borrowed from the writings of several of King's Gandhian advisors, it obscured the many contemporary sources of King's Gandhian beliefs. King's reading surely influenced his understanding of Gandhi, but equally important were King's personal and intellectual relationships with a variety of eminent American students of Gandhi, Mordecai Johnson being one of many.[58]

It is important to neither overstate nor ignore the significance of Gandhi for King before Montgomery. J. Pious Barber, editor of the *National Baptist Voice* and a family friend King often visited during his time at Crozer, remembered that King would often argue "all night" on behalf of "Gandhi and his methods against my thesis of coercion." In a letter written in February 1957, King stated that Gandhi had "a definite influence" upon his thinking and said that he had read most of Gandhi's major works before coming to Montgomery. In contrast, Gandhian pacifist Glenn Smiley remembered that a few months after the boycott had begun, he had told King, "I'm assuming that you're very familiar and have been greatly influenced by Mahatma Gandhi." King responded that in fact he knew "very little about the man" and expressed eagerness to learn more.[59]

It was the boycott itself that offered King the opportunity to make clear his commitment to Gandhi as a model and as a source of inspiration. King's first public address after the beginning of the boycott made no mention of Gandhi. Only a few weeks after the boycott began, however, the editor of the *Birmingham World,* a Black newspaper, wrote that King "often tells the story of how Mahatma Gandhi, the emaciated emancipator, liberated India with his nonviolence campaign."[60] When, in April 1957, King was asked to name the books and authors that had "strongly influenced" him, three of the five titles he listed were directly related to Gandhi: Louis Fischer's renowned biography of Gandhi, Richard Gregg's *The Power of Non-Violence,* and Gandhi's *Autobiography.*[61] What inspired and shaped King's burgeoning references to Gandhi? A week after the boycott began, Montgomery librarian Juliette Morgan wrote a letter to the editor of the *Montgomery Advertiser* comparing the protest positively with Gandhi's efforts in India.[62] The national and international press quickly identified the boycott as Gandhian, as did many activists, scholars, and religious figures who wrote King to encourage him to learn from Gandhi or to congratulate him for already having done so.[63] Several prominent Gandhian activists, most notably Glenn Smiley and Bayard Rustin, came to Montgomery to advise King in person. The public proliferation of highly positive comparisons between King and Gandhi, coupled with the private encouragement of many friends and advisors, played a crucial role in inspiring King to present himself as Gandhian. Through his personal connections with older Black students of Gandhi, such as Benjamin Mays and Mordecai Johnson, as well as through the ongoing resonance of Gandhi in Black civil society, King inherited and made his own a distinctly African American Gandhi. King's Gandhi, rooted in the long history of Black anticolonialism and much more than a symbol of nonviolence, embodied the power of colored cosmopolitanism wedded to the liberation theology of the Black church.

Many of the figures who wrote King regarding Gandhi stressed anticolonialism and civil disobedience as much as nonviolence. One of King's fraternity brothers, for example, wrote King, "In the hands of Gandhi civil disobedience proved to be a potent political weapon. It may also prove to be such in the hands of the Southern Negro."[64] Even many of the Gandhian pacifists who flocked to the movement stressed Gandhi's antiracism and his anticolonialism as much as his nonviolence. At the "Institute on Non-Violence and Social Change," hosted by King to mark the anniversary of the beginning of the bus boycott, Homer Jack, one of the founders of CORE and a Unitarian minister, declared of Gandhi, "If he did anything for the Indian people under imperialism, he took away from them all fear of their white masters."[65] FOR produced a documentary film that juxtaposed Montgomery's story with Gandhi's experiences in South Africa and India. Its title, *Walk to Freedom*, demonstrated the ongoing power of an expansive conception of freedom as a link between Black and Indian struggles.

For King, as for A. Philip Randolph and the members of CORE, Gandhi represented the courage to defy injustice as much as the moral imperative to do so nonviolently. King's early references to the Mahatma focused as much on the liberating potential of Gandhi's tactics as on their nonviolence. In March 1956 King told a large audience at Brooklyn's Concord Baptist Church, "Gandhi was able to break loose from the political and economic domination by the British and brought the British Empire to its knees." He challenged his audience to "use this method in the United States."[66] In 1958 King wrote, "Nonviolent resistance is not a method for cowards; it does resist." He explained, "This is why Gandhi often said that if cowardice is the only alternative to violence, it is better to fight."[67] For some Montgomery Blacks, Gandhi's pursuit of independence meant as much as his commitment to nonviolence. During a sermon in 1959, King declared, "I would say the first thing that we must see about this life is that Mahatma Gandhi was able to achieve for his people independence." One member of the congregation responded with a resounding "Yes" before King could complete the sentence with the phrase "through nonviolent means."[68]

King's emphasis on the active resistance of Gandhian satyagraha resulted in part from the fact that, unlike A. Philip Randolph, King found himself speaking on behalf of a movement that had already demonstrated discipline and nonviolence. Many of Montgomery's Blacks had developed their own commitment to nonviolence, inspired equally by common sense and a Christian conception of forbearance. One woman in Montgomery explained, "Gandhi's all right, but we get this straight from Jesus Christ."[69] Understanding what King or other high-profile leaders learned from Gandhi must not entail overlooking the wealth of indigenous protest traditions and local community organizing that drove much of the civil rights movement. Neither should Gandhi's legacy be understood as an elite inheritance. Although many of the advocates of Gandhian concepts were well traveled and well educated, the fact that King's Gandhi emerged within a Christian vocabulary and as a distinctly "colored" leader increased the potential resonance of Gandhi for many Blacks.

Many advisors encouraged King to understand Gandhi as a religious, if not distinctly Christian, figure. Benjamin Mays forwarded King a letter from Reverend Hazel Elora Foster, a former Morehouse professor with a PhD from the University of Chicago Divinity School, who had met Gandhi while in India during the period 1939–1941. In exuberant prose, Foster wrote, "I have wondered whether, now Gandhi has died, his ideas and ideals had died with him. You prove to me they have not. And as he was earnestly trying to follow the Sermon on the Mount, so you are folowing [sic] his grat [sic] example—Jesus."[70] Not all of King's advisors saw Gandhi and Christ as so tightly linked. George D. Kelsey, a professor of Christian ethics with whom King had studied at Morehouse, suggested that King make clear that "the movement which you so nobly led was Christian in motivation and substance." He wrote in the margins of a draft chapter of Stride Toward Freedom, King's account of the Montgomery boycott, "Christ furnished the spirit and motivation, while Gandhi furnished the method," a crucial line that King put in the final version.[71]

King marshaled long-established Christian readings of Gandhi to defend his relationship with the Mahatma. When King set up a tax-exempt organization to channel donations to the Southern Christian Leadership Conference (SCLC), he named it the "Gandhi Society for Human Rights." Harold Fey, editor of the *Christian Century,* criticized King for not choosing a "Christian" name. King responded, "I believe that in some marvelous way, God worked through Gandhi, and the spirit of Jesus Christ saturated his life. It is ironic, yet inescapably true, that the greatest Christian of the modern world was a man who never embraced Christianity."[72] In addition to defending Gandhi by linking him with Christ, King defended his own Christianity by linking it to Gandhi. In *Stride Toward Freedom,* King remembered a Methodist minister arguing that a church leader should not be encouraging a boycott but, rather, leading a congregation to "a glorious experience of the Christian faith." King responded, "We are only doing in a minor way what Gandhi did in India; and certainly no one referred to him as an unrepentant sinner; he is considered by many a saint."[73]

Without King, historian George Fredrickson declared, "There would have been civil rights movements but no Civil Rights Movement." King's ability to unify—far from perfect—owed much to his ability to inhabit Gandhi's legacy. King's connection to Gandhi strengthened his appeal to both Blacks and whites. Gandhi represented courage, civil disobedience, and the rising colored world to many Blacks while symbolizing nonthreatening nonviolence to whites.[74]

On February 2, 1959, the day before he embarked on his first and only journey to India, King spoke at the annual dinner of the War Resister's League in New York. "It may even be possible," King told the audience, "for the colored peoples through adherence to nonviolence, so to challenge the nations of the world that they will seriously seek an alternative to war and destruction." Did King's understanding of "colored peoples" transcend the borders of the United States and the racial borders of the word "Negro"? His decision to pluralize "peoples" indicated such a colored cosmopolitanism, as did a line in King's original draft that proclaimed, "This is the great hour for the Negro and the other colored peoples of the world."[75]

King repeatedly made clear that his understanding of "colored people" included Asians. The links between India and Africa, and in particular the use of civil disobedience in Ghana, contributed to King's understanding of India as a leader of the colored world.[76] During his trip to India,

King later wrote, he and his traveling companions had been looked upon "as brothers with the color of our skins as something of an asset." He explained that "the strongest bond of fraternity was the common cause of minority and colonial peoples in America, Africa and Asia struggling to throw off racialism and imperialism." According to one of the organizers of King's trip, James Bristol of the Quaker Center, Indians did not see King as an American but "as the champion of the oppressed peoples of the world—in America, Asia and Africa." King in turn portrayed Gandhi as a courageous colored man fighting for the freedom of his people. In his Palm Sunday sermon on Gandhi, King stressed that Indians were "humiliated and embarrassed and segregated in their own land." King told the story of Gandhi's expulsion from the first-class compartment of a train in South Africa: "They noticed that he was an Indian, that he had a brown face, and they told him to get out and move on to the third-class accommodation." King's portrayal of Gandhi as fighting against racial segregation and King's own colored cosmopolitanism make more significant the fact that King regularly referred to Gandhi as the "little brown man in India."[77]

King's trip to India solidified his standing as a Gandhian while diversifying his debt to Gandhi and India. The trip was organized by the Gandhi Smarak Nidhi (Gandhi Memorial Fund) and the American Friends Service Committee (AFSC). The Kings traveled through much of India, meeting eminent personalities such as Jawaharlal Nehru, the prime minister, Jayaprakash Narayan, the socialist freedom fighter who had dedicated his life to antipoverty community work, Rajendra Prasad, the president of India and a longtime Gandhian pacifist, and Sarvapalli Radhakrishnan, a world-renowned philosopher and India's vice president. Coretta Scott King remembered her husband comparing their itinerary to "meeting George Washington, Thomas Jefferson, and James Madison in a single day."[78]

During his first press conference in India, King declared, "To other countries I may go as a tourist, but to India I come as a pilgrim." Throughout the trip, King made clear that his was a pilgrimage primarily to the land of Gandhi. King spent the night in a home Gandhi often used in Bombay, visited Gandhi's Sabarmati Ashram, and met with Vinoba Bhave, then perhaps Gandhi's preeminent living disciple.[79] King's association with Gandhi contributed to the positive press he received in India. On January 30, 1958, the *Hindustan Times* published a tribute to Gandhi in which King compared the Mahatma to Abraham Lincoln. The editor added, "A Baptist clergyman in Montgomery, Alabama, Dr. King has been called 'the American Gandhi.'"[80]

What did it mean to be "the American Gandhi"? More than nonviolence, King's trip to India reinforced his commitment to economic justice. Mrs. King remembered, "The sign of emaciated human beings wearing only a dirty loincloth, picking through garbage cans, both angered and depressed my husband." Even before he visited India, King repeatedly praised the success of Gandhi's efforts to end the economic exploitation of India. Traveling in India sharpened King's appreciation of Gandhi's concern for the poor. In his Palm Sunday sermon on Gandhi, delivered in March 1959, King lamented the poverty of the Indian people under colonial rule and stressed Gandhi's determination to end poverty. In an account of his trip "to the land of Gandhi," published in *Ebony* in July 1959, King decried the economic inequality he witnessed in India and concluded, "The bourgeoisie—white, black or brown—behaves about the same the world over."[81]

Confronting the intersection of class and caste in India sharpened King's analysis of the structural inequalities of race and class in the United States. In his article for *Ebony*, King wrote that even India confronted "the problem of segregation." "We call it race in America; they call it caste in India," he wrote. "In both places it means that some are considered inferior, treated as though they deserve less."[82] Before the Kings had left for India, one of the organizers of the trip, G. Ramachandran, himself born into an Untouchable family, wrote King that he thought King "would be particularly interested to know how Gandhiji wrestled with the problem of untouchability in India and succeeded in showing the [way] out against the heaviest odds."[83] Such a framework for understanding the history of caste, in which Gandhi emerged as a hero, would remain central to King's own understanding. In his Palm Sunday sermon on Gandhi, King recalled seeing the poverty Dalits faced in India and stressed Gandhi's opposition to untouchability. King mentioned that Gandhi had adopted an untouchable girl and described Gandhi's 1932 fast, by which Gandhi successfully opposed granting separate electorates to Dalits, as a fast against untouchability. King overlooked the tensions between Gandhi and renowned supporters of separate electorates such as Dr. Ambedkar. In his article for *Ebony*, "My Trip to the Land of Gandhi," King mentioned that Gandhi took untouchables by the hand into temples, and declared, "To equal that, President Eisenhower would take a Negro child by the hand and lead her into Central High School in Little Rock."[84]

While King recognized the ongoing brutality of caste in India, he concluded that "India appears to be integrating its untouchables faster than the United States is integrating its Negro minority." Both nations had laws against discrimination, King explained, "But in India the leaders of Government, of religious, educational and other institutions, have publicly endorsed the integration laws." Furthermore, the Indian government had "set forth a constitutional provision making untouchability illegal" and had spent "millions of dollars a year in scholarships, housing, and community development to lift the standards of the untouchables."[85] In his book *Why We Can't Wait*, King recalled Jawaharlal Nehru's defense of India's policy of "reservations" for Dalits in government employment and education. When King's travel companion, Lawrence Reddick, asked if such an affirmative action policy constituted reverse discrimination, Nehru responded that it might but that it was still a necessary "way of atoning for the centuries of injustices we have inflicted upon these people."[86]

King's interest in caste continued after he returned from India. In April 1959 King asked William Stuart Nelson for "books or pamphlets" on the caste system, explaining that he was "making a study of untouchability." Nelson replied with materials, adding that Black protests were "proving a source of great encouragement to and re-awakening of people in India . . . thereby serving the cause of non-violence in the very country which has witnessed its most significant demonstration."[87] The First Southwide Institute on Nonviolent Resistance to Segregation, held in July 1959, featured speeches not only from King but also from Nelson and Richard Gregg. One of its resolutions stated, "We make common cause with the oppressed and submerged peoples of the world—particularly the unfreed peoples of Africa and the former 'untouchables' of India. We call upon them to adhere to the principles of nonviolence in our common world struggle."[88]

Poverty proved central to King's understanding of what united the "submerged peoples of the world." In a sermon on "The American Dream," delivered at Ebenezer Baptist Church on July 4, 1965, King recalled being introduced during a visit to a school for Dalits in the South Indian state of Kerala. The principal of the school proclaimed, "Young people, I would like to present to you a fellow untouchable from the United States of America." King explained that for a moment he was "a bit shocked and peeved" that he had been "referred to as an untouchable." But then, he told his congregation, he began to think about motels where he could not stay, lunch counters that would not serve Blacks, still segregated buses and schools, and the fact that "twenty million of my brothers and sisters were still smothering in an airtight cage of poverty in an affluent society," and that "these twenty million brothers and sisters were still by and large housed in rat-infested, unendurable slums in the big cities of our nation." Finally, King told his audience, "I said to myself, 'Yes, I am an untouchable, and every Negro in the United States of America is an untouchable.'" King's sermon bears a strong resemblance to an earlier account written by King's advisor, Benjamin Mays, of his own visit to a school for Dalits. That King borrowed the account from Mays matters less, however, than that King chose to introduce an emphasis on urban poverty that was in tune with his own experiences in India and his growing concerns about the structural racism of urban ghettos.[89]

In July 1957 W. E. B. Du Bois published an article on "Gandhi and the American Negroes" in the magazine *Gandhi Marg*. Du Bois prophesied that "it may well be that . . . real human equality and brotherhood in the United States will come only under the leadership of another Gandhi."[90] As an American Gandhi, Martin Luther King did much to inspire, to mobilize, and to unify the ongoing civil rights movement. A full understanding of Gandhi's legacy, however, requires recognizing the power of grassroots community organization. In the early 1960s it would be countless committed individuals, many inspired by Gandhi, working within the organizing traditions of local Black communities, who would drive the civil rights movement.

Nonviolence and Revolution

On February 1, 1960, four students from North Carolina A&T University sat down at the "whites only" lunch counter of the local Woolworth's variety store, sparking a wave of student-led "sit-ins." The four students had seen a documentary on Gandhi a few months earlier and had read some of Gandhi's writings while discussing what they could do to challenge segregation.[91] As with the bus boycott in Montgomery, news reports compared the sit-ins and Gandhian satyagraha. Even President Eisenhower was asked for his opinion on the recent "Gandhi-like passive resistance demonstrations."[92] This was not the first time that students had led sit-ins against Jim Crow segregation. In 1943 and 1944, for example, students at Howard University organized a series of sit-ins at segregated restaurants in the nation's capital. Pauli Murray, then a student at Howard Law, emerged as one of the leaders of the movement. Murray wrote Eleanor Roosevelt that the Howard protesters "were convinced they must find a technique which was uniquely American even though it might have Gandhian elements within it."[93]

Between 1940 and 1960 many Americans perceived Gandhi as a radical. Paradoxically, as the most confrontational Gandhian tactics swept the country in the early 1960s, Gandhian "nonviolence," not civil disobedience or colored solidarity, increasingly dominated the understanding of Gandhi among both movement activists and the general public. By embracing a notion of nonviolence that excluded armed self-defense, some civil rights advocates, including Martin Luther King, narrowed the public perception of Gandhian tactics, even while they themselves developed diverse and quite radical understandings of Gandhi's legacy. A narrow conception of nonviolence, coupled with the brutality of white supremacists and the slow, often inadequate response of federal authorities, undermined the perceived viability of nonviolent civil disobedience. Increasingly skeptical that nonviolent civil disobedience could change structures of injustice so deep and pervasive, some activists left the movement, while others began to promote violent rebellion.

A month after the first Greensboro sit-in, a group of students gathered at Shaw University in Raleigh, North Carolina, to discuss how to maintain and coordinate the momentum of the sit-ins. The name of the organization they created, the Student Nonviolent Coordinating Committee (SNCC), spoke to the centrality of nonviolence to their understanding of the movement. James Lawson, a theology graduate student at Vanderbilt, played a central role in shaping SNCC's understanding of nonviolence. Lawson joined FOR and CORE as a young man, spent fourteen months in prison for refusing to be drafted in 1951, and served for three years as a Methodist missionary in Nagpur, India. In February 1957 Martin Luther King encouraged Lawson to come to the South to help in the movement. After A. J. Muste created a position for him in FOR, Lawson settled in Nashville, where he began training local Black college students in nonviolent civil disobedience. Participants in Lawson's workshops read Gandhi and studied the Indian freedom struggle while preparing to launch nonviolent civil disobedience. When protests in Nashville began, John Lewis, a key SNCC leader and a regular participant in Lawson's workshops, added a note to the instructions given to protesters in Nashville: "Remember the teachings of Jesus, Gandhi, Thoreau, and Martin Luther King Jr." A group of Lawson's Nashville students, including Lewis, would play a central role in mobilizing and directing the future of SNCC.[94]

SNCC emerged as the vanguard of a larger student engagement with Gandhian nonviolent civil disobedience in the early 1960s. Student protesters learned of Gandhi through films and lectures at churches and schools and by reading Gandhi's autobiography and other Gandhian tracts. Richard Gregg's *The Power of Nonviolence* received top billing in a list of recommended books published in SNCC's *Student Voice* magazine.[95] Martin Luther King and the SCLC publicized the lessons of Gandhi, among other ways, by presenting the "Gandhi Award" annually to that person "doing the most during the year for better race relations through use of direct, non-violent action."[96] CORE also inspired young student activists to engage with Gandhi's legacy. In 1960 CORE delegates debated Gandhian nonviolence and its implications in Miami, and Charles R. Oldham, the national chairman of CORE, declared, "We must widen and deepen the understanding of nonviolent direct action so that soul force, the Satyagraha of Gandhi, develops and transforms our society."[97]

For student activists, as for Martin Luther King and A. Philip Randolph, the radical potential of civil disobedience remained an important element of Gandhi's legacy. One leaflet declared that the sit-in protesters had "revolutionized" the struggle "with the sophisticated technique of nonviolent protest, adopted from their patron saint, the Indian Mahatma Gandhi."[98] Many SNCC activists saw in Gandhi a leader who recognized the power of grassroots mobilization. Diane Nash, one of the leaders of the Nashville movement, later explained that the most important lesson she had learned from reading Gandhi was that, in the words of historian David Halberstam, "leaders did not expect others to do things they were not willing to do themselves." In July 1961, as he rushed to join a procession in which he would be savagely beaten, SNCC activist Bob Zellner remembered a quote he attributed to Gandhi: "There go my people. I have to go and run and catch up because I am their leader."[99]

Many student activists interpreted Gandhian concepts to reflect their own experiences in the movement. Jim Zwerg connected James Lawson's discussion of satyagraha or "soul-force" to the power of communal singing. Zwerg remembered "singing some of those freedom songs, and that bond starts building and that soul—that soul-force that Jim Lawson used to call it. And by golly there's *nothin'* that's gonna' stop you."[100] Gandhi, a consummate fan of spirituals, would have no doubt been gladdened by this connection between satyagraha and the collective singing so central to the civil rights movement. Jerome Smith, a twenty-one-year-old pacifist, remembered that his chapter of CORE in New Orleans had "a deep Gandhian philosophy." While Jim Zwerg had found "soul-force" in song, Smith understood Gandhi's legacy in terms of discipline and sacrifice. "In fact we spent hours talking about Gandhian philosophy and willingness to give our lives," Smith recalled. "We would not eat and talk for days as a means of acquiring discipline."[101] For Jim Bevel, Gandhi's decision to wear minimal clothing offered an opportunity to confront the challenges of Mississippi jails. When another student activist lamented the poor and minimal clothing they had been offered by prison authorities, Bevel responded that Gandhi had "wrapped a rag around his balls and brought down the entire British empire."[102]

Many student activists associated Gandhi primarily with the multifaceted word "nonviolence," which often meant much more than the absence of physical violence. SNCC's founding statement declared, "We affirm the philosophical or religious ideal of nonviolence as the foundation of our purpose, the presupposition of our faith, and the manner of our action."[103] When a new member in the movement, Bernice Johnson, asked veteran SNCC activists Charles Sherrod and Cordell Reagon what "nonviolent" meant in the title of SNCC, Reagon responded, "Nonviolence is love, love for your fellow man."[104] Jailed in Jackson, Mississippi, several students announced that they were going to go on a hunger strike. James Farmer remembered, "The enthusiasm of these college students ran high and they were full of Mahatma Gandhi and imbued with a sense of history in the making." Along with James Lawson, Farmer led a series of daily workshops on "nonviolence and Gandhi." Farmer remembered, "Those who mechanically 'bought' the mechanics of nonviolence were stung by its effectiveness and startled by the near-theology of its impact on them." In jail, Farmer explained, "[T]he injunctions of Gandhi acquired shape and size . . . and for the first time a word, 'nonviolence,' left the academic vocabulary and joined the real issue in the real world."[105]

What did it mean to recognize the "effectiveness" of nonviolence while imprisoned in jail? Student accounts of imprisonment offer little evidence that nonviolent protests changed the hearts or minds of southern jailers. Away from reporters and cameras, the suffering so many activists endured behind bars could have little immediate impact on national sentiment. Movement memoirs offer many examples of courage and personal transformation experienced behind bars. For most activists, however, personal transformation, while meaningful, was not sufficient. The goal remained to combat the inequalities and injustices of American society. While James Farmer felt that jail heightened the respect activists felt for Gandhian nonviolence, for some the vicious brutality of white supremacists made "nonviolence" seem all the more foreign and irrelevant. After four young girls were killed in the bombed-out basement of the 16th Street Baptist Church in Birmingham, SNCC veteran Anne Moody told another movement leader, "If Martin Luther King thinks nonviolence is really going to work for the South as it did for India, then he is out of his mind."[106]

Even many of those who remained committed to employing nonviolent civil disobedience chose to distinguish between nonviolence as a philosophy and as a tactic. According to SCLC leader Hosea Williams, "Nonviolence as a way of life was just as foreign to blacks as flying a space capsule would be to a roach." One SNCC member, Don Harris, estimated that between 50 and 75 percent of SNCC activists rejected "strict adherence to nonviolence" as early as 1961 and 1962.[107] King himself often distinguished between nonviolence as a method and as a way of life. In *Stride Toward Freedom,* King wrote, "Living through the actual experience of the protest, nonviolence became more than a method to which I gave intellectual assent; it became a commitment to a way of life."[108] King made clear that he did not believe that nonviolence would become a way of life for the majority of Blacks. He noted that many followers of Gandhi, including Nehru, had pursued nonviolence on largely tactical grounds. During his trip to India, King was asked, "Is non-violence with you a creed or a policy?" He responded, "I have come to believe in it as a way of life. Perhaps most people in America still treat it as a technique."[109]

What did it mean to believe in nonviolence as "a way of life"? In both the United States and India, Gandhians differed in their interpretation of a nonviolent life. For Gandhi, nonviolence entailed vegetarianism. King, when asked in India if his conception of nonviolence included vegetarianism, responded with the single word, "No."[110] King's personal commitment to nonviolence became most evident in his persistent antimilitarism, exemplified by his courageous and controversial opposition to the war in Vietnam. In his tribute to Gandhi, published in the *Hindustan Times,* King wrote, "If we fail, on an international scale, to follow the Gandhian principle of non-violence, we may end up destroying ourselves through the misuse of our own instruments. The choice is no longer between violence and non-violence. It is now either non-violence or non-existence."[111] King discussed the potential for a nonviolent international politics with Nehru. Although he believed in nonviolence between individuals, Nehru argued that one nation could not survive if it embraced nonviolence when facing a violent threat. In remarks broadcast on All-India Radio, King disagreed. "It may be that just as India had to take the lead and show the world that national independence could be achieved nonviolently," King declared, "so India may have to take the lead and call for universal disarmament."[112] King's statement demonstrated the gap between India's foreign policy and the ideals of Gandhi, a gap made evident in an interchange between Black pacifist Bill Sutherland and the president of India, Rajendra Prasad. Prasad told Sutherland that he regretted resigning from an honorary position he had held in the War Resister's League. With a smile, Prasad explained that he could not represent the War Resister's League and be the commander in chief of the Indian armed forces.[113]

King's understanding of nonviolence changed over time, in part as a result of the influence of Gandhian pacifists. When Bayard Rustin visited

King's home during the early days of the Montgomery boycott, he found armed guards on the porch and weapons scattered throughout the house. Did this mean that King had yet to embrace nonviolence? Rustin later stated, "The fact of the matter is that when I got to Montgomery, Dr. King had very limited notions about how a nonviolent protest should be carried out." Rustin reported to colleagues that King was "developing a decidedly Gandhi-like view" and was "eagerly learning all that he can about nonviolence."[114] Glenn Smiley also strove to influence King's relationship to Gandhi and nonviolence. Along with Smiley and other Gandhian pacifists, Rustin convinced King to embrace a conception of nonviolence that was explicitly opposed to armed self-defense. The career of Robert F. Williams, a charismatic leader suspended from the NAACP for advocating armed self-defense, exemplifies the lost opportunities that resulted from the dichotomization of Black freedom struggles into oversimplified notions of violence and nonviolence. Armed self-defense and nonviolent protest were not mutually exclusive. Rather, the ability of nonviolent activists to mobilize Black communities depended largely on the capacity of local Blacks to physically defend activists. At the same time the willingness of nonviolent protesters to suffer brutal assaults brought national and international pressure to bear on the federal government. Nonviolent tactics and armed self-defense worked together to channel white violence into less deadly and more politically useful situations.[115]

Obscuring the practical symbiosis between nonviolent civil disobedience and armed self-defense, Gandhi's legacy became reduced to a narrow notion of nonviolence that was increasingly marginalized by calls for more "militant" resistance. In 1962 poet LeRoi Jones (later Amiri Baraka) criticized "the idea of 'passive' resistance" as "an Indian 'rope trick' that cannot be applied in this scientific country."[116] In 1965 novelist John Killens wrote in *Black Man's Burden*, "Please do not give us the example of India and Mohandas Karamchand Gandhi." He declared, "The situations are not similar; they could not be more dissimilar."[117] Meeting in Baltimore in 1966, CORE delegates voted to eliminate a commitment to the "technique of nonviolence in direct action" as a requirement for chapters. Floyd McKissick, CORE's chairman, attacked nonviolence as a "dying philosophy" that had "outlived its usefulness" and asserted, "I think nonviolence in the future will only be a technique and a strategy."[118] In 1969, well after many of its original members had left, SNCC changed its name to the Student *National* Coordinating Committee. The burgeoning Black Power movement, despite drawing heavily on transnational linkages with the Third World, turned away from Gandhi and India to violent revolutions in Cuba, China, and North Vietnam. The

nonviolent nationalism of the Indian freedom movement had little significance for many Black nationalists of the 1960s and 1970s.

Recent scholarship has challenged accounts of a sharp break in the
civil rights movement in the mid-1960s to the late 1960s by demonstrating that much of what is associated with Black Power had developed
earlier, especially in the cities of the North and the West.[119] The history of
African American connections to Gandhi both supports and challenges
this new assessment. On the one hand, the history of Black anticolonialism and Third World solidarity, so evident in early references to Gandhi
and India, linked Black Power with early struggles. Both A. Philip Randolph and Martin Luther King led all-Black organizations while expressing solidarity with the colored world. On the other hand, the tendency
for some Black Power advocates to embrace violence, at least on a sym-
bolic and rhetorical level, should be distinguished from the nonviolent
conceptions of struggle that dominated the movement until at least the
mid-1960s. Paradoxically, the rejection of Gandhian nonviolence resulted in part from the centrality it attained in the self-presentation of
both King and the early SNCC. As nonviolence became increasingly contrasted with armed self-defense, advocates of the latter became associated
with overt violence, whether urban riots or armed rebellions. The fruitful
balance between colored solidarity and white support and between nonviolent civil disobedience and armed self-defense became increasingly
untenable.

All the Blacks of the World

In September 1963 the Bombay-based journal *United Asia* reported on
the March on Washington for Jobs and Freedom during which Martin
Luther King delivered his iconic speech, "I Have a Dream." In 1859, two
years after the Sepoy Rebellion, known by some as the First War of Indian
Independence, the white abolitionist John Brown was hanged after attempting to foment rebellion among the six million slaves living in the American
South. Noting the wrong year and confusing John Brown and his friend,
the renowned African American abolitionist Frederick Douglass, the
United Asia editorial stated, "Frederick Douglas was the abolitionist negro killed in the year 1857—the year in which the brown-skin Indians of
Asia rose in their first mighty revolution against the white imperialism of
the British." Thus *United Asia* used the racial dimensions of British colonialism to connect its readers to the struggles of African Americans.
Bringing this race/colony comparison forward in time, the editorial declared, "The atrocities on negro demonstrators reminded people in India

of their experience of the British methods of suppression during Gandhi-ji's great movements of 1920, 1930 and 1942." The editorial concluded, "These memories of the past rose up to our minds and we could almost feel physically the pain, the anguish, the suffering of the negroes." The editorial simultaneously recognized that a race/caste comparison remained to challenge Indians:

> The millions of untouchables in India might as well regard the negroes' struggle for equality and human dignity as their own struggle. . . . Their struggle against the high caste tyranny is almost identical in content with the great battle the negroes of America are fighting. It may be that the American negro is fighting not only for himself and for his brethren in America but for all the submerged castes, for all the blacks of the world whether they be in America or in India.[120]

King's "I Have a Dream" speech and his legacy more generally have become neatly contained in a national story in which the goals for which King fought are presented as having all been accomplished. King's engagement with caste reveals a more expansive understanding of the ongoing African American struggle, a struggle that continues to have relevance for, as the editors of United Asia put it, "all the blacks of the world."

Even as the influence of Gandhi declined among African Americans, the legacy of Martin Luther King took on new meaning in India. In 1969 the Indian Postal Service issued a commemorative stamp that memorialized Dr. King, and the United States Information Service, New Delhi, distributed a twenty-six-page tribute to King.[121] On June 16 of that year, J. J. Singh, the influential businessman who had defended the rights of Indian Americans in the 1940s, sent his friend Jayaprakash Narayan an impassioned letter. During his trip to India, King had met Narayan, who had dedicated his life to eradicating poverty via Gandhian community organizing. Narayan had become a vocal critic of the government's failure to effectively reduce poverty and had recently been quoted in the press seeming to condone violent opposition to the government. In 1968 J. J. Singh had presided over a discussion on "Black Power" at the India International Center in Delhi. In his letter to Narayan, he turned to the lessons of Black Power to convince Narayan "that man will remain close to the animal so long as he is unable to eschew violence." Singh wrote, "Negro leaders in America will tell you that but for the violence methods adopted by the negroes, no advancement of the coloured people would have taken place." Singh granted, "This may be so," but added that "some people must think and work for the ultimate good of the human race which can be achieved only be eschewing violence. Martin Luther King kept on talking of non-violence notwithstanding the fact that almost all negroes decried his stand."[122]

Viewed from the subcontinent, the Black Power and civil rights movements overlapped within a shared struggle for human rights that transcended national notions of freedom. On March 15, 1970, Kamaladevi Chattopadhyaya published an articled entitled "Black Power on the Move" in the Bombay-based newspaper *The Bharat Jyoti*. Rather than focus on recent events, Kamaladevi demonstrated the continuity of Black Power with earlier assertions of colored solidarity. She narrated her own encounters in the 1940s with Indian Muslims who had journeyed to the United States to forge links with African American Muslims.[123] In June 1972 a group of young Dalits formed the Dalit Panthers in Bombay. On August 15, 1973, the twenty-sixth anniversary of Indian independence, the Dalit Panthers organized a march of some two hundred people through the streets of Bombay in a celebration of what they called "Black Independence Day" (*"Kala Swatantrya Din"*). Drawing on the legacy of the Black Panthers, the Dalit Panthers challenged a narrative in which "independence" had already come to the Indian people. The very name "Dalit Panthers" marshaled notions of blackness and Black Power to present Dalit resistance as militantly unbounded by the triumphant complacency of self-proclaimed "democratic" nation states. A Dalit Panther manifesto declared:

> Due to the hideous plot of American imperialism, the Third Dalit World, that is, oppressed nations, and Dalit people are suffering. Even in America, a handful of reactionary whites are exploiting blacks. To meet the force of reaction and remove this exploitation, the Black Panther movement grew. From the Black Panthers, Black Power emerged. . . . We claim a close relationship with this struggle.

Popular publications, ranging from *Time* to the Dalit magazine *Asmitadarsha,* contributed to Dalit knowledge of the Black Panthers. Much like their American namesake, the Dalit Panthers found their political and economic goals stymied by official repression and undermined by internal disagreement but nevertheless left a significant cultural and literary mark on the ongoing Dalit struggle.[124]

Just as the legacy of Gandhi in the civil rights movement extended well beyond Martin Luther King, so the involvement of South Asians in the movement extended beyond Gandhi. As the example of Krishnalal Shridharani makes evident, many South Asians played central roles in translating Gandhian satyagraha into the American context. Others publicized South Asian opposition to American racial oppression, thus helping frame civil rights as a crucial front in the Cold War. South Asians did more, however, than speak in defense of civil rights protests; they joined them. Although too few in number to have a major influence on the course of the civil rights movement, several South Asians utilized their racial ambiguity to make evident the arbitrary and constructed nature of Jim Crow.

Traveling through the American South in the early 1950s, Rammanohar Lohia, a leading Indian socialist, encouraged African Americans to employ nonviolent civil disobedience. As the secretary of the All-India Congress Committee's Foreign Department, Lohia had written W. E. B. Du Bois in 1936 to establish "the closest relations with our Negro comrades of America."[125] In 1951 Lohia lectured on "the Awakening of Asia and Africa" at Fisk University's annual race relations institute. He also spoke at the Highlander Folk School, an innovative and racially integrated community organizing center in the hills of Tennessee. Lohia was accompanied on his travels by Harris Wofford, a white lawyer who had studied at Howard University and had lived in India for several years. After Lohia returned to India, Wofford wrote him, "Maybe one of these days some of your prescriptions for [the] USA will be carried out. I'm sure civil disobedience would be the best thing for our health—but it must be a healthy dose of it." Wofford helped prepare such a "healthy dose" of civil disobedience. In 1951 he published a book on Lohia's travels, further publicizing Lohia's call for civil disobedience.[126] A few years later, in November 1955, Wofford asked an audience at the Hampton Institute, "Do not we here, in carrying on the work which the lawyers of the NAACP have started so well, need to adopt and adapt the principles and practices which Gandhi demonstrated in South Africa?" Wofford's speech was noted in the Black press and reproduced widely. One copy made its way to E. D. Nixon, soon to become a driving force behind the Montgomery bus boycott. A longtime member of A. Philip Randolph's Brotherhood of Sleeping Car Porters, Nixon would have recognized in Wofford's speech a continuation of Randolph's earlier efforts. Nixon passed on the speech to King, who would himself find Wofford a valuable advisor.[127]

When the Montgomery bus boycott began, Jawaharlal Nehru had for over twenty years expressed solidarity with African American freedom struggles. It was thus not surprising that in December 1956 Nehru "responded with enthusiasm" to the opportunity to meet King, an opportunity that proved elusive for the time being. A few years later, King gave Nehru a copy of *Stride Toward Freedom* in which he wrote, "We hope that as the march to the sea ushered in mass action leading to India's independence, so our efforts here may become a part of the great liberation movement changing the face of the world." Nehru responded in January 1959, thanking King for sending *Stride Toward Freedom* and saying that he hoped to meet King in India soon. Nehru added, "I have long been interested in the work that you have been doing and, more especially, in the manner of doing it." In October 1960, just a year after meeting King in New Delhi, Nehru, now in New York, received a citation celebrating the birthday of Gandhi from CORE leaders who were themselves working to implement Gandhian satyagraha in the United States. While accepting the citation, Nehru stated that he was "all for racial equality" and was "proud" and "pleased" that Gandhi's legacy was contributing to its achievement in the United States.[128]

Prominent South Asian visitors to the United States repeatedly expressed solidarity with the civil rights movement. In 1958 Kaka Kalelkar, a close associate of Gandhi's and a member of the Indian parliament, visited Montgomery. Kalelkar spoke at a mass meeting and later wrote King, "I have no doubt about the ultimate success of the coloured people. The American constitution is on your side, and so are justice and the spirit of the Times with you. Need I add that the prayers of millions of my country folk are also on your side?" Kalelkar encouraged Indians to support the Montgomery protest by proclaiming that both Martin and Coretta Scott King were "pious people after the heart of Mahatma Gandhi."[129] The Indian ambassador M. C. Chagla strongly endorsed the sit-ins and other movement protests. In April 1960, speaking alongside Howard University's president, Mordecai Johnson, at Washington's elite Cosmos Club, Chagla called racial prejudice "anachronistic" and "antediluvian." At Kansas University Chagla praised "massive non-violent, non-cooperation" and compared sit-ins to the Indian struggle for independence.[130] Chagla often compared race and caste. In 1959 he praised Martin Luther King in an address to some six hundred cadets at the Maxwell Air Force Base in Montgomery, Alabama. He compared the Indian government's efforts to eliminate caste oppression to the federal government's response to Jim Crow segregation.[131] By comparing race and caste, Chagla challenged Indians and Americans to achieve their democratic ideals.

Indian newspapers and magazines offered regular and consistently sympathetic coverage of the civil rights movement. In October 1956 the weekly *Mankind*, affiliated with Rammanohar Lohia, published an article by Harris Wofford on "civil disobedience in Alabama." One of the editors of *Mankind* solicited several articles on African American struggles for an edition on "World Satyagraha" scheduled for publication in 1960.[132] In Bombay *United Asia* closely covered the civil rights movement, often noting the use of Gandhian techniques. An editorial in October 1962 praised SNCC for utilizing "the technique of non-violent mass resistance to injustice, oppression, and exploitation which Gandhiji evolved in India." "Gandhi does not live in the pontifical sermons of Indian leaders, nor does he live in the statues of stone," the editorial declared. "He lives today in the brave non-violent action of American Negroes."[133]

In addition to expressing solidarity with the civil rights movement through the media, some Indians met directly with movement activists. In 1960 Sucheta and Jivatram Bhagwandas (J. B.) Kripalani visited the United States. Eminent Gandhian activists, both Kripalanis had been actively involved in anticolonial protests and after independence remained prominent figures in Indian politics. In the United States the Kripalanis spoke on the Montgomery bus boycott and the sit-ins and met with veteran Gandhians Mordecai Johnson and William Stewart Nelson at a small gathering at the Indian Embassy.[134] In Atlanta they participated in a SNCC training at Morehouse College, where they met with Martin Luther King and Coretta Scott King, with whom they had dined in India. At Morehouse the Kripalanis spoke about their time working with Gandhi to end violent riots between Hindus and Muslims. One participant remembered the Kripalanis stressing "how they were absolutely terrified, but did it nonetheless," a sentiment that would have reverberated for young SNCC activists confronting the threat of violence day after day.[135]

South Asian support for the Black freedom struggle extended beyond famous leaders. Two of the participants at the Kripalani SNCC training were Jaswant Krishnayya and Ahmed Meer, Indian students at MIT who decided to spend their summer vacation in the South learning about the civil rights movement from student activists. Meer remembered, "We were both concerned with the plight of the American Blacks and found it inconsistent with the American image and ideals we had come to admire in the short time we had been in the US." Meer and Krishnayya traveled through Tennessee, Georgia, Alabama, and Louisiana. They established close connections with student activists throughout the South, who offered support and guidance. After the trip had concluded, Meer and Krishnayya sent a letter to the friends they had made in the South. "It would be trite perhaps," they wrote, "to say that we think this is a historic time in the story of democracy (as is, for example, the Indian experiment)." Meer and Krishnayya positioned Black efforts and "the Indian experiment" side by side within the global struggle for democracy. Back at MIT, Krishnayya published an editorial in *The Boston Globe,* condemning violence in the South and defending the civil rights movement as a struggle for "simple human rights."[136]

On May 28, 1964, more than a decade after he had traveled through the American South encouraging African Americans to embrace Gandhian civil disobedience, Rammanohar Lohia, now a prominent member of the Indian parliament, himself offered satyagraha in Jackson, Mississippi. Lohia relished the opportunity to be arrested for confronting Jim Crow. He had been turned away from Morrison's Cafeteria the night before his arrest and chose to return in order to court arrest. Dressed in sparkling-white cloth that distinguished him as Indian, Lohia attempted to enter the restaurant for the second time. When the manager asked him to leave, Lohia replied, "I tell you with greatest humility, I am not leaving." The police arrested him, put him in a paddy wagon, and drove him away from the restaurant before releasing him. The State Department promptly sent a formal apology to the Indian ambassador. Decrying his treatment as "tyranny against the United States Constitution," Lohia told reporters that both the State Department and the Indian Embassy "may go to hell." Segregation was a moral issue, he stressed, not a political one. When told that the American ambassador to the United Nations, former Senator Adlai Stevenson, would offer his apologies, Lohia replied that Stevenson should apologize to the Statue of Liberty.[137]

Like the Kripalanis, Lohia understood the American civil rights movement as part of a global struggle for justice. Describing Lohia as a "short, brown-skinned political leader," *The Chicago Defender* reported that Lohia understood protests in Mississippi as part of a worldwide "revolution against color inequality." This was the twenty-first time that Lohia had been arrested. "The fact that I had not been arrested in America," Lohia explained, "was something of a blemish on my record."[138] Lohia understood the connections between discrimination based on color throughout the world. In January 1960 Lohia wrote a close friend, decrying the treatment of "the Negroes and the coloured peoples" and connecting this discrimination to color prejudice within India. He had "been speaking on the colour of the skin being no criterion of beauty," Lohia explained, "but there is either not much of a comprehension or else the dark ones have imbibed the teaching of the white colour being superior in such a deep way that they cannot easily get rid of it."[139] Lohia tackled caste discrimination as well. The Socialist Party that Lohia helped found mandated that 60 percent of its officials belong to the "scheduled castes" and other minorities in India. After his arrest, Lohia frequently emphasized that the problem he was confronting in Mississippi, what he called "the challenge of colour and caste," also existed in India. Lohia told one journalist, "Let me make it perfectly clear that I am not trying to uncover or publicize something foul in American life. Such foul spots exist everywhere—also in India."

Like many southern establishments, Morrison's Cafeteria would normally have served an Indian dignitary on the grounds that he was both foreign and not "a Negro." Why then was Lohia twice refused entry? Lohia's treatment came as a response on the part of Morrison's management to the efforts of two South Asian professors at Tougaloo College. For months before Lohia arrived, Hamid Kizilbash, a Pakistani professor, and Savithri Chattopadhyay, an Indian professor, had actively engaged in efforts to desegregate Jackson. In a particularly fitting example, Kizilbash and Chattopadhyay, along with other Tougaloo faculty, had accompanied a group of Black students to see *Lord of the Flies* at the whites-only Capri Theater. Kizilbash tried to buy tickets for the group, explaining that his students had studied the book. The manager refused, but did offer to show the film for free in the "colored theater." On a different night, an interracial group was able to gain admission at the segregated Paramount Theater, although a white teacher wondered if the fact that Chattopadhyay had dressed in a sari "was the acceptance factor." Chattopadhyay's Indian identity did not, however, always shield her from racial discrimination. On Palm Sunday she was forcibly expelled from Galloway Methodist Church, which allowed only "whites" to worship God.[140]

A few days before Lohia arrived in Jackson, Jerrodean Davis, a Black Tougaloo student, Chattopadhyay, and a white faculty member went to Morrison's downtown cafe where, to their great surprise, they were served. The following day Jawaharlal Nehru died. Chattopadhyay and another Indian faculty member went to Jackson to send a cablegram to India to express their grief. On the way home they were refused service at a different branch of Morrison's, the same chain of cafes in which Chattopadhyay had been served alongside a Black student only the night before. When questioned, the manager explained that the previous day no one had known whether Jerrodean Davis was Black or Indian, and it was only that racial confusion that had led to the group being served. Once the restaurant's management learned that Davis was Black, orders were issued to all chains to not serve any South Asians, perhaps out of recognition that the racial boundary between "Negro" and "Indian" was too difficult to establish on sight, or perhaps out of retribution for the protest activities of South Asian faculty members at Tougaloo. Unfortunately for the management at Morrison's, they had chosen to institute this unusual extension of Jim Crow, a ban on South Asians, only a few days before Lohia arrived in town.[141] Lohia was excluded not because he was mistaken for Black but because the whites of Jackson had learned to see South Asians as a danger to Jim Crow segregation.

The South Asian faculty members at Tougaloo challenged the borders of race and nation, not only by actively engaging in civil rights protests but by doing so together. Indians and Pakistanis worked together with white and Black Americans to confront Jim Crow. The day after Lohia's arrest, Hamid Kizilbash was attacked while driving home from a civil rights rally with Reverend Ed King. Forced to stop by a caravan of angry whites, Kizilbash, King, and the other passengers locked the doors of their car and prayed. The threatening mob produced clubs, guns, and a can that appeared to contain gasoline. When one man threatened to break the windows of the car, Kizilbash rolled down his window to bargain for their safety. He was immediately struck on the side of the head, while his attackers began to pry open his door. As blood began running down Kizilbash's face, Reverend King screamed, "He's not Negro, he is Indian." The attackers immediately stopped their assault. Perhaps after considering that Kizilbash might be the famous dignitary who had been arrested only the day before, the mob decided to let the car go with a warning to never return. Undaunted by his beating, Kizilbash reported the incident to the Mississippi Highway Patrol and to the local sheriff, although neither did anything to apprehend his assailants. Kizilbash's case did find mention in a publication of the United States Commission on Civil Rights, which reported that Kizilbash had told investigators that he believed he would have been killed if he was not South Asian, a fact that Kizilbash deemed "the greatest irony of my existence here."[142] At first mistaken for Black, the Pakistani professor had ultimately been saved by being mistaken for a leading Indian. Only a year before India and Pakistan would go to war for the second time, the potential unity of South Asia found hopeful expression on a lonely stretch of road outside Jackson, Mississippi.

Conclusion

The Reflection of What Is

Poets, prophets, and reformers are all picture makers—and
this ability is the secret of their power and of their achievements.
They see what ought to be by the reflection of what is, and
endeavor to remove the contradiction.

—Frederick Douglass, "Pictures"

EGINNING IN THE LATE nineteenth century, South Asians and
African Americans learned from each other in ways that not
only advanced their respective struggles for freedom but helped
define what freedom could and should mean. This transnational exchange did not entail the clean transfer of ideas, practices, or identities.
Rather, a complex process of self-transformation through self-recognition
bridged struggles that were themselves internally diverse. Looking abroad
and seeing oneself involved reflection in both senses of the word—a partial mirroring and a great amount of thought and practice.

Proponents of unity between South Asians and African Americans often wrote as if such unity already existed and merely had to be revealed.
The long history of efforts to build meaningful transnational solidarities
remained obscure to the vast majority of those involved. This absence of
historical awareness is echoed in the now-routine invocations of friendship between India and the United States. Paeans to the achievements of
"the world's largest democracies" often fail to recognize the generations
of shared struggle that brought both countries closer to achieving their
democratic principles. Judged by the expansive imagination of their pre-
decessors, Indians and Americans have only begun to realize the potential of words such as freedom and democracy. Comparisons between
President Barack Obama and Chief Minister Kumari Mayawati, the

---

Frederick Douglass, "Pictures," quoted in John Stauffer, *The Black Hearts of Men:
Radical Abolitionists and the Transformation of Race* (Cambridge, Mass.: Harvard
University Press, 2001), 45.

female Dalit leader of India's most populous state, while marking progress, should also remind us that African Americans and Dalits remain disproportionately poor and marginalized. The full promise of the struggles for Indian independence and American racial equality has yet to be fulfilled.[1]

In the late nineteenth century, the global juxtaposition of emancipation and empire inspired social reformers in the United States and India to imagine transnational notions of freedom that were both anti-imperial and antiracist. At the intersection of the African and Indian diasporas, racial diplomats, most notably Marcus Garvey, utilized interracial alliances to construct transnational but firmly racial identities. In the aftermath of the First World War, racial diplomats promoted alliances between South Asians and African Americans that maintained, and at times rigidified, racial boundaries between "the Negro race" and "the Indian people." In contrast, colored cosmopolitans such as W. E. B. Du Bois, Cedric Dover, and Kamaladevi Chattopadhyaya envisioned the solidarity of the dark world without employing chauvinistic notions of race and while recognizing fissures within and across the boundaries of color. Racial diplomacy and colored cosmopolitanism are best understood as two ends of a continuum in which individual actors took various positions at different times and within particular contexts.

At their best, colored cosmopolitans defied the stale dichotomy between assimilation and separatism and challenged conceptions of cosmopolitanism as necessarily "post-racial" or "post-ethnic." By establishing transnational, transracial alliances, they made claims upon the nation-state that were, in the words of Cedric Dover, "both 'racial' and antiracial at the same time."[2] In order to confront colonialism, racism, sexism, poverty, and other inequalities and injustices, many thinkers became cosmopolitans with a cause, locating their cosmopolitanism in relation to a more limited set of loyalties. Du Bois and other advocates of colored solidarity embodied the ambivalences of a cosmopolitan counterracist racialism while demonstrating the broader point that many historical agents chose to be, in Anthony Appiah's words, "partial cosmopolitans."[3] Their cosmopolitanism was "partial" in that it was "colored," biased toward "the colored world." Many colored cosmopolitans demanded a solidarity not of sameness but of similitude, not of chauvinism but of resistance to hierarchies within, as well as beyond, the cosmos of the colored world.

During the Second World War, antiracist activists in the United States used colored cosmopolitanism to link Indian anti-imperialism and American antiracism in opposition to fascism and in pursuit of a global double victory. Their success depended on the degree to which American politicians cared about Indian support and believed that such support could be threatened by American racial oppression. In the aftermath of Indian independence and the onset of the Cold War, Walter White and other advocates of global double victory leveraged Indian opinion to make the attainment of American racial justice a Cold War necessity. Intellectuals and activists such as Du Bois and Walter White, as well as the 22,000 Black soldiers who fought in India during the Second World War, all contributed to fostering Indian opposition to American racism. Beginning in the first half of the twentieth century and taking shape during the Second World War, the link between the Cold War and the civil rights movement was largely built by African Americans themselves with tools forged through transnational debates on race and color.

Translating global double victory into the context of the Cold War entailed narrowing a broad human rights movement into a more limited struggle for "civil rights." The effort to link American victory in the Cold War to the achievement of racial equality contributed to the red-baiting of renowned African American public figures such as Du Bois and Paul Robeson. International diplomacy simultaneously limited the support Indian leaders, including Jawaharlal Nehru and Vijayalakshmi Pandit, offered African American struggles. The emerging Third World, in contrast to earlier visions of a united Colored World, left ambivalent the place of African Americans and other "colored" minorities within the First and Second Worlds, as well as the status of Dalits and other minorities within "colored" countries such as India. In 1936 Du Bois had warned against substituting "for the exploitation of colored by white races, an exploitation of colored races by colored men."[4] His warning grew increasingly relevant in the wake of decolonization. The *trans*national nature of the colored world envisioned by Du Bois was largely overshadowed in distinctly *inter*national gatherings such as the Asian-African conference at Bandung.

The sudden importance of many "Third World" countries to American foreign policy, while endowing Indian solidarity with African Americans with greater meaning at the same time weakened that solidarity. In the United States the ability of South Asians to distinguish themselves as foreign and thus beyond Jim Crow norms took on new meaning now that many South Asian visitors were no longer subjects of the British Empire but citizens and, at times, official representatives of postcolonial nations. In the winter of 1951 an Indian farmer named Amar Singh visited Carroll County, Georgia. After talking with a group of African American veterans, Singh told a reporter, "They used to think they couldn't go where white men went because they had dark skins. But then they saw that I was accepted everywhere. They said they always thought that colored people all over the world were united."[5] Singh's ambivalent grammar failed to indicate whether the Black veterans with whom he talked were inspired to challenge Jim Crow, having seen Singh being treated as "white," or were saddened to discover that the bonds of color did not prevent many South Asians from enjoying the privileges of whiteness. The capacity of South Asians in certain contexts and at certain times to distinguish themselves from other "colored" people makes evident that cultural difference—or, more precisely, perceived cultural difference—can at times be used to gain some of the privileges of citizenship precisely by marking one as foreign.[6] While "culture" has been mobilized to police the borders of belonging, cultures themselves have been forged and re-forged through movements across such borders. The construction of colored cosmopolitanism supports Edward Said's contention that "cultures are too intermingled, their contents and histories too interdependent and hybrid, for surgical separation into large and mostly ideological oppositions like Orient and Occident."[7]

The transnational history of nonviolent civil disobedience makes evident not only the hybridity of culture but also the way in which that hybridity facilitated the flow of ideas and protest strategies across the seemingly rigid borders of nations, religions, and, indeed, cultures themselves. Beginning in the midst of the Second World War, a variety of civil rights activists realized the prophecy that Gandhi had offered in 1936 to his African American visitors, the Thurmans and the Carrolls: "It may be through the Negroes that the unadulterated message of nonviolence is delivered to the world."[8] While Gandhi waged his final nonviolent *satyagraha* against British rule, Pauli Murray, James Farmer, Bayard Rustin, A. Philip Randolph, and many others adapted Gandhi's techniques of resistance for the struggle against Jim Crow. The reputation of Gandhi's tactics as radical hampered efforts to employ Gandhian methods on a mass scale in the 1940s. Beginning a decade later, however, African Americans made the achievement of racial justice a Cold War imperative by using Gandhian nonviolent civil disobedience to force their struggles onto the world stage. Dr. Martin Luther King Jr. and other civil rights leaders built upon the long history in which African Americans had come to view Gandhi as a colored leader opposing white oppression and as a religious figure embodying Christian liberation theology. Tracing the history of African American engagement with Gandhi reveals the continuity between early Black nationalism and later notions of Black Power while demonstrating that Black Power did not always entail a rhetoric of violence.

After 1965 a dramatic increase in South Asian immigration to the United States exacerbated tensions between South Asian Americans and African Americans while also inspiring novel forms of connection. The public visibility of affluent South Asian doctors, scientists, and computer engineers contributed to the "model minority myth," the idea that South Asian migrants had, through thrift and hard work, excelled while less enterprising minorities had fallen behind. The model minority myth ignored both the large numbers of poor and working-class South Asian Americans and the fact that the statistically higher levels of affluence and education among South Asian Americans derived in large part from the dictates of American immigration policy. The contrast between the model minority myth and colored cosmopolitanism should be assessed in relation to South Asian efforts to benefit from affirmative action, South Asian and African American joint participation in the anti-apartheid movement, and South Asian American hip-hop culture.[9] Also deserving of greater attention are more recent collaborative efforts to respond to the racial profiling that Blacks have long suffered and that South Asians came to face in the wake of the terrorist attacks of September 11, 2001.

The story of a young lawyer, Vanita Gupta, illustrates the potential for colored cosmopolitanism to continue to inspire an interconnected struggle for justice in the United States. Only months after graduating from law school, Gupta began investigating the case of forty-six African Americans who had been convicted in a drug case that hinged on the testimony of a single white police officer in the small town of Tulia, Texas. After countless hours of research, Gupta proved that the officer had perjured himself on multiple occasions. The presiding judge recommended the release of all forty-six defendants. "I feel my identity as a South Asian is closely linked to my identity as a person of color," Gupta told a reporter for the South Asian web portal Rediff.com. Echoing the many South Asian and African American advocates of colored cosmopolitanism, and speaking for a new generation of progressive South Asian American activists, Gupta declared, "We have a duty to take on issues that affect all communities of color."[10]

To a great extent, assessing the significance of the solidarity that linked South Asian and African American freedom struggles means probing the power of words. Neither South Asian nor African American leaders were in the position to offer the money, materials, and armies that the governments of certain powerful nations such as the United States or the Soviet Union used to try to shape the world.[11] The link between the Cold War and the civil rights movement, contingent as it was upon the growing clout of recently decolonized nations, might be taken as evidence that solidarities mattered only when backed with economic and military power. Tracing the origins of Afro-Indian solidarity back to the construction of colored cosmopolitanism yields a more subtle and balanced understanding of how solidarities, even those expressed by marginalized minorities, came to matter. Transnational solidarities gained political significance when alliances built over generations took on new meaning as a result of global events such as the Second World War, decolonization, and the Cold War. Assessing the history of transnational solidarities requires tracking the interplay of evolving ideas and identities with changing political and economic structures.

It is vital to recognize, even though we cannot fully measure, the hope that came from feeling connected to a worldwide movement. The mutual solidarities expressed by African Americans and South Asians often manifested a transnational conception of self, what historian Penny Von Eschen has called a "marvelously fluid sense of 'we-ness.' "[12] It is difficult to evaluate the inspirational significance of statements of solidarity such as those Gandhi sent to *The Crisis* or that Du Bois contributed to *Chand*. It is even more challenging to assess the influence of grassroots declarations of support, especially those that have been filtered through observers, such as the excited discussions of Indian independence that Horace Cayton reported hearing in poolrooms in wartime Chicago. Nevertheless, to treat solidarities as significant only when they could be leveraged in the realm of global power politics is to flatten the thickness of transnational encounter and to ignore the human dimension of the protests that propelled freedom movements in both India and the United States.

Many of the central figures in this book—W. E. B. Du Bois, Marcus Garvey, Pauli Murray, and Mahatma Gandhi, to name a few—linked South Asian and African American freedom struggles without traveling in person the distance covered by their words and actions. Their contributions mattered no less because they made them from a distance. Indeed, transnational analogies often served national or local purposes. It was to Indian audiences that both Gandhi and Ambedkar argued that caste oppression in India was worse than racial oppression in the United States. Gandhi, as we have seen, argued the opposite when questioned by an American. Even transnational analogies that were blatantly inaccurate, such as Garvey's depiction of the Moplah Rebellion as an example of Hindu-Muslim unity, were often wielded in pursuit of just ends. The significance of such analogies must be traced primarily to their impact on local audiences. Nevertheless, understanding the context of both ends of the analogy sheds light on the choices that forged the analogy and the missed opportunities involved in those choices. It matters that when Du

Bois noted the tendency of Indians to claim Aryan ancestry, he over-looked the fact that his critique applied most directly to higher-caste and Northern-born Indians. By treating Indians as a unified bloc, Du Bois missed the opportunity to speak out against caste oppression.

Missed opportunities should not overshadow the impact of transna-tional analogies. Martin Luther King's decision to follow Benjamin Mays in embracing the label "untouchable," for example, facilitated King's in-creasing opposition to the structural inequalities of race and class. By self-identifying as an "untouchable," King did not intend to inspire an alliance between Blacks and Dalits. He aimed primarily to name and thus undermine inequalities of power within the United States. Neverthe-less, his language demonstrates the power of analogy to indict multiple injustices.

Examining the history of analogies between Indian and African Ameri-can freedom struggles reveals the tendency of even the most sympathetic transnational witnesses to treat the sufferings of others as a blank screen upon which to project their own sufferings. At times, activist intellectuals associated their experiences with the sufferings of others by simplifying complexities in order to minimize differences. When Pauli Murray com-pared A. Philip Randolph and Jawaharlal Nehru, she chose not to discuss the fact that Randolph envisioned freedom within the American nation, while Nehru focused on attaining an independent nation-state. Rather, when Nehru demanded "full and equal freedom for all the countries of Asia" and "the recognition of Indian independence," Murray told her readers that Nehru "might easily have been A. Philip Randolph." Murray explained, "Change the word 'Asia' to 'Negro' and the word 'indepen-dence' to 'equality' and the comparison is complete." Murray made the most of the fact that Randolph and Nehru both used certain key terms. She used capacious words such as "freedom," "independence," and "equal-ity" to bring together for her audience the solidarities she would later make evident on a bus in Virginia.[13]

Connecting social movements never entails only the communication of ideas but always involves the active reinterpretation of concepts to fit new contexts. Translation, not transmission, linked struggles that were themselves heterogeneous products of creative synthesis. Thus while Du Bois played a prominent role in inspiring a variety of Indian leaders to embrace colored cosmopolitanism, Indian figures themselves, ranging from Cedric Dover to Kamaladevi Chattopadhyaya to Rammanohar Lohia, invented and reinterpreted notions of color before sharing their interpretations once again across the divides of race and nation. Gandhi's transition from advocate of Aryan civilization to champion of colored peoples, while not without its inconsistencies, demonstrates the ability of a self-conscious individual to grow from exposure to transnational discourse. Gandhi learned from African American struggles, especially from the life and work of Booker T. Washington. The Washingtonian limitations of Gandhi's approach to caste, limitations inherited in part by Martin Luther King, reveal that transnational learning was always partial and often replete with missed opportunities. The multifaceted African American engagement with Gandhian nonviolent civil disobedience should be seen as part of a long, multidirectional process of exchange and creative re-adaptation. As Harris Wofford told King, Ralph Abernathy, and E. D. Nixon, "You have already proved yourselves master artists of non-violent direct action. It would not be Gandhian at all if you were merely copying Gandhi. He was, like you, a creator, not a copier."[14]

Recognizing the continuity and collective impact of the many connections between South Asian and African American freedom struggles should not entail glossing over the many discontinuities in time and space that marked the history of those connections. Comparisons between race and caste provide perhaps the best example of the potential of transnational comparisons to erase important differences. Comparing the practice of caste in Tamil Nadu and Gujarat or what race has meant in Chicago and New Orleans is challenging enough. Yet for over one hundred years a range of Americans and South Asians have juxtaposed race and caste. Tracking the history of these comparisons reveals that race and caste have long been intertwined with each other and with other forms of human identification, such as gender, class, religion, and nation. These identities have been defined and redefined within particular political and intellectual projects, often in resistance to hierarchies that were themselves defined in dynamic interrelation. Understanding the history of race and caste requires not only recognizing that these identifications have changed but analyzing when, how, and for whom they have changed. Indian claims to whiteness often relied not just on racial but on caste-based hierarchies, with which high-caste Hindus distinguished themselves not just from "non-white" Americans but also from low-caste Indians. Colored cosmopolitanism, on the other hand, offered antiracist activists the opportunity to confront the intersection of multiple oppressions.

Assessing the significance of generations of transnational exchanges requires dispensing with the coarse claims made by boosters of easy solidarity, whether "racial" or otherwise—claims that too often rendered invisible internal differences of caste, class, and gender. The financial costs of travel, education, and perhaps, above all, time away from remunerative work help explain why many of the African Americans and South

Asians in this book were relatively affluent, male elites. Mass migration, inexpensive newspapers, and the movement of soldiers provided fuel for the transnational imagination and initiative of impoverished African Americans and South Asians who themselves contributed to this history. Future work will undoubtedly reveal more grassroots linkages between these struggles but without diminishing the inequalities in access and power that gave elites disproportionate power to shape these connections. Similarly, while many women in both the United States and South Asia were denied the opportunity to assume positions of power, the influence of Kamaladevi Chattopadhyaya, Vijayalakshmi Pandit, Pauli Murray, and the other women who figure predominantly in these pages should speak both to the absence and the presence, the silence and the many voices, of the dynamic women whose leadership has yet to be recognized.

To dichotomize transnational unity and local diversity, the history of elites and that of subalterns, would be to miss one of the central arguments of this book. Transnational and subaltern histories can meaningfully intersect only when the whole and the fragment are not opposed but understood in dynamic and historical relation. The fragmentation of the United States and India in terms of race, caste, gender, class, region, and religion, while complicating transnational unities, simultaneously opened new channels of connection. In the words of Chandra Mohanty, "In knowing differences and particularities, we can better see the connections and commonalities because no border or boundary is ever complete or rigidly determining."[15]

It is a testament to the creativity of colored cosmopolitanism that it has been in fiction and poetry that transracial notions of color have been most successfully paired with respect for intraracial or nonracial notions of difference. In his poem "Negro, My Brother," Ali Sardar Jafri, a renowned contemporary Urdu poet, celebrated the beauty and multiplicity of blackness. "In this forest of ivory," Jafri wrote, "his black body,/Like a swirling black cloud,/Like a flash of black lightning,/A sea of black limbs." In the original Urdu, the word for "black" begins three consecutive lines, each time conjugated to match the gender and plurality of its accompanying noun: "kaalaa," "kaali," "kaale." Thus the poem speaks to the unity and diversity of blackness. In a separate piece, entitled "Paul Robeson," Jafri told the famous singer, "Our lands lie far apart,/But not our hearts,/Your garden lies beyond mine." Crossing boundaries of both race and religion, the poem ends by telling Robeson, "Your song is the song of Krishna,/The evening of Gokul./Let me embrace you,/That you too are black."[16]

Historically, race has functioned to include as well as to exclude. Witness Swami Vivekananda's embrace of his "black-skinned Negroid" ancestors or Kamaladevi Chattopadhyaya's defiant stance on that train in Louisiana. When she refused to move and told the conductor, "I am a coloured woman," Kamaladevi made evident what Paul Gilroy has called "the processes of cultural mutation and restless (dis) continuity that exceed racial discourse and avoid capture by its agents."[17] Nevertheless, as Kamaladevi's example makes equally clear, the success of transnational antiracist initiatives derived in part from racial pride—pride both strengthened and complicated by transnational connections. Finding hope in the struggles of other "dark" or "colored" peoples, South Asians and African Americans forged a race-based nationalism that complicated the boundaries of both race and nation.

At sunrise on July 4, 1898, on a houseboat in the Kashmir valley, Swami Vivekananda recited a poem he had written to celebrate the anniversary of the American Declaration of Independence. His poem concluded:

> Move on, O Lord, in thy resistless path!
> Till thy high noon o'erspreads the world,
> Till every land reflects thy light,
> Till men and women, with uplifted head,
> Behold their shackles broken, and
> Know, in springing joy, their life renewed!

The Swami's audience, a small group of largely American disciples, included one of his most devoted students, Sister Nivedita. Born in Ireland as Margaret Elizabeth Noble, Sister Nivedita had left London for Calcutta only six months earlier, in January 1898. There, Vivekananda gave her the name Nivedita, "devoted to God." In Kashmir, Sister Nivedita and the Swami set about organizing a surprise celebration for their American companions, complete with an impromptu flag hastily fashioned by a local tailor. She later described the early morning scene: "The stars and stripes were very crudely represented, I fear, on the piece of cotton that was nailed, with branches of evergreens to the head of the dining-room-boat, when the Americans stepped on board for early tea, on Independence Day!"

Reading his poem at dawn, Vivekananda began by linking the rise of the sun and of a new nation: "Behold, the dark clouds melt away." He praised the United States for spreading "the light of Freedom," and spoke with epic imagery to both the grandeur of his Himalayan surroundings and the patriotism of his audience. Vivekananda's desire that American liberty "o'erspreads the world" spoke most immediately to the British Raj. He challenged imperial legitimacy by praising the freedom of Britain's former colony. His long and complex relationship with the United States, however, complicates an attempt to read his poem as simple praise for all things American. He knew that the land of the free itself had "shackles" that needed breaking.[18]

Vivekananda imagined that others might "behold their shackles broken" and thus reimagined his own struggles in a global context. Like many of the figures in this book, he employed the rhetoric of slavery and freedom to contest inequality and injustice on a global scale. Beginning in an age of emancipation and empire, when expansive notions of freedom conflicted with persistent forms of inequality, social reformers utilized comparisons between Indians and African Americans in order to pursue particular notions of freedom. Recovering their efforts is even more important in a contemporary world saturated with hollow invocations of freedom and democracy. "Freedom today," Robin Kelley has written, "is practically a synonym for free enterprise." The omnipresence of "freedom" in the media, politics, and public discourse of both the United States and India only underscores the importance of engaging both the limitations and the unredeemed potentialities of what Kelley has fittingly called "freedom dreams."[19] The history of connections between African American and South Asian freedom struggles calls for the kind of "reflection" that Frederic Douglass invoked in 1864: "Poets, prophets, and reformers are all picture makers—and this ability is the secret of their power and of their achievements. They see what ought to be by the reflection of what is, and endeavor to remove the contradiction."[20] Understanding the "picture makers" of the past who struggled to make real their reflections can help us navigate from "what is" to "what ought to be."

In June 1964 in Neshoba County, Mississippi, three young civil rights workers—James Chaney, Michael Schwerner, and Andrew Goodman—were abducted and killed.[21] Three weeks earlier, on a similar stretch of highway in the same county, Hamid Kizilbash escaped death, in part because the mob that had mistaken him for Black was told that he was Indian. A few days before they were murdered, Chaney, Schwerner, and Goodman had left a large gathering of other young people who had volunteered to spend the summer working for racial justice in Mississippi. When Bob Moses learned that the three young men had disappeared, he told an audience of some three hundred volunteers that he believed that Chaney, Schwerner, and Goodman were dead and that everyone who volunteered that summer was risking his or her life. In the silence that followed, SNCC staff member Jean Wheeler began singing from the back of the room a song whose chorus speaks to the courage and stubborn persistence that inspired freedom struggles in the United States and South Asia:

> They say that freedom is a constant struggle
> They say that freedom is a constant struggle
> Oh lord, we've struggled so long
> We must be free . . .

Note on Usage

References to "South Asia" and "South Asians" signal the inclusion of non-Indian and especially Pakistani histories of the post-1947 period. When referring specifically to events before 1947, I refer to "India" and "Indians," with due respect for the internal diversity of India then and now. Although it gained popularity only in the 1970s, I use the word Dalit, from the Marathi for "broken" or "crushed," to refer to those once labeled "untouchable" and still too often oppressed at the bottom of the caste hierarchy in India and other parts of South Asia. Similarly, I use Black or African American even for periods of time when Negro was the term of choice for many African Americans. I have chosen to capitalize "Black," largely in order to signal the comparability of Black and Indian conceptions of community. I have chosen to keep "white" lowercased, in part because the capitalization of "white" and the de-capitalization of "Negro" long signified white supremacy and in part to register, albeit in a small way, the many historical differences between being Black and being white.

Notes

Introduction

1. Kamaladevi Chattopadhyaya, *Inner Recesses, Outer Spaces: Memoirs* (New Delhi: Navrang, 1986), 253; Nico Slate, "'I am a coloured woman': Kamaladevi Chattopadhyaya in the United States, 1939–41," *Contemporary South Asia* 17, no. 1 (March 2009): 7–19.
2. Raymond Williams, *Keywords: A Vocabulary of Culture and Society* (New York: Oxford University Press, 1976); Daniel Rodgers, *Contested Truths: Keywords in American Politics since Independence* (New York: Basic Books, 1987).
3. Daniel Immerwahr, "Caste or Colony? Indianizing Race in the United States," *Modern Intellectual History* 4, no. 2 (2007): 275–301; Balmurli Natrajan and Paul Greenough, eds., *Against Stigma: Studies in Caste, Race, and Justice since Durban* (Hyderabad: Orient Blackswan Press, 2009); Kamala Visweswaran, *Un/common Cultures: Racism and the Rearticulation of Cultural Difference* (Durham: Duke University Press, 2010).
4. Sugata Bose, *A Hundred Horizons: The Indian Ocean in the Age of Global Empire* (Cambridge, Mass.: Harvard University Press, 2006); Kris Manjapra, "The Mirrored World: Cosmopolitan Encounter between Indian Anti-Colonial Intellectuals and German Radicals, 1905–1939" (PhD diss., Harvard University, 2007); Claude Markovits, *The Global World of Indian Merchants, 1750–1947: Traders of Sind from Bukhara to Panama* (Cambridge: Cambridge University Press, 2000).
5. Jonathan Rosenberg, *How Far the Promised Land?: World Affairs and the American Civil Rights Movement from the First World War to Vietnam* (Princeton: Princeton University Press, 2006); Nikhil Pal Singh, *Black Is a Country: Race and the Unfinished Struggle for Democracy* (Cambridge, Mass.: Harvard University Press, 2004); Bill V. Mullen, *Afro Orientalism* (Minneapolis:

University of Minnesota Press, 2004); Carol Anderson, *Eyes Off the Prize: The United Nations and the African American Struggle for Human Rights, 1944–1955* (Cambridge: Cambridge University Press, 2003); Marc Gallicchio, *The African American Encounter with Japan and China: Black Internationalism in Asia, 1895–1945* (Chapel Hill: University of North Carolina Press, 2000); Penny Von Eschen, *Race against Empire: Black Americans and Anticolonialism, 1937–1957* (Ithaca, N.Y.: Cornell University Press, 1997); Brenda Gayle Plummer, *Rising Wind: Black Americans and U.S. Foreign Affairs, 1935–1960* (Chapel Hill: University of North Carolina Press, 1996).

6. Peter van der Veer, *Imperial Encounters: Religion and Modernity in India and Britain* (Princeton: Princeton University Press, 2001), 8. I am indebted to those scholars who have most closely examined the interconnected histories of South Asians and African Americans. See Sudarshan Kapur, *Raising Up a Prophet: The African American Encounter with Gandhi* (Boston: Beacon Press, 1992); Vijay Prashad, *The Karma of Brown Folk* (Minneapolis: University of Minnesota Press, 2000), and *Everybody Was Kung Fu Fighting: Afro-Asian Connections and the Myth of Cultural Plurality* (Boston: Beacon Press, 2001); Gerald Horne, *The End of Empires: African Americans and India* (Philadelphia: Temple University Press, 2008).

7. Thomas Bender, "Historians, the Nation, and the Plenitude of Narratives," in *Rethinking American History in a Global Age*, ed. Thomas Bender (Berkeley: University of California Press, 2002), 1–22; David A. Hollinger, "The Historian's Use of the United States and Vice Versa," in *Rethinking American History in a Global Age*, ed. Thomas Bender, 381–396; Andrew Rotter, *Comrades at Odds: The United States and India, 1947–1964* (Ithaca, N.Y.: Cornell University Press, 2000); Robert J. McMahon, *The Cold War on the Periphery: The United States, India, and Pakistan* (New York: Columbia University Press, 1994); Dennis Kux, *India and the United States: Estranged Democracies, 1941–1991* (Washington, D.C.: National Defense University Press, 1992); H. W. Brands, *India and the United States: The Cold Peace* (Boston: Twayne, 1990); Dennis Merrill, *Bread and the Ballot: The United States and India's Economic Development, 1947–1963* (Chapel Hill: University of North Carolina Press, 1990).

8. On the long history of efforts to forge solidarities between communities of color within the United States and abroad, see Thomas Guglielmo, "Fighting for Caucasian Rights: Mexicans, Mexican Americans, and the Transnational Struggle for Civil Rights in World War II Texas," *Journal of American History* 92 (March 2006): 1212–1237; Scott Kurashige, *The Shifting Grounds of Race: Black and Japanese Americans in the Making of Multiethnic Los Angeles* (Princeton: Princeton University Press, 2008); Allison Varzally, *Making a Non-White America: Californians Coloring Outside Ethnic Lines, 1925–1955* (Berkeley: University of California Press, 2008); Mark Brilliant, *The Color of America Has Changed: How Racial Diversity Shaped Civil Rights Reform in California, 1941–1978* (New York: Oxford University Press, 2010); Neil Foley, *Quest for Equality: The Failed Promise of Black-Brown Solidarity* (Cambridge, Mass.: Harvard University Press, 2010).

9. On the relationship between the nation-state and transnational activism, see Sidney Tarrow, *The New Transnational Activism* (Cambridge: Cambridge University Press, 2005).

10. Leslie McCall, "The Complexity of Intersectionality," *Journal of Women in Culture and Society* (November 2007): 1771–1800; Kimberlé Crenshaw, "Mapping the Margins: Intersectionality, Identity Politics, and Violence against Women of Color," *Stanford Law Review* 43, no. 6 (1991): 1241–1299.

1. Race, Caste, and Nation

1. David Brion Davis, *Inhuman Bondage: The Rise and Fall of Slavery in the New World* (Oxford: Oxford University Press, 2006); Rayford Whittingham Logan, *The Negro in American Life and Thought: The Nadir, 1877–1901* (New York: Dial Press, 1954).

2. See Brent Hayes Edwards, *The Practice of Diaspora: Literature, Translation, and the Rise of Black Internationalism* (Cambridge, Mass.: Harvard University Press, 2003); Earl Lewis, "To Turn as on a Pivot: Writing African Americans into a History of Overlapping Diasporas," *The American Historical Review* 100, no. 3 (June 1995): 765–787.

3. C. A. Bayly, *The Birth of the Modern world, 1780–1914: Global Connections and Comparisons* (Malden, Mass.: Blackwell, 2004), 199.

4. George M. Fredrickson, *Racism: A Short History* (Princeton: Princeton University Press, 2002); Kenneth Ballhatchet, *Race, Sex and Class under the Raj* (London: Weidenfeld and Nicholson, 1980); Eric Stokes, *The English Utilitarians and India* (Oxford: Clarendon Press, 1959), 288–310; Mrinalini Sinha, *Colonial Masculinity: The "Manly Englishman" and the "Effeminate Bengali" in the Late Nineteenth Century* (Manchester: Manchester University Press, 1995), 33–63; Thomas R. Metcalf, *Ideologies of the Raj* (Cambridge: Cambridge University Press, 1994), 203–214.

5. Paul Kramer, "Empires, Exceptions, and Anglo-Saxons: Race and Rule between the British and United States Empires, 1880–1910," *Journal of American History* 88, no. 4 (March 2002): 1315–1353; Rudyard Kipling, "Take Up the White Man's Burden," *McClure's Magazine* (February 1899); Teddy Roosevelt, "The Expansion of the White Races," in *The Works of Theodore Roosevelt, National Edition* (New York: Charles Scribner's Sons, 1925), vol. 16, 258–278; Thomas G. Dyer, *Theodore Roosevelt and the Idea of Race* (Baton Rouge: Louisiana State University, 1980); Frank Ninkovich, "Theodore Roosevelt: Civilization as Ideology," *Diplomatic History* 10 (Summer 1986): 221–245.

6. Randall Kennedy, *Nigger: The Strange Career of a Troublesome Word* (New York: Pantheon Books, 2002); Niall Ferguson, *Empire: How Britain Made the Modern World* (London: Allen Lane, 2003), 165; Helen Bannerman, *The Story of Little Black Sambo* (London: Grant Richards, 1899); Andrew Rotter, *Comrades at Odds: The United States and India, 1947–1964* (Ithaca, N.Y.: Cornell University Press, 2000), 150–151.

7. Robert Knox, *The Races of Men: A Fragment* (Philadelphia: Lea and Blanchard, 1850), 149–150.

8. Bruce Baum, *The Rise and Fall of the Caucasian Race: A Political History of Racial Identity* (New York: New York University Press, 2006), especially 73–94.

9. See Thomas R. Trautmann, *Aryans and British India* (Berkeley: University of California Press, 1997), and *Languages and Nations: The Dravidian Proof in Colonial Madras* (Berkeley: University of California Press, 2006); Susan Bayly, *Caste, Society, and Politics in India from the Eighteenth Century to the Modern Age* (Cambridge: Cambridge University Press, 1999), 114; Christophe Jaffrelot, *India's Silent Revolution: The Rise of the Lower Castes in North India* (London: Hurst & Co., 2003), 151–152; Peter van der Veer, *Imperial Encounters: Religion and Modernity in India and Britain* (Princeton: Princeton University Press, 2001), 134–157.

10. The idea that racial differences defined the Aryans finds little support in the Vedas themselves. Romila Thapar, "The Image of the Barbarian in Early India," *Comparative Studies in Society and History* 13, no. 1 (October 1971): 408–436. See also Trautmann, *Aryans and British India*, 176, 211–216; Edwin F. Bryant and Laurie L. Patton, eds., *The Indo-Aryan Controversy: Evidence and Inference in Indian History* (London: Routledge, 2005).

11. Quoted in Trautmann, *Aryans and British India*, 170, 175.

12. William Wilson Hunter, *The Indian Empire: Its People, History, and Products* (London: Trubner & Co., 1882), 75, 54.

13. Quoted in Nicholas Dirks, "Recasting Tamil Society," in *Caste Today*, ed. C. J. Fuller, 265 (Delhi: Oxford University Press, 1996).

14. H. H. Risley, *The People of India* (Calcutta: Thacker, Spink & Co.; London, W. Thacker & Co., 1908), reprinted in 1991 (New Delhi: Munshiram Manoharlal, 1991), 5, 33–34, 45, and chap. 6.

15. Arthur Anthony Macdonell and Arthur Barriedale Keith, *Vedic Index of Names and Subjects*, vol. 2 (London: John Murray, 1912), 267. See also Trautmann, *Aryans and British India*, 206–211.

16. Jotirao Govindrao Phule, *Slavery in the Civilised British Government under the Cloak of Brahmanism*, trans. P. G. Patil (Bombay: Education Department, Government of Maharashtra, 1991); Gail Omvedt, "Jotirao Phule and the Ideology of Social Revolution in India," *Economic and Political Weekly*, September 11, 1971; Gail Omvedt, *Cultural Revolt in a Colonial Society: The Non-Brahman Movement in Western India 1873–1930* (Bombay: Scientific Socialist Education Trust, 1976); Rosalind O'Hanlon, *Caste, Conflict, and Ideology: Mahatma Jotirao Phule and Low Caste Protest in Nineteenth-Century Western India* (Cambridge: Cambridge University Press, 1985).

17. "The British Empire in the East, Part II," *Hunt's Merchant's Magazine and Commercial Review* 20 (May 1849): 481.

18. The influence of Uncle Tom's Cabin extended to China. See Michael Hunt, *The Making of a Special Relationship: The United States and China to 1914* (New York: Columbia University Press, 1983), 45–50; Dilip Menon, *The Blindness of Insight: Essays on Caste in Modern India* (Pondicherry and

New Delhi: Navayana, 2006), 89; Jotirao Phule, *Selected Writings of Jotirao Phule*, edited and with annotations and an introduction by G. P. Deshpande (New Delhi: Leftword, 2002), 222.

19. Amanda Smith, *An Autobiography: The Story of the Lord's Dealings with Mrs. Amanda Smith, The Colored Evangelist* (Chicago: Christian Witness Co., 1893), iv–viii, 300, 311, 318–319.

20. Adrienne Moore, *Rammohun Roy and America* (Calcutta: Satis Chandra Chakravarti, 1942), 164.

21. "Duty of Disobeying Laws [1]," and "Duty of Disobeying Laws [2]," *Indian Opinion*, September 7 and 14, 1907, translated from Gujarati, *The Collected Works of Mahatma Gandhi* (CWMG). The CWMG is available online at www.gandhiserve.org/cwmg/cwmg.html.

22. Van Gosse, "'As a Nation, the English Are Our Friends': The Emergence of African American Politics in the British Atlantic World, 1772–1861," *The American Historical Review* 113, no. 4 (October 2008): 1003–1028.

23. Joseph Cephas Holly, "Freedom's Champions," in *Freedom's Offering* (Freeport, N.Y.: Books for Libraries Press, 1971) and James Madison Bell, "The Dawn of Freedom," in *The Poetical Works of James Madison Bell* (Freeport, N.Y.: Books for Libraries Press, 1970), both available via Proquest: African-American Poetry Full-Text Database.

24. Du Bois, "Gandhi and American Negroes," *Gandhi Marg* (July 1957): 1–4; Du Bois, *Dusk of Dawn: An Essay toward an Autobiography of a Race Concept* (New York: Schocken Books, 1968), 47.

25. Mark Twain, *The Autobiography of Mark Twain*, as arranged and edited and with Introduction and Notes by Charles Neider (New York: Perennial Library, 1975), 314; Mark Twain, *Mark Twain's Notebook* (New York: Harper, 1935), 270–271 and 280–281.

26. Mark Twain, *Following the Equator: A Journey around the World*, vol. 2 (New York and London: Harper & Brothers, 1897 and 1899), 28, 23, 63.

27. Twain, *Following the Equator*, 29, emphasis in original.

28. "Dear Alasinga," July 1, 1895, *The Complete Works of Swami Vivekananda* (CWSV), vol. 5; "To Miss Josephine MacLeod," September 1895, CWSV vol. 8; *The Life of Swami Vivekananda by His Eastern and Western Disciples*, 6th ed. (Calcutta: Advaita Ashrama, 1989), 406–407, 467; The CWSV is available online at www.ramakrishnavivekananda.info/vivekananda/complete_works.htm.

29. *The Life of Swami Vivekananda*, 456; "Sayings and Utterances," CWSV vol. 9, from Sister Nivedita, *The Complete Works of Sister Nivedita*, vol. 1 (Calcutta: Advaita Ashrama, 1982), 153.

30. For examinations of Vivekananda's time in the United States, see Sukalyan Sengupta and Makarand Paranjape, eds., *The Cyclonic Swami: Vivekananda in the West* (New Delhi: Samvad India Foundation, in association with the Center for Indic Studies, University of Massachusetts at Dartmouth, 2005); Carl T. Jackson, *Vedanta for the West: The Ramakrishna Movement in the United States* (Bloomington: Indiana University Press, 1994); Marie Louise Burke, *Swami Vivekananda in America: New Discoveries*, 3rd ed., 6 vols. (Calcutta: Advaita Ashrama, 1983–1987).

31. "From Far Off India," *Saginaw Courier Herald,* March 22, 1894, "Reports in American Newspapers," CWSV vol. 2; "The Way to the Realisation of a Universal Religion," CWSV vol. 2; "The Great Teachers of the World," February 3, 1900, CWSV vol. 4.

32. "Dear Sir," 17, August 1889, CWSV vol. 6; Tapan Raychaudhuri, "Swami Vivekananda's Construction of Hinduism," in William Radice, ed. *Swami Vivekananda and the Modernization of Hinduism* (New York: Oxford University Press, 1998), 1–16; "Vedanta in Its Application to Indian Life," CWSV vol. 3; "To Pramada Das Mitra from Almora," May 30, 1897, CWSV vol. 6; "Buddhistic India," February 2, 1900, CWSV vol. 3.

33. "Sayings and Utterances," CWSV 9, from Sister Nivedita, *The Complete Works of Sister Nivedita,* vol. 1 (Calcutta: Advaita Ashrama, 1982), 153; "Aryans and Tamilians," CWSV vol. 4.

34. "My Plan of Campaign," CWSV vol. 3.

35. B. N. Goswami, "Malik Ambar: A Remarkable Life," *The Tribune,* August 13, 2006; Pashington Obeng, *Shaping Membership, Defining Nation: The Cultural Politics of African Indians in South Asia* (Lanham, Md.: Lexington Books, 2007); R. R. S. Chauhan, *Africans in India: From Slavery to Royalty* (New Delhi: Asian Publication Services, 1995); Shanti Sadiq Ali, *The African Dispersal in the Deccan: From Medieval to Modern Times* (London: Sangam, 1996).

36. Joseph E. Harris, "Expanding the Scope of African Diaspora Studies: The Middle East and India, a Research Agenda," *Radical History Review* 87 (Fall 2003): 157–168.

37. For another example of Washington's international prominence, see Sven Beckert, "From Tuskegee to Togo: The Problem of Freedom in the Empire of Cotton," *The Journal of American History* 92 (September 2005): 501. Also see Louis Harlan, *Booker T. Washington: The Wizard of Tuskegee, 1901–1915* (New York: Oxford University Press, 1983), 279; Anagarika H. Dharmapala to Booker T. Washington, June 20, 1903, Louis R. Harlan and Raymond W. Smock, eds., *The Booker T. Washington Papers* (BTW Papers), vol. 13, 507–508. The BTW Papers are available online at www.historycooperative.org/btw.

38. Mohandas Gandhi, "From Slave to College President," *Indian Opinion,* October 9, 1903, CWMG.

39. Dharmapala to BTW, June 20, 1903, BTW Papers, vol. 13, 507–508; BTW, "Industrial Education in Africa," *Independent* 60 (March 15, 1906): 616–619. In BTW Papers, vol. 8, 548–552.

40. BTW, *My Larger Education,* BTW Papers, vol. 1, 456, 445.

41. The Library of Congress holds several South Asian translations of Washington's works. See Mahadev Hari Modak to BTW, September 5, 1913, BTW Papers, vol. 12, 178–179; Harlan, *The Wizard of Tuskegee,* 277–278.

42. Maureen Swan, *Gandhi: The South African Experience* (Johannesburg: Ravan Press, 1985), 112. Also see Anil Nauriya, *The African Element in Gandhi* (New Delhi: National Gandhi Museum and Gyan Publishing House, 2006); James D. Hunt, "Gandhi and the Black People of South Africa," reprinted in

Hunt, *An American Looks at Gandhi: Essays in Satyagraha, Civil Rights and Peace* (New Delhi: Promilla & Co., 2005).

43. Gandhi, "Speech at Public Meeting, Bombay," September 26, 1896, CWMG.

44. Gandhi, "Open Letter," before December 19, 1894, CWMG, emphasis in original.

45. See William Manning Marable, *African Nationalist: The Life of John Langalibalele Dube* (Michigan: UMI Dissertation Services, 1976); R. Hunt Davis Jr., "John L. Dube: A South African Exponent of Booker T. Washington," *Journal of African Studies* 2, no. 4 (1976)

46. Raojibhai Patel, "Gandhiji Ki Sadhana," cited in *Sushila Nayar, Mahatma Gandhi: Satyagraha at Work, Volume IV* (Ahmedabad: *Navajivan Publishing House*, 1989), 714. See also Davis, "John L. Dube," 508; E. S. Reddy, *Gandhiji's Vision of a Free South Africa* (New Delhi: Sanchar Publishing House, 1995), 49; Hunt, *An American Looks at Gandhi*, 84.

47. Gandhi, "The Kaffirs of Natal," *Indian Opinion*, September 2, 1905, translated from the Gujarati, CWMG.

48. *Indian Opinion*, March 17, 1906, translated from Gujarati, CWMG

49. See "Cable to Secretary of State for Colonies" and "Cable to Viceroy of India," both September 8, 1906, CWMG.

50. Gandhi, "To the Colonial-Born Indian," *Indian Opinion*, July 15, 1911, CWMG.

51. *People v. Hall*, 4 Cal. 399 (1854).

52. Amitava Kumar, *Passport Photos* (Berkeley: University of California Press, 2000), 63.

53. "Meet Walter Simon," newspaper clipping from an English-language Ceylonese newspaper (title and date obscured), *Walter Augustus Simon Papers*, Box 2, Folder "USIS Colombo, Ceylon, 1966–68," Manuscript, Archives, and Rare Book Library, Emory University.

54. See Harold A. Gould, *Sikhs, Swamis, Students, and Spies: The India Lobby in the United States, 1900–1946* (New Delhi: Sage, 2006); Joan Jensen, *Passage from India: Asian Indian Immigrants in North America* (New Haven: Yale University Press, 1988).

55. Jensen, *Passage from India*, 52, 101; Mae Ngai, *Impossible Subjects: Illegal Aliens and the Making of Modern America* (Princeton: Princeton University Press, 2004), 18, 37; Richard White, *"It's Your Misfortune and None of My Own": A History of the American West* (Norman: University of Oklahoma Press, 1991); Patricia Nelson Limerick, *The Legacy of Conquest: The Unbroken Past of the American West* (New York: Norton, 2006).

56. The frequency of marriage between Punjabi migrants and Mexican Americans demonstrates that Indian migrants were not unwilling to marry outside the Indian community. Joan M. Jensen, "Apartheid: Pacific Coast Style," *The Pacific Historical Review* 38, no. 3 (August 1969): 340; Rajani Kanta Das, *Hindustani Workers on the Pacific Coast* (Berlin: W. de Gruyter, 1923), 109–116; Karen Leonard, *Making Ethnic Choices: California's Punjabi-Mexican Americans* (Philadelphia: Temple University Press, 1994).

57. See Gould, *Sikhs, Swamis, Students, and Spies*, 268.

58. Circuit Court of Appeals, Fifth Circuit, *United States v. Dolla*, March 1, 1910.

59. *United States v. Balsara*. (C. C. A. 1910) 180 Fed. 694.

60. Jensen, *Passage from India*, 248.

61. See re Halladjian et al. (174 Fed. 834).

62. Bruce La Brack, "The Sikhs of Northern California: A Socio-Historical Study," unpublished PhD thesis (Syracuse University, 1980), 130. Quoted in Ronald Takaki, *Strangers from a Different Shore: A History of Asian Americans* (Boston: Little, Brown, 1989), 128–129.

63. *Thirteenth Census of the United States Taken in the Year 1910*, vol. 1 (Washington, D.C.: Government Printing Office, 1912), 126.

64. United States Immigration Commission, *Dictionary of Races or Peoples* (Washington, D.C.: Government Printing Office, 1911), 30, 97.

65. *In Re Akhay Kumar Mozumdar* (E. D. Wash. 1913) 207 F.

66. *United States v. Bhagat Singh Thind*, 261 U.S. 204 (1923).

67. Jensen, *Passage from India*, 246, 259; also see Emma Lue Sayers, "Negro Should Create His Own God: Hindu Lawyer Says He Should Be Himself and Not Imitate the White Man," *New York Amsterdam News*, December 29, 1926, 20.

68. See "Sidat-Singh Proves To Be Mister Webb," *Chicago Defender*, October 30, 1937, 2; "Sidat-Singh Out of Maryland Game," *New York Amsterdam News*, October 30, 1937, 17; "Sidat-Singh Leads Syracuse To Win Over Penn State," *Pittsburgh Courier*, November 6, 1937, 18; "Sidat-Singh Paces Syracuse's Victory," *Chicago Defender*, November 13, 1937, 8; "Syracuse Rally Upsets Cornell," *Atlanta Constitution*, October 16, 1938; Al Monrow, "Dixie Coach Not to Demand Sidat-Singh Bar," *Chicago Defender*, October 29, 1938; "Arlington Burial for Sidat-Singh," *New York Amsterdam News*, July 3, 1943; Gerald Horne, *The End of Empires: African Americans and India* (Philadelphia: Temple University Press, 2008), 93–96.

69. Rash Behari Day, *My Days with Uncle Sam* (Italla, Kuti, Tipperah, Bengal, India: Author, 1919), Preface, 8, 70, 75, emphasis in original.

70. Day, *My Days with Uncle Sam*, 20, 205–206, 214.

71. Day, *My Days with Uncle Sam*, 188, 206–208.

72. Shridhar V. Ketkar, *History of Caste in India* (Jaipur: Rawat Publications, 1979), 11, 100–115.

73. Ketkar, *History of Caste*, 143.

74. Ketkar, *History of Caste*, 77–78, 169. See also Shridhar V. Ketkar, "Radical Defects of Ethnology," *American Anthropologist*, n.s., 11, no. 2 (1911): 321–322.

75. "One Tenth of Student Body Are Foreigners," *The Tech*, January 23, 1922, 1–2; Bharatan Kumarappa, *My Student Days in America* (Bombay: Padma Publications, 1945), 82–83.

76. Kumarappa, *My Student Days in America*, 3–7, 81, 84–85.

2. Racial Diplomacy

1. "War!" *The African Times and Orient Review*, n.s., 1, no. 20 (August 4, 1914): 450; John Edward Bruce, *The Selected Writings of John Edward Bruce: Militant Black Journalist*, compiled and edited by Peter Gilbert (New York: Arno Press, 1971), 152–153.

2. Sudarshan Kapur, *Raising Up a Prophet: The African American Encounter with Gandhi* (Boston: Beacon Press, 1992); Sean Chabot, "Framing, Transnational Diffusion and African American Intellectuals in the Land of Gandhi," supplement, *International Review of Social History* 49, supplement no. 12 (2004): 19–40.

3. Sugata Bose, *A Hundred Horizons: The Indian Ocean in the Age of Global Empire* (Cambridge, Mass.: Harvard University Press, 2006), especially chap. 4; Graham Smith, *When Jim Crow Met John Bull* (New York: St. Martin's Press, 1987), 7.

4. Erez Manela, *The Wilsonian Moment: Self-Determination and the International Origins of Anticolonial Nationalism* (Oxford: Oxford University Press, 2007); and Michael Adas, "Contested Hegemony: The Great War and the Afro-Asian Assault on the Civilizing Mission Ideology," *Journal of World History* 15, no. 1 (2004): 31–63.

5. Herbert Naeem Gul Rathore, "Indian Nationalist Agitation in the United States: A Study of Lala Lajpat Rai and the India Home Rule League of America, 1914–1920" (PhD diss., Columbia University, 1965), 73–74; N. S. Hardikar, *Lala Lajpat Rai in America* (New Delhi: Servants of the People Society, 1966); Parso (or Parson) to Du Bois, September 25, 1917, Reel 5, Du Bois Papers (hereafter cited as DBP).

6. "Explosion of Asia as Menace to Peace," *New York Evening Post*, September 22, 1917, 14. Quoted in Dohra Ahmad, "'More Than Romance': Genre and Geography in Dark Princess," *ELH* 69, no. 3 (2002): 775–803.

7. "India's Saint," *The Crisis* 22 (July 1921): 124–125; John Haynes Holmes, *I Speak for Myself: The Autobiography of John Haynes Holmes* (New York: Harper & Brothers, 1959); K. D. Shastri to Du Bois, January 22, 1918, and Du Bois to Shastri, February 7, 1918, Reel 6, DBP.

8. "Overseas," *The Crusader* 3, no. 5 (January 1921): 17.

9. Friends of Freedom for India Pamphlet (1916), Slide 403, Reel 5, DBP; Du Bois, "The Woes of India," *The Crisis* 22 (May 1921): 27.

10. Lala Lajpat Rai, *The United States of America: A Hindu's Impressions and a Study* (Calcutta: Brahmo Mission Press, 1916), iii.

11. Lajpat Rai, *Young India: An Interpretation and a History of the Nationalist Movement from Within* (New York: B. W. Huebsch, 1916), and *The Arya Samaj: An Account of Its Origin, Doctrines, and Activities, with a Biographical Sketch of the Founder* (London: Longmans, Green, 1915); Kenneth Jones, *Socio-Religious Reform Movements in British India* (Cambridge: Cambridge University Press, 1989).

12. Lajpat Rai, *The United States of America*, 103, 157.

13. Ibid., 89, 104.

14. Ibid., 73, 77, 390.

15. Ibid. , 391, 393, 394.

16. Joginder Singh Dhanki, *Perspectives on Indian National Movement: Selected Correspondence of Lala Lajpat Rai* (New Delhi: National Book Organization, 1998), 99–101.

17. Lajpat Rai, *Young India,* 35, 39; Lajpat Rai, *Young India* vol. 1 (1918): 5.

18. March 14, 1918, Slide 598, Reel 6, DBP; Du Bois, "The League of Nations," *The Crisis* 19 (November 1919): 336–337.

19. *The Crisis* covered the massacre: "The Looking Glass," *The Crisis* 20 (August 1920): 187–189.

20. Blanche Watson, " 'Saint' Gandhi: The Greatest Man in the World," and W. E. B. Du Bois, "As the Crow Flies," *The Brownies' Book* 2, no. 12 (December 1921): 344–345.

21. *The Crisis* 22 (August 1921): 170; "The Affairs of India," *The Crisis* 24, no. 2 (June 1922): 82–83.

22. Basanta Koomar Roy, "Oppressed India, Great Britain's Dixieland," *The Chicago Defender,* April 15, 1922, 15.

23. "India Independence Fund," *The Crusader* 5, no. 3 (November 1921): 17. See also "The Soviet Successes," *The Crusader* 2, no. 11 (July 1920): 10–11; "A Few Notes on Tactics," *The Crusader* 6, no. 1 (January–February 1922): 9; "Talking Points," *The Crusader* 3, no. 4 (December 1920): 15; Cyril V. Briggs, "Americans?" *The Crusader* 1, no. 110 (June 1919): 5.

24. Blanche Watson, "Gandhi and Non-Violent Resistance," *The Messenger* (May 1922): 405–406.

25. Du Bois, "Gandhi and India," *The Crisis* (March 1922): 203–207.

26. Reverdy C. Ransom, "Gandhi, Indian Messiah and Saint," *A. M. E. Church Review* 38 (October 1921): 87–88.

27. A. L. Jackson, "Mahatma Gandhi, *The Chicago Defender,* December 24, 1921, 16; James Weldon Johnson, "Gandhi a Prisoner," *New York Age,* March 25, 1922, in *The Selected Writings of James Weldon Johnson,* vol. 1: The New York Age Editorials (1914–1923), ed. Sondra Kathryn Wilson, 243 (New York: Oxford University Press, 1995). Also see Lala Lajpat Rai, "Gandhi and Non-Cooperation," *A. M. E. Church Review* 39 (October 1922): 80–81.

28. E. Franklin Frazier, "The Negro and Non-Resistance," *The Crisis* 27, no. 5 (March 1924): 213–214; *The Crisis* 28, no. 2 (June 1924): 58–59.

29. Du Bois, "World Leaders," *The Crisis* 28, no. 2 (June 1924): 59.

30. On the Khilafat movement, see Gail Minault, *The Khilafat Movement: Religious Symbolism and Political Mobilization in India* (New York: Columbia University Press, 1982); Ayesha Jalal, *Self and Sovereignty: Individual and Community in South Asian Islam since 1850* (London: Routledge, 2000).

31. "India's Saint," *The Crisis* 22 (July 1921): 124–125. See also "Sedition Growing in India," *Norfolk Journal and Guide,* March 18, 1922, 4; J. Cogdell, "Look Out! England Is Up to Her Old Tricks Again!" *The Messenger* (October 1922): 504–505; "The Mystic Gandhi Imprisoned," *Norfolk Journal and Guide,* April 1, 1922, 4. One exception is Fred H. Williams, "Quien Sabe (Who Knows)," *The Crusader* 4, no. 1 (March 1921): 19.

32. Shahid Amin, *Event, Metaphor, Memory: Chauri Chaura, 1922–1992* (Berkeley: University of California Press, 1995).

33. See "Gandhi in Prison Is Able Force," *The Chicago Defender,* June 3, 1922, 13; "Indian Rebellion Plot Revealed at Trial," *The Negro World,* January 14, 1928, 2; "East India Determined To Be Free," *The Negro World,* January 14, 1928, 4.

34. Winston James, *Holding Aloft the Banner of Ethiopia: Caribbean Radicalism in Early Twentieth-Century America* (London: Verso, 1998).

35. See Tony Martin, *Race First: The Ideological and Organizational Struggles of Marcus Garvey and the Universal Negro Improvement Association* (Westport, Conn.: Greenwood Press, 1976); Robert A. Hill, ed., *The Marcus Garvey and Universal Negro Improvement Association Papers* (Berkeley: University of California Press, 1983) (hereafter cited as MGUNIA); Colin Grant, *Negro with a Hat: The Rise and Fall of Marcus Garvey* (Oxford: Oxford University Press, 2008).

36. MGUNIA 2: 500, 502; 3: 734–736. See also MGUNIA 4: 267, 523; 5: 601–603, 636.

37. MGUNIA 2: 340; 4: 184.

38. See MGUNIA 4: 51–52; *The Negro World,* September 17, 1921, 9.

39. A. H. Maloney, "Persecution of Gandhi and Hon. Marcus Garvey Likened," *The Negro World,* March 25, 1922, 3; J. Jackson Tilford, "South African Revolt and Native Tolerance," *The Negro World,* March 25, 1922, 5; "Parallels," *The Negro World,* March 18, 1922, 4; MGUNIA 5: 119, 253; 6: 258.

40. On May 31, 1930, Mudgal became "acting managing editor" of *The Negro World.* Later in life he moved to India, becoming a member of Parliament before being forced to resign in 1951 after a Parliamentary Committee found him guilty of accepting bribes. See H. C. [*sic*] Mudgal, "Who Will Help?" *The Negro World,* February 1, 1930, 4; Hucheswar G. Mudgal, *Marcus Garvey: Is He the True Redeemer of the Negro* (New York: H.G. Mudgal, 1932); *The Mudgal Case* (New Delhi: Parliament Secretariat, 1951).

41. Kapur, *Raising Up a Prophet,* 21–22; *The Negro World,* May 6, 1922, 2; Haridas Muzumdar, "Gandhi the Apostle of Freedom," *The Negro World,* May 6, 1922, 2l; MGUNIA 4: 891.

42. MGUNIA 4: 451–452.

43. MGUNIA 3: 49; File BS 202600–667, RG 65, FBI files, USNA; MGUNIA 1: lxx–lxxviii.

44. MGUNIA 4: 477.

45. MGUNIA 4: 333–334, 4: 379, 6: 180, 277.

46. MGUNIA 4: 567–573.

47. MGUNIA 3: 587; 4: 567–569.

48. MGUNIA 5: 645; Gandhi, "Negroes' Sympathy," August 21, 1924, CWMG.

49. See Paul Gilroy, *Against Race: Imagining Political Culture beyond the Color Line* (Cambridge, Mass: Belknap Press of Harvard University Press, 2000); note 13 in MGUNIA 7: 642.

50. In 1934 Du Bois embraced aspects of segregation, leading to his separation from the NAACP. Sounding very much like Garvey, Du Bois declared, "It is

the race-conscious black man cooperating together in his own institutions and movements who will eventually emancipate the colored race." See Charles Spurgeon Johnson, "After Garvey—What?" *Opportunity* 1, no. 8 (August 1923): 231–233; MGUNIA 2: 500–502; MGUNIA 3: 734–736; MGUNIA 5: 356; Du Bois, "Segregation," *The Crisis* 41 (January 1934): 20; "The Board of Directors on Segregation," *The Crisis* 41 (May 1934): 149; Du Bois, "A Negro Nation within the Nation," *Current History* 42 (June 1935): 265–270.

51. Horace Mann Bond, "Temperament," *The Crisis* 30, no. 2 (June 1925): 83–86; "A Word from India," *The Crisis* 30, no. 5 (September 1925): 229–230.

52. Kelly Miller, "Unrest among Weaker Races," in *The Everlasting Stain* (Washington, D.C.: Associated Publishers, 1924), 101, 103

53. Spencer Lavan, *The Ahmadiyah Movement: A History and Perspective* (Delhi: Manohar Book Service, 1974); Richard Brent Turner, "The Ahmadiyya Mission to Blacks in the United States," *The Journal of Religious Thought* 44, no. 2 (Winter–Spring 1988): 50–67; Richard Brent Turner, *Islam in the African American Experience,* 2d ed. (Bloomington: Indiana University Press, 2003), 127; Martin, *Race First,* 75–76.

54. MGUNIA 1: 519–521; Robert A. Hill, "The First England Years and After, 1912–1916," in *Marcus Garvey and the Vision of Africa,* ed. John Henrik Clarke and Amy Jacques Garvey (New York: Random House, 1974), 38–76; Dusé Mohamed Ali, "Foreign Affairs," *The Negro World,* March 25, 1922, 4; May 20, 1922, 4.

55. "The Only Solution of Color Prejudice," *Moslem Sunrise* 1, no. 2 (October 1921): 41; Turner, *Islam in the African American Experience,* xviii.

56. "True Salvation of the American Negroes," "Brief Report of the Work in America," "Moslem View of Color Line," and "Equality," *Moslem Sunrise* 2, nos. 2 and 3 (April/July 1923): 184, 190, 192, 194, 204.

57. Turner, *Islam in the African American Experience,* 92–93 and chap. 5 and 6; Robert Dannin, *Black Pilgrimage to Islam* (Oxford: Oxford University Press, 2005).

58. Lajpat Rai, "Presidential Address at the Bombay Hindu Conference," in *Lala Lajpat Rai: Writings and Speeches,* vol. 2, ed. Vijaya Chandra Joshi, 245 (Delhi: University Publishers, 1966).

59. Khurshid Ahmad Khan Yusufi, ed., *Speeches, Statements, and Messages of the Quaid-e-Azam,* vol. 1 (Lahore: Bazm-e-Iqbal, 1996).

60. See Taraknath Das to J. T. Sunderland, June 17, 1925, in *Taraknath Das: Life and Letters,* 267; Taraknath Das to J. T. Sunderland, October 25, 1925, JT Sunderland Papers, NMML; Gupta, "Indians in the United States," *The Modern Review* (July 1924): 16.

61. "Tagore to Myron N. Phelps," in *Selected Letters of Rabindranath Tagore,* ed. Krishna Dutta and Andrew Robinson, 74–77 (Cambridge: Cambridge University Press, 1997).

62. Katherine Mayo, *Mother India* (London: Jonathan Cape, 1927), and *The Isles of Fear: The Truth about the Philippines* (New York: Harcourt Brace and Company, 1925); Mrinalini Sinha, *Specters of Mother India: The Global Restructuring of an Empire* (Durham: Duke University Press, 2006); K. A.

Natarajan, *Rejoinder to "Mother India"* (Bombay: The Tatva-Vivechaka Press, 1927), 55; C. S. Ranga Iyer, *Father India: A Reply to Mother India* (London: Selwyn & Blount, 1927), 90; Dhan Gopal Mukerji, *A Son of Mother India Answers* (New York: E. P. Dutton & Company, 1928), 62; Kanhaya Lal Gauba, *Uncle Sham: Being the Strange Tale of a Civilisation Run Amok* (Lahore: The Times Publishing Company, 1929), 36–41.

63. Dilip Singh Saund, *My Mother India* (Stockton: Pacific Coast Khalsa Diwan Society, 1930).

64. Varnashrama Dharma refers to the order or duties associated with the division of society into varnas (castes) and ashramas (life stages). See Sisir K. Bose, ed., *Netaji: Collected Works,* vol. 5 (Calcutta: Netaji Research Bureau, 1985), 255–257.

65. "Interviews with Foreigners," before March 1, 1929, CWMG.

66. Public killings of Dalits have occurred all too frequently up to the present day. See Susan Bayly, *Caste, Society and Politics in India from the Eighteenth Century to the Modern Age* (Cambridge: Cambridge University Press, 1999), especially chap. 9.

67. Joginder Singh Dhanki, ed., *Perspectives on Indian National Movement: Selected Correspondence of Lala Lajpat Rai* (New Delhi: National Book Organization, 1998), 409–410; Du Bois to Lajpat Rai, November 9, 1927, Reel 22, DBP.

68. Lala Lajpat Rai, *Unhappy India* (Calcutta: Banna, 1928), 113, 124.

69. Ibid., lix, 140, 87.

70. Bhimrao Ramji Ambedkar, "Which Is Worse? Slavery or Untouchability?" in *Dr. Babasaheb Ambedkar: Writings and Speeches* 12 (Bombay: Government Central Press, 1989): 741–759. Also see *Dr. Babasaheb Ambedkar: Writings and Speeches* 5: 9–18, 75–88.

71. Ambedkar, "Which Is Worse? Slavery or Untouchability?" 742, 745, 749–50, 752, 754; Ambedkar, "Negroes and Slavery," in *Dr. Babasaheb Ambedkar: Writings and Speeches* 5: 80–88.

72. Katherine Mayo, "Mahatma Gandhi and India's 'Untouchables,'" 1930, in *The Americanization of Gandhi: Images of the Mahatma,* ed. Charles Chatfield, 250 (New York: Garland, 1976). Also see Harry H. Field, *After Mother India* (New York: Harcourt, Brace and Company, 1929), 250.

73. Gandhi to Amy Jacques Garvey, May 12, 1926, CWMG; Amy Jacques Garvey, *Garvey and Garveyism* (New York: Octagon Books, 1968), 168; Gandhi, "Race Arrogance," *Young India,* October 14, 1926, CWMG.

74. Dohra Ahmad, "More Than Romance: Genre and Geography in Dark Princess," *ELH* 69, no. 3 (2002): 775–803.

75. "Garvey the Master Architect of Ethiopia, Says Hindu Patriot," *The Negro World,* February 11, 1922.

3. Colored Cosmopolitanism

1. W. E. B. Du Bois, "To the Nations of the World," (1900), in *The Oxford W. E. B. Du Bois Reader,* ed. Eric J. Sundquist, 625 (New York: Oxford University Press, 1996); Du Bois, *The Souls of Black Folk* (New York: Penguin Books, 1989), 13.

2. W. E. B. Du Bois, *The Negro* (New York: Oxford University Press, 2007), 110.

3. Pratap Bhanu Mehta, "Cosmopolitanism and the Circle of Reason," *Political Theory* 28, no. 5 (October 2000): 620; David Hollinger, *Cosmopolitanism and Solidarity: Studies in Ethnoracial, Religious, and Professional Affiliation in the United States* (Madison: University of Wisconsin Press, 2006), xviii–xix. Also see Kwame Anthony Appiah, *Cosmopolitanism: Ethics in a World of Strangers* (New York: Norton, 2006) and *The Ethics of Identity* (Princeton: Princeton University Press, 2005); Seyla Benhabib, *Another Cosmopolitanism* (Oxford: Oxford University Press, 2006); Steven Vertovec and Robin Cohen, eds., *Conceiving Cosmopolitanism: Theory, Context, Practice* (New York: Oxford University Press, 2002).

4. Leslie McCall, "The Complexity of Intersectionality," *Journal of Women in Culture and Society* (November 26, 2007): 1771–1800; Kimberlé Crenshaw, "Mapping the Margins: Intersectionality, Identity Politics, and Violence against Women of Color," *Stanford Law Review* 43, no. 6 (1991): 1241–1299.

5. Herbert Aptheker, *"One Continual Cry": David Walker's Appeal to the Colored Citizens of the World (1829–1830): Its Setting, Its Meaning* (New York: Humanities Press, 1965), 79–80, 106, emphasis in original.

6. Alexander Crummell, *Africa and America: Addresses and Discourses* (Springfield, Mass.: Wiley & Co., 1891), 375–376, emphasis in original.

7. Judith Shklar, "Subversive Genealogies," *Daedalus* 101, no. 1 (Winter 1972): 129–154.

8. "India," *The Horizon: A Journal of the Color Line* 1, no. 1 (January 1907): 8, reprinted in *The Rare Periodicals of W. E. B. Du Bois, Volume 2, Part 1,* compiled, indexed, and reprinted by Paul G. Partington (Whittier, Calif.: Paul G. Partington, 1991).

9. "India," *The Horizon: A Journal of the Color Line* 1, no. 2 (January 1907): 8–9, reprinted in Partington, *The Rare Periodicals of W. E. B. Du Bois.*

10. In South Africa the term "coloured" has come to identify people of "mixed" ethnoracial origin. See "Speech at Y.M.C.A." May 18, 1908, CWMG. Also see *Indian Opinion,* June 4, 1910, CWMG.

11. Dusé Mohamed Ali, "The Coloured Man in Art and Letters," *Indian Opinion,* October 21, 1911. Quoted in Anil Nauriya, *The African Element in Gandhi* (New Delhi: National Gandhi Museum and Gyan Publishing House, 2006), available online at http://www.anc.org.za/ancdocs/history/people/gandhi/anil.html.

12. See "Foreword" and "A Word to Our Brothers," *The African Times and Orient Review* 1, no. 1 (July 1912): 1, 4.

13. "Our Symposium and Why" and "Symposium," *African Times and Orient Review* 1, no. 1 (July 1912): 13–18; *African Times and Orient Review* 1, no. 3 (September 1912): 79–80.

14. W. E. B. Du Bois, "World War and the Color Line," *The Crisis* 9, no. 1 (November 1914): 29.

15. Du Bois, "Egypt and India," *The Crisis* 18, no. 2 (June 1919): 62. See also Du Bois, "Bleeding Ireland," *The Crisis* 21, no. 5 (March 1921): 200.

16. Marcus Garvey, "The Negro's Greatest Enemy," *Current History* 18, no. 6 (September 1923): 951–957, reprinted in Amy Jacques Garvey, ed., *The Philosophy and Opinions of Marcus Garvey II* (New York: Universal Publishing House, 1923), especially 127–128; Tony Martin, *Race First: The Ideological and Organizational Struggles of Marcus Garvey and the Universal Negro Improvement Association* (Westport, Conn.: Greenwood Press, 1976), 273–333, 344–355 (hereafter cited as MGUNIA). For an exception, see MGUNIA 4: 184.

17. MGUNIA 4: 567–569.

18. Peter V. Fernandes, "Englishmen and the Darker Races," *The Negro World,* July 2, 1921, 4.

19. See "Announcement," *The Negro World,* March 25, 1922, 4; Dusé Mohamed Ali, "Foreign Affairs," *The Negro World,* June 17, 1922, 4. See also Ali, "Foreign Affairs," *The Negro World,* April 1, 1922, 4.

20. J. Jackson Tilford, "South African Revolt and Native Tolerance," *The Negro World,* March 25, 1922, 5.

21. Hubert Harrison, "The Brown Man Leads the Way," *The Negro World,* October 29, 1921, 8.

22. See Martin, *Race First,* 9–10, and "Unrest among the Negroes," British Home Office (Directorate of Intelligence), October 7, 1919, 133, cited in W. F. Elkins, "'Unrest among the Negroes,' A British Document of 1919," *Science and Society* XXXII, no. 1 (Winter 1968): 77–78.

23. Hubert Henry Harrison, *When Africa Awakes: The "Inside Story" of the Stirrings and Strivings of the New Negro in the Western World* (New York: Porro Press, 1920), 40, 96–97; Jeffrey B. Perry, ed., *A Hubert Harrison Reader* (Middletown, Conn.: Wesleyan University Press, 2001), 99–101, 127, 139–140, 213–214, 216–219, 231–234, and note 9 on 443; Kevin Gaines, *Uplifting the Race: Black Leadership, Politics, and Culture in the Twentieth Century* (Chapel Hill: University of North Carolina Press, 1996), 234–246; Winston James, *Holding Aloft the Banner of Ethiopia: Caribbean Radicalism in Early Twentieth-Century America* (London: Verso, 1998), 123–134.

24. John Edward Bruce, *The Selected Writings of John Edward Bruce: Militant Black Journalist,* compiled and edited by Peter Gilbert (New York: Arno Press, 1971), 125, 139–145, 147, 152–153, emphasis in the original.

25. *The World Forum,* January 1919, in RG 165, File 10218–296, Records of the War Department General and Special Staffs, Correspondence of the Military Intelligence Division Relating to "Negro Subversion," M1440, Reel 5. Also see Beverly Lowry, *Her Dream of Dreams: The Rise and Triumph of Madam C. J. Walker* (New York: Alfred A. Knopf, 2003), 404–405; A'Lelia Bundles, *On Her Own Ground: The Life and Times of Madam C. J. Walker* (New York: Scribner, 2001), 257–258; Brenda Gayle Plummer, *Rising Wind: Black Americans and U.S. Foreign Affairs, 1935–1960* (Chapel Hill: University of North Carolina Press, 1996), 16, 20.

26. "WP-enemy Propaganda," subject file, 1911–1927, Naval Records Collection, RG 45, USNA; "Talking Points," *The Crusader* 2, no. 11 (July 1920): 7; "Black and Brown Races," *The Crusader* 4, no. 4 (June 1921): 6; "Liberating

Africa," *The Crusader* 4, no. 6 (August 1921): 8; "Overseas Correspondence," *The Crusader* 2, no. 8 (April 1920): 31; A. L. Jackson, "The Onlooker," *The Chicago Defender* 25 (March 1922): 12; "The Mystic Gandhi Imprisoned," *Norfolk Journal and Guide,* April 1, 1922, 4; Du Bois, "Opinion," *The Crisis* 23, no. 6 (April 1922): 247; Du Bois, "Opinion," *The Crisis* 24, no 1 (May 1922): 7.

27. *The Crisis* 28, no. 2 (June 1924): 58–59. Also see "Gandhi Arrested," *The Messenger* (March 1922): 368–369; "America's India," *The Messenger* (June 1922): 418.

28. Du Bois, "The Hegemony of Race," *The Crisis* 31, no. 5(March 1926): 248.

29. Du Bois, "The Outer Pocket," *The Crisis* 30, no. 2 (June 1925): 94. See also Abdur Raoof Malik to Du Bois, Reel 22, Du Bois Papers (hereafter cited as DBP).

30. Du Bois, "The Outer Pocket," *The Crisis* 30, no. 2 (June 1925): 93–94. Chaturvedi's last name was incorrectly identified as "Matiovedi."

31. Chaturvedi to Du Bois, January 19, 1925 and September 15, 1925, and Du Bois to Chaturvedi, October 15, 1925, Reel 15, DBP.

32. Amiya Kanti Das to Du Bois., October 23, 1925, Reel 16, DBP.

33. Du Bois to Amiya Kanti Das, December 10, 1925, Reel 16, DBP.

34. Shripad R. Tikekar to Du Bois, December 23, 1927, Reel 23, DBP.

35. See Khan to Du Bois, September 29, 1927, Reel 23, DBP.

36. W. E. B. Du Bois, *Dark Princess: A Romance* (New York: Harcourt, Brace, 1928), 22. Also see Bill Mullen, "Du Bois, Dark Princess, and the Afro-Asian International," *Positions: East Asia Cultures Critique* 11, no. 1 (Spring 2003): 217–239.

37. Du Bois, *Dark Princess,* 7–8, 17, 19, 227–228. Also see Du Bois, "Egypt and India," *The Crisis* 18, no. 2 (June 1919): 62.

38. Du Bois, *Dark Princess,* 9, 239.

39. Ibid., 16, 21.

40. See Herbert Aptheker, *The Literary Legacy of W. E. B. Du Bois* (White Plains, N.Y.: Kraus International Publications, 1989), 205; Jane Reitell, *Annals of the American Academy of Political and Social Science* (November 1928): 347–348; Du Bois, *Dark Princess,* 21–22, 24.

41. Du Bois, *Dark Princess,* 256–257.

42. Contrast this reading with Herman Beavers, "Romancing the Body Politic: Du Bois's Propaganda of the Dark World," *The Annals of the American Academy of Political and Social Science* 568 (March 2000), reprinted in *W. E. B. Du Bois: Modern Critical Views,* ed. Harold Bloom, 211–226 (Philadelphia: Chelsea House Publishers, 2001); Du Bois, *Dark Princess,* 33, 96.

43. I am grateful to Adam Ewing for suggesting this comparison. See Michelle Ann Stephens, *Black Empire: The Masculine Global Imaginary of Caribbean Intellectuals in the United States, 1914–1962* (Durham: Duke University Press, 2005).

44. Du Bois, *Dark Princess,* 245, 210, 220–221, 308, 311. Also see Edward J. Blum, *Du Bois: American Prophet* (Philadelphia: University of Pennsylvania Press, 2007), especially 169–173.

45. Du Bois, "As the Crow Flies," *The Crisis* 36, no. 1 (January 1929): 5; "The Browsing Reader," *The Crisis* 36, no. 5 (May 1929): 175.

46. Feroz Chand to Du Bois, December 13, 1928, Reel 26; Du Bois to the editor of *The People,* January 19, 1929, Reel 29, DBP.

47. *The Aryan Path* was published by the Theosophy Company. In keeping with its transnational message, Du Bois published part of the article in the African American newspaper *The Pittsburgh Courier.* See Du Bois, "The Clash of Colour," *The Aryan Path* 7, no. 3 (March 1936): 111–115; Du Bois, "Indians and Negroes," in "A Forum of Fact and Opinion," *Pittsburgh Courier,* April 11, 1936, 2. Also see "India," *Freedomways,* memorial issue (First Quarter, 1965): 115–117.

48. The 1921 Pan-African Congress included three delegates from India. See Slide 368, Reel 10, DBP; Du Bois, "The Clash of Colour," 111–115.

49. Marcus Garvey, "The Negro's Greatest Enemy," *Current History* 18, no. 6 (September 1923): 951–957, reprinted in Amy Jacques Garvey, ed., *The Philosophy and Opinions of Marcus Garvey* II (New York: Universal Publishing House, 1923), 128.

50. Du Bois, "The Clash of Colour," 111–115.

51. Ibid., 114–115.

52. *The Aryan Path* 7, no. 3 (March, 1936): 105 and N. S. Subba Rao, *The Aryan Path* 7, no. 5 (May 1936): 213–216.

53. N. S. Subba Rao, *The Aryan Path* 7, no. 5 (May, 1936): 213–216.

54. W. E. B. Du Bois, "The Union of Colour," *Aryan Path* 7, no. 10 (October 1936): 483–484.

55. N. S. Subba Rao, "A Rejoinder to Dr. Du Bois," *Aryan Path* 7, no. 10 (October 1936): 484–485.

56. S. Natarajan to Du Bois, October 2, 1936, Reel 45, DBP. See also "Concept and Symbol," *Indian Social Reformer* (September 5, 1936): 4–5.

57. Rammanohar Lohia to Du Bois, July 20, 1936, Reel 45, DBP.

58. See Herbert Aptheker, *A Documentary History of the Negro Peoples in the United States,* vol. 3 (New York: Citadel Press, 1969), 488–493.

59. Nico Slate, "A Coloured Cosmopolitanism: Cedric Dover's Reading of the Afro-Asian World," in *Cosmopolitan Thought Zones: New Approaches to South Asian Intellectual History,* ed. Kris Manjapra and Sugata Bose, 213–235 (New York: Palgrave Macmillan, 2010).

60. Cedric Dover, *Cimmerii? Or Eurasians and Their Future* (Calcutta: The Modern Art Press, 1929), 19, 36

61. Cedric Dover, *Half-Caste* (London: M. Secker and Warburg, 1937), 52.

62. See A. B. V. Drew, "Half-Caste," *Man* 38 (September 1938): 156; William O. Brown, "The Present and Future of the Mixed Blood," *The Journal of Negro Education* 7, no. 4 (October 1938): 556–557. See also *Perez v. Sharp,* 32 Cal. 2d 711; 198 P.2d 17 (1948).

63. "Race Scientist Debunks White Superiority Thesis," *The Chicago Defender,* national edition December 4, 1937, 24.

64. See Dover to Du Bois, August 1, 1937, and Du Bois to Dover, September 7, 1937, in Reel 47, DBP.

65. Dover to Du Bois on December 1, 1937, and December 21, 1937, Reel 47; Du Bois to Dover, January 5, 1938, Reel 48; Dover to Du Bois, February 3, 1938, Reel 48; Dover to Jawaharlal Nehru, undated, Reel 48, DBP.

66. Dover to Jawaharlal Nehru (JN), May 16, 1936, vol. 18, JN Papers, Nehru Memorial Museum and Library, Delhi.

67. Nehru later met Padmore, who sent Nehru an autographed copy of his *Life and Struggles of Negro Toilers.* See JN to Dover, July 15 and September 3, 1936, vol. 18, JN Papers, NMML; Padmore to JN, July 9, 1938, vol. 78, JN Papers, NMML.

68. Dover to JN, undated and May 18, year not given, vol. 18, JN Papers, NMML.

69. Jawaharlal Nehru, *Autobiography* (London: John Lane, 1936), 500.

70. Dover, *Feathers in the Arrow: An Approach For Coloured Writers and Readers* (Bombay: Padma Publications, 1947), 32.

71. For example, Dover worked to publish Claude McKay's poetry in England and India. See Carl Cowl to John Dewey, August 21, 1947, *Claude McKay Papers,* Box 2, Folder 49, Yale University Beinecke Library. See also Dover to Du Bois, October 21, 1946, *The Papers of W. E. B. Du Bois,* Reel 58 (Sanford, N.C.: Microfilming Corporation of America, 1980–1981).

72. Dover, "The Terminology of Homotypes of Insects," *Science* 60, no. 1565 (December 1924); "The Classification of Man," *Proceedings of the Indian Academy of Science,* Section A, vol. 8 (August 1952): 209–213; "The Black Knight," *Phylon* 15, no. 1 (First Quarter, 1954); "The Black Knight: Part II," *Phylon* 15, no. 2 (Second Quarter, 1954); *Brown Phoenix* (London: The College Press, 1950).

73. Dover, "Books as Ambassadors," *The Crisis* 54, no. 12 (December, 1947): 368–369.

74. Dover, "Towards Coloured Unity," *Congress Socialist* (January 23, 1937), reprinted in *Pan-Africa* (February 1947): 30–32.

75. Dover, *Half-Caste,* 19.

76. See "Bill Would Admit Hindus as Citizens," *The Negro World,* February 11, 1928, 3.

77. "A Hindu Speaks His Mind About Us," *The Chicago Defender,* November 29, 1930, 14.

78. "One Hindu Speaks," *The Chicago Defender,* December 6, 1930, 14.

79. Frank St. Claire, "Page Mr. Hindu," *The Chicago Defender,* December 6, 1930, 14.

80. J. Dalton Gilmore, "Page Mr. Romola," *The Chicago Defender,* December 13, 1930, 12; Dorothy M. Holmes, "They're Not So Hot," *The Chicago Defender,* December 27, 1930, A2; Mrs. E. O. Harris, "They're Still Talking About Mr. Romola," *The Chicago Defender,* December 27, 1930, A2.

81. W. H. Beecher, "Mahatma Gandhi's Burden," *The Chicago Defender,* December 13, 1930, 12.

82. Moxley W. Willis, "This Is Courage!" *The Chicago Defender,* January 17, 1931, 14.

83. "Another Hindu Writes," *The Chicago Defender,* December 13, 1930, 12.

84. Rao offered a possible explanation for Romola's sour mood when he asked, "By the way, is this the same Mr. Chowbury who is known as Romola, a flamboyant dreamer whose vision of marketing oriental perfumes failed miserably?" See "One Hindu to Another," *The Chicago Defender,* December 20, 1930, 12.

85. D. G. Madho Singh, "This Makes the Hindu Question Unanimous," *The Chicago Defender,* December 27, 1930, A2; D. G. Madho Singh, "India Speaks," *The Chicago Defender,* January 31, 1931, 14.

86. L. Rahman, "No Color Line in Islam," *The Chicago Defender,* December 20, 1930, 12.

87. Penny Von Eschen, *Race against Empire: Black Americans and Anticolonialism, 1937–1957* (Ithaca, N.Y.: Cornell University Press, 1997), 22–23.

88. "International Council Holds Public Meeting," *The Chicago Defender,* August 16, 1924, 10.

89. Frank R. Crosswaith, *The Negro World,* January 25, 1930, 6.

4. Soul Force

1. "Mrs. Naidu, Noted East Indian Poetess, at Great U.N.I.A. Mass Meeting in Capetown, South Africa, Lauds Principles and Leadership of the Association," *The Negro World,* May 17, 1924.

2. Sudarshan Kapur, *Raising Up a Prophet: The African American Encounter with Gandhi* (Boston: Beacon Press, 1992).

3. See Margaret Chatterjee, *Gandhi and the Challenge of Religious Diversity: Religious Pluralism Revisited* (New Delhi: Promilla & Co., in association with Bibliophile South Asia, 2005); Uma Majmudar, *Gandhi's Pilgrimage of Faith: From Darkness to Light* (Albany: State University of New York Press, 2005); J. T. F. Jordens, *Gandhi's Religion: A Homespun Shawl* (New York: St. Martin's Press, 1998).

4. Sarojini Naidu, *Sarojini Naidu: Selected Letters, 1890s to 1940s,* edited by Makarand Paranjpe (New Delhi: Kali for Women, 1996), 212–216.

5. Richard B. Gregg to Du Bois, November 19, 1926, Reel 18, W. E. B. Du Bois Papers (hereafter cited as DBP) and Du Bois, "Gandhi and American Negroes," *Gandhi Marg* (July 1957): 1–4.

6. See David McI. Gracie, *Gandhi and Charlie: The Story of a Friendship As Told through the Letters and Writings of Mohandas K. Gandhi and the Rev'd Charles Freer Andrews* (Cambridge, Mass: Cowley Publications, 1989); Hugh Tinker, *The Ordeal of Love: C. F. Andrews and India* (Oxford: Oxford University Press, 1998).

7. "Overseas," *The Crisis* 29, no. 4 (February 1925): 182.

8. Du Bois to C. F. Andrews, c/o Bishop Jones, The Fellowship of Reconciliation, February 19, 1929; Andrews to Du Bois, February 26, 1929, Reel 29, DBP.

9. C. F. Andrews, "Christianity and Race Prejudice," *The Crisis* 36, no. 8 (August 1929): 271, 284.

10. Mahatma Gandhi, "To the American Negro," *The Crisis* 36, no. 7 (July 1929): 225. See also "Message from Gandhi Published in *Crisis,*" *New York Amsterdam News,* July 19, 1929, 20.

11. Kelly Miller, *Race Adjustment and the Everlasting Stain* (New York: Arno Press, 1968), 295–298. Also see Walter White, *Rope and Faggot: A Biography of Judge Lynch* (Notre Dame: Notre Dame University Press, 1929), 137.

12. Amiya Chakravarty to Du Bois, July 12, 1929, Reel 30, DBP. "A Message for the American Negro from Rabindranath Tagore," *The Crisis* 36, no. 10 (October 1929): 333–334. *The Crisis* printed excerpts of Tagore's writings in 1931 and 1932 as well. See *The Crisis* 38, no. 7 (July 1931): 224; *The Crisis* 39, no. 12 (December 1932): 372. Also see Bolton Smith to Du Bois, September 21, 1929; Du Bois to Smith, August 28, 1929, Reel 30, DBP.

13. Du Bois, *Against Racism: Unpublished Essays, Papers, Addresses, 1887–1961*, edited by Herbert Aptheker (Amherst: University of Massachusetts Press, 1985), 315–316. Also see Mulk Raj Anand to Du Bois, September 30, 1960; Du Bois to Anand, October 14, 1960, Reel 74, DBP.

14. Du Bois to A. C. Chakravarty, September 15, 1931, Reel 36, DBP.

15. Du Bois, "India and Africa," in *The Golden Book of Tagore: A Homage to Rabindranath Tagore from India and the World in Celebration of His Seventy-Fifth Birthday*, ed. Ramanandra Chatterjee (Calcutta: The Golden Book Committee, 1931), Reel 87, DBP.

16. R. R. Moton to N. S. Hardikar, June 24, 1922; A. L. Holsey to N. S. Hardikar, September 19, 1922, in N. S. Hardikar Papers, NMML.

17. "Dinabandhu in America," *Young India*, February 28, 1929, CWMG.

18. "Indian Poet Meets Head of Tuskegee," *The Chicago Defender*, November 15, 1930, 2.

19. *Tuskegee Messenger*, March 9, 1929, quoted in Benarsidas Chaturvedi and Marjorie Sykes, *Charles Freer Andrews: A Narrative* (New York: Harper & Brothers, 1950), 238.

20. J. T. Sunderland, "Rev. C. F. Andrews in America," *The Modern Review* 47 (June 1930): 682–684; "Shriyut Andrewski America-Yatra," *Hindi Pravas Bharatiya*, dated "7 1930," I/D 250, Benarsidas Chaturvedi Papers, National Archives of India (NAI), New Delhi.

21. "Tuskegeeme Shriyut Andrews," *Vishaal Bharat*, I/D 247, Benarsidas Chaturvedi Papers, NAI.

22. I/A 87, Benarsidas Chaturvedi Papers, NAI. Also see I/A 88, Benarsidas Chaturvedi Papers, NAI.

23. I/A 91, Benarsidas Chaturvedi Papers, NAI.

24. "Negroes Welcome Rev. Andrews, Missionary from India," *The Daily Chronicle*, June 17, 1929, I/D 231, Benarsidas Chaturvedi Papers, NAI.

25. Quoted in Kapur, *Raising Up a Prophet*, 77.

26. GWC to CFA, February 24, 1929, Reel 11, the George Washington Carver Papers at Tuskegee Institute (GWCP).

27. Anil Nauriya, *The African Element in Gandhi* (New Delhi: National Gandhi Museum and Gyan Publishing House, 2006).

28. Barry Mackintosh, for example, claimed that Carver was "completely apolitical." See Barry Mackintosh, "George Washington Carver: The Making of a Myth," *Journal of Southern History* 42, no. 4 (1976): 526. For a more balanced assessment of Carver, see Linda O. McMurry, *George Washington Carver: Scientist and Symbol* (New York: Oxford University Press, 1981).

29. See Vinay Lal, "Nakedness, Nonviolence, and Brahmacharya: Gandhi's Experiments in Celibate Sexuality," *Journal of the History of Sexuality* 9, no. 1/2 (January 2000): 105–136; Jordens, *Gandhi's Religion*, chap. 11, 185–198. Also see Joseph S. Alter, *Gandhi's Body: Sex, Diet, and the Politics of Nationalism* (Philadelphia: University of Pennsylvania Press, 2000).

30. Mohandas Gandhi, "What Is Brahmacharya?" *Young India* (June 5, 1924), quoted in Lal, "Nakedness, Nonviolence, and Brahmacharya," 105.

31. M. K. Gandhi, *An Autobiography or The Story of My Experiments with Truth* (Ahmedabad: Navajivan, 1958), 152. See also CWMG, MG to Bhaishir Chhaganlal, December 10, 1928; MG to Rameshchandra, December 13, 1927; MG to Mahadev Desai, November 30, 1928; MG to Richard B. Gregg, January 28, 1929.

32. "Kegee Savant Makes Up Menu for Gandhi," *The Baltimore Afro-American*, November 22, 1930, Reel 60, GWCP.

33. "Dr. Carver Makes Up Menu for Gandhi," November 28, 1930, National Press Clipping Bureau, Reel 60, GWCP. See also W. Hughes Tapley, "Slave Boy Who Was Sold for a Horse, Became One of the World's Greatest Scientists," *The Chicago Defender*, May 4, 1935.

34. *Norfolk Journal and Guide*, "Says Gandhi Gets Strength from Peanuts," April 24, 1937.

35. Gandhi, *An Autobiography*, 201.

36. CFA to GWC, February 28, 1929, Reel 11, GWCP.

37. See M. K. Gandhi, *Satyagraha in South Africa* (Madras: S. Ganesan, 1928), especially the chapter entitled "The Advent of Satyagraha"; see also Jordens, *Gandhi's Religion*, 37.

38. See Gandhi, *An Autobiography*, 114; McMurry, *George Washington Carver*, 96–97, 106.

39. Kapur, *Raising Up a Prophet*, 75.

40. MG to CFA, October 16, 1933, CWMG.

41. On the legend that Carver had been offered a large salary by Thomas Edison, see McMurry, *George Washington Carver*, 176–178.

42. Charles Freer Andrews, "George Carver of Tuskegee," *Harijan* (April 6, 1934). The *Vishaal Bhaarat* article on "Andrews in Tuskegee" also dwelled in detail on George Washington Carver. See "Tuskegeeme Shriyut Andrews," *Vishaal Bharat*, I/D 247, Benarsidas Chaturvedi Papers, NAI.

43. Andrews, "George Carver of Tuskegee,"

44. Gregg to GWC, May 24, 1935, Reel 17, GWCP. For more on Gregg, see Joseph Kip Koseck, "Richard Gregg, Mohandas Gandhi, and the Strategy of Nonviolence," *The Journal of American History* 91, no. 4 (2005): 1318–1348.

45. See CWMG, "An Example to Copy," July 29, 1933; *Harijan* (May 18, 1934–July 6, 1934); CWMG, "Speech at Town Hall, Hassan," August 3, 1927.

46. GWC to MG, July 27, 1935, Reel 17, GWCP. I have not been able to locate Carver's first letter to Gandhi or Gandhi's "card."

47. Desai to GWC, September 2, 1935, Reel 17, GWCP.

48. See "How to Grow the Peanut and 105 Ways of Preparing It for Human Consumption," Bulletin 31 (1916); "How to Make and Save Money on the Farm," Bulletin 39 (1927); "Twelve Ways to Meet the New Economic Conditions

Here in the South," Bulletin 33 (1917), Reel 46, GWCP. Also see McMurry, *George Washington Carver,* 78–80.

49. Louis Fischer, *A Week with Gandhi* (New York: Duell, Sloan, and Pearce, 1942); Ramachandra Guha, *An Anthropologist among the Marxists and Other Essays* (Delhi: Permanent Black, 2001), 11–23; M. K. Gandhi, *Village Industries,* compiled by R. K. Prabhu (Ahmedabad: Navajivan, 1960).

50. McMurry, *George Washington Carver,* 106–107; GWC, "The Love of Nature," *Guide to Nature 5* (December 1912): 16–18; CWMG, "The Same Old Argument," October 7, 1926; M. K. Gandhi, *Economics of Khadi* (Ahmedabad: Navajivan, 1941); Emma Tarlo, *Clothing Matters: Dress and Identity in India* (Chicago: University of Chicago Press, 1996).

51. Carver, "Three Delicious Meals Every Day for the Farmer," Bulletin 32 (1916), Reel 46, GWCP; Ranajit Guha, *Dominance without Hegemony: History and Power in Colonial India* (Cambridge, Mass.: Harvard University Press, 1998), 37–38.

52. Linda O. Hines, "White Mythology and Black Duality: George Washington Carver's Response to Racism and the Radical Left," *The Journal of Negro History* 62 (1977): 136–137.

53. Between 1930 and 1932 *The Chicago Defender* alone published eighty articles mentioning Gandhi. *The Pittsburgh Courier* published forty-seven, the *New York Amsterdam News* thirty-five, and *The Atlanta Daily World* fourteen. These figures were attained using the search engine provided by ProQuest Historical Newspapers and include any article that mentioned the word "Gandhi."

54. W. E. B. Du Bois, "As the Crow Flies," *The Crisis* 37, no. 4 (April 1930): 113, emphases in original. See also W. E. B. Du Bois, "As the Crow Flies," *The Crisis* 37, no. 5 (May 1930): 149.

55. On May 17, 1930, *The Chicago Defender* published a large photo of Sarojini Naidu, stating "Poetess becomes leader of East Indian revolt against British rule." See also "Woman, Leader of Rebels, Sentenced," *The Chicago Defender,* May 31, 1930, 1; H. G. Mudgal, "Mrs. Sarojini Naidu: The Joan of Arc of India," *The Negro World,* May 24, 1930, 6.

56. See, for example, John W. Watts, "Speaking for Frederick Douglass," *The Chicago Defender,* May 31, 1930, 14.

57. See Cleveland G. Allen, "New Yorkers to Fight War Dept. Color Line," *The Chicago Defender,* June 13, 1931, 3; R. L. Mays, "We Need a Ghandi [*sic*] in America, Says Mays," *The Chicago Defender,* May 10, 1930, 13.

58. Kelly Miller, "Passive Resistance of Gandhi," *The New York Amsterdam News,* April 2, 1930, 20.

59. Drusilla Dunjee Houston, "That Little Man Gandhi," *The Chicago Defender,* December 12, 1931, 14.

60. Langston Hughes, "Goodbye, Christ," in *The Collected Poems of Langston Hughes,* ed. Arnold Rampersad and David Roessel, 166–167(New York: Knopf, 1994).

61. Langston Hughes, *The Big Sea* (New York: Knopf, 1940), 275.

62. Langston Hughes, "Merry Christmas," in *The Collected Poems,* 132.

63. George Schuyler, "Views and Reviews," *The Pittsburgh Courier,* March 29, 1930; September 12, 1931; P.T.O., "Schuyler on Gandhi," *The Pittsburgh Courier,* September 19, 1931; Schuyler, "Views and Reviews," *The Pittsburgh Courier,* September 19, 1931.

64. W. E. B. Du Bois, "India," *The Crisis* 37, no. 7 (July 1930): 246.

65. See Du Bois, *Dark Princess,* 243, 246.

66. Du Bois to M. K. Gandhi, October 28, 1931, Reel 36, DBP.

67. "Gandhi and Jimmie," *The New York Amsterdam News,* September 30, 1931, 8.

68. William Pickens, "Gandhi-ism and Prayer Will Not Solve Negro's Problem," *The New York Amsterdam News,* February 10, 1932, 8.

69. Arthur S. Gray, "Gandhi-izing America," *The Chicago Defender,* August 30, 1930, 14.

70. Arthur S. Gray, "India Gives Reasons for Declaring of Her Independence," *The Negro World,* April 12, 1930, 4.

71. H. G. Mudgal, "Foreign Affairs," *The Negro World,* March 8, 1930, 4; Mudgal, "What Does 1930 Hold for [the] Negro? Will It Be a Happy New Year?" *The Negro World,* January 4, 1930, 4; Mudgal, "Foreign Affairs," *The Negro World,* February 15, 1930, 4; Mudgal, "India in 1930: A Policy of Blunders," *The Negro World,* January 11, 1930, 2; January 18, 1930, 4; January 25, 1930, 2; Mudgal, "Foreign Affairs," *The Negro World,* March 8, 1930, 4.

72. "Let's Learn Doggedness and Patience from Gandhi," *The Negro World,* June 14, 1930, 1.

73. *The Negro World* made clear its interest in violent revolution in India by printing over several weeks "A Brief History of the Hindustan Gadar Party," a lengthy article written by Rattan Singh for the League against Imperialism. See *The Negro World,* December 28; January 4. Also see "The End of British Imperialism," *The Negro World,* April 26, 1930, 4; "Fighting in India," *The Negro World,* May 3, 1930, 4.

74. Mary Church Terrell, *Unpublished Papers of Mary Church Terrell* (Alexandria, Va.: Alexander Street Press, 2004), 258–259.

75. "Hail Gandhi a 'Second Moses' in U.S," *The Chicago Defender,* October 17, 1931, 13.

76. Du Bois, "India," *The New York Amsterdam News,* October 7, 1931, 8; "Europe in India," *The New York Amsterdam News,* October 14, 1931, 8.

77. "Students to Hear Gandhi Follower," *The Atlanta Daily World,* October 27, 1932.

78. "Noted Hindu Speaks Here This Sunday," *The Atlanta Daily World,* February 24, 1934.

79. Two of the African American religious leaders who traveled to India in the mid-1930s, Howard Thurman and Benjamin Mays, would both have an important influence on King's understanding of Gandhi. See Chapter 7.

80. I am indebted to Sudarshan Kapur for several of the sources in the following section, as my notes make evident. His main argument, that the connections between Gandhi and Black Americans owed much to a similar religious outlook, is also important to my analysis. The following section differs from

Kapur in making analogies between race and caste more central to the history of these interactions. See Kapur, *Raising Up a Prophet,* 82–100.

81. Kapur, *Raising Up a Prophet,* 83.

82. Howard Thurman, *With Head and Heart* (New York: Harcourt Brace Jovanovich, 1979), 106–108.

83. Thurman, *With Head and Heart,* 104, 113–114, 123–125. Also see Howard Thurman, "What We May Learn from India," in *A Strange Freedom: The Best of Howard Thurman on Religious Experience and Public Life,* ed. Walter Earl Fluker and Catherine Tumber, 205 (Boston: Beacon Press, 1998).

84. Thurman, "What We May Learn from India," 206, 209–210.

85. Thurman, *With Head and Heart,* 128; Mahadev Desai, "With Our Negro Guests," *Harijan* (March 14, 1936).

86. Thurman, *With Head and Heart,* 131–135; Desai, "With Our Negro Guests," *Harijan* (March 14, 1936); Kapur, *Raising Up a Prophet,* 91–93.

87. See Howard Thurman to Miss Mabel E. Simpson, "India Miscellaneous File," Box 65, Howard Thurman Papers, Boston University; Kapur, *Raising Up a Prophet,* 82.

88. Thurman, *With Head and Heart,* 131–135.

89. Benjamin E. Mays, "The Color Line around the World," *The Journal of Negro Education* 6, no. 2 (April 1937): 134–143; Benjamin E. Mays, *Born to Rebel: An Autobiography* (New York: Scribner, 1971), 153.

90. Mays, *Born to Rebel,* 155.

91. "Interview to Professor Mays," CWMG, extracted from Mahadev Desai, "A Discourse on Nonviolence," *Harijan* (March 20, 1937); Mays, "The Color Line around the World," 134–143.

92. Mays, *Born to Rebel,* 156–159.

93. Sudarshan Kapur places Tobias at the meeting between Mays and Gandhi, although Mays says nothing of Tobias attending the meeting in his autobiography, and Mahadev Desai and Gandhi's *Collected Works* separate Gandhi's discussions with Mays and Tobias, stating that the former occurred before the latter.

94. "Interview to Dr. Tobias," CWMG, extracted from Mahadev Desai, "A Discourse on Nonviolence," *Harijan* 5, no. 6 (March 20 1937): 41–43.

95. See "India Wants National Independence, Says Dr. Channing H. Tobias," *The Chicago Defender,* March 6, 1937, 24; "Tobias Finds Little Talk of War or of Wally-Edward Romance on Trip to India," *The Atlanta Daily World,* January 4, 1937, 2; "Dr. C. H. Tobias Sees No Visible Signs of War in European Countries," *The Pittsburgh Courier,* January 9, 1937, 5; "India's Color Thrills Tobias," *The New York Amsterdam News,* March 13, 1937, 15.

96. Ambedkar, *What Congress and Gandhi Have Done to the Untouchables* (Bombay: Thacker & Co., 1945), especially 176, 185, 270–271.

97. "Colour Prejudice," *Indian Opinion,* February 7, 1910, CWMG.

98. "Interviews with Foreigners," before March 1, 1929, CWMG.

99. "In the Grip of Untouchability," *Young India,* April 29, 1926, CWMG

100. Gandhi, "Race Arrogance," *Young India,* October 14, 1926, CWMG.

101. *India and the World,* vol. 2 (August 1933): 222–224.

102. CWMG, "An Example to Copy," July 29, 1933

103. "Letter to G. Ramachandra Rao," April 14, 1933; "Letter to N. R. Malkani," August 23, 1934; "Discussion with D. Ramaswami," August 3, 1944, CWMG.

104. CWMG, "An Example to Copy," July 29, 1933.

105. *Adi Karnatakas,* or "original Karnatakas," is a designation for Kannada-speaking Dalits.

106. CWMG, "Speech at Wardha," October 22, 1937.

107. "Interview to Harijan Workers," *Harijan* (July 6, 1934); "Self-Supporting Education," *Young India,* July 11, 1929; "An Example to Copy," July 29, 1933, CWMG.

108. Gandhi, "A Catechism," *Young India,* October 14, 1926; Speech at Wardha," October 22, 1937; Gandhi, *Autobiography,* 163; "An Example to Copy," July 29, 1933, CWMG.

109. CWMG, "Talk with a Harijan Sevak," before June 15, 1935.

110. I/A 110 (a), Benarsidas Chaturvedi Papers, NAI. See also Daniel Immerwahr, "Caste or Colony? Indianizing Race in the United States," *Modern Intellectual History* 4, no. 2 (2007): 275–301.

111. Du Bois, "As the Crow Flies," *The Crisis* 39 (November 1932): 342. Also see "Gandhi Strikes a Snag," *The Pittsburgh Courier,* September 22, 1934, 10.

112. "Speech at Untouchability Conference," December 27, 1924; "Speech at Public Meeting, Madras," March 22, 1925; "To Remove a Misgiving," *Hindi Navajivan,* July 16, 1925; "Letter to Manishankar Ganpatram," October 7, 1932; "A Letter," October 11, 1932; "Implications of Anti-Untouchability," *Harijan,* (March 23, 1934), all in CWMG.

113. Kapur, *Raising Up a Prophet,* 78–79.

114. "Gandhi Hits U.S. Bar," *Baltimore Afro-American,* June 16, 1934, 1, quoted in Kapur, *Raising Up a Prophet,* 78–79.

115. "Discussion with John R. Mott," November 13/14, 1936, CWMG; "Speech at Gandhi Seva Sangh Meeting, Hudli-IV," April 20, 1937, CWMG; "Caste Hindu Marries Harijan Girl," *Harijan* (June 22, 1940), CWMG; "Marriages between Harijans and Non-Harijans," *Harijan,* (July 7, 1946).

116. *Satyagraha in South Africa,* chap. 10, CWMG.

5. Global Double Victory

1. Gandhi to Franklin Roosevelt, July 1, 1942, *Collected Works of Mahatma Gandhi* (hereafter cited as CWMG).

2. *PM,* December 7, 1941.

3. *The Pittsburgh Courier,* February 7 and 14, 1942; Thomas J. Sugrue, *Sweet Land of Liberty: The Forgotten Struggle for Civil Rights in the North* (New York: Random House, 2008), 77–84; Beth T. Bates, "'Double V for Victory' Mobilizes Black Detroit, 1941–1946," in *Freedom North: Black Freedom Struggles Outside the South, 1940–1980,* ed. Jeanne Theoharis and Komozi Woodard (New York: Palgrave Macmillan, 2003), 17–40.

4. India was one of several geographic pillars of the global double victory movement. Civil rights activists also argued that American racism would complicate relations with China, the Philippines, Mexico, and other parts of the world. See Thomas Guglielmo, *Race War: World War II and the Crisis of American Democracy* (New York: Oxford University Press, forthcoming). Also see Sugata Bose, *A Hundred Horizons: The Indian Ocean in the Age of Global Empire* (Cambridge, Mass.: Harvard University Press, 2006), chap. 5; Leonard A. Gordon, *Brothers against the Raj: A Biography of Indian Nationalists Sarat and Subhas Chandra Bose* (New York: Columbia University Press, 1990); Reginald Kerney, *African American Views of the Japanese: Solidarity or Sedition?* (Albany: State University of New York Press, 1998), especially 101; Gerald Horne, *Race War: White Supremacy and the Japanese Attack on the British Empire* (New York: New York University Press, 2004); Marc Gallicchio, *The African American Encounter with Japan and China: Black Internationalism in Asia, 1895–1945* (Chapel Hill: University of North Carolina Press, 2000); Ernest Allen Jr. "Waiting for Tojo: The Pro-Japan Vigil of Black Missourians, 1932–1943," *Gateway Heritage* (Fall 1994): 16–32. On the war in the Pacific as a "racial war," see John Dower, *War without Mercy: Race and Power in the Pacific War* (New York: Pantheon Books, 1986); Christopher Thorne, *Allies of a Kind: The United States, Britain, and the War against Japan* (New York: Oxford University Press, 1978), especially, 3–11, 726–730.

5. Unlike the number of American soldiers in India at a particular time, the larger total that served in India over the course of the war is difficult to estimate. One contemporary source puts the total number of U.S. soldiers that served in India over the course of the war at 400,000. While 400,000 may be an overestimate, the army reported that there were 183,920 American soldiers serving in the India-Burma theater in November 1944 alone. This figure does not include troops that had left India before November or that came after, and thus can be taken as a safe minimum estimate for the number of American soldiers serving in India-Burma during the war. See Eugene B. Vest, "Native Words Learned by American Soldiers in India and Burma in World War II," *American Speech* 23, no. 3/4 (October–December 1948): 223–231; also see the United States Army's official three-volume history of the China-Burma-India (CBI) theater of the Second World War, Charles F. Romanus and Riley Sunderland, *Stilwell's Mission to China* (Washington, D.C.: Office of the Chief of Military History, Dept. of the Army, 1953); *Stilwell's Command Problems* (Washington, D.C.: Office of the Chief of Military History, Dept. of the Army, 1956); and *Time Runs Out in CBI* (Washington, D.C.: Office of the Chief of Military History, Dept. of the Army, 1959).

6. Twenty-two thousand is the figure given for the "maximum" number of Black troops serving in India in August 1945 and thus underestimates the total that served in India over the course of the war. See "Participation of Negro Troops in the Post-War Military Establishment," from the Headquarters of the India Burma Theater to the Adjutant General, War Department, Washington, D.C., August 29, 1945, Box 57, File 291.1, the National Archives of the United States (hereafter cited as NAUS).

7. Roosevelt's secretary of state, Cordell Hull, later remembered, "While for the sake of good relations with Britain we could not tell the country what we were saying privately, we were saying everything that the most enthusiastic supporters of Indian freedom could have expected and we were convinced that the American people were with us." What the Roosevelt administration told the British government regarding India was, however, never so weighty as to inspire anything more than cosmetic changes in British policy, as demonstrated by the weak proposals Cripps was allowed to offer. Historian Dennis Merrill has concluded that, taken as a whole, "America extended only muted sympathy for independence in India," a judgment largely supported by other historians. See Cordell Hull, *The Memoirs of Cordell Hull*, vol. 2 (New York: Macmillan, 1948), 1483; Dennis Merrill, "The Ironies of History: The United States and the Decolonization of India," in *The United States and Decolonization: Power and Freedom*, ed. David Ryan and Victor Pungong, 102–110 (New York: St. Martin's Press, 2000); Kenton J. Clymer, *Quest for Freedom: The United States and India's Independence* (New York: Columbia University Press, 1995); M. S. Venkataramani and B. K. Shrivastava, *Quit India: The American Response to the 1942 Struggle* (New Delhi: Vikas, 1979), and *Roosevelt, Gandhi, Churchill: America and the Last Phase of India's Freedom Struggle* (New Delhi: Radiant, 1983); Christopher Thorne, *Allies of a Kind: The United States, Britain, and the War against Japan* (New York: Oxford University Press, 1978); Gary R. Hess, *America Encounters India, 1941–1947* (Baltimore: Johns Hopkins University Press, 1971); United States Department of State, *Foreign Relations of the United States, 1942*, vol. 1, *General; the British Commonweath; the Far East* (Washington, D.C.: U.S. Government Printing Office, 1942), especially 619–662.

8. "What You Have to Do in Order to Win," *Baltimore Afro-American*, April 11, 1942, 12.

9. See "India, Jan.–May, 1942," Box A320, NAACP Papers, Library of Congress (LOC).

10. Davis to White, April 30, 1942, "India, Jan.–May, 1942," Box A320, NAACP Papers, LOC.

11. Murphy to White, May 4, 1942, "India, Jan.–May, 1942," Box A320, NAACP Papers, LOC.

12. Du Bois to White, May 2, 1942, Reel 54, Du Bois Papers (hereafter cited as DBP).

13. *People's Voice*, May 2, 1942. Quoted in Horne, *Race War*, 122.

14. Lanier to White, May 5, 1942, "India, Jan.–May, 1942," Box A320, NAACP Papers, LOC.

15. Randolph to White, May 7, 1942, White to Randolph, May 11, 1942, and Randolph to White, May 14, 1942, all in "India, Jan.–May, 1942," Box A320, NAACP Papers, LOC.

16. Phelps Stokes to White, May 29, 1942, "India, Jan.–May, 1942," Box A320, NAACP Papers, LOC.

17. See White to Willkie, May 11, 1942, "India, Jan.–May, 1942," Box A320, NAACP Papers, LOC; "Willkie Says War Liberates Negro," *New York Times*,

July 20, 1942; "Dixie's Three Stooges Rap Willkie on India," *The New York Amsterdam News*, November 7, 1942.

18. See Gallicchio, *The African American Encounter with Japan and China*, 140, 161.

19. Despite her differences with White, Buck did much to promote Indian independence and the rights of African Americans. See Buck to White, on May 5, "India, Jan.–May, 1942," Box A320, NAACP Papers, LOC; "Pearl Buck's 10 Points," *Baltimore Afro-American*, June 13, 1942, 1, 4; Gallicchio, *The African American Encounter with Japan and China*, 159–162; Post War World Council, *Freedom for India Now!* (New York: Post War World Council, 1942); Pearl S. Buck, *American Unity and Asia* (New York: The John Day Company, 1942); Pearl S. Buck, *Freedom for All* (New York City: The Post War World Council, 1942); Roi Ottley, *"New World A-Coming": Inside Black America* (Boston: Houghton Mifflin, 1943), 326, 237.

20. Curie refused to let White show the memo to President Roosevelt. See "Office Memorandum," May 5, and Curie to White in "India, Jan.–May, 1942," Box A320, NAACP Papers, LOC.

21. Elizabeth Borgwardt, *A New Deal for the World: America's Vision for Human Rights* (Cambridge, Mass.: Belknap Press of Harvard University Press, 2005).

22. White kept a clipping of a *New York Herald Tribune* article entitled "Rajagopalachari Urges India to Fight if Country Is Invaded," May 5, 1942, in "India, Jan.–May, 1942," Box A320, NAACP Papers, LOC.

23. Wilkins to White, May 5, 1942, "India, Jan.–May, 1942," Box A320, NAACP Papers, LOC; White to Roosevelt, May 4, 1942, included in Walter White to W. E. B. Du Bois, May 12, 1942, Reel 54, DBP.

24. Walter White to W. E. B. Du Bois, May 12 and June 5, 1942, Reel 54, DBP; Welles to Roosevelt, May 22, 1942, Folder 14, Box 151, Welles Papers, Franklin Delano Roosevelt Library.

25. White to Buck, June 5, 1942, "India, June–Dec., 1942," Box A320, NAACP Papers, LOC.

26. White to Shridharani, June 8, 1942, and "Messages Received by CTF for Mr. White," June 10, 1942, in "India, June–Dec., 1942," Box A320, NAACP Papers, LOC.

27. White to Berle, June 24, 1942, Note by the Division of Near Eastern Affairs, and Berle to White, July 1, 1942, 845.00/1369, State Department Files, NAUS, quoted in Venkataramani and Shrivastava, *Quit India*, 295–296.

28. There is circumstantial evidence that White may have helped encourage Sumner Welles to oppose racism and imperialism as related evils. See White, "Memo from the Secretary," June 9, 1942, and Davis to White, June 8, 1942, in "India, June–Dec., 1942," Box A320, NAACP Papers, LOC; Christopher D. O'Sullivan, *Sumner Welles, Postwar Planning, and the Quest for a New World Order, 1937–1943* (New York: Columbia University Press, 2007), chap. 6.

29. See Drew Pearson, "Washington-Merry-Go-Round," *The Washington Post*, December 22, 1942, B5; Pearson, "Washington-Merry-Go-Round," March 31, 1943; George Padmore, *The Chicago Defender*, January 2, 1943, 1.

30. John Robert Badger, "World View," *The Chicago Defender,* April 10, 1943, 15; Charley Cherokee, "National Grapevine," *The Chicago Defender,* May 15, 1943, 15.

31. *PM,* July 19, 1942.

32. Robinson to White, April 7, 1942, "India, Jan.–May, 1942," Box A320, NAACP Papers, LOC.

33. "Discussion with Dr. John," February 8, 1942, CWMG; Mahadev Desai, "British and American Nazism," *Harijan* (February 15, 1942).

34. Interview to Preston Grover, June 21, 1942, CWMG.

35. John Davies, memo, "The Indian Problem: Fall and Winter 1942–43," 8–10, 17, 29–31, Calcutta, January 23, 1943, Joseph Stilwell Papers, Box 52, Folder 14, Hoover Institution Archives. Also see William Phillips to Secretary of State, February 19, 1943, in *Foreign Relations of the United States, 1943,* vol. 4 *The Near East and Africa* (Washington, D.C.: U.S. Government Printing Office, 1943), 196–197.

36. Mr. Pereira to the Department of State, September 3, 1943, Record Group 59, Decimal File 811.4016.707, NAUS, and Airgram No. 953, the American Consulate, Bombay, India, to Secretary of State, July 19, 1943, Record Group 59, Decimal File 811.4016/654, NAUS.

37. Seventy-Sixth Congress, "Hearings on Repeal of Chinese Exclusion Act, House Committee on Immigration and Naturalization," May 19–June 3, 1943, 33–42, quoted in Tapan K. Mukherjee, *Taraknath Das: Life and Letters of a Revolutionary in Exile* (Calcutta: National Council of Education, Bengal, 1997), 207–208.

38. Kamaladevi Chattopadhyaya, *Inner Recesses, Outer Spaces: Memoirs* (New Delhi: Navrang, 1986), 232.

39. N. Sangulee to Lord Zetland, Indian Political Intelligence (IPI) 16, Microfiche no. 570, File 635 (1939), Oriental and Indian Office Collections, British Library.

40. Note to "Mr. Silver," IPI 16, Microfiche no. 570, File 635 (1939), Oriental and Indian Office Collections, British Library.

41. Chattopadhyaya, *Inner Recesses,* 238–240; "Radio Today," *New York Times,* April 7, 1941.

42. "Britain Is Assailed for Plight of India," *New York Times,* December 18, 1939, 18.

43. "Events Today," *New York Times,* January 3, 1940, 19.

44. James Williams to Nehru, March 6, 1940, vol. 103, Jawaharlal Nehru (hereafter JN) Papers, Nehru Memorial Museum and Library (hereafter NMML), New Delhi; Nehru to Kamaladevi, September 25, 1940, vol. 38, JN Papers, NMML. Also see "Britain Is Assailed for Plight of India," *New York Times,* December 18, 1939, 18.

45. Folder 1, Box A 379, NAACP Papers, LOC; Kamaladevi Chattopadhyaya, *America: The Land of Superlatives* (Bombay: Phoenix Publications, 1946), iv; *The Chicago Defender,* March 23, 1940, 10; *The Bombay Chronicle,* June 17, 1940, quoted in Jamila Brij Bhushan, *Kamaladevi Chattopadhyaya: Portrait of a Rebel* (New Delhi: Abhinav Publications, 1976), 91.

46. Gallicchio, *The African American Encounter with Japan and China,* 172–173; Horne, *Race War,* 225.

47. See Chapter 6 in this book.

48. K. A. Abbas, *An Indian Looks at America* (Bombay: Thacker & Co., 1943), 62, 66.

49. Abbas, *An Indian Looks at America,* 64–65, 67–69; Confidential, War Department, HQ Second Service Command, ASF, Security and Intelligence Division, November 14, 1944. Subject "Ethiopian World Federation, Local 26, 290 Lenox Avenue, New York, NY," NAUS.

50. Cedric Dover, *Know This of Race* (London: Secker & Warburg, 1939), 3.

51. Cedric Dover, "Paul Robeson," in *Talking to India: A Selection of English Language Broadcasts to India,* ed. George Orwell, 18 (London: George Allen & Unwin, 1943).

52. Dover, *Know This of Race,* 43.

53. Dover, "Paul Robeson," 17. Also see Dover to Du Bois, June 20, 1943, DBP, Reel 55.

54. Cedric Dover, *Hell in the Sunshine* (London: M. Secker & Warburg, 1943), 83, 186.

55. Du Bois, *Black Reconstruction in America* (New York: S. A. Russell Company, 1956), 15–16.

56. Du Bois, *Dusk of Dawn: An Essay toward an Autobiography of a Race Concept* (New York, Harcourt, Brace & co. 1940), 96, 117, 151.

57. *The Selected Works of Jawaharlal Nehru* (New Delhi: Orient Longman Limited, 1982), vol. 11, 397.

58. "Events Scheduled for Today," *New York Times,* March 8, 1941, 17.

59. "Dictated to CTF," June 19, 1942, "India, June–Dec., 1942," Box A320, NAACP Papers, LOC.

60. In July 1938 Eslanda Robeson wrote Nehru introducing him to Langston Hughes, explaining that she had already introduced Hughes to Yusuf Meherally. She sent Nehru the summary of the National Negro Congress as well as her own book. See the letters between Nehru and Eslanda Goode Robeson in vol. 88, JN Papers, NMML.

61. Rajni Patel to Jawaharlal Nehru, May 6 and July 14, 1939, vol. 80, JN Papers, NMML.

62. Rajni Patel to Jawaharlal Nehru, August 19, 1939, vol. 80, and Robeson to Jawaharlal Nehru, April 10, 1940, vol. 88, JN Papers, NMML.

63. All in vol. 80, JN Papers, NMML.

64. Rajni Patel to Jawaharlal Nehru, March 2, 1942, vol. 80, JN Papers, NMML.

65. Rajni Patel to Jawaharlal Nehru, November 18, 1939, vol. 80, JN Papers, NMML.

66. "Speech at A.I.C.C. Meeting," August 7, 1942, CWMG.

67. *Selected Works of Jawaharlal Nehru,* vol. 12, 458–459.

68. Thomas J. Anderson and eighty-six others to Roosevelt, September 26, 1942, 845.00/1640, State Department Files, NAUS, cited in Venkataramani and Shrivastava, *Quit India,* 295.

69. Horace Cayton, "Fighting for White Folks?" *The Nation,* September 26, 1942; "India Justified in Freedom Fight, Readers Declare," *The Pittsburgh Courier,* October 10, 1942.

70. "Push 2-Speared Attack on Vote Bans in South: Seek End of White Primary, Poll Tax Senate Committee Hears Arguments for Passage of Pepper Bill," *The Chicago Defender,* August 8, 1942, 1.

71. Alan Murray to White, August 3, 1942, and White to Murray, August 10, 1942, "India, June–Dec., 1942," Box A320, NAACP Papers, LOC.

72. See White to Roosevelt, August 31, 1942, "India, June–Dec., 1942," Box A320, NAACP Papers, LOC; "U.S. Mediation of Indian Crisis Sought By NAACP," *The Chicago Defender,* August 15, 1942, 1; "Makes India Plea," *The Chicago Defender,* August 22, 1942, 3; "British Hypocrisy," *The Chicago Defender,* August 22, 1942, 14.

73. H. W. Sewing to Walter White, August 21, 1942, in "India June–Dec., 1942," Box A320, NAACP Papers, LOC.

74. Charles Stevenson to Wilkins, September 10, 1942, "India, June–Dec., 1942," Box A320, NAACP Papers, LOC.

75. A. M. Wendell Malliet, "Colored World Watches India as British Face Fateful Hour," *The New York Amsterdam Star News,* August 15, 1942, 1–2.

76. Ottley, *"New World A-Coming,"* 342.

77. Frederick L. Schuman, *Time* (August 31, 1942). See also Oswald Garrison Villard, "The Final Hour in India," *The Christian Century* 59 no. 30 (July 29, 1942): 933–934; Carey McWilliams, *Brothers under the Skin* (Boston: Little, Brown and Company, 1943), 5, 20; "Color: Unfinished Business of Democracy," special issue, *Survey Graphic* 31, no. 11 (November 1942).

78. Walter White, "War Emergency Conference Speech," NAACP Papers.

79. Unknown author to White, September 28, 1942, "India, June–Dec., 1942," Box A320, NAACP Papers, LOC.

80. Deton J. Brooks Jr., "Ghandi's [*sic*] Stand Threatens Allied Crisis," *The Chicago Defender,* August 8, 1942, 1–2.

81. See A. M. Wendell Malliet, "World Watches India This Week; Gandhi in Challenge," *The New York Amsterdam Star News,* August 8, 1942, 1, 5.

82. "The Atlantic Charter and India," *The Chicago Defender,* August 22, 1942, 14. Also see A. M. Wendell Malliet, "Colored World Watches India As British Face Fateful Hour," *The New York Amsterdam Star News,* August 15, 1942, 1–2; A. C. MacNeal, "Under the Lash: Criticism of Men and Conditions Which Make or Mar the Future of a Race," *The Chicago Defender,* August 15, 1942, 13.

83. Quoted in McWilliams, *Brothers under the Skin,* 20, 42.

84. "Democracy's Voice Speaks," *People's Voice,* New York, May 22, 1943. Reprinted in *Paul Robeson Speaks: Writings, Speeches, Interviews, 1918–1974,* ed. (and with introduction and notes by) Philip S. Foner, 144 (New York: Brunner/Mazel, 1978).

85. See Albert Parker, "The Struggle for India: How It Affects Black Americans," *Militant* (August 22, 1942); George Breitman, "How to Destroy Fascism Abroad and Prevent It at Home," *Militant* (October 31, 1942), in *Fighting*

Racism in World War II, ed. Fred Stanton, 246–248, 277–278 (New York: Pathfinder, 1980).

86. See *Daily Worker* (London), November 16, 1942; Max Yergan to Roosevelt, August 12, 1942, 845.00/1576, State Department Files, NAUS, both quoted in Venkataramani and Shrivastava, *Quit India,* 295.

87. "India and Africa in Forum Discussion," *The New York Amsterdam Star News,* August 29, 1942, 2. On Goshal, see Leonard Gordon, "Bridging India and America: The Art and Politics of Kumar Goshal," *Amerasia Journal* 15, no. 2 (1989): 68–88.

88. "Robeson to Talk at Aid-India Rally," *The New York Amsterdam Star News,* August 29, 1942, 2; "Chinese Y Agent Pleads for India and Negroes," *The New York Amsterdam News,* September 12, 1942, 2.

89. See, for example, John Robert Badger, "World View: Gandhi and Gandhism," *The Chicago Defender,* February 20, 1943, 15.

90. Gandhi to Joshi, June 11, 1944; Joshi to Gandhi, June 14, 1944; Gandhi to Joshi, July 30, 1944, CWMG.

91. White to Indian National Congress (INC), "India, Jan.–May, 1942"; White to Singh, September 16, 1942, "India, June–Dec., 1942"; Singh to White, February 17, 1943, "India General 43–45"; NAACP to Churchill, February 20, 1943, "India General 43–45"; "3 Major Radio Chains Refused to Carry Nehru Speech, NAACP Learns"; James Fly to Walter White, August 1, 1942, "India, June–Dec., 1942," all in Box A320, NAACP Papers, LOC.

92. Singh had spoken at the National Convention of the NAACP in Los Angeles earlier that summer. Singh to White, September 11, 1942, "India, June–Dec., 1942," Box A320, NAACP Papers, LOC, emphasis in original; Countee Cullen, "Karenge ya Marenge," in *My Soul's High Song: The Collected Writings of Countee Cullen,* 318, edited by Gerald Early (New York: Anchor Books, 1991).

93. Langston Hughes, "Here to Yonder," *The Chicago Defender,* January 30, 1943, 14; "Ghandi [*sic*] Is Fasting," *The Collected Poems of Langston Hughes,* ed. Arnold Rampersad, associate ed. David Roessel, 578 (New York: Knopf; distributed by Random House, 1994).

94. Krishnaya to White, July 18, 1944, and White to Krishnaya, July 20, 1944, "India General 43–45," Box A320, NAACP Papers, LOC.

95. Goshal, "To the Allied Leaders," *The Pittsburgh Courier,* August 21, 1943, 6.

96. See Goshal's columns in *The Pittsburgh Courier* on October 10, 1942, 12; October 24, 1942, 13; September 11, 1943, 6. Also see Goshal, "Jawaharlal Nehru, Leader of the Indian Masses and Foe of British Imperialism," *The Pittsburgh Courier,* November 14, 1942, 7.

97. See Goshal, "Imperialism and Discrimination Must Be Eliminated to Have Peace on Earth," *The Pittsburgh Courier,* December 26, 1942, 12; "Compared to America, Indians Show Amazing Unanimity for Freedom," *The Pittsburgh Courier,* July 22, 1944, 6.

98. Gunnar Myrdal, with the assistance of Richard Sterner and Arnold Rose, *An American Dilemma: The Negro Problem and Modern Democracy* (New York: Harper & Brothers, 1944), 997, 1006, 1015–1016.

99. See Romanus and Sunderland, *Time Runs Out*, 301; "Ram Ram, Jad Jao: Yanks in India Master Lingo and Learn How to Get Along," *Newsweek* (January 4, 1943): 21–23.

100. See William Phillips to President Roosevelt, April 19, 1943, in *Foreign Relations of the United States*, 1943, vol. 4, *The Near East and Africa*, 218–219; Phillips to Secretary of State, February 12, 1943, and February 19, 1943, ibid., 191–192, 196–197.

101. Maggi M. Morehouse, *Fighting in the Jim Crow Army: Black Men and Women Remember World War II* (Lanham, Md.: Rowman and Littlefield, 2000); Philip McGuire, ed., *Taps for a Jim Crow Army: Letters from Black Soldiers in World War II* (Lexington, Ky.: University Press of Kentucky, 1993); A. Russell Buchanan, *Black Americans in World War II* (Santa Barbara, Calif.: Clio Books, 1977); Ulysses Grant Lee, *The Employment of Negro Troops* (Washington, D.C.: Office of the Chief of Military History, U.S. Army, 1966).

102. Mary Penick Motley, ed., *The Invisible Soldier: The Experience of the Black Soldier, World War II*, with a foreword by Howard Donovan Queen (Detroit: Wayne State University Press, 1975), 117–119; Houston T. Campbell Memoirs (AFC/2001/001/294), 21; Ira Pottard (AFC/2001/001/49545), Veterans History Project (hereafter cited as VHP), American Folklife Center, Library of Congress. See also Deton J. Brooks, "India Troops Hit Slander," *The Chicago Defender*, April 7, 1945, 1.

103. Deton J. Brooks, "No Color Problem in India Red Cross Club," *The Chicago Defender*, December 2, 1944, 6; Deton J. Brooks, "GI's Dream Comes True—Scribe Finds Base in India with No Color Problem," *The Chicago Defender*, April 21, 1945, 4; Deton J. Brooks, "Calcutta Social Whirl Happy Escape from Burma Jungle for Colored GIs," *The Chicago Defender*, January 27, 1945, 6; Brooks, "Famed Pianist, Cholera Victim, Dies in India," *The Chicago Defender*, May 26, 1945, 11.

104. Joseph Davis Collection (AFC/2001/001/38558), VHP.

105. Louis Douglas (AFC/2001/001/16649), VHP. See also Charles William Whalen Jr. Memoirs (AFC/2001/001/26457), VHP.

106. Evelio Grillo (AFC/2001/001/13404), VHP.

107. Brendan I. Koerner, *Now the Hell Will Start: One Soldier's Flight from the Greatest Manhunt of World War II* (New York: Penguin Press, 2008); Deton J. Brooks, "U.S. Soldier Hangs in India," *The Chicago Defender*, April 7, 1945, 10.

108. "Participation of Negro Troops in the Post-War Military Establishment," 5–7.

109. "The Enclosure of the Army Air Forces," in "Participation of Negro Troops in the Post-War Military Establishment."

110. Technical Intelligence Report, November 21, 1944, "Inadequate Recreational Facilities for Negro Troops; Sources of Dissension among Negro Troops," NAUS.

111. Deton J. Brooks, "First Negro MPs in India-Burma Theatre," *The Chicago Defender*, April 28, 1945.

112. "4155th Quartermaster Truck Company," 4, in "Participation of Negro Troops."

113. "Base Section," 7, in "Participation of Negro Troops."

114. Brooks, "Negro GI's Jim Crowed in India; Red Cross Worker Quits in Protest," *The Chicago Defender,* July 14, 1945, 1; Deton J. Brooks, "Negro GIs Snub U.S. Jim Crow Pool in India; Swim with British Troops," *The Chicago Defender,* July 28, 1945, 5.

115. "Report of the Headquarters," 18–19, in "Participation of Negro Troops."

116. Colonel Lewis P. Jordan to the Commanding General of the Service of Supply of the Army, December 16, 1942, File 291.2, Box 30, Adjutant General, General Correspondence, USNA; Gandhi, "Foreign Soldiers in India," Joseph Stilwell Papers, Box 25, Folder 27, Hoover Institution Archives; "CBI History, Chapter 1: Historical and Political Setting," 30, Joseph Stilwell Papers, Box 19, Folder 9, Hoover Institution Archives.

117. White to Osborn, "India, June–Dec., 1942," Box A320, NAACP Papers, LOC; Speech by Walter White, June 16, 1942, Roll 1, Section 3, no. 0154, FBI File on the NAACP; Thomas Hachey, "Walter White and the American Negro Soldier in World War II: A Diplomatic Dilemma for Britain," *Phylon* 39, no. 3 (Third Quarter, 1978): 241–249.

118. Herbert L. Matthews, *The New York Times,* "U.S. Forces Build India Repair Depot, November. 18, 1942, pg. 12.

119. Dan Burley, "A Negro-American Meets India," *The New York Amsterdam News,* September 1, 1945, reprinted in *Pan-Africa* (January 1947), 9–12.

120. "Enclosure from the Headquarters of Advance Section," 8; "Enclosure of the Intermediate Section," 5; "The Enclosure of the Army Air Forces," 7; "47th Quartermaster Battalion," all in "Participation of Negro Troops."

121. Without providing specific evidence, the Aarmy's official history concluded, "Incidents between Negroes and Indians were out of proportion to the number of Negro troops." File 890-F.E./44 and File 741(9) F.E. /44, National Archives of India, New Delhia; *Time Runs Out,* 297; File 233/45, Home (Political) Files, Confidential, 1945, West Bengal State Archives, Kolkata.

122. Motley, *The Invisible Soldier,* 120.

123. "Negro Soldiers in India and Ireland," *The Chicago Defender,* June 20, 1942, pg. 1.

124. Deton J. Brooks, Jr. "Burma Missionary Sets Up Red Cross Club Ffor Negroes Aat India Base," *The Chicago Defender,* October. 14, 1944, 11.

125. Sajjad Zaheer, "Meeting American Seamen," *People's War,* August 23, 1942, page 4 and "Behind Negro-White Riot in Detroit, U.S.A." *People's War,* July 14, 1943, page 4.

126. "Report of the Headquarters of the CBI Theatre," 16; "Statement Regarding Troops of the 49th Ordnance Battalion (Negro)," 4; "591st Ordnance Ammunition," 3; "The Enclosure of the Army Air Forces," 6, all in "Participation of Negro Troops."

127. "U.S. Negro Troops in Calcutta," Technical Intelligence Report, December 6, 1944, Army Service Forces Office of the Commanding General, RG 107, Assistant Secretary of War Civilian Aide, Box 265, NAUS.

128. "News From America," *The Statesman*, Feb 1, 1943; "Negroes in U.S. Army," *The Statesman*, Mar 2, 1943; "Racial Riots in Detroit," *The Statesman*, June 23, 1943; "U.S. Army," Amrita Bazar Patrika, Mar 2, 1943; "By the Way," Amrita Bazar Patrika, June 24, 1943.

129. J. Saunders Redding, *An American in India: A Personal Report on the Indian Dilemma and the Nature of Her Conflicts* (Indianapolis: Bobbs-Merrill, 1954), 170–171.

130. Ibid., 169–171.

131. See Justin Hart, "Making Democracy Safe for the World," *Pacific Historical Review* 73 (February 2004): 49–84.

132. Interview to Stuart Gelder, July 4, 1944, CWMG.

133. Quoted in McWilliams, *Brothers under the Skin*, 20.

134. Deton J. Brooks, "*Defender* Reporter Visits Gandhi," *The Chicago Defender*, June 16, 1945, 1. Also see "Message to Shanti Sena Dal," September 5, 1947, CWMG.

6. Building a Third World

1. St. Clair Drake, "Brother India," *The Pittsburgh Courier*, August 3, 1946, 7.

2. Kumar Goshal, "Attitudes of Some Indian Leaders," *The Pittsburgh Courier*, August 17, 1946, 6; Goshal, "Clash of Reactionary and Progressive Interests," *The Pittsburgh Courier*, August 24, 1946, 7.

3. Andrew Rotter, *Comrades at Odds: The United States and India, 1947–1964* (Ithaca, N.Y.: Cornell University Press, 2000), 150–187; Mary Dudziak, *Cold War Civil Rights: Race and the Image of American Democracy* (Princeton: Princeton University Press, 2000); Thomas Borstelmann, *The Cold War and the Color Line: American Race Relations in the Global Arena* (Cambridge, Mass.: Harvard University Press, 2001); Azza Salama Layton, *International Politics and Civil Rights Policies in the United States, 1941–1960* (New York: Cambridge University Press, 2000).

4. See Carol Anderson, *Eyes Off the Prize: The United Nations and the African American Struggle for Human Rights, 1944–1955* (Cambridge: Cambridge University Press, 2003); Penny Von Eschen, *Race against Empire: Black Americans and Anticolonialism, 1937–1957* (Ithaca, N.Y.: Cornell University Press, 1997); Gerald Horne, *Black and Red: W. E. B. Du Bois and the Afro-American Response to the Cold War, 1944–1963* (Albany: State University of New York Press, 1986).

5. See Charlee Cherokee, "National Grapevine," *The Chicago Defender*, October 4, 1947, 13, 21; Cherokee, "Indian Speaks," *The Chicago Defender*, March 7, 1948, 15.

6. Dover to Du Bois, October 21 and 25, 1946, Reel 58, Du Bois Papers (hereafter cited as DBP), emphasis in original.

7. Dover to Du Bois, November 29, 1947, Reel 59, DBP.

8. Cedric Dover, "Introduces This Number," in "Special Symposium on the American Negro," *United Asia* 5, no. 3 (June 1953): 149.

9. Dover to Du Bois, May 15, 1947, Reel 59, DBP. Meherally met with Eslanda Goode Robeson in London in 1938. She gave him a letter of introduction to Langston Hughes. During his travels, Meherally collected the business cards of African American philosopher Alain Locke, as well as several influential Pan-African figures, including George Padmore, T. K. Makonnen, and Jomo Kenyatta. See Robeson to Nehru, July 19, 1938, vol. 88, JN Papers, NMML, and S. No. 5, "Other Papers," Yusuf Meherally Papers, NMML.

10. Dover to Du Bois, June 8, 1948; Du Bois to Dover, June 23, 1948, Reel 61, DBP.

11. Dover to Du Bois, Reel 61, DBP. The letter from Nehru was dated June 23, 1948.

12. Dover, *Feathers in the Arrow: An Approach for Coloured Writers and Readers* (Bombay: Padma Publications, 1947), 5. Dover to Du Bois, November 1, 1946; Dover to Du Bois, November 25, 1946; Du Bois to Dover, November 22, 1946; Dover to Du Bois, November 25, 1946, all Reel 58, DBP. Also see Dover to Du Bois, November 29, 1947, Reel 59, DBP.

13. See Nico Slate, "A Coloured Cosmopolitanism: Cedric Dover's Reading of the Afro-Asian World," in *Cosmopolitan Thought Zones: South Asia and the Global Circulation of Ideas,* ed. Sugata Bose and Kris Manjapra (New York: Palgrave Macmillan, 2010), 213–235.

14. Dover, "Notes on Coloured Writing," *Phylon* 8, no. 3 (Third Quarter, 1947): 222.

15. A Jewish writer, born in Poland, Glicksberg was well aware of the consequences of "the racist doctrines of the Nazis." His critique of Dover may have been partially inspired by Dover's links to British fascist Oswald Mosley. At least a few articles were published under Dover's name in Mosley's newspaper, *Union,* although it is unclear, given Dover's history of opposing anti-Semitism, why he chose to grace the pages of such a disreputable publication. Charles I. Glicksberg, "Eurasian Racialism," *Phylon* 12, no. 1 (1951): 13–19. On Dover's links to Mosley, see Issai Hosiosky to Bryn Hovde, January 1, 1950, and Saul Padover to Louis Wirth, February 15, 1950, both in the files of Clara Mayer, New School University Archives.

16. Dover, "The Snail Regrets," *Phylon* 12, no. 4 (1951): 347–356; Dover to Du Bois, July 14, 1951, Reel 66, DBP.

17. "Special Symposium on the American Negro," *United Asia* 5, no. 3 (June 1953). Also see Dover, "The Bantu Hits Back," *United Asia* 2, no. 3 (December 1949): 209–211; "The Vast Similitude," *United Asia* 3, no. 3 (1951): 189; "What Is a Race Riot?" *United Asia* 11, no. 3 (1959): 235–237.

18. Dover, "In This Number," in Special Symposium on the American Negro," 141.

19. Charles Johnson, "Foreword: The Negro Today," in "Special Symposium on the American Negro," 147.

20. George V. Allen, "The American Negro: A Postscript," in "Special Symposium on the American Negro," 197–198.

21. Dover, "Introduces This Number," in "Special Symposium on the American Negro," 148–149.

22. Kamaladevi Chattopadhyaya, *America: The Land of Superlatives* (Bombay: Phoenix Publications, 1946), 170–209, especially 177, 205.

23. Ibid., 70, 113–141, 144–145, 177–178, 184–187, 192–204, 209.

24. Lucas to White, April 19, 1953, "India General 1953–1955," Box A320, NAACP Papers, Library of Congress (LOC).

25. See Kenneth R. Janken, "From Colonial Liberation to Cold War Liberalism: Walter White, the NAACP, and Foreign Affairs, 1941–1955," *Ethnic and Racial Studies* 21, no. 6 (November 1998): 1074–1095.

26. White to Singh, June 27, 1944, Subject File 35, JJ Singh Papers, NMML.

27. JJ Singh to Vijayalakshmi Pandit, August 23, 1944, JJ Singh Papers, NMML.

28. Walter White, "The Work of the India League," *The Chicago Defender*, February 24, 1945, 11.

29. Hemendra K. Rakhit to White, September 5, 1945, Box A378, NAACP Papers.

30. Walter White to JJ Singh, June 9, 1947, JJ Singh Papers, NMML.

31. Several examples from Devadas Gandhi's paper, the *Hindustan Times*, are offered later in this chapter. See also Frenise A. Logan, "Racism and Indian-U.S. Relations, 1947–1953: Views in the Indian Press," *Pacific Historical Review* 54 (February 1985): 71–79.

32. Ralph Izard, "Gandhi's Son Asks Negro Aid for People of India," *The Chicago Defender*, May 18, 1946, 1, 6; "Gandhi's Son in U.S.," *The Chicago Defender*, May 25, 1946, 13. Also see Singh and Walsh to White, May 20, 1946; White to John Sengstacke, Ira F. Lewis, and Carl Murphy, all June 3, 1946; Edmondson to *The Chicago Defender*, June 3, 1946, all in Box A378, NAACP Papers.

33. See Walter White to JJ Singh, November 1, 1949; Singh to White, November 2, 1949; White to Singh, March 14, 1950; Singh to White, March 18, 1950; White to Singh, March 24, 1950, JJ Singh Papers, NMML. Also see White's letters to President Truman, Assistant Secretary of State George C. McGhee, and Walter Reuther, in "India: Famine Conditions 1950–51 March," Box A319, NAACP Papers.

34. White to Senators Connally and Gillette, February 9, 1951, in "India: Famine Conditions 1950–51 March," Box A319, NAACP Papers.

35. See White to Mitchell, February 15, 1951, in "India: Famine Conditions 1950–51 March," Box A319, NAACP Papers.

36. White to Singh, May 18, 1949, Folder 3, "India League of America 1949," Box A379, NAACP Papers. Also see Walter White to JJ Singh, September 12, 1952, JJ Singh Papers, NMML.

37. JJ Singh to Jawaharlal Nehru, April 10, 1942, JJ Singh Papers, NMML.

38. Poppy Cannon, *A Gentle Knight: My Husband, Walter White* (New York: Popular Library, 1956), 119–120.

39. American Consulate General, Bombay, India, to Secretary of State, March 28, 1947, RG 59, Decimal File 811.4016/3–2847, USNA. Also see Layton, *International Politics and Civil Rights Policies*, 135.

40. See Reed Harris to White, October 28, 1952; White to Harris, October 31, 1952; Cousins to White, November 24, 1952; White to Cousins, November 26, 1952, all in "India, 1949–1952," Box A320, NAACP Papers.

41. See Brendan Saxton to White, September 19, 1952, with attachment from Argus J. Tressider, public affairs officer, American Embassy, Colombo, to editor, *Ammunition*, August 4, 1952; and White to Saxton, September 23, 1952, in "India, 1949-1952," Box A320, NAACP Papers.

42. See Howard B. Schaffer, *Chester Bowles: New Dealer in the Cold War* (Cambridge, Mass.: Harvard University Press, 1993).

43. Bowles to White, November 15, 1951; White to Bowles, September 19, 1951, Folder 5, Box A379, NAACP Papers.

44. Bowles to White, February 13, 1952, and April 7, 1952, "India, 1949-1952," Box A320, NAACP Papers.

45. Chester Bowles, *Ambassador's Report* (New York: Harper, 1954), 31, 384-387, 395-397.

46. Ralph McGill, "Chester Bowles Makes Sense," *The Atlanta Constitution*, December 27, 1951. Also see McGill, "Imperialism Always Doomed," *The Atlanta Constitution*, December 9, 1951.

47. Ralph McGill, "One-Man Gallup Poll," *The Atlanta Constitution*, January 1, 1952.

48. Chester Bowles, "Racial Minorities in American Life," *United Asia* 5, no. 1 (February 1953): 15-19.

49. P. L. Prattis, "Seventeen Days in Independent India," *The Pittsburgh Courier*, September 17, 1949, 12.

50. P. L. Prattis, "Seventeen Days in Independent India," *The Pittsburgh Courier*, September 3, 1949, 12.

51. See P. L. Prattis, "Seventeen Days in Independent India," *The Pittsburgh Courier*, October 8, 1949, 7; October 15, 1949, 7; October 22, 1949, 7; December 10, 1949, 21.

52. P. L. Prattis, "Seventeen Days in Independent India," *The Pittsburgh Courier*, October 1, 1949, 7.

53. Kamaladevi Chattopadhyaya, "Determining Social Status by Color . . . Antiquated: East Indian Woman Leader Decries Age of Irrationalism," *The Pittsburgh Courier*, October 1, 1949, 8.

54. Kenesaw M. Landis, graphics by Tom P. Barrett, *Segregation in Washington* (Chicago: National Committee on Segregation in the Nation's Capital, 1948): especially 4-10.

55. Layton, *International Politics and Civil Rights Policies*, 134.

56. Nehru, "Note for Asaf Ali and K. P. S. Menon," January 22, 1947, K. P. S. Menon Papers, NMML.

57. Frank E. Bolden, "Nehru Finds India's Problems Akin to U.S. Negroes'—Bolden," *The Pittsburgh Courier*, August 11, 1945, 1.

58. Ralph Izard, "Nehru Sees World Upheaval," *The Chicago Defender*, August 31, 1946, 1.

59. Lillian Scott, "Cut Negroes from Nehru Visit Here," *The Chicago Defender*, October 15, 1949, 1.

60. Langston Hughes, "To Understand America, Nehru Should Visit Negro Ghettos Too," *The Chicago Defender*, November 5, 1949, 6. Also see Trezzvant W. Anderson, "Will Nehru See Everything Here?" *The Pittsburgh Courier*, October 22, 1949, 5.

61. Roy Wilkins to "Your Excellency," September 16, 1949; White to Oram, Moon, and Smith, September 16, 1949; memo from White to Wilkins and Onam, October 7, 1949; "Draft of Letter," all in Folder 3, "India League of America, 1949," Box A379, NAACP Papers.

62. "Prime Minister Nehru Gets First Hand Briefing on Problem; Dr. Bunche, Walter White Serve As Chairmen of Meeting," *The Atlanta Daily World,* November 9, 1949, 1; Brenda Gayle Plummer, *Rising Wind Black Americans and U.S. Foreign Affairs, 1935–1960* (Chapel Hill: University of North Carolina Press, 1996), 219; "Nehru Presented Life Membership in NAACP," *The Atlanta Daily World,* November 11, 1949, 2; "Jawaharlal Nehru Joins the NAACP," *The New York Amsterdam News,* November 12, 1949, 1.

63. Robert Shelby, "Nehru Shook My Hand," *The Chicago Defender,* November 5, 1949, 6.

64. Vijayalakshmi Pandit, *The Scope of Happiness: A Personal Memoir* (New York: Crown, 1979), 191–192; Toki Schalk, "Madame Pandit, Indian Leader, Found Happiest Hour in Harlem," *The Pittsburgh Courier,* April 14, 1945, 5.

65. Schalk, "Madame Pandit, Indian Leader, Found Happiest Hour in Harlem," 5. Also see "'We Must Break Down Color Barriers,' Warns Mme. Pandit," *The Pittsburgh Courier,* April 14, 1945, 1; "Indian Children Impoverished— Madame Pandit," *The New York Amsterdam News,* March 3, 1945, 1A.

66. Walter White, "People, Politics and Places," *The Chicago Defender,* June 30, 1945, 13; W. E. B. Du Bois, "DuBois, White Run from Photo with Indian Stooges," *The Chicago Defender,* May 12, 1945, 5; Drake, "Brother India," 7.

67. "Society, Literary Crowd Gathers to Discuss Eslanda Robeson's New Book," *The New York Amsterdam News,* August 18, 1945, 8; Pandit, *Scope of Happiness,* 217.

68. Harry Greene, *Washington Star,* November 23, 1950, in S. No. 5, Press Clippings, First Installment, Vijayalakshmi Pandit Papers, NMML; Lawrence C. Burr, "Madam Pandit Leads Fight for Minorities," *The Atlanta Daily World,* December 21, 1946, 1; Jawaharlal Nehru, *The Selected Works of Jawaharlal Nehru,* second series, vol. 1 (New Delhi: Jawaharlal Nehru Memorial Fund, 1984), 475. See also *Baltimore Afro-American,* December 21, 1946.

69. Du Bois to Pandit, September 18, 1947, Reel 60, DBP.

70. Dover to Smythe, October 24, 1947; Smythe to Dover, November 3, 1947; Smythe to Dover, December 10, 1947; Dover to Smythe, December 19, 1947; Du Bois, "A Short Statement . . . for the Indian Delegation," Reel 60, DBP.

71. Mordecai Johnson, "Citation for Pandit," S. No. 5, Subject Files, First Installment, Vijayalakshmi Pandit Papers, NMML.

72. "Howard Honors Distinguished Three," *The Washington Post,* June 4, 1949, in S. No. 5, Subject Files, First Installment, Vijayalakshmi Pandit Papers, NMML; Mordecai Johnson to Nayantara Sahgal, September 16, 1970, Nayantara Sahgal Papers, NMML.

73. "Dr. Bunche Receives Spingarn Medal Here," *Los Angeles Examiner,* July 18, 1949; "Medal Presented Bunche at Rally," *Los Angeles Times,* July 18, 1949; "Honors Given World Figures," *Charleston Daily Mail,* May 29, 1950; "Mrs. Pandit Assails Prejudices in Talk," St. Louis *Post-Dispatch,* June 6, 1950, all in S. No. 5, Press Clippings, First Installment, Vijayalakshmi Pandit Papers, NMML.

74. "Panel Calls for More Jobs, More Doctors, Democracy," *The Atlanta Daily World,* November 29, 1950, S. No. 5, Press Clippings, First Installment, Vijayalakshmi Pandit Papers, NMML.

75. Du Bois, "As The Crow Flies," mailed August 5, 1950, Reel 84, DBP.

76. Toki Schalk Johnson, "Madame Pandit: India's Voice in America," *Pittsburgh Courier Magazine,* May 19, 1951, in S. No. 5, Press Clippings, First Installment, Vijayalakshmi Pandit Papers, NMML; Schalk, "Madame Pandit, Indian Leader, Found Happiest Hour in Harlem," 5; Schalk, "Toki Types," *The Pittsburgh Courier,* December 29, 1945, 8; Du Bois, "DuBois, White Run from Photo with Indian Stooges," 5; Walter White, "Portrait of Mme. Pandit," *The Chicago Defender,* June 30, 1945, 13.

77. "Mme. Pandit Warns U.S. of Disunity Dangers," *The Chicago Defender,* November 10, 1945, 10; Toki Schalk, "National Council of Negro Women Outlines Aims for a Full and Diversified Program Reaching Women throughout the World," *The Pittsburgh Courier,* November 10, 1945, 8.

78. Liliane R. Davidson, "U.S. Spirit Inspires New Republic, Says Mme. Pandit," *Daytona Beach Evening News,* April 3, 1951, S. No. 5, Press Clippings and S. No. 14, Subject Files, First Installment, Vijayalakshmi Pandit Papers, NMML; S. No. 39, Subject Files, First Installment, Vijayalakshmi Pandit Papers, NMML; "Panel Calls for More Jobs, More Doctors, Democracy," *The Atlanta Daily World,* November 29, 1950, S. No. 5, Press Clippings, First Installment, Vijayalakshmi Pandit Papers, NMML; "Honors Given World Figures," *Charleston Daily Mail,* May 29, 1950, S. No. 5, Press Clippings, First Installment, Vijayalakshmi Pandit Papers, NMML.

79. Dunbar S. McLaurin, "India Would Welcome Negro Ambassador," *The Pittsburgh Courier,* March 4, 1950, 1.

80. Helen Laville and Scott Lucas, "The American Way: Edith Sampson, the NAACP, and African American Identity in the Cold War," *Diplomatic History* 20, no. 4 (Fall 1996): 565–590. Also see Walter White, "Foreign Peoples Curious About U.S. Race Question," *The Chicago Defender,* September. 10, 1949, pg. 7.

81. Quoted in Kathleen E. Gordon, "Edith S. Sampson: First African American Delegate to the United Nations, First Black Woman Elected Judge in the U.S.," American Women's Legal History, May 13, 1997, available online at http://www.stanford.edu/group/WLHP/papers/edith.html#27. Also see "Answer," *Time,* August 28, 1950.

82. P. L. Prattis, "The Horizon," *The Pittsburgh Courier,* September 2, 1950, 20.

83. Carl Rowan, *Breaking Barriers: A Memoir* (Boston: Little, Brown and Company, 1991), 123–124.

84. Carl Rowan, *The Pitiful and the Proud* (New York: Random House, 1956), 49–50, 146, 224.

85. Ibid., 30–33, 55–56, 143–145, 147–148.

86. Jay Saunders Redding, *An American in India* (New York: The Bobbs-Merrill Company, 1954), 11–13, 35–36, 169, 275, emphasis in original. Also see Redding, "Report from India," *American Scholar* (Autumn 1953): 441–449.

87. Redding, *An American in India,* 18–19, 191–192, 218.

88. Polly Cowan, "Interview with Dorothy Height," in *The Black Women Oral History Project,* vol. 5, ed. Ruth Edmonds Hill, 124–125 (Westport, Conn.: Meckler, 1991).

89. Ibid., 125–126.

90. Dorothy Height, *Open Wide the Freedom Gates: A Memoir* (New York: PublicAffairs, 2003), 220.

91. Rowan, *The Pitiful and the Proud,* 66.

92. Redding, *An American in India,* 184, 33.

93. Ibid., 48–53.

94. Height became acquainted with several powerful Indian women, including future Prime Minister Indira Gandhi. See Height, *Open Wide the Freedom Gates,* 219; also see Cowan, "Interview," 123.

95. Quoted in Dudziak, *Cold War Civil Rights,* 34.

96. Quoted in Laville and Lucas, "The American Way," 572.

97. Rowan, *The Pitiful and the Proud,* 33, 76–77, 79, 82, 154–156, emphasis in original.

98. Schuyler, "Views and Reviews," *The Pittsburgh Courier,* August 26, 1950, 21.

99. Schuyler, "Views and Reviews," *The Pittsburgh Courier,* September 30, 1950, 15.

100. B. R. Ambedkar, *Address Delivered on the 101st Birthday Celebration of Mahadev Govind Ranade* (Bombay: Thacker & Co., 1943).

101. Ambedkar to Du Bois, circa July 1946, Reel 58, DBP.

102. D. C. Ahir, *Dr. Ambedkar and the Indian Constitution* (Lucknow: Buddha Vihara, 1973); B. R. Ambedkar, *States and Minorities: What Are Their Rights and How to Secure Them in the Constitution of Free India* (Bombay: Thacker and Co., 1947). Also see M. Ramaswamy, *Fundamental Rights: A Constitutional and Juridical Study with Particular Reference to India in the Light of the Experience of the United States of America and the United Kingdom* (Delhi: Indian Council of World Affairs, 1946), 213.

103. C. Rajagopalachari, *Ambedkar Refuted,* 2d ed. (Bombay: Hind Kitab, 1946), 15.

104. Schalk, "Madame Pandit, Indian Leader, Found Happiest Hour in Harlem," 5.

105. Bolden, "Nehru Finds India's Problems Akin to U.S. Negroes'—Bolden," 1. Also see "India Must Have Political Freedom before Ridding Itself of Caste System," *The Pittsburgh Courier,* January 9, 1943, 7.

106. Izard, "Nehru Sees World Upheaval," 1.

107. Lin Yutang, "Color: Unfinished Business of Democracy," special issue, *Survey Graphic* 31, no. 11 (November 1942): 560.

108. National Committee on Segregation in the Nation's Capital, *Segregation in Washington,* 4.

109. Bowles to White, November 15, 1951, and White to Bowles, September 19, 1951, Folder 5, Box A379, NAACP Papers.

110. Anonymous review of *Segregation* by Robert Penn Warren, *United Asia* 9, no. 6 (December 1957): 417.

111. Bharatan Kumarappa, *My Student Days in America* (Bombay: Padma Publications, 1945), preface, 78–81.

112. Oliver Cromwell Cox, *Caste, Class, and Race: A Study in Social Dynamics* (New York: Modern Reader Paperbacks, 1948): ix, 21, 83, 426, 453, 468, 502.

113. Ibid., 332.

114. See Anderson, *Eyes Off the Prize;* Von Eschen, *Race against Empire;* Glenda Gilmore, *Defying Dixie: The Radical Roots of Civil Rights, 1919–1950* (New York: Norton, 2008), For a defense of the NAACP's anticommunism, see Manfred Berg, "Black Civil Rights and Liberal Anticommunism: The NAACP in the Early Cold War," *JAH* 94, no. 1 (June 2007).

115. Laville and Lucas, "The American Way," 571; Rowan, *The Pitiful and the Proud,* 19–21; McGill, "Chester Bowles Makes Sense."

116. Quoted in *Thirty Years of Treason: Excerpts from Hearings before the House Committee on Un-American Activities, 1938–1968,* ed. Eric Bentley, 770 (New York: Viking Press, 1971).

117. W. James Ellison, "Paul Robeson and the State Department," *The Crises* LXXXIV (May 1977): 184–189; Pandit, *Scope of Happiness,* 217.

118. L. N. Rao to Du Bois, November 9, 1953, and Du Bois to Rao, November 24, 1953, Reel 79; Anand to Du Bois, September 30, 1960, and Du Bois to Anand, October 1960, Reel 74; Du Bois to Dover, February 14, 1951, and Dover to Du Bois, dated only March 1951; Du Bois to Dover, March 30, 1951, and Dover to Du Bois, June 1, 1951, Reel 66, DBP.

119. Dover to Du Bois, July 23, 1951, and Du Bois to Dover, September 27, 1951, Reel 66, DBP.

120. Dover to Du Bois, September 6, 1951, and "A MESSAGE TO DR. W. E. B. DU BOIS FOR OCTOBER 2, 1951," Reel 66, emphasis in original; Dover to Shirley Graham Du Bois, July 7, 1958, and Dover to Du Bois, July 12, 1958, Reel 73, DBP.

121. Du Bois to Nehru, November 7, 1946, Reel 59, DBP.

122. The letter was dated October 10, 1949, Reel 63, DBP.

123. Du Bois, "As the Crow Flies," mailed August 5, 1950, Reel 84, DBP.

124. L. N. Rao to Du Bois, November 9, 1953, and Du Bois to Rao, November 24, 1953, Reel 79, DBP.

125. Du Bois to Nehru, December 26, 1956, Reel 72, DBP.

126. Paul Robeson, "Here's My Story," *Freedom* (October 1951), in *Paul Robeson Speaks: Writings, Speeches, Interviews, 1918–1974,* ed. Philip S. Foner (New York: Brunner/Mazel, 1978), 288.

127. Speech at convention of National Negro Labor Council, Cincinnati, Ohio, October 27, 1951, *The Atlanta Daily World,* April 8, 1976, in *Paul Robeson Speaks,* 291.

128. "Here's My Story," *Freedom* (May 1953), in *Paul Robeson Speaks,* 350; also see "Their Victories for Peace Are Also Ours," *New World Review* (November 1955): 16–17, in *Paul Robeson Speaks,* 408.

129. Although unofficial representatives of South Africa's African National Congress attended, only Ethiopia, Liberia, and the Gold Coast (Ghana) represented sub-Saharan Africa.

130. White to Nehru, January 5, 1955, and White to Pandit, January 21, 1955, both in "India General 1953–1955," Box A320, NAACP Papers.

131. Kenneth Robert Janken, *White: The Biography of Walter White, Mr. NAACP* (New York: New Press, 2003): 358–359.

132. Quoted in Plummer, *Rising Wind,* 249.

133. See Rowan, *The Pitiful and the Proud,* 387; Rowan, *Breaking Barriers,* 124, 145–146.

134. Quoted in Max Yergan, "Blast U.S. Segregation: African-Asian Policy Mapped in Indonesia," *The Pittsburgh Courier,* April 30, 1955, 1.

135. Max Yergan, "Max Yergan: 'Africans Not among Bandung Sponsors,'" *The Pittsburgh Courier,* June 11, 1955; Max Yergan, "Africans, Asians in Bandung Talks," *The Pittsburgh Courier,* April 23, 1955, 1.

136. "Color and Politics at Bandung," *The Pittsburgh Courier,* April 30, 1955, 24; Marguerite Cartwright, "Report on the Asian-African Conference," *The New York Amsterdam News,* May 7, 1955, 5, and "Who Will Attend the Bandung Conference," *The New York Amsterdam News,* April 9, 1955, 1.

137. George McTurnan Kahin, *The Asian-African Conference: Bandung, Indonesia, April 1955* (Ithaca, N.Y.: Cornell University Press, 1956), 39, 81, 84.

138. Ethel L. Payne, "Afro-Asia Meet First Confab of World's Darker Peoples," *The Chicago Defender,* April 16, 1955, 12. Also see "The Issue at Bandung," *The New York Amsterdam News,* April 2, 1955, 16; "Rogers Says: Bandung Is Product of 500 Years," *The Pittsburgh Courier,* April 23, 1955, 24.

139. "NAACP Sends Greetings to Bandung Confab," *The Atlanta Daily World,* April 20, 1955, 1.

140. Adam Clayton Powell, "Not 'Anti-American,' Eastern Parley Criticizes US Policy," *The Atlanta Daily World,* April 26, 1955; Marguerite Cartwright, "Who Will Attend the Bandung Conference," *The New York Amsterdam News,* April 9, 1955, 1. Also see "Adam Clayton Powell Meets Red China's Premier," *The Atlanta Daily World,* April 24, 1955, 1; "Powell Tells Why He'll Defy Afro-Asia Meet Ban," *The Chicago Defender,* April 9, 1955, 2; Yergan, "Blast U.S. Segregation, 1.

141. Richard Wright, *The Color Curtain: A Report on the Bandung Conference* (Jackson: University Press of Mississippi, 1995), 13, 140, 165. Also see Cedric Dover's sharp critique of Wright, "Bandung—Through a Curtain," *United Asia* 8, no. 3 (June 1956).

142. For an alternative view of Bandung, see Vijay Prashad, *The Darker Nations: A People's History of the World* (New York: New Press, 2007), 31–50.

143. William A. Rutherford, "India and Black America," *United Asia* 3, no. 2 (1950): 139–140.

7. Nonviolence and the Nation

1. Pauli Murray, *Song in a Weary Throat: An American Pilgrimage* (New York: Harper & Row, 1987), 138, 144.

2. See "The Boycott Movement against Jim Crow Streetcars in the South, 1900–1906," *Journal of American History* 55 (March 1969): 745–775; Lizabeth Cohen, *A Consumers' Republic: The Politics of Mass Consumption in Postwar America* (New York: Knopf, 2003), 44–61.

3. Clayborne Carson, *In Struggle: SNCC and the Black Awakening of the 1960* (Cambridge, Mass.: Harvard University Press, 1981); Charles M. Payne, *I've Got the Light of Freedom: The Organizing Tradition and the Mississippi Freedom Struggle* (Berkeley: University of California Press, 1995).

4. "Notes taken by P.M. on Non-violence," dated March 1940, "Petersburg Bus Incident," File 86, Box 4, Pauli Murray Papers (hereafter PMP).

5. Murray's letter to Jean and Pan, April 9, 1940, "Petersburg Bus Incident," File 87, Box 4, PMP; Murray, *Song in a Weary Throat,* 143–146.

6. Murray to Dame, March 24, 1940, "Petersburg Bus Incident," Folder 85, Box 4, PMP.

7. Robert H. Cooley Jr. to Murray and McBean, April 8, 1940, "Petersburg Bus Incident," Folder 85, Box 4, PMP.

8. On the overlap between nonviolent direct action and legal strategies to end racial inequality, see the preface to Adam Fairclough, *Race and Democracy: The Civil Rights Struggle in Louisiana, 1916–1972,* 2d ed. (Athens: University of Georgia, 2008); Thomas J. Sugrue, *Sweet Land of Liberty: The Forgotten Struggle for Civil Rights in the North* (New York: Random House, 2008), 169–170.

9. Glenda Gilmore, *Defying Dixie: The Radical Roots of Civil Rights, 1919–1950* (New York: Norton, 2008), 287–288, 315–329; John D'Emilio, *Lost Prophet: The Life and Times of Bayard Rustin* (New York: Free Press, 2003); Daniel Levine, *Bayard Rustin and the Civil Rights Movement* (New Brunswick, N.J.: Rutgers University Press, 2000).

10. In her notes on nonviolence, Murray wrote "War Without Violence" near the top of the page and underlined it twice. Later that year she wrote a friend asking for a copy in order to review the book for the Black press. See Murray, *Song in a Weary Throat,* 138; "Notes taken by P.M. on Non-violence," dated March 1940; Murray to Jean and Pan, April 2, 1940, "Petersburg Bus Incident," File 86, Box 4, PMP; Krishnalal Shridharani, *War without Violence: A Study of Gandhi's Method and Its Accomplishments* (New York: Harcourt Brace, and Company, 1939).

11. Murray to Jean and Pan, April 9, 1940, "Petersburg Bus Incident," File 87, Box 4, PMP.

12. "Methodists V. Viceroy," *Time* (April 22, 1940); "Non-Political Missions," *Time* (November 25, 1940).

13. Joseph Kip Kosek, *Acts of Conscience: Christian Nonviolence and Modern American Democracy* (New York: Columbia University Press, 2009), 185–186; Paul R. Dekar, *Creating the Beloved Community: A Journey with the Fellowship of Reconciliation,* foreword by Donald B. Kraybill, preface by Pat Clark (Telford, Pa.: Cascadia Publishing, 2005), chap. 3; David Scott Cooney, "A Persistent Witness of Conscience: Methodist Nonviolent Activists, 1940–1970" (PhD diss., Illiff School of Theology, 2000); "Ruth Reynolds," in *Voices for Independence: Portraits of Notable Individuals in the Struggle for Puerto Rican Independence,* ed. Jean Zwickel (Pittsburg, Calif.: White Star Press, 1988); Jay Holmes Smith, "A Memorandum Concerning a New York Ashram," Box 13, Series A-3 (correspondence of A. J. Muste), Section II, Fel-

lowship of Reconciliation (FOR) Papers, Swarthmore College Peace Collection (hereafter SCPC); Smith, "Ministers and the Revolution," Box 4, Series A-3 (correspondence of A. J. Muste), Section II, FOR Papers, SCPC; Muste to Jones, July 3, 1942, "General Correspondence," Box 4, Series A-3 (correspondence of A. J. Muste), Section II, FOR Papers, SCPC.

14. The Harlem Ashram to the Board of Directors of the YMCA of NY, August 12, 1941, and the Harlem Ashram to a "fellowship friend," October 4, 1941, Box 13, Series A-3 (correspondence of A. J. Muste), Section II, FOR Papers, SCPC; "Background for Action Projects" September 23, 1944, Box 13, Series A-3 (correspondence of A. J. Muste), Section II, FOR Papers, SCPC.

15. "The Work of the Harlem Ashram" and Smith to Muste, November 18, 1944, Box 13, Series A-3 (correspondence of A. J. Muste), Section II, FOR Papers, SCPC.

16. Brochure, September 9, 1942, Harlem Ashram Papers (hereafter HAP), SCPC Collected Documents Group. See also J. Holmes Smith to "Dear Friend," March 14, 1946, HAP.

17. Muste to Jones, July 3, 1942, General Correspondence, "Smith, J. Holmes," Box 4, Series A-3, FOR Papers, SCPC.

18. James Farmer, *Lay Bare the Heart: An Autobiography of the Civil Rights Movement* (New York: Arbor House, 1985), 149.

19. "Diary Excerpts, 1940–42," Folder 26, Box 1, PMP.

20. "History/Beginnings"; Allen Bacon, "Recollections of Ahimsa Farm," May 4, 1989; "Ahimsa," *Antiochian* 5, no. 7 (October 4, 1940); "Aggressive Pacifism," August 1940 all in Ahimsa Farm Papers, SCPC.

21. The larger history of swimming pool desegregation, like so much of the history of civil rights activism in the North, is a story of defeat in the face of white intransigence and residential segregation heightened by white flight to suburbia. See "A Project in Satyagraha," in "History and Documents" and "To the Youth Council of the NAACP," July 29, 1941, Direct Action Projects Folder, Ahimsa Farm Papers; Larry Gara and Lena Mae Gara, "Ahimsa Farm: A Gandhian Experiment in Ohio," *Fellowship* (May–June 1996); Sugrue, *Sweet Land of Liberty,* especially chap. 5–7.

22. Farmer, *Lay Bare the Heart,* 134–136, 355–356; August Meier and Elliott Rudwick, *CORE: A Study in the Civil Rights Movement, 1942–1968* (New York: Oxford University Press, 1973), 6, 13; "The Work of the Harlem Ashram," Box 13, Series A-3 (correspondence of A. J. Muste), Section II, FOR Papers, SCPC.

23. Meier and Rudwick, *CORE,* 5; D'Emilio, *Lost Prophet;* Levine, *Bayard Rustin.*

24. "Randolph Plans 'Civil Disobedience' Campaign Patterned after Ghandi's [sic] Resistance to British Regime in India," *The New York Amsterdam News,* January 9, 1943, 1; "Randolph to Adopt Gandhi Technique," *The Chicago Defender,* January 9, 1943, 4.

25. "On Mr. Randolph's Proposal for Negro Action," *The Atlanta Daily World,* January 19, 1943.

26. "Citizens Repudiate Non-Violence Program: Feel Gandhi's Way Is Not Comparable to U.S. Situation," *The Pittsburgh Courier,* April 24, 1943, 4. Also see "Civil Disobedience," *The Pittsburgh Courier,* January 23, 1943, 6.

27. W. E. B. Du Bois, "As the Crow Flies," *The New York Amsterdam News,* March 13, 1943, 10.

28. Ralph Templin, "Non-Violence Method Called 'All-Sided Sword,'" *The New York Amsterdam News,* May 29, 1943, 10.

29. Muste to Randolph, January 11, 1943; Randolph to Muste, January 25, 1943; Pauli Murray to Randolph, May 13, 1943, all in Box 27, A. Philip Randolph Papers (hereafter APRP).

30. See Jay Holmes Smith to Randolph, June 27, 1943, Smith to Randolph, November 18, 1943, and Randolph to Smith, December 1, 1943, all in Box 27, APRP.

31. Burton to Randolph, March 16, March 22, and April 21, 1943, Box 27, APRP.

32. "Randolph Blames Roosevelt for U.S. Wave of Rioting," *The Chicago Defender,* July 10, 1943; "MOWM Asks Roosevelt to Appoint Race Commission," *The Pittsburgh Courier,* July 10, 1943. See also Jones to Randolph, May 18, 1943, and Randolph to Jones, May 25, 1943, Box 27, APRP.

33. "MOWM Asks Roosevelt to Appoint Race Commission," *The Pittsburgh Courier,* July 10, 1943.

34. Reinhold Niebuhr, *Moral Man and Immoral Society: A Study in Ethics and Politics* (New York: C. Scribner's Sons, 1932), 254.

35. James Farmer, ed., "Civil Disobedience: Is It the Answer to Jim Crow?" *Non-Violent Action News Bulletin* 2/3 (n.d.), Folder 400, Box 18, PMP.

36. "Randolph Blasts Courier as 'Bitter Voice of Defeatism,'" *The Chicago Defender,* June 12, 1943.

37. "Randolph Urges Powerful Negro Political Bloc," *The Atlanta Daily World,* May 17, 1943, 1; "Randolph Tells Technique of Civil Disobedience," *The Chicago Defender,* June 26, 1943.

38. "Randolph Refutes Cry of 'Calamity Howlers,'" *The Chicago Defender,* February 6, 1943, 6.

39. "Randolph Blasts Courier as 'Bitter Voice of Defeatism,'" *The Chicago Defender,* June 12, 1943. Also see George M. Houser, *Erasing the Color Line,* foreword by A. Philip Randolph (New York: Fellowship Publications, 1945).

40. Horace R. Cayton, "N.A.A.C.P.—M.O.W.M.," *The Pittsburgh Courier,* June 19, 1943, 13; Nancy and Dwight MacDonald, "Memo: Two Outsiders Look at the M.O.W.," June 20, 1943, Box 27, APRP.

41. Muste to Randolph, June 9, 1948, APRP.

42. August Meier, Elliott Rudwick, and Francis L. Broderick, eds., *Black Protest Thought in the Twentieth Century* (Indianapolis: Bobbs-Merrill, 1971): 276–277.

43. Randolph's decision earned criticism from pacifists. See James Peck to Randolph, August 15, 1948, George Houser to Randolph, August 15, 1948, and Randolph to Houser, April 26, 1949, all in APRP.

44. Art Preis, "Permanent Organization Established," *Militant* (October 3, 1942), in *Fighting Racism in World War II*, ed. Fred Stanton, 261 (New York: Pathfinder, 1980).

45. "Randolph Makes Plea For India," *The Chicago Defender*, October 24, 1942, 8.

46. William Hefner to General Lewis B. Hershey, June 24, 1943, and Bronson Clark to William Hefner, May 1942, Ahimsa Farm Papers.

47. "Free India Committee," report as recalled by William K. Hefner, Ahimsa Farm Papers.

48. "The Work of the Harlem Ashram," Box 13, Series A-3 (correspondence of A. J. Muste), Section II, FOR Papers, SCPC.

49. Murray to Jean and Pan, April 2, 1940, "Petersburg Bus Incident," File 86, Box 4, PMP; "Indian Youth Leader," *The New York Amsterdam News*, March 23, 1940; "Indian Student to Tell of His Land's Struggle," *The Chicago Defender*, March 23, 1940; "New Orleans Prepares for Youth Conference," *The Chicago Defender*, April 6, 1940; Pauli Murray to Krishnalal Shridharani, August 24, 1942, Box 102, PMP; Murray, *Song in a Weary Throat*, 195; Pauli Murray to the editor of the *New York Herald Tribune*, August 12, 1942, "Howard Civil Rights Committee," File 395, Box 18, PMP.

50. W. E. B. Du Bois, "As the Crow Flies," *The New York Amsterdam News*, April 10, 1943, 10.

51. W. E. B. Du Bois, "As the Crow Flies," *The New York Amsterdam News*, February 26, 1944, 1. See also W. E. B. Du Bois, "As the Crow Flies," *The New York Amsterdam News*, September 12, 1942, 6.

52. "Civil Disobedience," *The Pittsburgh Courier*, January 23, 1943, 6.

53. "Colored Folk the World Over Now Feel Akin," *The Chicago Defender*, July 17, 1943, 1.

54. Pauli Murray, "An American Negro Views the Indian Question," *The Call*, September 4, 1942, 4.

55. Pauli Murray to APR, August 9, 1942, and August 24, 1942, Box 27, APRP, LOC.

56. See Randolph's foreword to George M. Houser, *Erasing the Color Line* (New York: Fellowship Publications, 1945); Randolph, "Why Should We March?" "Color: Unfinished Business of Democracy," special issue, *Survey Graphic* 31, no. 11 (November 1942): 488–489; Matha Biondi, *To Stand and Fight: The Struggle for Civil Rights in Postwar New York City* (Cambridge, Mass.: Harvard University Press, 2003), 15, 20; "Urge Race to Support India," *Baltimore Afro-American*, August 22, 1942; "Randolph Tells Philosophy Behind 'March' Movement," *The Chicago Defender*, June 19, 1943.

57. John Robert Badger, "World View," *The Chicago Defender*, March 13, 1943, 15; Krishnalal Shridharani, *Warning to the West* (New York: Duell, Sloan and Pearce, 1942); John Robert Badger, "World View," *The Chicago Defender*, July 17, 1943; "Confirmation," *The Pittsburgh Courier*, July 17, 1943.

58. David J. Garrow, *Bearing the Cross: Martin Luther King, Jr. and the Southern Christian Leadership Conference* (New York: Vintage Press, 1988), 111–112;

Keith D. Miller, *Voice of Deliverance: The Language of Martin Luther King, Jr. and Its Sources* (New York: The Free Press, 1992).

59. Garrow, *Bearing the Cross*, 41, 43; Martin Luther King Jr., *Stride Toward Freedom: The Montgomery Story* (New York: Harper and Row, 1958), 96; *The Papers of Martin Luther King, Jr. Volume III: Birth of a New Age, December 1955–December 1956*, eds. Clayborne Carson, Stewart Burns, Susan Carson, Dana Powell, and Peter Holloran (Berkeley: University of California Press, 1997), 171; King to George Hendrick, February 5, 1957, *The Papers of Martin Luther King, Jr. Volume IV: Symbol of the Movement, January 1957–December 1958*, eds. Clayborne Carson, Susan Carson, Adrienne Clay, Virginia Shadron, and Kieran Taylor (Berkeley: University of California Press, 2000), 184.

60. Quoted in Garrow, *Bearing the Cross*, 32.

61. King to Lawrence M. Byrd, April 25, 1957, King Papers, vol. IV, 183–184.

62. King, *Stride Toward Freedom*, 85.

63. A comparison of the citations for "Gandhi" in the indexes of the second and third volume of the King Papers demonstrates the sudden emergence of comparisons between Gandhi and King in the aftermath of the bus boycott. See "The Ghost of Gandhi Walks Montgomery Streets," *The New Republic*, March 12, 1956; "Attack on the Conscience," *Time* (February 18, 1957); Dr. Samuel Dubois Cook to King, March 23, 1956, King Papers, vol. III, 203–204; J. Martin England to King, April 29, 1956, King Papers, vol. III, 232.

64. William Stuart Nelson to King, March 21, 1956, King Papers, vol. III, 182–183. See also Lillian Smith to King, ibid., 181–182.

65. Jack repeatedly compared Gandhi and King in speeches, including one for India's ambassador to the United States, G. L. Mehta. See "Great Soul: The Mahatma and Montgomery," delivered December 7, 1956; "Gandhi Alive!" delivered October 2, 1963; "The Legacy of Gandhi Today," n.d., all in "Speeches, Gandhi," Box 4, Series IV, Homer Jack Papers, SCPC. Also see King to Homer Alexander Jack, August 20, 1956, King Papers, vol. III, 350–351.

66. "King Speaks at Big Rally in Brooklyn," *Montgomery Advertiser*, March 26, 1956; Stanley Rowland Jr., "2,500 Here Hail Boycott Leader," *New York Times*, March 26, 1956, 27.

67. King, *Stride Toward Freedom*, 102.

68. "Palm Sunday Sermon on Mohandas K. Gandhi," March 22, 1959, *The Papers of Martin Luther King, Jr. Volume V: Threshold of a New Decade, January 1959–December 1960*, eds. Clayborne Carson, Tenisha Armstrong, Susan Carson, Adrienne Clay, and Kieran Taylor (Berkeley: University of California Press, 2005), 145–157.

69. Harris Wofford, *Of Kennedys and Kings: Making Sense of the Sixties* (New York: Farrar, Straus, Giroux, 1980), 118–123.

70. Foster to King, April 29, 1956, King Papers, vol. IV, 233–234. Also see Richard Gregg to King, May 20, 1956, King Papers, vol. III, 267–269.

71. George D. Kelsey to King, April 4, 1958, King Papers, vol. IV, 394–395; King, *Stride Toward Freedom*, 85.

72. E. Stanley Jones had earlier called Gandhi "one of the most Christlike men in history." See Harold Fey, "A Gandhi Society?" *Christian Century* 79 (1962): 735–736; Garrow, *Bearing the Cross*, 200; Louis Fischer, *The Life of Mahatma Gandhi* (New York: Harper, 1950), 334.

73. Martin Luther King Jr., "Six Talks in Outline," November 23, 1949, in *The Papers of Martin Luther King, Jr. Volume 1: Called To Serve, January 1929–June 1951*, ed. Clayborne Carson, Ralph E. Luker, and Penny A. Russell, 249 (Berkeley: University of California Press, 1992); King, *Stride Toward Freedom*, 117.

74. George M. Fredrickson, *Black Liberation: A Comparative History of Black Ideologies in the United States and South Africa* (Oxford: Oxford University Press, 1996), 253; Marc Gallicchio, *The African American Encounter with Japan and China: Black Internationalism in Asia, 1895–1945* (Chapel Hill: University of North Carolina Press, 2000), 208; Meier and Rudwick, *CORE*, xx.

75. Delivered February 2, 1959, King Papers, vol. V: 120–125.

76. King, "Non-Aggression Procedures to Interracial Harmony," King Papers, vol. III, 321–328; "The Rising Tide of Racial Consciousness," King Papers, vol. V, 499–508; Richard Gregg to King, April 2, 1956, King Papers, vol. III, 211–212; King, "The Birth of a New Nation," April 7, 1957, King Papers, vol. IV, 155–167; King to Nkrumah, April 17, 1959, King Papers, vol. V, 85–86; Kevin Gaines, *American Africans in Ghana: Black Expatriates and the Civil Rights Era* (Chapel Hill: University of North Carolina Press, 2006), 83.

77. King, "My Trip to the Land of Gandhi"; Quoted in King Papers, vol. V, 11; King, "Palm Sunday Sermon on Mohandas K. Gandhi"; King, "The 'New Negro' of the South: Behind the Montgomery Story," "Non-Aggression Procedures to Interracial Harmony," King Papers, vol. III, 280–286, 321–328.

78. Coretta Scott King, *My life with Martin Luther King, Jr.* (New York: Holt, Rinehart and Winston, 1969), 176.

79. Reddick, "Account of Press Conference in New Delhi on 10 February 1959," King Papers, vol. V, 126; Vinoba Bhave, "Dr. Martin Luther King with Vinoba," *Bhoodan* 3 (March 18, 1959): 369–370; "Mahatma's Spirit Lives in India," *Hindustan Times*, March 9, 1959.

80. *Hindustan Times*, January 30, 1958; *Peace News*, January 31, 1958; "Dr. King Will Make Study of Gandhism," *Hindustan Times*, February 11, 1959; "Gandhian Methods: Dr. Martin Luther King's Views," *India News* 3, no. 4 (March 1, 1959): 3, in Subject File 64, MC Chagla Papers, Nehru Memorial Museum and Library (NMML), New Delhi; King Papers, vol. IV, 354–355.

81. Scott King, *My Life*, 173; King, "Some Things We Must Do," King Papers, vol. IV, 341–342; King, "The 'New Negro' of the South," 280–286, 321–328; "Palm Sunday Sermon on Mohandas K. Gandhi," March 22, 1959, King Papers, vol. V, 145–157; "My Trip to the Land of Gandhi," *Ebony* (July 1959), in King Papers, vol. V, 231–238.

82. King, "My Trip to the Land of Gandhi."

83. King was not alone in portraying Gandhi as a heroic opponent of untouchability. See Homer Jack, "Great Soul: The Mahatma and Montgomery," in

"Speeches, Gandhi," Box 4, Series IV, Homer Jack Papers, SCPC; G. Ramachandran to King, December 27, 1958, King Papers, vol. V, 553.

84. King, "My Trip to the Land of Gandhi," King Papers, vol. V, 236.

85. King, "Statement upon Return from India," March 18, 1959, King Papers, vol. V, 143; King, "The Rising Tide of Racial Consciousness," September 6, 1960, King Papers, vol. V, 499–508.

86. King, *Why We Can't Wait* (New York: Signet Classic Edition, 2000), 125; Note 4 in King, "Address at the Religious Leaders Conference," May 11, 1959, King Papers, vol. V, 197–198.

87. King to Nelson, April 7, 1959, King Papers, vol. V, 181.

88. King Papers, vol. V, 262.

89. "The American Dream," July 4, 1965, in *A Knock at Midnight: Inspiration from the Great Sermons of Reverend Martin Luther King, Jr.*, ed. Clayborne Carson and Peter Holloran (New York: Warner Books, 1998), 79–100; Daniel Immerwahr, "Caste or Colony? Indianizing Race in the United States," *Modern Intellectual History* 4, no. 2 (2007): 275–301.

90. W. E. B. Du Bois, "*Gandhi and the American Negroes,*" Gandhi Marg 1, no. 3 (July 1957): 177. Also see Du Bois, *Will the Great Gandhi Live Again? National Guardian,* February 11, 1957; "Crusader without Violence," *National Guardian,* November 9, 1959, in *W. E. B. Du Bois: A Reader,* ed. David Levering Lewis (New York: Henry Holt & Company, 1995), 358–362.

91. Martin Oppenheimer, *The Sit-In Movement of 1960* (Brooklyn: Carlson, 1989), 37.

92. "The President's News Conference," March 16, 1960.

93. Murray, *Song in a Weary Heart,* 208–209; Mordecai Johnson to Leon A. Ransom, May 2, 1944, the Howard Civil Rights Committee to Ransom, May 2, 1944, and Murray to Roosevelt, May 4, 1944, all in File 396, "Howard Civil Rights Committee," Box 18, PMP.

94. Garrow, *Bearing the Cross,* 89–90; Wesley C. Hogan, *Many Minds, One Heart: SNCC's Dream for a New America* (Chapel Hill: University of North Carolina Press, 2007), chap. 1.

95. *Student Voice* (August 1960): 2, referenced in David L. Chappell, *A Stone of Hope: Prophetic Religion and the Death of Jim Crow* (Chapel Hill: University of North Carolina Press, 2004), 84; also see Harvard Sitkoff, *The Struggle for Black Equality: 1954–1980* (New York: Hill and Wang, 1981), 83; Howard Zinn, *SNCC: The New Abolitionists,* 2d ed. (Boston: Beacon Press, 1965), 38–39.

96. "CORE Will Convene in St. Louis," *The New York Amsterdam News,* June 25, 1960.

97. Meier and Rudwick, *CORE,* 113.

98. Simon Wendt, *The Spirit and the Shotgun: Armed Resistance and the Struggle for Civil Rights* (Gainesville: University Press of Florida, 2007), 111; Mary King, *Freedom Song: A Personal Story of the 1960s Civil Rights Movement* (New York: Morrow, 1987), 295.

99. David Halberstam, *The Children* (New York: Random House, 1998), 10, 268, 406.

100. "One Man's Civil Rights Story," lecture by Jim Zwerg at Beloit College, Beloit, Wisconsin, September 18, 2002, transcript pages 1–2, 4–5, 25, transcript courtesy of Ann Bausum.

101. Meier and Rudwick, *CORE*, 116.

102. Halberstam, *The Children*, 343.

103. Zinn, *SNCC*, 220–221.

104. Henry Hampton and Steve Fayer, *Voices of Freedom: An Oral History of the Civil Rights Movement from the 1950s through the 1980s* (New York: Bantam Books, 1990), 99.

105. Farmer, *Lay Bare the Heart*, 11–12; James Farmer, preface to Ralph T. Templin, *Democracy and Nonviolence: The Role of the Individual in World Crisis* (Boston: P. Sargent, 1965), 24.

106. Anne Moody, *Coming of Age in Mississippi* (New York: Dial Press, 1968).

107. Aldon Morris, *The Origins of the Civil Rights Movement: Black Communities Organizing for Change* (New York: Free Press, 1984), 158; Emily Stoper, *The Student Nonviolent Coordinating Committee: The Growth of Radicalism in a Civil Rights Organization* (Brooklyn, N.Y.: Carlson, 1989), 28.

108. King, *Stride Toward Freedom*, 101.

109. King Papers, vol. V, 119, 127.

110. Ibid., 127.

111. King, "His Influence Speaks to World Conscience," King Papers, vol. IV.

112. "Notes for Conversation between King and Nehru" and King, "Farewell Statement," March 9, 1959, King Papers, vol. V, 130, 135–136. Vinoba Bhave helped inspire King's statement on unilateral disarmament. See Scott King, *My Life*, 177.

113. Bill Sutherland and Matt Meyer, *Guns and Gandhi in Africa: Pan-Africanist Insights on Nonviolence, Armed Struggle and Liberation* (Trenton, N.J.: Africa World Press, 2000), 45.

114. D'Emilio, *Lost Prophet*, 230; Garrow, *Bearing the Cross*, 72.

115. Wendt, *The Spirit and the Shotgun;* Timothy B. Tyson, "Robert F. Williams, 'Black Power,' and the Roots of the African American Freedom Struggle," *The Journal of American History* 85, no. 2 (September 1998): 540–570.

116. LeRoi Jones, *Home: Social Essays* (New York: William Morrow & Company, 1966), 85.

117. John Oliver Killens, *Black Man's Burden* (New York: Simon and Schuster, 1965), 108–110, 120.

118. Meier and Rudwick, *CORE*, 414–415; Wendt, *The Spirit and the Shotgun*, 140.

119. Peniel E. Joseph, *Waiting 'til the Midnight Hour: A Narrative History of Black Power in America* (New York: Henry Holt and Co., 2006); Matthew Countryman, *Up South: Civil Rights and Black Power in Philadelphia* (Philadelphia: University of Pennsylvania Press, 2006).

120. "The Freedom March," unsigned editorial, *United Asia* 15, no. 9 (September 1963): 600–602.

121. N. Krishnan to G. L. Mehta, January 18, 1969, G. L. Mehta Papers and File 75, Pamphlets, Sucheta Kripalani Papers, NMML.

122. Singh to Jayaprakash Narayan, February 23, 1968 and June 16, 1969, JJ Singh Papers, NMML.

123. Kamaladevi Chattopadhyaya, "Black Power on the Move," *The Bharat Jyoti,* March 15, 1970.

124. Lata Maurugkar, *Dalit Panther Movement in Maharashtra: A Sociological Approach* (London: Sangam Books, 1991), 44, 237; V. S. Naipaul, *India: A Million Mutinies Now* (New York: Penguin Books, 1992), 116; Jayashree Gokhale, *From Concessions to Confrontation: The Politics of an Indian Untouchable Community* (Bombay: Popular Prakashan, 1993), 264; N. M. Aston, ed., *Dalit Literature and African American Literature* (Delhi: Prestige Books, 2001); Vijay Prashad, "Afro-Dalits of the Earth, Unite!" *African Studies Review* 43 (2000): 189–201.

125. Rammanohar Lohia to Du Bois, July 20, 1936, Reel 45, Du Bois Papers.

126. Harris Wofford, *Of Kennedys and Kings: Making Sense of the Sixties* (New York: Farrar, Straus, Giroux, 1980), 110; Wofford to Lohia, Socialist Party Papers, Subject Number 86, May 1952–December 1952, Correspondence Received, NMML; Harris Wofford, *Lohia and America Meet* (Mt. Rainer, Md.: 1951); Muste to Lohia, August 13 and August 17, 1952, Socialist Party Papers, Subject Number 86, May 1952–December 1952, Correspondence Received, NMML.

127. Wofford discussed Gandhi with Nixon, whom he called "a Gandhi-with-gun." See "Gandhi Methods Urged for Civil Rights Fight," *The Atlanta Daily World,* November 22, 1955; "People, Places, and Things," *The Chicago Defender,* December 3, 1955; Garrow, *Bearing the Cross,* 83–84; David J. Garrow, ed., *Martin Luther King, Jr.: Civil Rights Leader, Theologian, Orator* (Brooklyn, N.Y.: Carlson, 1989), 1151; Wofford, *Of Kennedys and Kings,* especially 104–105.

128. Dorothy M. Steere to King, January 5, 1957, and Homer Jack to King, December 27, 1956, King Papers, vol. III, 496, 498; King Papers, vol. V: 107–108; "Nehru 'Pleased' by Sit-In Movement," *The New York Amsterdam News,* October 15, 1960, 8.

129. Kaka Kalelkar and Sarojini Nanavati to King, September 9, 1958, King Papers, vol. IV, 493–494.

130. Rosemary Donihi, "Non-Violence Is Best Route Out," *The Washington Post,* April 28, 1960, Subject File 61, MC Chagla Papers, NMML; "Coexistence Theme Urged by an Envoy," *The Kansas City Star,* May 10, 1960; "Chagla Tells KU Coexistence Best," *Lawrence Daily Journal World,* May 10, 1960, Subject File 61, MC Chagla Papers, NMML; "Chagla Assails China for Naked Aggression," *Hindustan Times,* May 11, 1960, Subject File 62, MC Chagla Papers, NMML.

131. Brenda Gayle Plummer, *Rising Wind: Black Americans and U.S. Foreign Affairs, 1935–1960* (Chapel Hill: University of North Carolina Press, 1996), 314; Ann Moyer, "Ambassador Notices India, U.S. Likeness," *The Daily Nebraskan,* April 19, 1960, Subject File 61; "Present Is 'Decade of African Freedom'—Indian Ambassador," *The Lincoln Star,* Wednesday April 20, 1960, Subject File 62, MC Chagla Papers, NMML.

132. "Correspondence carried out with the foreign/Indian contributors to do articles for World Satyagraha number of 'Mankind,'" Subject Number 753, Socialist Party Papers, NMML.

133. "Non-Violent Struggle in America," *United Asia* 14, no. 10 (October 62): 550. Also see K. T. Narasimha Char, "Mahatma Gandhi's Concept of Passive Resistance and Its Efficacy at the Present Day," *United Asia* 20, no. 5 (September–October 1968): 265; J. Shaffer, "Satyagraha's Twenty-fifth Anniversary in the United States," *United Asia* 17, no. 1 (January–February 1965): 5–7.

134. David Gale to Acharya Kripalani, May 16, 1960, in "Tour of the USA," Subject File 66, Sucheta Kripalani Papers, NMML. Also see "Wife Gives Him Two Votes," *The Washington Post*, April 18, 1960, Subject File 61, MC Chagla Papers, NMML.

135. E-mail correspondence from Jaswant Krishnayya and Ahmed Meer to the author.

136. "Student from India Forewarned Of Price South Puts on Freedom," *The Boston Globe*, May 23, 1961.

137. "Mississippi Ousts Indian Politician from a Cafeteria," *New York Times*, May 29, 1964; "U.S. Plans an Apology," *New York Times*, May 29, 1964; "Jackson, Miss., Hit by Indian Socialist," *New York Times*, May 30, 1964; Edwin King, "Lohia and the American Civil Rights Movement," *Gandhi Marg* 59 (1971): 270–277.

138. "Color Arrest Pleases Man from India," *The Chicago Defender*, June 3, 1964.

139. Rammanohar Lohia to Roma Mitra, January 28, 1960, Rammanohar Lohia Papers, NMML.

140. Clarice T. Campbell, *Civil Rights Chronicle: Letters from the South* (Jackson: The University Press of Mississippi, 1997), 199, 204, 209.

141. Campbell, *Civil Rights Chronicle*, 218–219.

142. Moody, *Coming of Age*, 376; United States Commission on Civil Rights, *A Report on Equal Protection in the South* (Washington, D.C.: Government Printing Ofice, 1965), 22–23.

Conclusion

1. See Harish S. Wankhede, "Margins to Centre," *Tehelka* (November 21, 2008); Jeremy Kahn, "India's Anti-Obama," *Newsweek* (April 27, 2009); Ashutosh Varshney, "Obama and India," *Seminar* 593 (January 2009).

2. David Hollinger has made clear that his own conception of "post-ethnic" retains room for "communities of descent whose progeny choose to devote their energies to these communities even after experiencing opportunities for affiliating with other kinds of people." See David Hollinger, *Postethnic America: Beyond Multiculturalism* (New York: Basic Books, 2005), 13, 118, 197; Cedric Dover, "Notes on Coloured Writing," *Phylon* 8, no. 3 (3rd Quarter, 1947), 222.

3. Kwame Anthony Appiah, *The Ethics of Identity* (Princeton: Princeton University Press, 2005), 242. On cosmopolitan anticolonial nationalism, see

Louise Blakeney Williams, "Overcoming the 'Contagion of Mimicry': The Cosmopolitan Nationalism and Modernist History of Rabindranath Tagore and W. B. Yeats," *American Historical Review* 112, no. 1 (February 2007): 69–100. For a compelling defense of cosmopolitan patriotism, see Jonathan M. Hansen, *The Lost Promise of Patriotism: Debating American Identity, 1890–1920* (Chicago: University of Chicago Press, 2003).

4. Du Bois, "The Clash of Colour," *The Aryan Path* 7, no. 3 (March 1936): 114–115.

5. "Amar Singh Discovers America," *American Unity* (November/December 1951); "India General, 1949–1952," Box A320, NAACP Papers.

6. On "cultural citizenship," see Renato Rosaldo, "Cultural Citizenship, Inequality, and Multiculturalism," in *Latino Cultural Citizenship: Claiming Identity, Space, and Rights,* ed. William V. Flores and Rina Benmayor, 27–38 (Boston: Beacon Press, 1997); Aihwa Ong, "Cultural Citizenship as Subject-Making," *Current Anthropology* 37, no. 5 (1996): 737–762.

7. Edward Said, *Representations of the Intellectual* (London: Vintage, 1994), xii.

8. "Interview to American Negro Delegation," February 21, 1936, CWMG.

9. See Nitasha Sharma, *Hip Hop Desis: South Asian Americans, Blackness, and a Global Race Consciousness* (Durham: Duke University Press, 2010); Sunaina Marr Maira, *Desis in the House: Indian American Youth Culture in New York City* (Philadelphia: Temple University Press, 2002).

10. Gupta's story will be conveyed in a film in which she will be played by leading African American actress Halle Berry. "Vanita: Sworn to Justice," and "Vanita Spelt [*sic*] Hope for Defendants," *Rediff India Abroad* (December 8, 2004).

11. Odd Arne Westad, *The Global Cold War: Third World Interventions and the Making of Our Times* (Cambridge: Cambridge University Press, 2005).

12. Von Eschen, *Race against Empire*, 22–23.

13. Pauli Murray, "An American Negro Views the Indian Question," *The Call,* September 4, 1942, 4.

14. Harris Wofford to King, Abernathy, Nixon, and "Company," April 25, 1956, King Papers, vol. III, 225–226.

15. Chandra Mohanty, "'Under Western Eyes' Revisited: Feminist Solidarity through Anticapitalist Struggles," *Signs: Journal of Women in Culture and Society* 28, no. 2 (2002): 505.

16. Ali Sardar Jafri, *My Journey: Selected Urdu Poems of Ali Sardar Jafri,* edited and translated by Baidar Bakht and Kathleen Grant Jaeger (New Delhi: Sterling Publishers, 1999), 324–327.

17. Paul Gilroy, *The Black Atlantic: Modernity and Double Consciousness* (Cambridge, Mass.: Harvard University Press, 1993), 2.

18. "To the Fourth of July," July 4, 1898, CWSV, and Sister Nivedita, *Notes of Some Wanderings with Swami Vivekananda* (Calcutta: Udbodhan Office, 1922), 76–77.

19. Robin D. G. Kelley, *Freedom Dreams: The Black Radical Imagination* (Boston: Beacon Press, 2002), xi. Also see Eric Foner, *The Story of American Freedom* (New York: W. W. Norton, 1998).

20. Frederick Douglass, "Pictures," quoted in John Stauffer, *The Black Hearts of Men: Radical Abolitionists and the Transformation of Race* (Cambridge, Mass.: Harvard University Press, 2001), 45.
21. Wesley C. Hogan, *Many Minds, One Heart: SNCC's Dream for a New America* (Chapel Hill: University of North Carolina Press, 2007), 163.

Acknowledgments

This book began as a humble research paper in a seminar taught by James T. Kloppenberg. From the beginning, Professor Kloppenberg has given me the perspective to see past my immediate preoccupations to the larger purpose of my work as a historian. Lizabeth Cohen amazed me with the time and energy she gave to this project. Her twentieth-century dissertation reading group, a vital academic community that shaped much of this book, embodies her commitment to advancing scholarship and supporting her students. Through his teaching and his scholarship, Sugata Bose deepened my commitment to exploring histories that cross disciplinary as well as national boundaries. Evelyn Higginbotham supported and guided this project from its beginnings. My attention to the intersections of race, caste, class, and gender owes much to her inspiration.

Many scholars at Harvard University gave me their advice and support. I do not have the space to thank them fully or even adequately. For making Harvard an ideal place to pursue my interests in the transnational history of social movements, I am especially grateful to Sana Aiyar, David Armitage, Sven Beckert, Vincent Brown, Courtney Bucher, Angus Burgin, Joyce Chaplin, Nancy Cott, Antara Datta, Evan Dawley, Adam Ewing, Denise Ho, Akira Iriye, Erez Manela, Kris Manjapra, Lisa McGirr, Elizabeth More, Uche Nwamara, Vernie Oliveiro, Anne Porter, Daniel Sargent, Eren Tasar, Tryg Throntveit, Van Tran, Benjamin Waterhouse, and everyone involved in organizing Harvard's annual Graduate Student Conference in International History.

I am grateful for the support of my colleagues in the Department of History at Carnegie Mellon University. Joe Trotter read the entire manuscript and offered invaluable support and guidance. I cannot imagine a more supportive environment for a young scholar than what I have found at Carnegie Mellon.

Librarians and archivists are my guardian angels. I am grateful, in particular, to Barbara Burg at Harvard's Widener Library; Sue Collins at Carnegie Mellon's Hunt Library; David Giordano, Richard Boylan, and Walter Hill of the National

Archives of the United States; Randall Burkett at Emory University's Manuscript, Archives, and Rare Book Library; Dr. N. Balakrishnan and the entire staff of the Nehru Memorial Museum and Library; J. K. Bhatnagar at the Gandhi National Museum, New Delhi; and Hena Basu in Kolkata.

I had the privilege of being able to discuss my work with several scholars working within the growing and vibrant fields of transnational African American and South Asian history. I am particularly grateful to Carol Anderson, Ann Bausum, Manu Bhagavan, Gurminder Bhambra, Tim Borstelmann, Suchetana Chattopadhyay, Mary Dudziak, Oz Frankel, Kevin Gaines, Marc Gallicchio, Tom Guglielmo, Gerald Horne, Daniel Immerwahr, Vicky Margree, Gyan Prakash, Lara Putnam, Barbara Ransby, Robbie Shilliam, and Narendra Subramanian.

I have a special debt of gratitude to Ramachandra Guha, Paul Kramer, and Enuga Reddy, for reading the entire manuscript and offering detailed and extremely helpful suggestions. Anil Nauriya and S. Anand both graciously offered their guidance. Jaswant Krishnayya and Ahmed Meer generously shared their memories and photos. Maureen Alexander allowed me to spend many days looking through books and papers in her attic.

Finally, to my editor, Joyce Seltzer, and Jeannette Estruth of Harvard University Press, whose enthusiasm and expertise have been so consistently remarkable, to the anonymous reviewers who gave invaluable suggestions, and to Andrea Nightingale, Ed Sparks, Shirley and Alex Scopelitis, Brittany Herrera, Matt Coffman, Afam, Kanayo, Terri, and Chuma Agbodike, Uncle Dan and all the Slates, Jonathan Nassim, Albert Cho, Dawn, Pearl, Aleyamma, and Golda Philip, Emily Ann Mohn, and Karena and Peter Slate—thank you.

Index